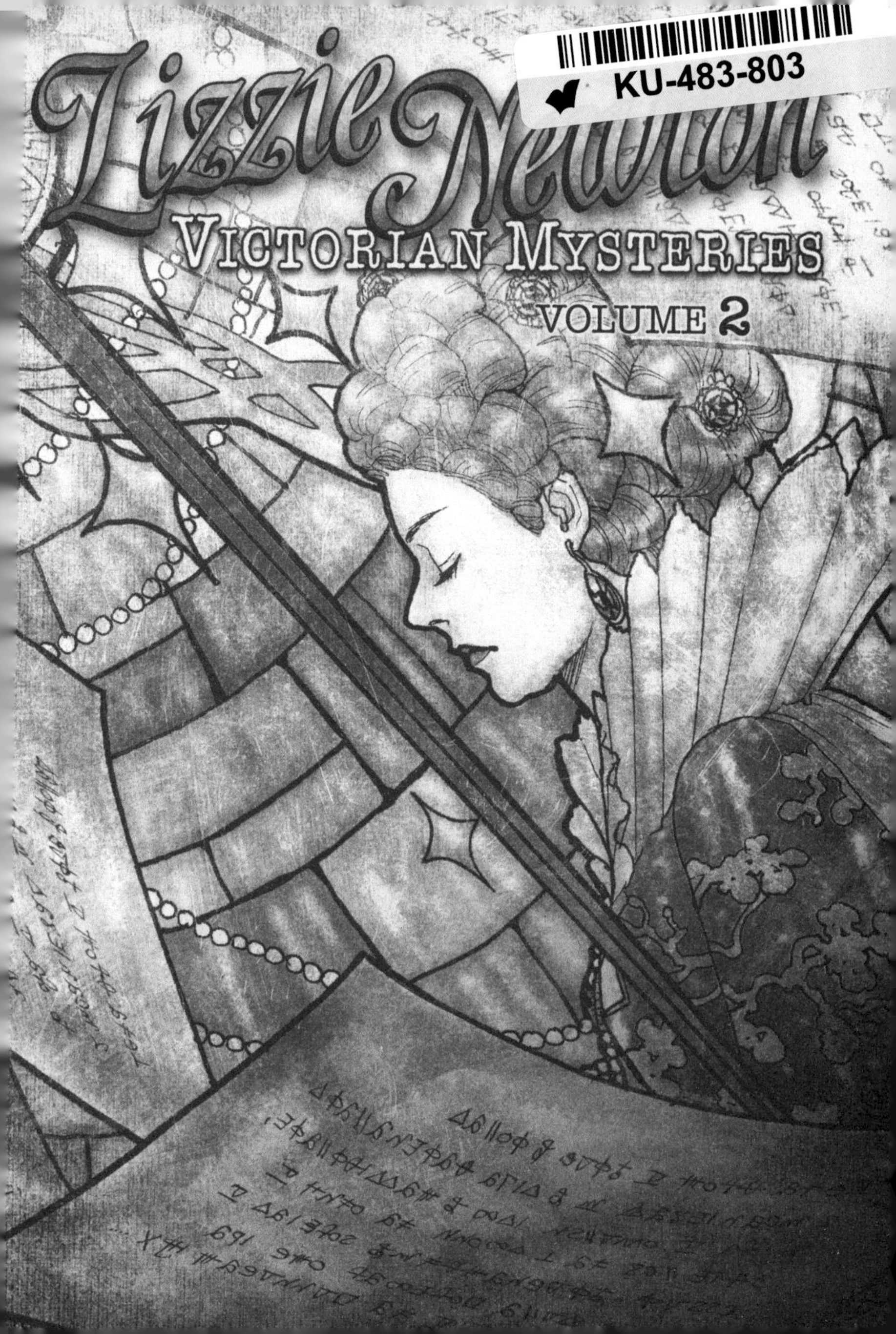
Lizzie Newton
Victorian Mysteries
Volume 2

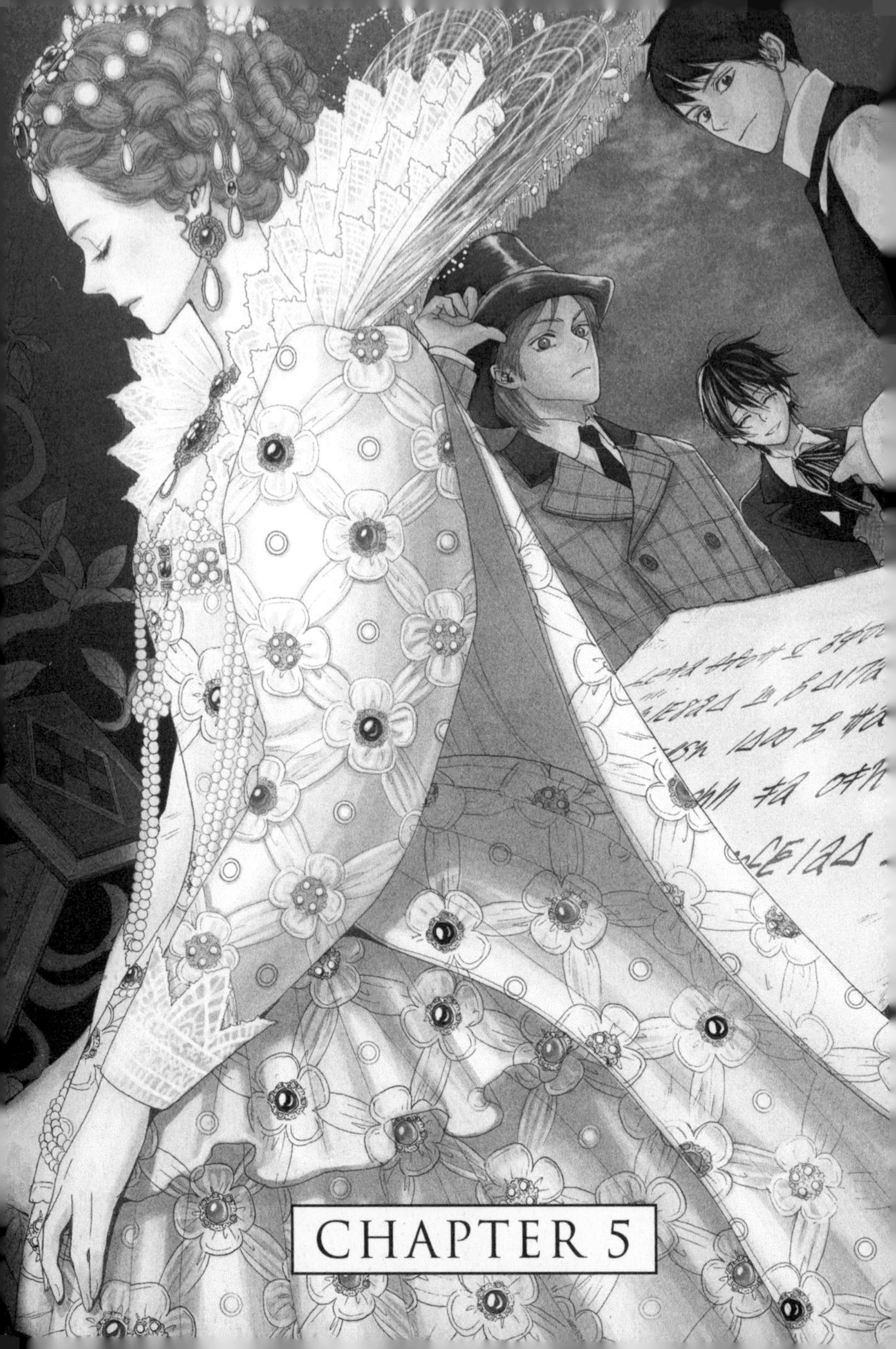
CHAPTER 5

Lizzie Newton

Victorian Mysteries

VOLUME 2

000000802335

Story
Hey-jin Jeon

Art
Ki-ha Lee

Lizzie Newton
VICTORIAN MYSTERIES
VOLUME 2

art by **Hey-jin Jeon**
story by **Ki-ha Lee**

STAFF CREDITS

translation	**Lauren Na**
adaptation	**Janet Houck**
lettering	**Roland Amago**
layout	**Bambi Eloriaga-Amago**
book design	**Nicky Lim**
assistant editor	**Shanti Whitesides**
editor	**Adam Arnold**
publisher	**Jason DeAngelis** **Seven Seas Entertainment**

LIZZIE NEWTON: VICTORIAN MYSTERIES VOL. 2
©2011 by JEON Hey-jin, LEE Ki-ha, Daewon C.I. Inc.
All rights reserved. First published in Korea as A LADY DETECTIVE VOL. 2
in 2011 by Daewon C.I. Inc. English translation rights arranged by
Daewon C.I. Inc. through Topaz Agency Inc.

ISBN: 978-1-937867-08-9

Printed in Canada

First Printing: February 2013

10 9 8 7 6 5 4 3 2 1

FOLLOW US ONLINE: www.gomanga.com

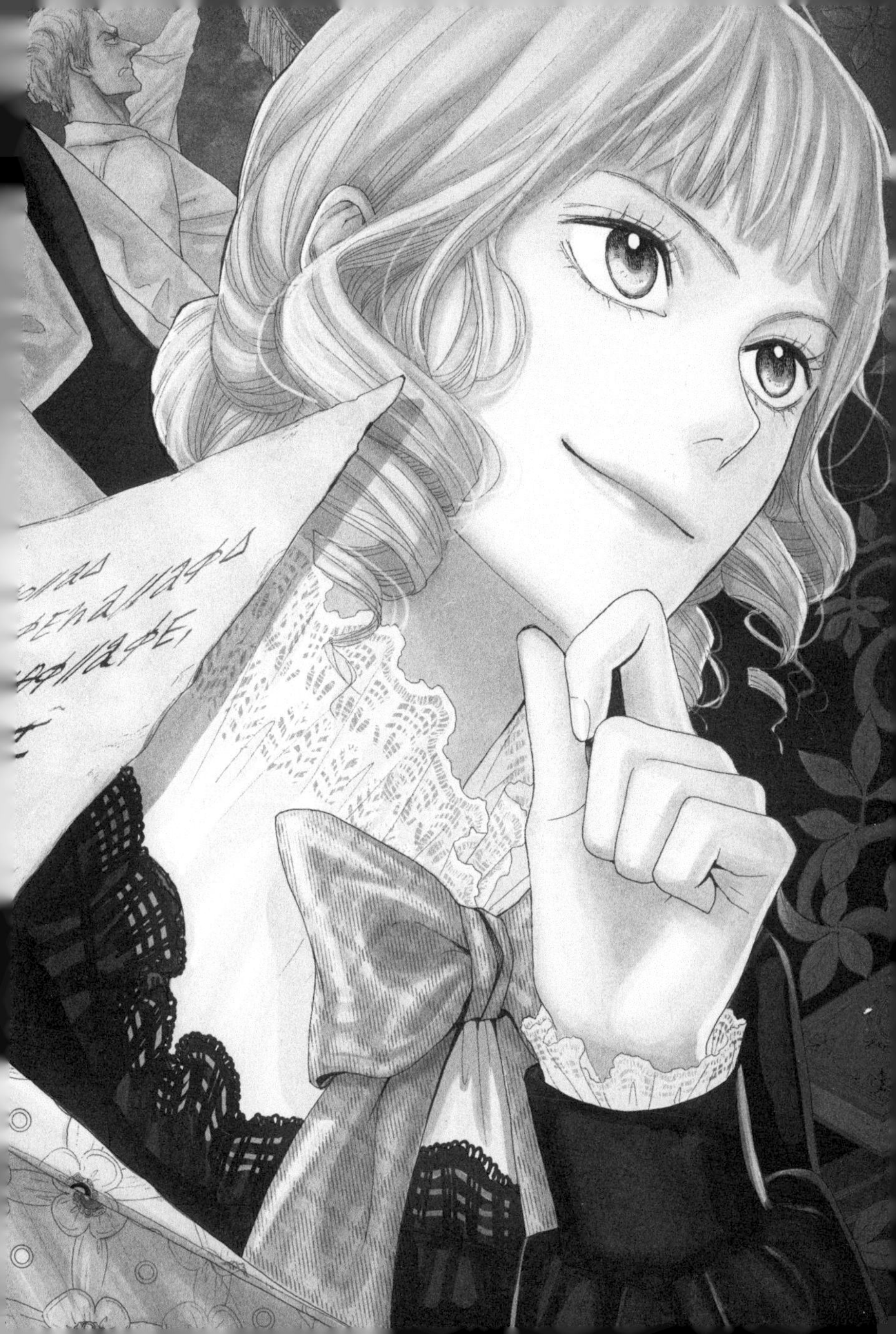

Lizzie Newton
Victorian Mysteries

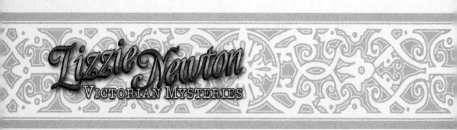

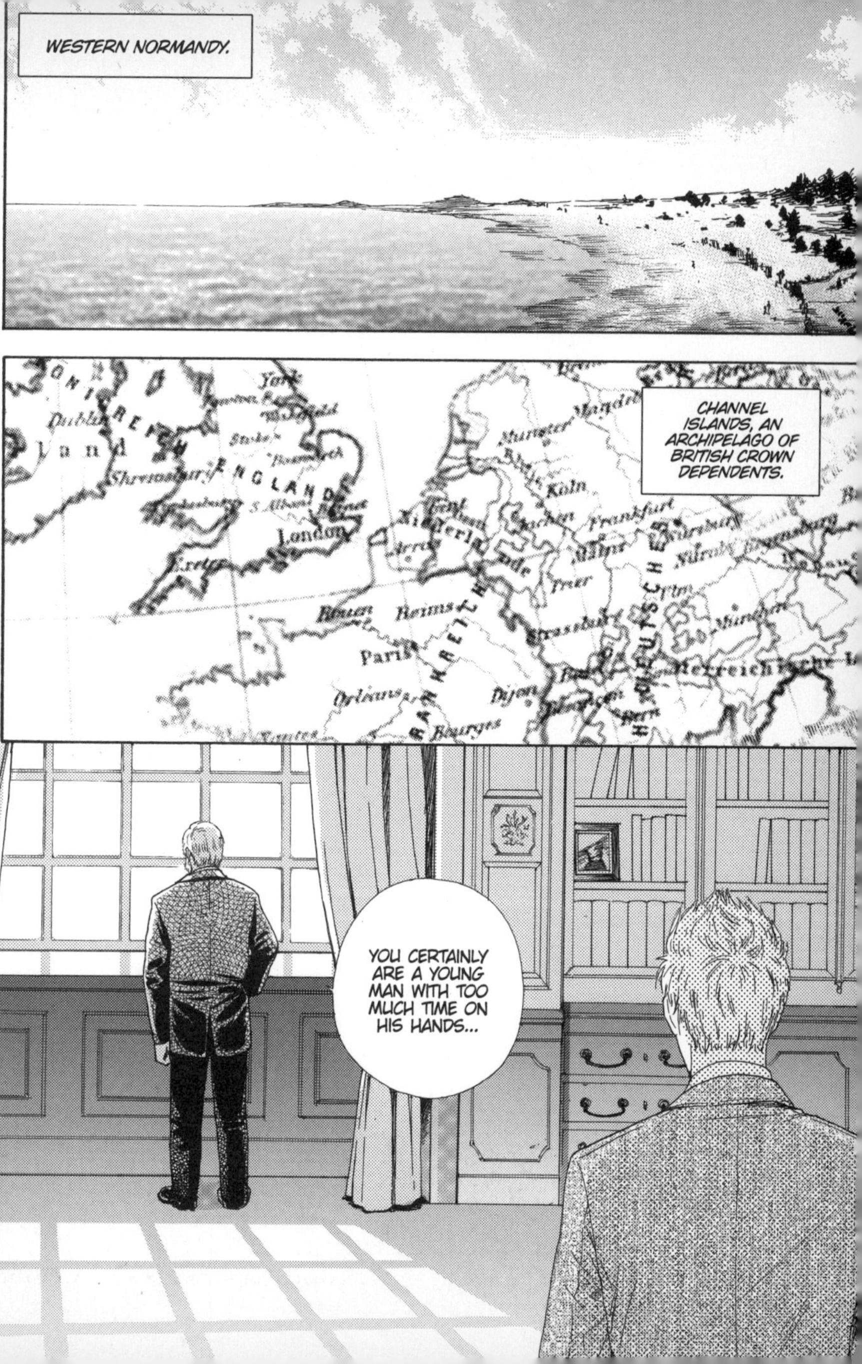
WESTERN NORMANDY.
CHANNEL ISLANDS, AN ARCHIPELAGO OF BRITISH CROWN DEPENDENTS.
YOU CERTAINLY ARE A YOUNG MAN WITH TOO MUCH TIME ON HIS HANDS...

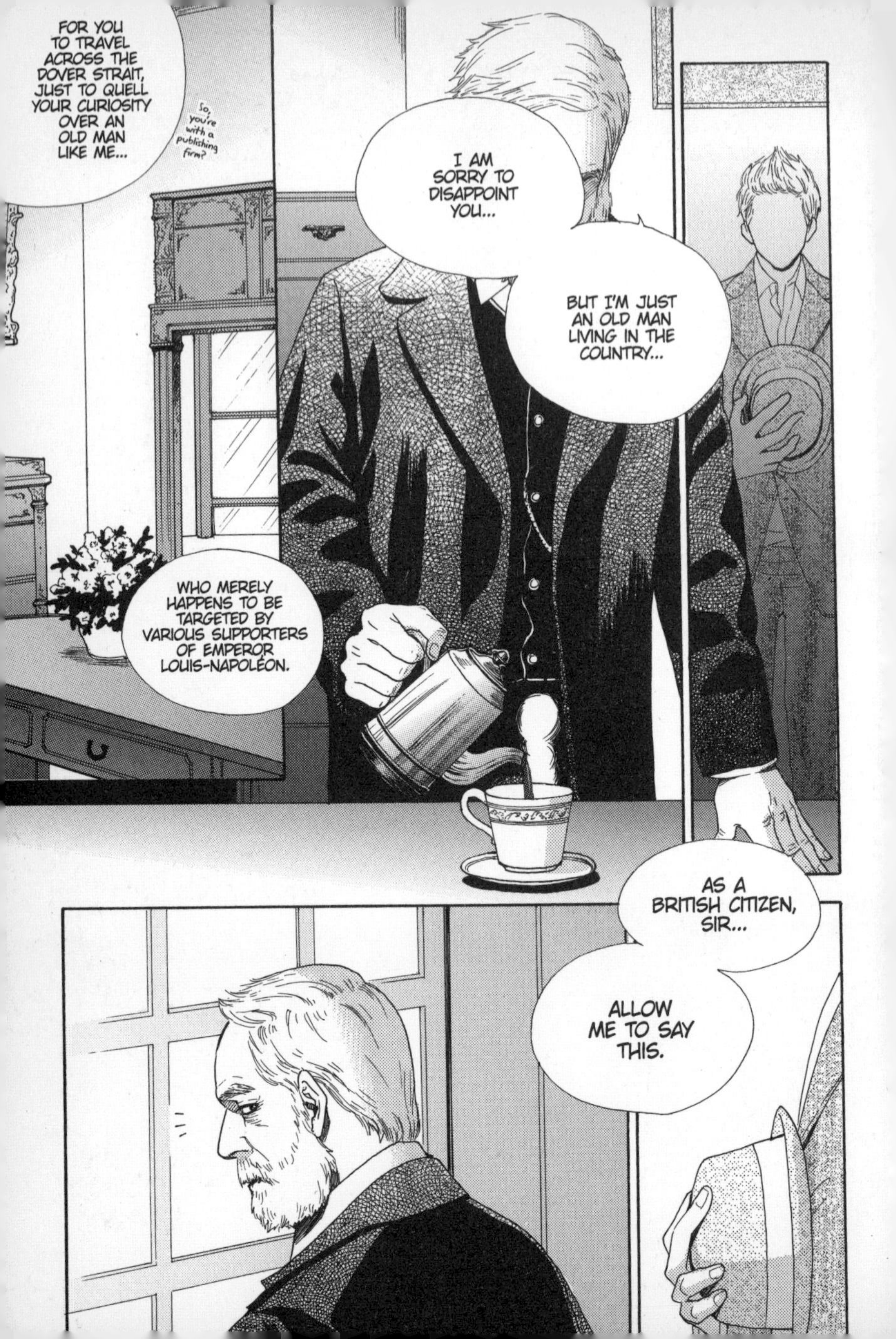
FOR YOU TO TRAVEL ACROSS THE DOVER STRAIT, JUST TO QUELL YOUR CURIOSITY OVER AN OLD MAN LIKE ME...
So, you're with a publishing firm?
I AM SORRY TO DISAPPOINT YOU...
BUT I'M JUST AN OLD MAN LIVING IN THE COUNTRY...
WHO MERELY HAPPENS TO BE TARGETED BY VARIOUS SUPPORTERS OF EMPEROR LOUIS-NAPOLÉON.
AS A BRITISH CITIZEN, SIR...
ALLOW ME TO SAY THIS.

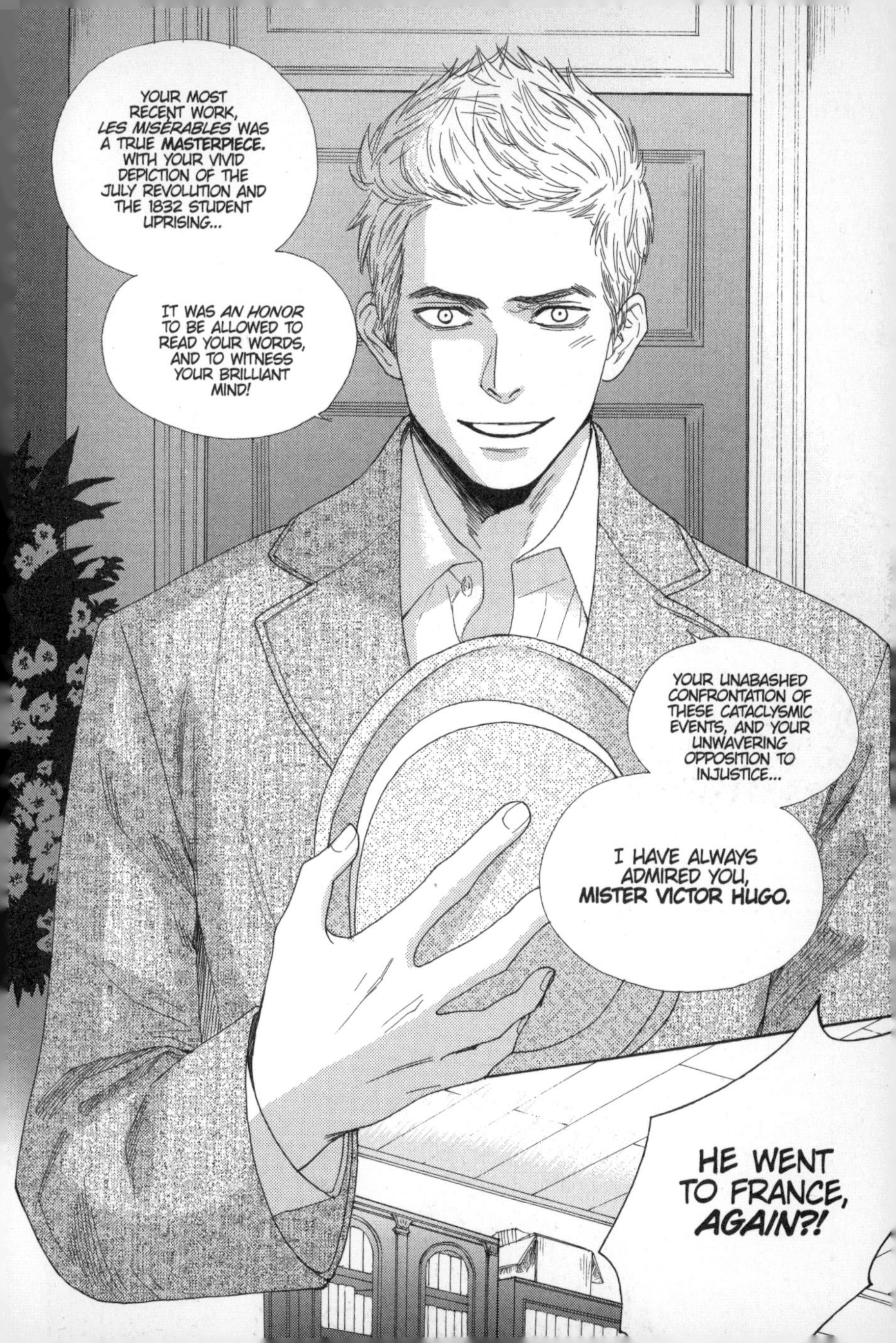
YOUR MOST RECENT WORK, *LES MISÉRABLES* WAS A TRUE **MASTERPIECE.** WITH YOUR VIVID DEPICTION OF THE JULY REVOLUTION AND THE 1832 STUDENT UPRISING...
IT WAS *AN HONOR* TO BE ALLOWED TO READ YOUR WORDS, AND TO WITNESS YOUR BRILLIANT MIND!
YOUR UNABASHED CONFRONTATION OF THESE CATACLYSMIC EVENTS, AND YOUR UNWAVERING OPPOSITION TO INJUSTICE...
I HAVE ALWAYS ADMIRED YOU, **MISTER VICTOR HUGO.**
HE WENT TO FRANCE, *AGAIN?!*

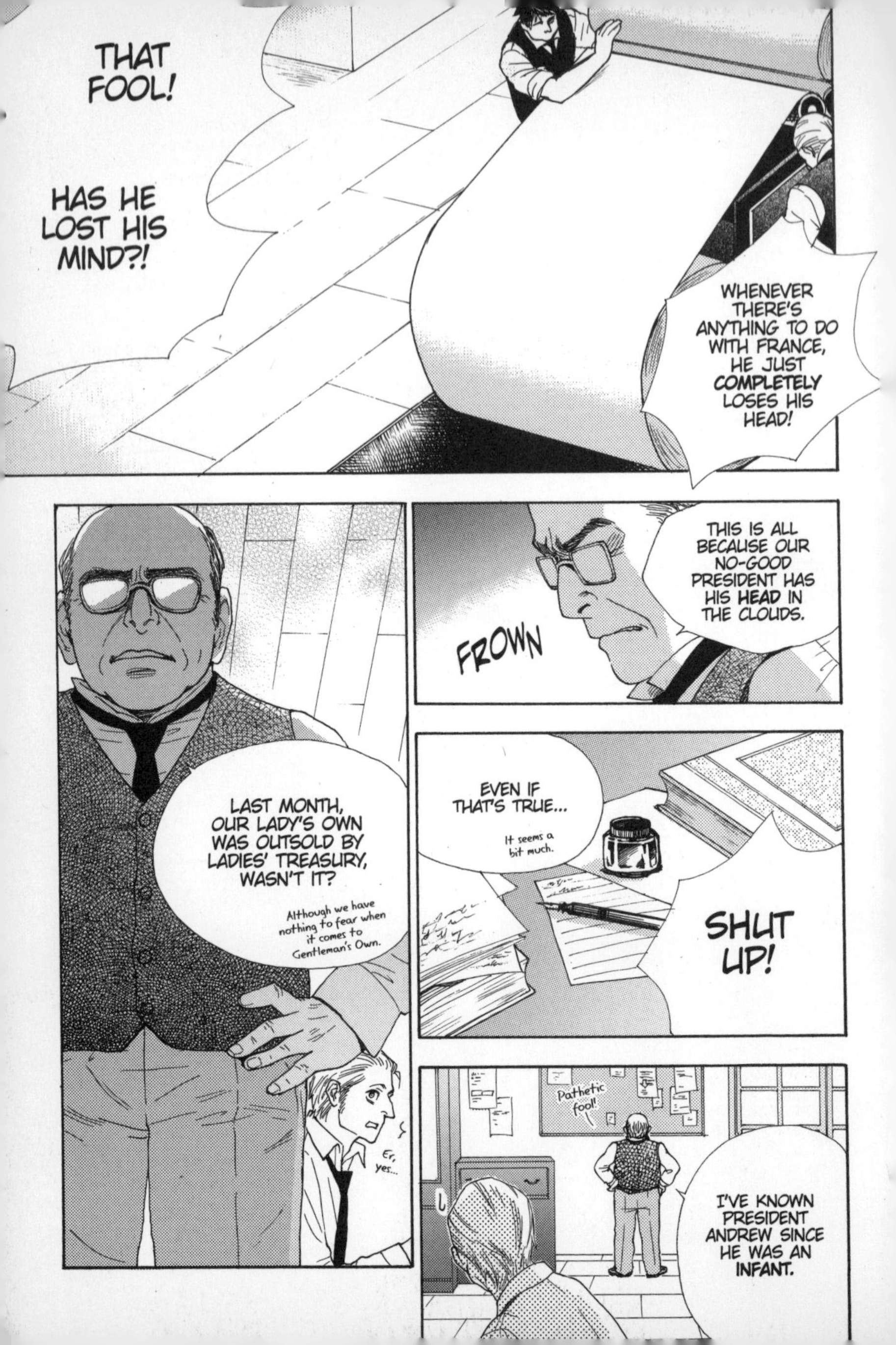
THAT FOOL!
HAS HE LOST HIS MIND?!
WHENEVER THERE'S ANYTHING TO DO WITH FRANCE, HE JUST COMPLETELY LOSES HIS HEAD!
LAST MONTH, OUR LADY'S OWN WAS OUTSOLD BY LADIES' TREASURY, WASN'T IT?
Although we have nothing to fear when it comes to Gentleman's Own.
Er, yes...
FROWN
THIS IS ALL BECAUSE OUR NO-GOOD PRESIDENT HAS HIS HEAD IN THE CLOUDS.
EVEN IF THAT'S TRUE...
It seems a bit much.
SHUT UP!
Pathetic fool!
I'VE KNOWN PRESIDENT ANDREW SINCE HE WAS AN INFANT.

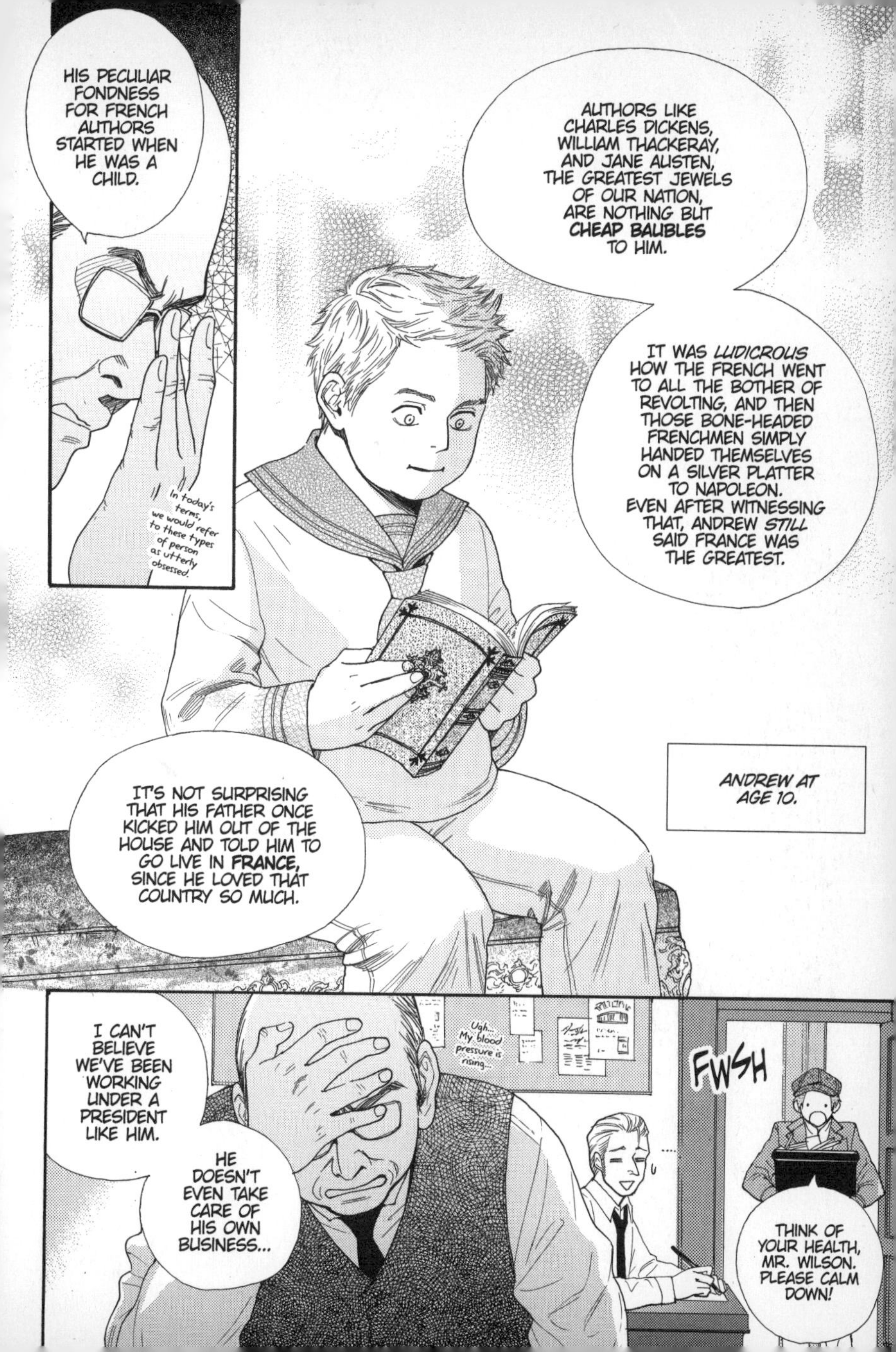
HIS PECULIAR FONDNESS FOR FRENCH AUTHORS STARTED WHEN HE WAS A CHILD.
In today's terms, we would refer to these types of person as utterly obsessed.
AUTHORS LIKE CHARLES DICKENS, WILLIAM THACKERAY, AND JANE AUSTEN, THE GREATEST JEWELS OF OUR NATION, ARE NOTHING BUT **CHEAP BAUBLES** TO HIM.
IT WAS *LUDICROUS* HOW THE FRENCH WENT TO ALL THE BOTHER OF REVOLTING, AND THEN THOSE BONE-HEADED FRENCHMEN SIMPLY HANDED THEMSELVES ON A SILVER PLATTER TO NAPOLEON. EVEN AFTER WITNESSING THAT, ANDREW *STILL* SAID FRANCE WAS THE GREATEST.
IT'S NOT SURPRISING THAT HIS FATHER ONCE KICKED HIM OUT OF THE HOUSE AND TOLD HIM TO GO LIVE IN **FRANCE,** SINCE HE LOVED THAT COUNTRY SO MUCH.
ANDREW AT AGE 10.
I CAN'T BELIEVE WE'VE BEEN WORKING UNDER A PRESIDENT LIKE HIM.
HE DOESN'T EVEN TAKE CARE OF HIS OWN BUSINESS...
Ugh... My blood pressure is rising...
FWSH
...
THINK OF YOUR HEALTH, MR. WILSON. PLEASE CALM DOWN!

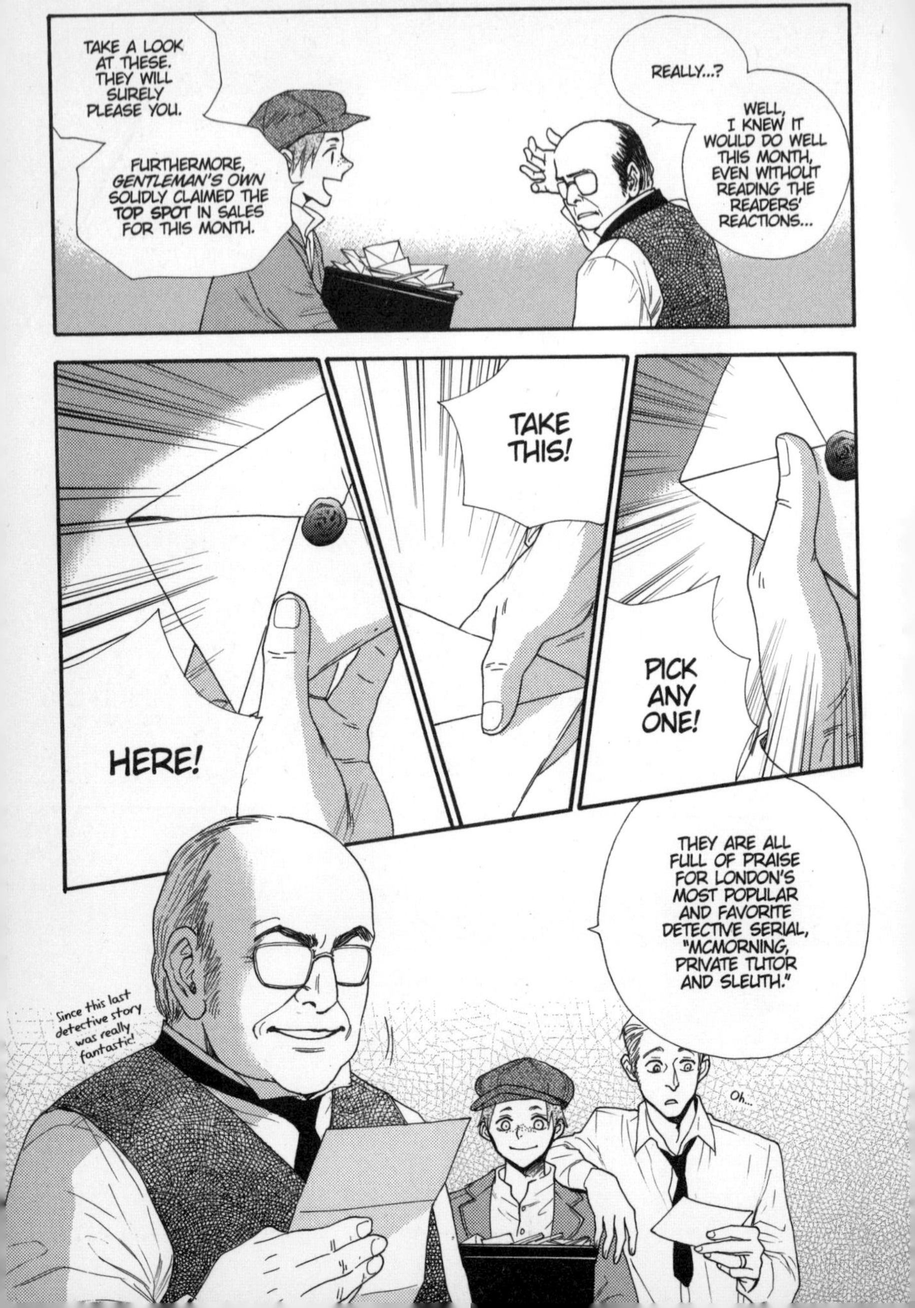

TAKE A LOOK AT THESE. THEY WILL SURELY PLEASE YOU.
FURTHERMORE, *GENTLEMAN'S OWN* SOLIDLY CLAIMED THE TOP SPOT IN SALES FOR THIS MONTH.
REALLY...?
WELL, I KNEW IT WOULD DO WELL THIS MONTH, EVEN WITHOUT READING THE READERS' REACTIONS...
HERE!
TAKE THIS!
PICK ANY ONE!
THEY ARE ALL FULL OF PRAISE FOR LONDON'S MOST POPULAR AND FAVORITE DETECTIVE SERIAL, "MCMORNING, PRIVATE TUTOR AND SLEUTH."
Since this last detective story was really fantastic!
Oh...

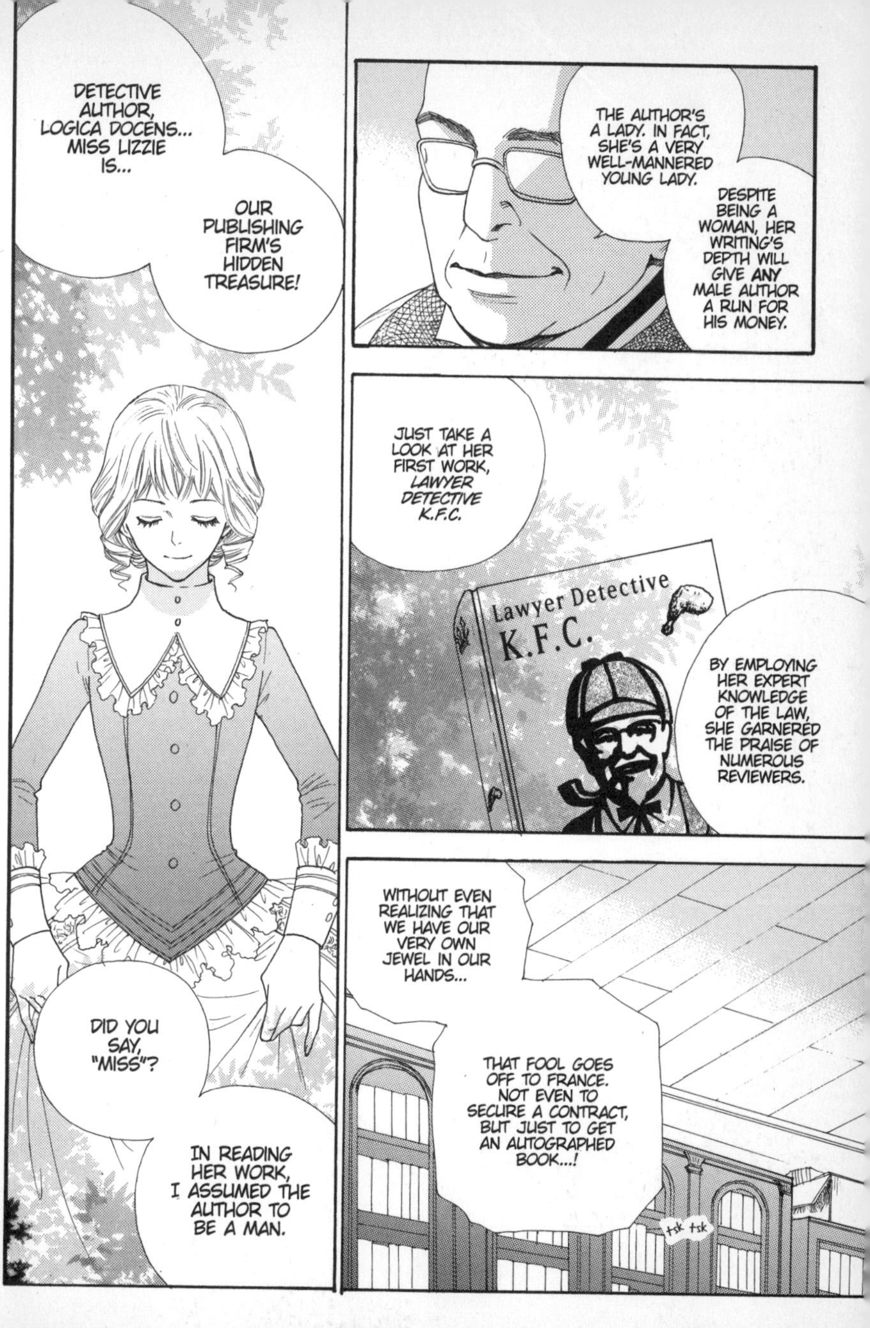
DETECTIVE AUTHOR, LOGICA DOCENS... MISS LIZZIE IS...
OUR PUBLISHING FIRM'S HIDDEN TREASURE!
DID YOU SAY, "MISS"?
IN READING HER WORK, I ASSUMED THE AUTHOR TO BE A MAN.
THE AUTHOR'S A LADY. IN FACT, SHE'S A VERY WELL-MANNERED YOUNG LADY.
DESPITE BEING A WOMAN, HER WRITING'S DEPTH WILL GIVE ANY MALE AUTHOR A RUN FOR HIS MONEY.
JUST TAKE A LOOK AT HER FIRST WORK, *LAWYER DETECTIVE K.F.C.*
Lawyer Detective K.F.C.
BY EMPLOYING HER EXPERT KNOWLEDGE OF THE LAW, SHE GARNERED THE PRAISE OF NUMEROUS REVIEWERS.
WITHOUT EVEN REALIZING THAT WE HAVE OUR VERY OWN JEWEL IN OUR HANDS...
THAT FOOL GOES OFF TO FRANCE. NOT EVEN TO SECURE A CONTRACT, BUT JUST TO GET AN AUTOGRAPHED BOOK...!
tsk tsk

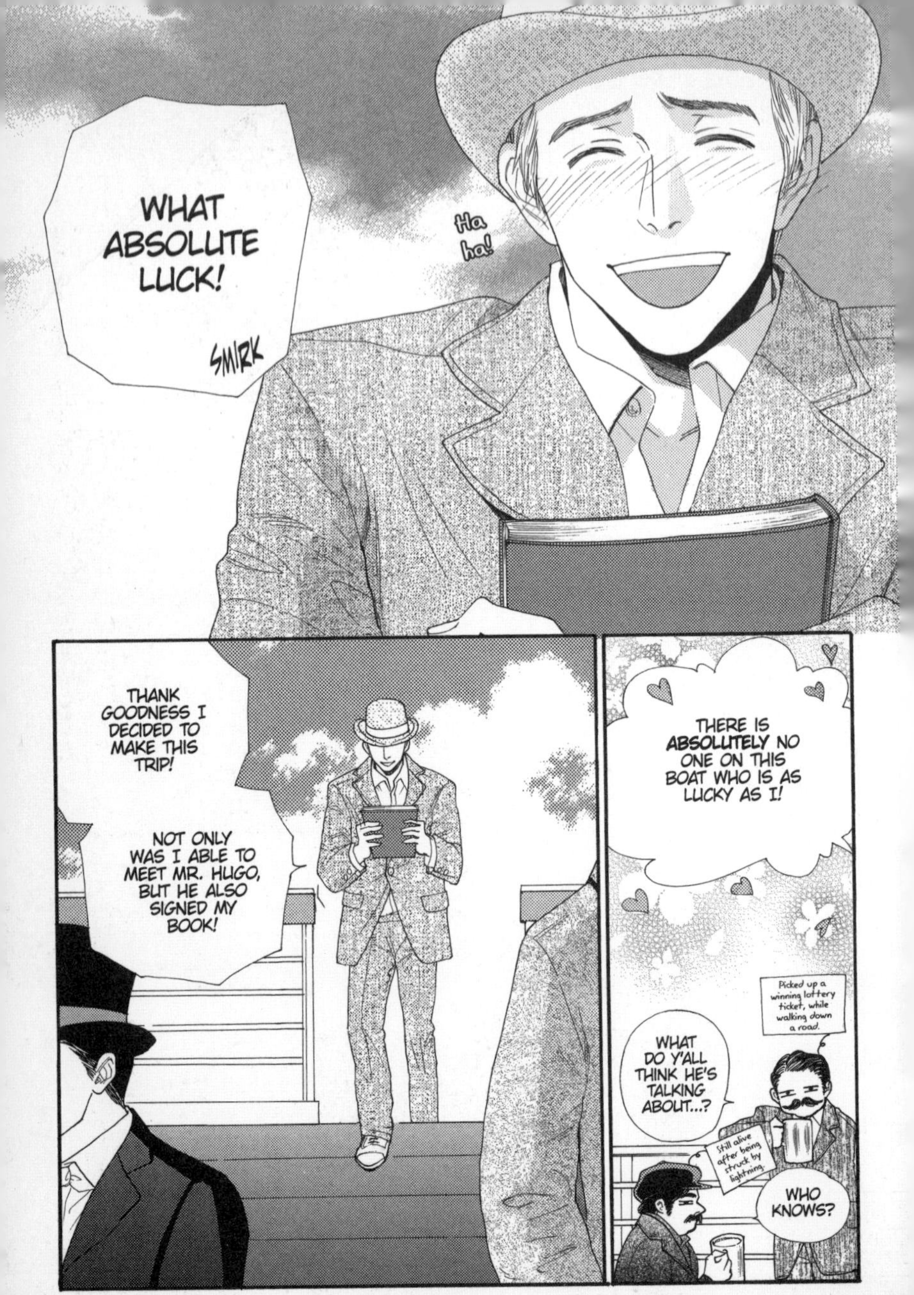
WHAT ABSOLUTE LUCK!
SMIRK
Ha ha!
THANK GOODNESS I DECIDED TO MAKE THIS TRIP!
NOT ONLY WAS I ABLE TO MEET MR. HUGO, BUT HE ALSO SIGNED MY BOOK!
THERE IS **ABSOLUTELY** NO ONE ON THIS BOAT WHO IS AS LUCKY AS I!
Picked up a winning lottery ticket, while walking down a road.
WHAT DO Y'ALL THINK HE'S TALKING ABOUT...?
Still alive after being struck by lightning.
WHO KNOWS?

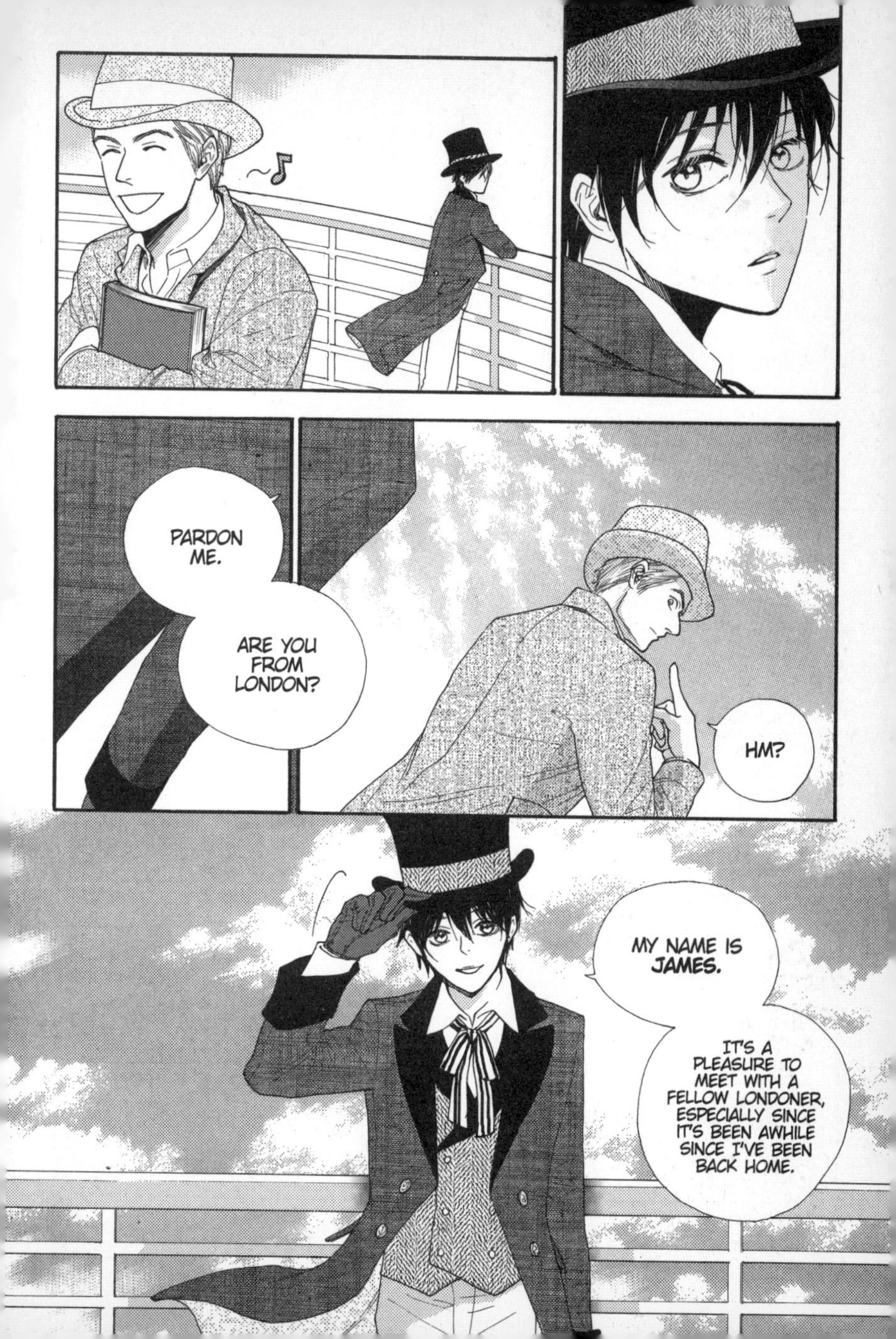
PARDON ME.
ARE YOU FROM LONDON?
HM?
MY NAME IS JAMES.
IT'S A PLEASURE TO MEET WITH A FELLOW LONDONER, ESPECIALLY SINCE IT'S BEEN AWHILE SINCE I'VE BEEN BACK HOME.

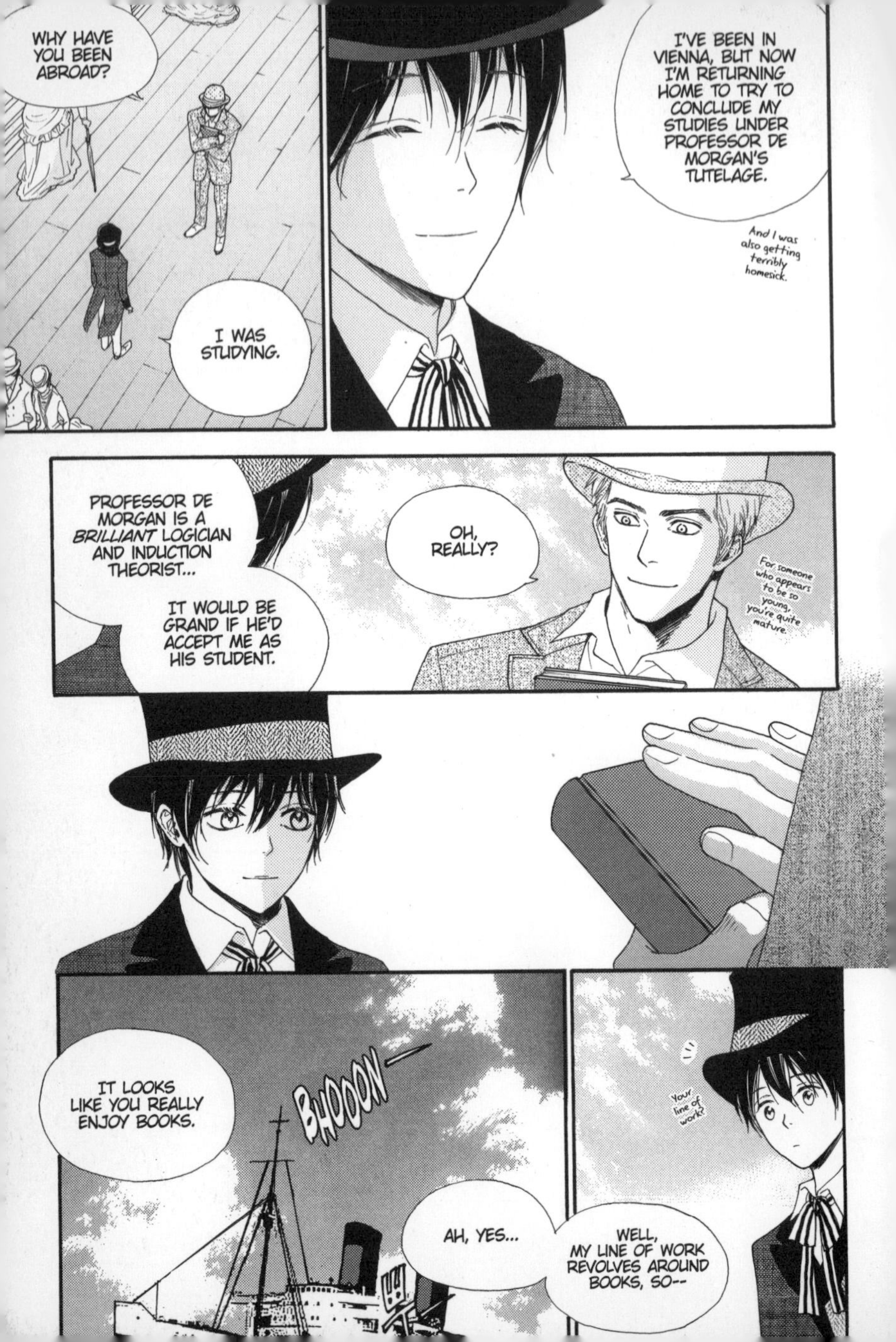
WHY HAVE YOU BEEN ABROAD?
I WAS STUDYING.
I'VE BEEN IN VIENNA, BUT NOW I'M RETURNING HOME TO TRY TO CONCLUDE MY STUDIES UNDER PROFESSOR DE MORGAN'S TUTELAGE.
And I was also getting terribly homesick.
PROFESSOR DE MORGAN IS A *BRILLIANT* LOGICIAN AND INDUCTION THEORIST...
IT WOULD BE GRAND IF HE'D ACCEPT ME AS HIS STUDENT.
OH, REALLY?
For someone who appears to be so young, you're quite mature.
IT LOOKS LIKE YOU REALLY ENJOY BOOKS.
BHOOON—
AH, YES...
Your line of work?
WELL, MY LINE OF WORK REVOLVES AROUND BOOKS, SO--

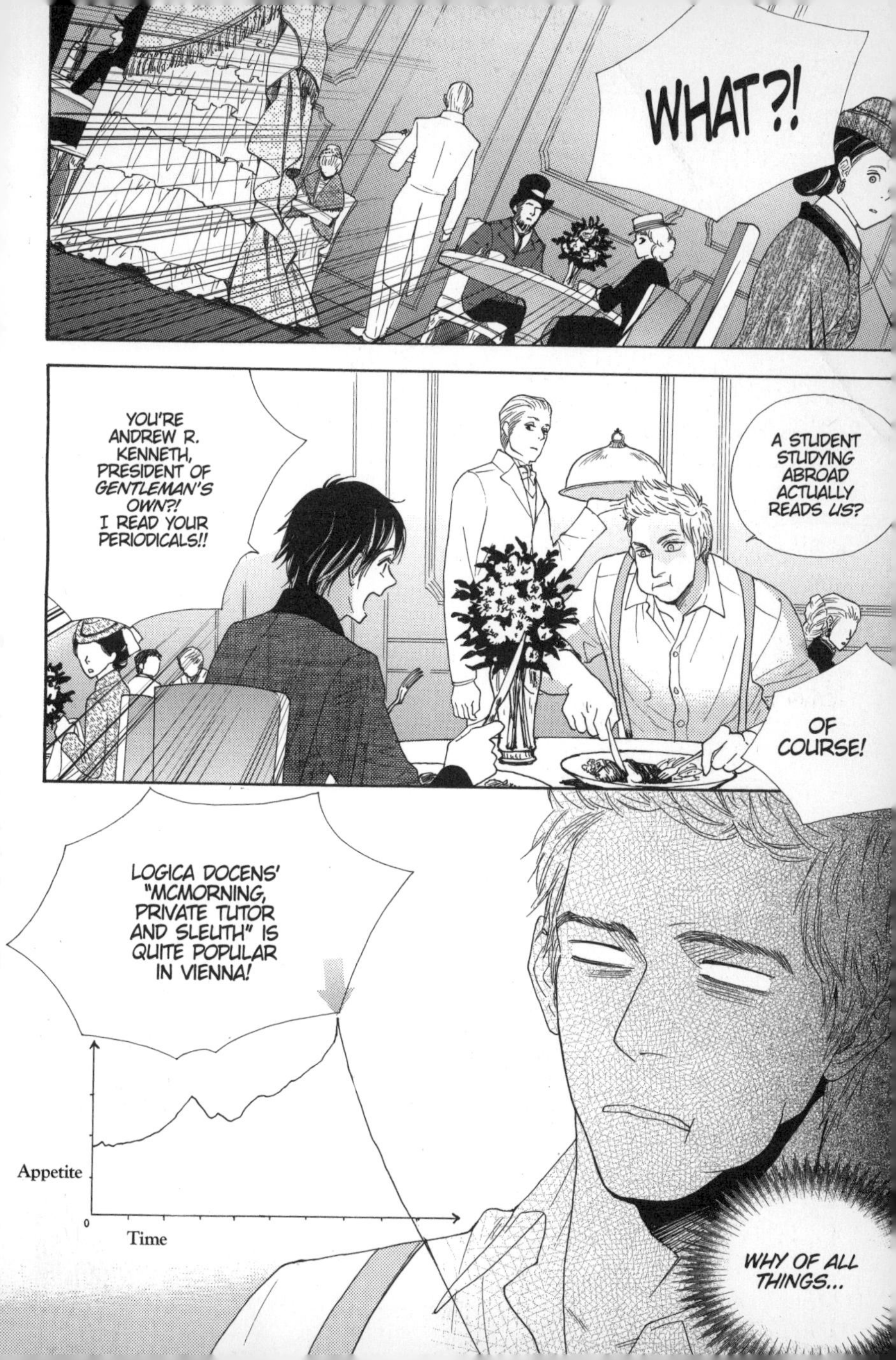
WHAT?!
YOU'RE ANDREW R. KENNETH, PRESIDENT OF GENTLEMAN'S OWN?! I READ YOUR PERIODICALS!!
A STUDENT STUDYING ABROAD ACTUALLY READS US?
OF COURSE!
LOGICA DOCENS' "MCMORNING, PRIVATE TUTOR AND SLEUTH" IS QUITE POPULAR IN VIENNA!
Appetite
0
Time
WHY OF ALL THINGS...

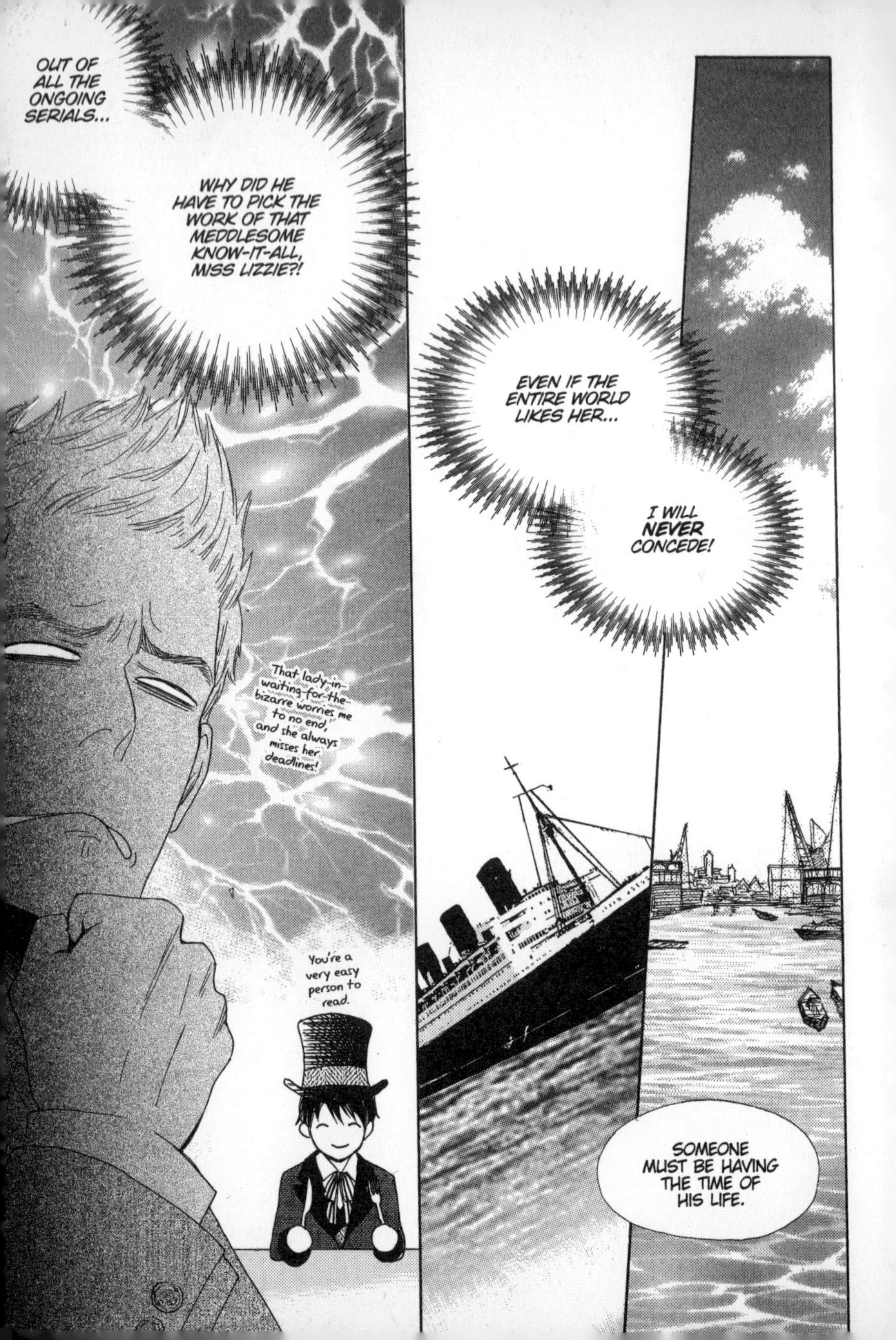
OUT OF ALL THE ONGOING SERIALS...
WHY DID HE HAVE TO PICK THE WORK OF THAT MEDDLESOME KNOW-IT-ALL, MISS LIZZIE?!
That lady-in-waiting-for-the-bizarre worries me to no end, and she always misses her deadlines!
You're a very easy person to read.
EVEN IF THE ENTIRE WORLD LIKES HER...
I WILL NEVER CONCEDE!
SOMEONE MUST BE HAVING THE TIME OF HIS LIFE.

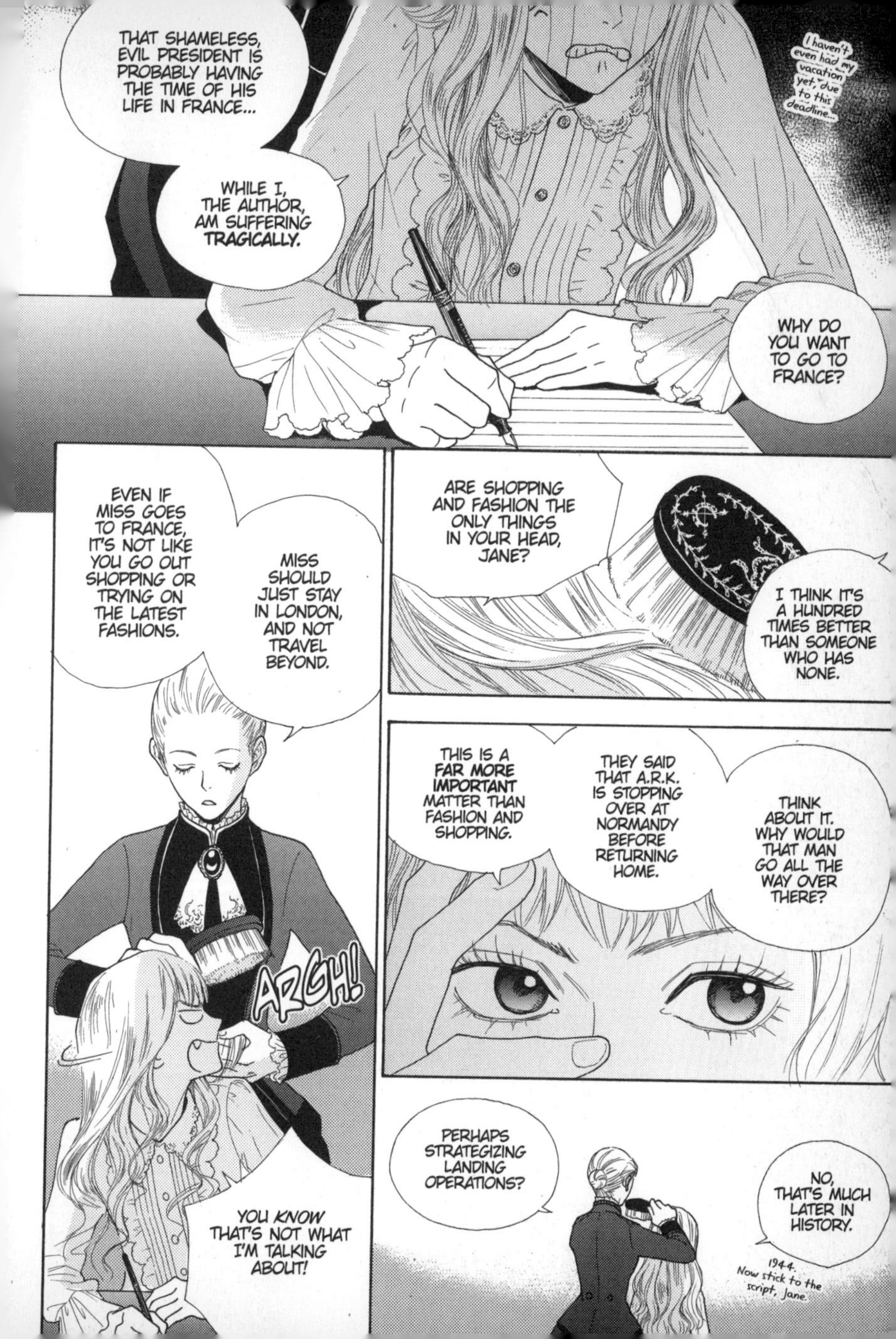
THAT SHAMELESS, EVIL PRESIDENT IS PROBABLY HAVING THE TIME OF HIS LIFE IN FRANCE...
WHILE I, THE AUTHOR, AM SUFFERING **TRAGICALLY.**
I haven't even had my vacation yet, due to this deadline...
WHY DO YOU WANT TO GO TO FRANCE?
EVEN IF MISS GOES TO FRANCE, IT'S NOT LIKE YOU GO OUT SHOPPING OR TRYING ON THE LATEST FASHIONS.
MISS SHOULD JUST STAY IN LONDON, AND NOT TRAVEL BEYOND.
ARGH!
YOU *KNOW* THAT'S NOT WHAT I'M TALKING ABOUT!
ARE SHOPPING AND FASHION THE ONLY THINGS IN YOUR HEAD, JANE?
I THINK IT'S A HUNDRED TIMES BETTER THAN SOMEONE WHO HAS NONE.
THIS IS A **FAR MORE IMPORTANT** MATTER THAN FASHION AND SHOPPING.
THEY SAID THAT A.R.K. IS STOPPING OVER AT NORMANDY BEFORE RETURNING HOME.
THINK ABOUT IT. WHY WOULD THAT MAN GO ALL THE WAY OVER THERE?
PERHAPS STRATEGIZING LANDING OPERATIONS?
NO, THAT'S MUCH LATER IN HISTORY.
1944. Now stick to the script, Jane.

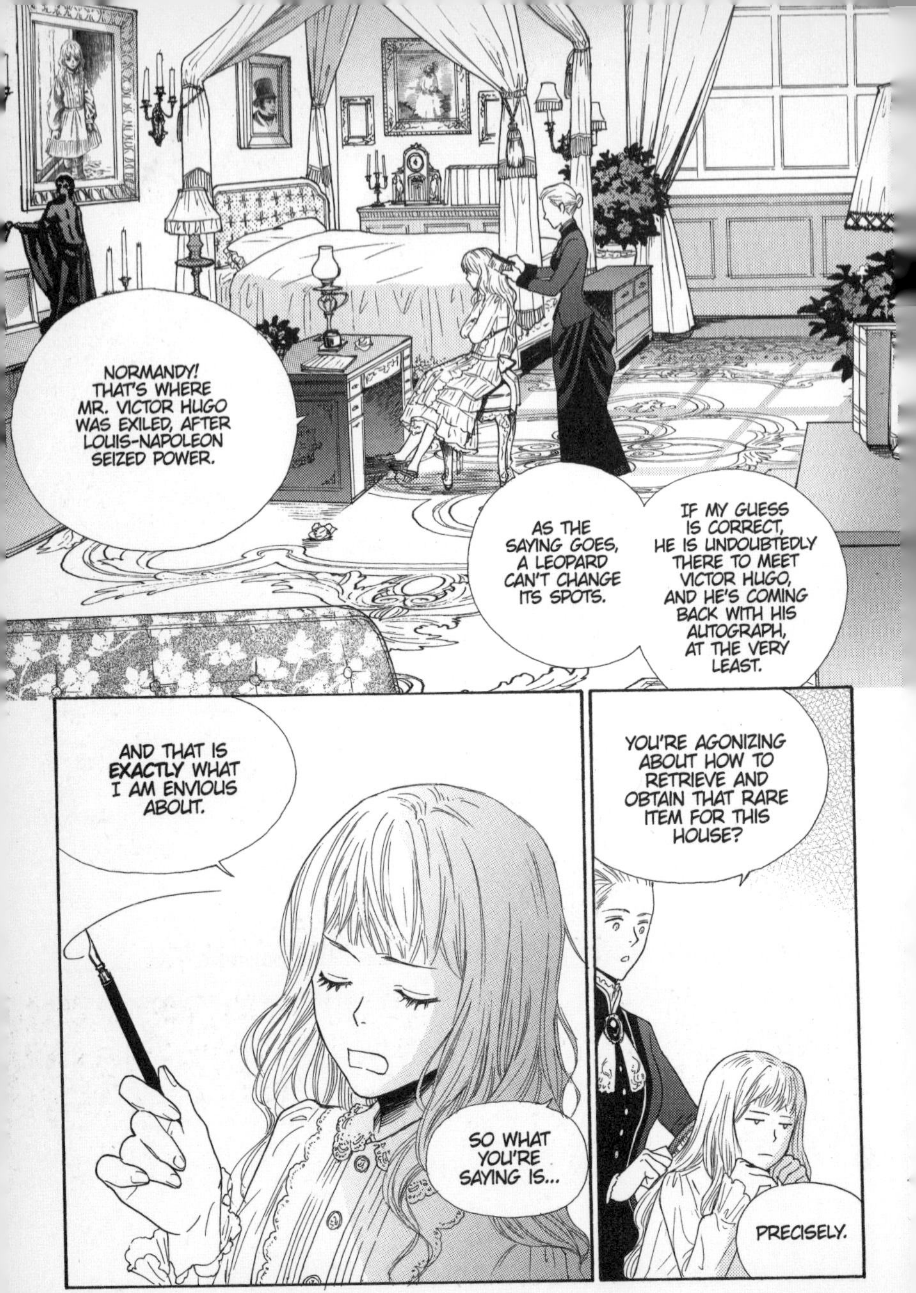
NORMANDY! THAT'S WHERE MR. VICTOR HUGO WAS EXILED, AFTER LOUIS-NAPOLEON SEIZED POWER.
AS THE SAYING GOES, A LEOPARD CAN'T CHANGE ITS SPOTS.
IF MY GUESS IS CORRECT, HE IS UNDOUBTEDLY THERE TO MEET VICTOR HUGO, AND HE'S COMING BACK WITH HIS AUTOGRAPH, AT THE VERY LEAST.
AND THAT IS **EXACTLY** WHAT I AM ENVIOUS ABOUT.
SO WHAT YOU'RE SAYING IS...
YOU'RE AGONIZING ABOUT HOW TO RETRIEVE AND OBTAIN THAT RARE ITEM FOR THIS HOUSE?
PRECISELY.

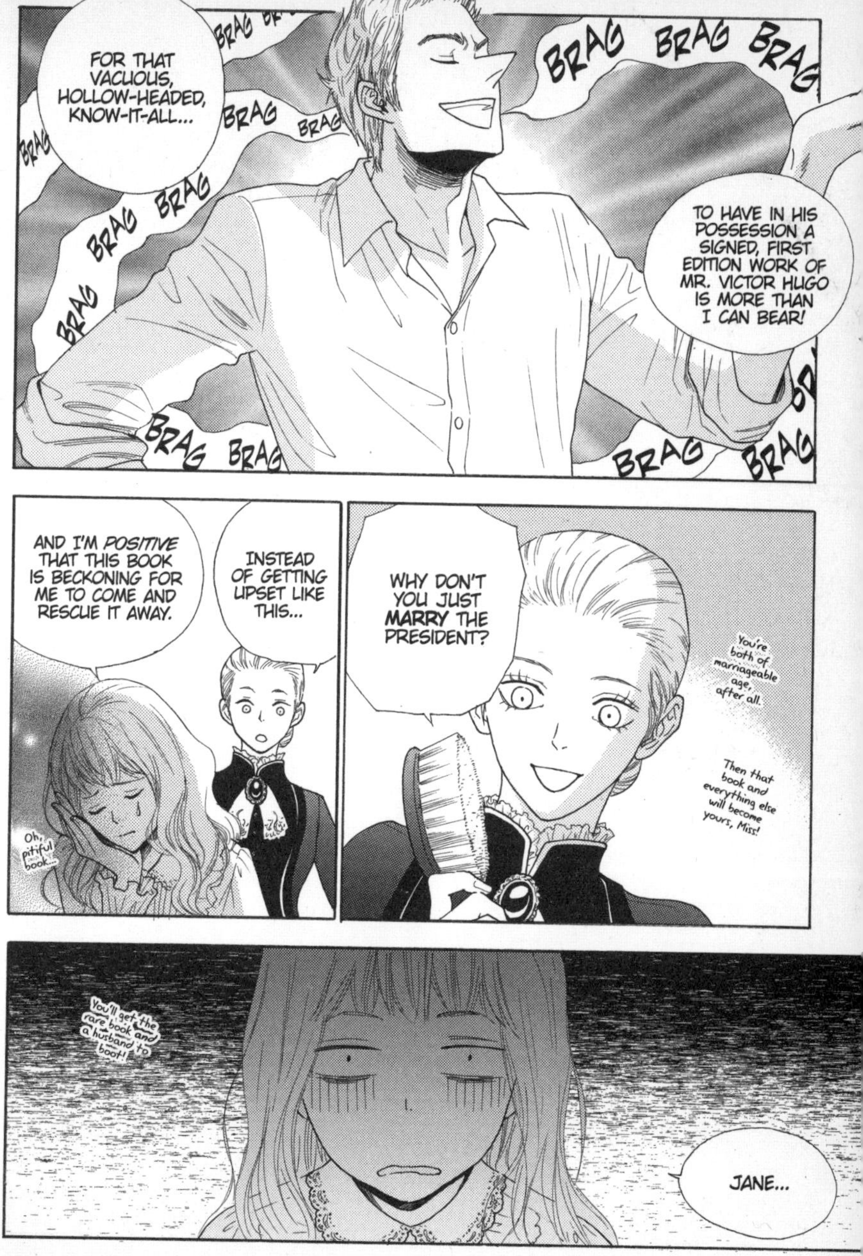
FOR THAT VACUOUS, HOLLOW-HEADED, KNOW-IT-ALL...
BRAG BRAG BRAG BRAG BRAG BRAG
BRAG BRAG BRAG
TO HAVE IN HIS POSSESSION A SIGNED, FIRST EDITION WORK OF MR. VICTOR HUGO IS MORE THAN I CAN BEAR!
BRAG BRAG BRAG BRAG
AND I'M *POSITIVE* THAT THIS BOOK IS BECKONING FOR ME TO COME AND RESCUE IT AWAY.
Oh, pitiful book...
INSTEAD OF GETTING UPSET LIKE THIS...
WHY DON'T YOU JUST **MARRY** THE PRESIDENT?
You're both of marriageable age, after all.
Then that book and everything else will become yours, Miss!
You'll get the rare book and a husband to boot!
JANE...

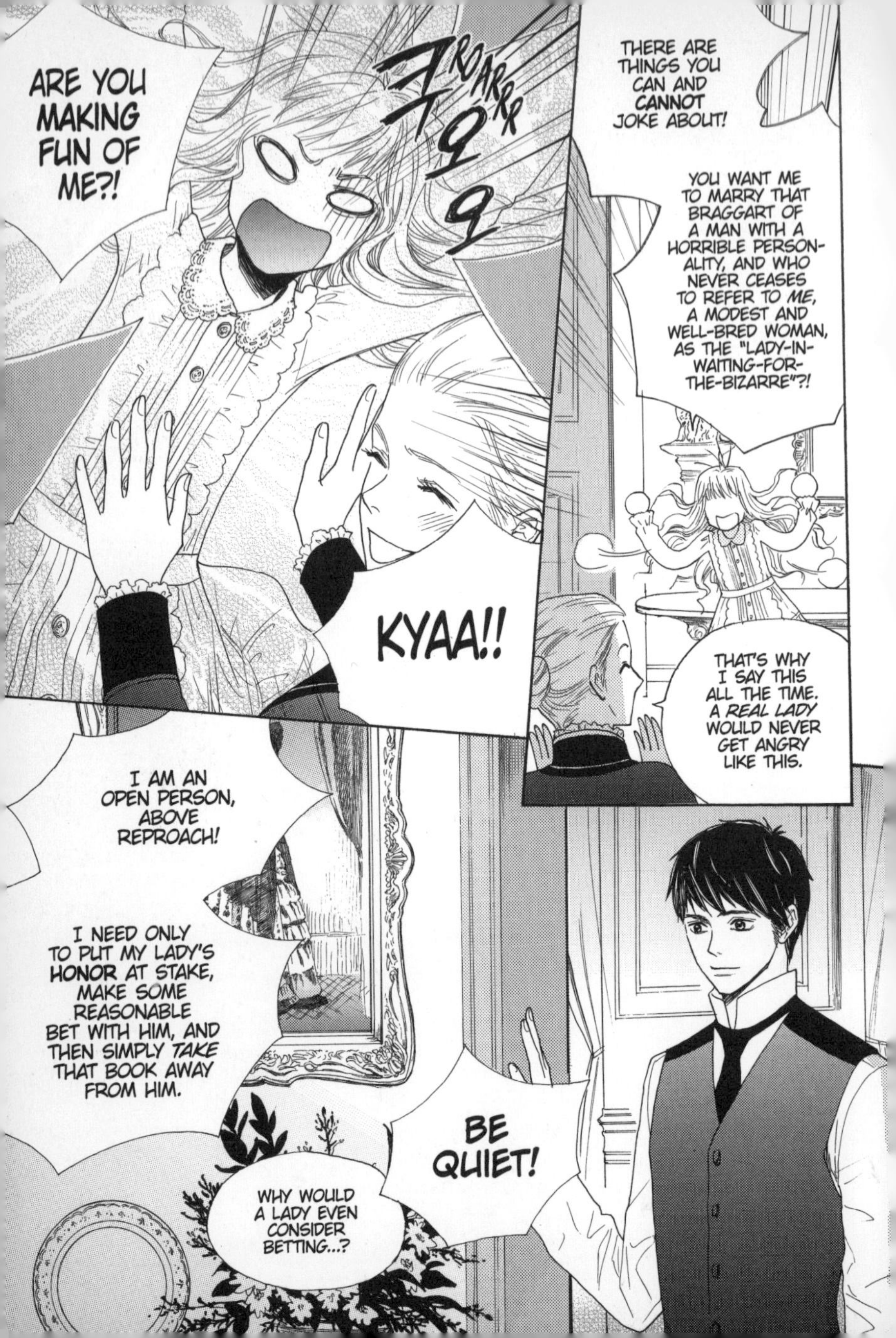
ARE YOU MAKING FUN OF ME?!
ROARRR
KYAA!!
THERE ARE THINGS YOU CAN AND CANNOT JOKE ABOUT!
YOU WANT ME TO MARRY THAT BRAGGART OF A MAN WITH A HORRIBLE PERSON-ALITY, AND WHO NEVER CEASES TO REFER TO *ME*, A MODEST AND WELL-BRED WOMAN, AS THE "LADY-IN-WAITING-FOR-THE-BIZARRE"?!
THAT'S WHY I SAY THIS ALL THE TIME. A *REAL LADY* WOULD NEVER GET ANGRY LIKE THIS.
I AM AN OPEN PERSON, ABOVE REPROACH!
I NEED ONLY TO PUT MY LADY'S **HONOR** AT STAKE, MAKE SOME REASONABLE BET WITH HIM, AND THEN SIMPLY *TAKE* THAT BOOK AWAY FROM HIM.
BE QUIET!
WHY WOULD A LADY EVEN CONSIDER BETTING...?

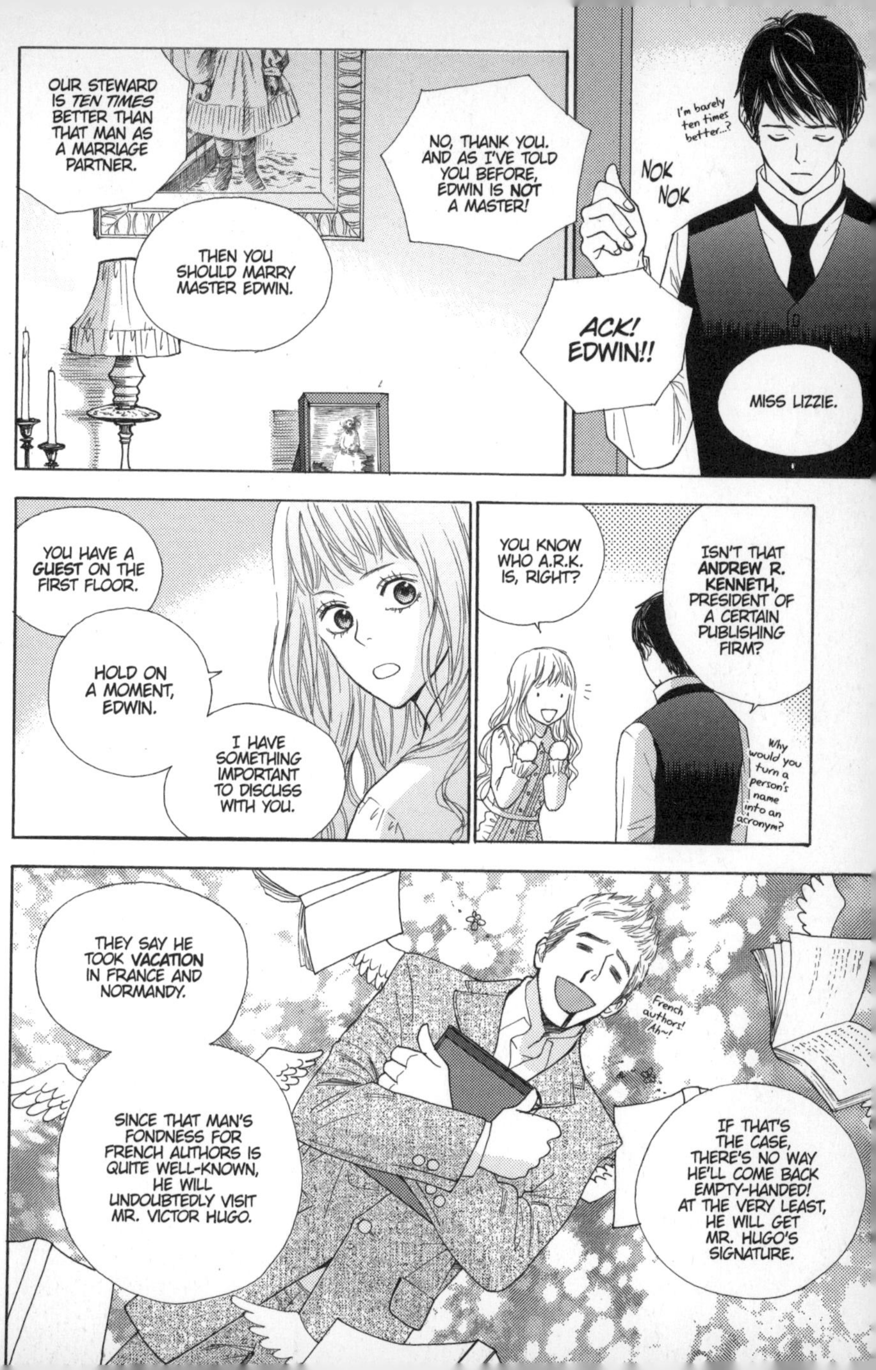
OUR STEWARD IS TEN TIMES BETTER THAN THAT MAN AS A MARRIAGE PARTNER.
THEN YOU SHOULD MARRY MASTER EDWIN.
NO, THANK YOU. AND AS I'VE TOLD YOU BEFORE, EDWIN IS NOT A MASTER!
I'm barely ten times better...?
NOK NOK
ACK! EDWIN!!
MISS LIZZIE.
YOU HAVE A GUEST ON THE FIRST FLOOR.
HOLD ON A MOMENT, EDWIN.
I HAVE SOMETHING IMPORTANT TO DISCUSS WITH YOU.
YOU KNOW WHO A.R.K. IS, RIGHT?
ISN'T THAT ANDREW R. KENNETH, PRESIDENT OF A CERTAIN PUBLISHING FIRM?
Why would you turn a person's name into an acronym?
THEY SAY HE TOOK VACATION IN FRANCE AND NORMANDY.
SINCE THAT MAN'S FONDNESS FOR FRENCH AUTHORS IS QUITE WELL-KNOWN, HE WILL UNDOUBTEDLY VISIT MR. VICTOR HUGO.
French authors! Ah~!
IF THAT'S THE CASE, THERE'S NO WAY HE'LL COME BACK EMPTY-HANDED! AT THE VERY LEAST, HE WILL GET MR. HUGO'S SIGNATURE.

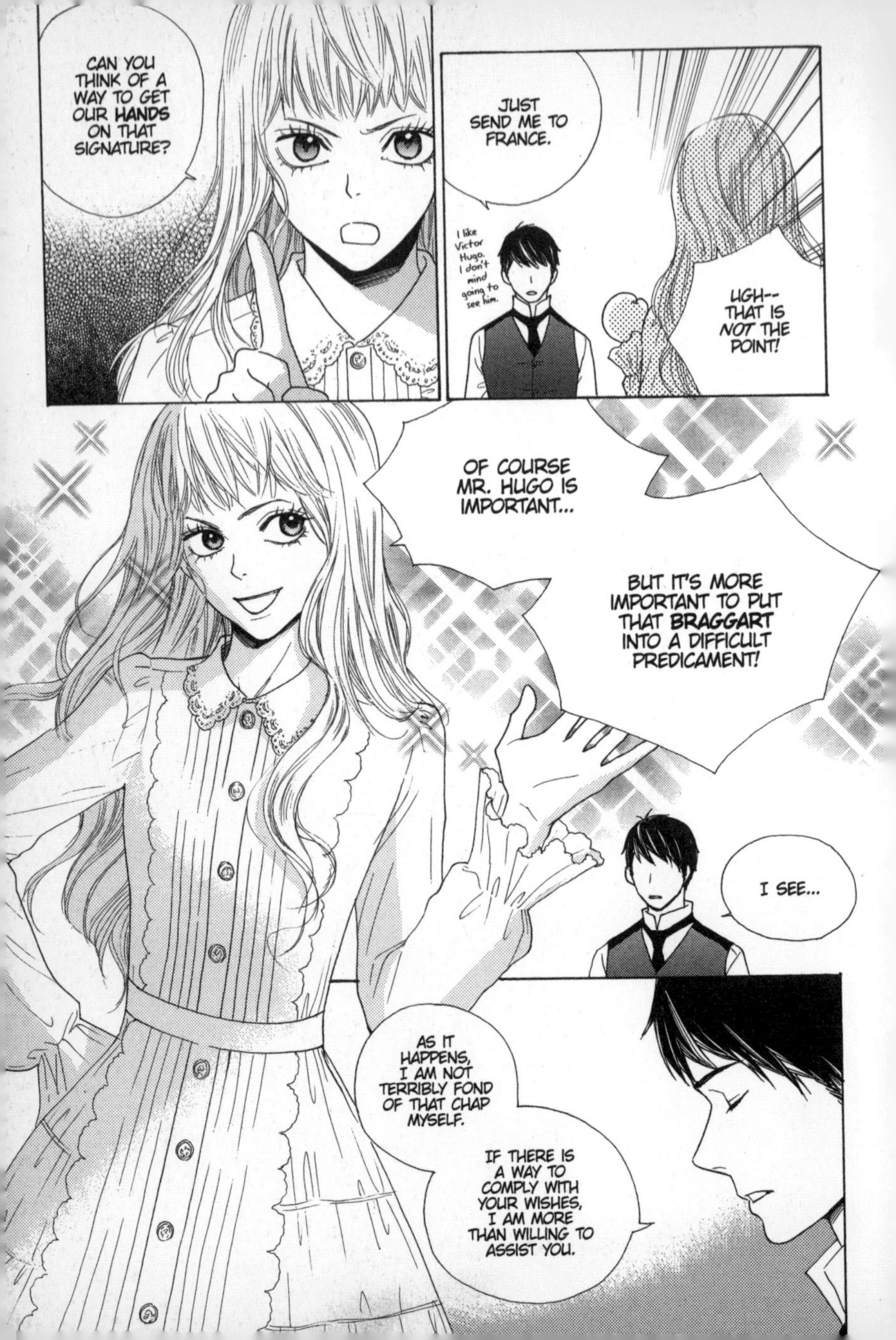
CAN YOU THINK OF A WAY TO GET OUR **HANDS** ON THAT SIGNATURE?
JUST SEND ME TO FRANCE.
I like Victor Hugo. I don't mind going to see him.
UGH-- THAT IS *NOT* THE POINT!
OF COURSE MR. HUGO IS IMPORTANT...
BUT IT'S MORE IMPORTANT TO PUT THAT **BRAGGART** INTO A DIFFICULT PREDICAMENT!
I SEE...
AS IT HAPPENS, I AM NOT TERRIBLY FOND OF THAT CHAP MYSELF.
IF THERE IS A WAY TO COMPLY WITH YOUR WISHES, I AM MORE THAN WILLING TO ASSIST YOU.

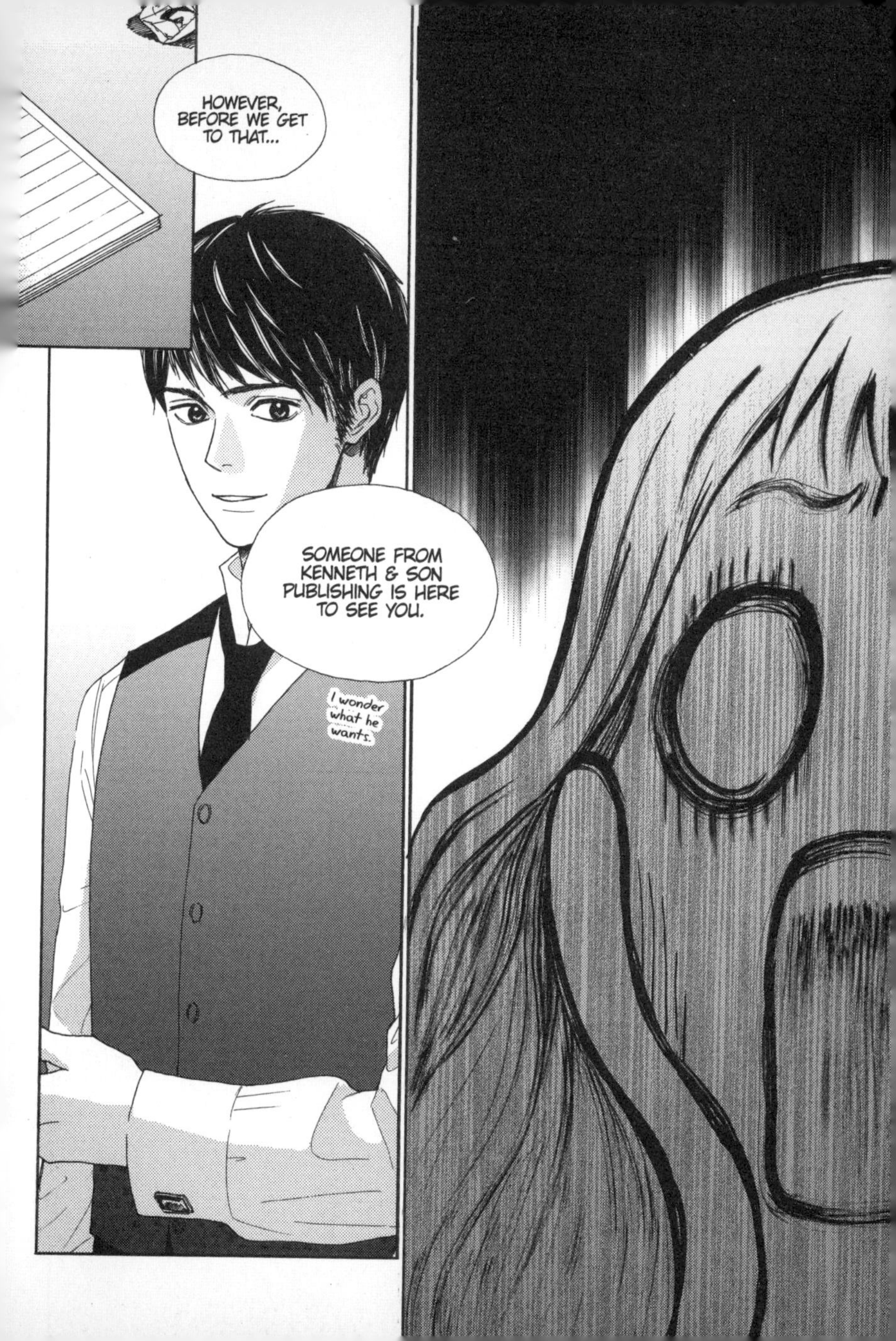
HOWEVER, BEFORE WE GET TO THAT...
SOMEONE FROM KENNETH & SON PUBLISHING IS HERE TO SEE YOU.
I wonder what he wants.

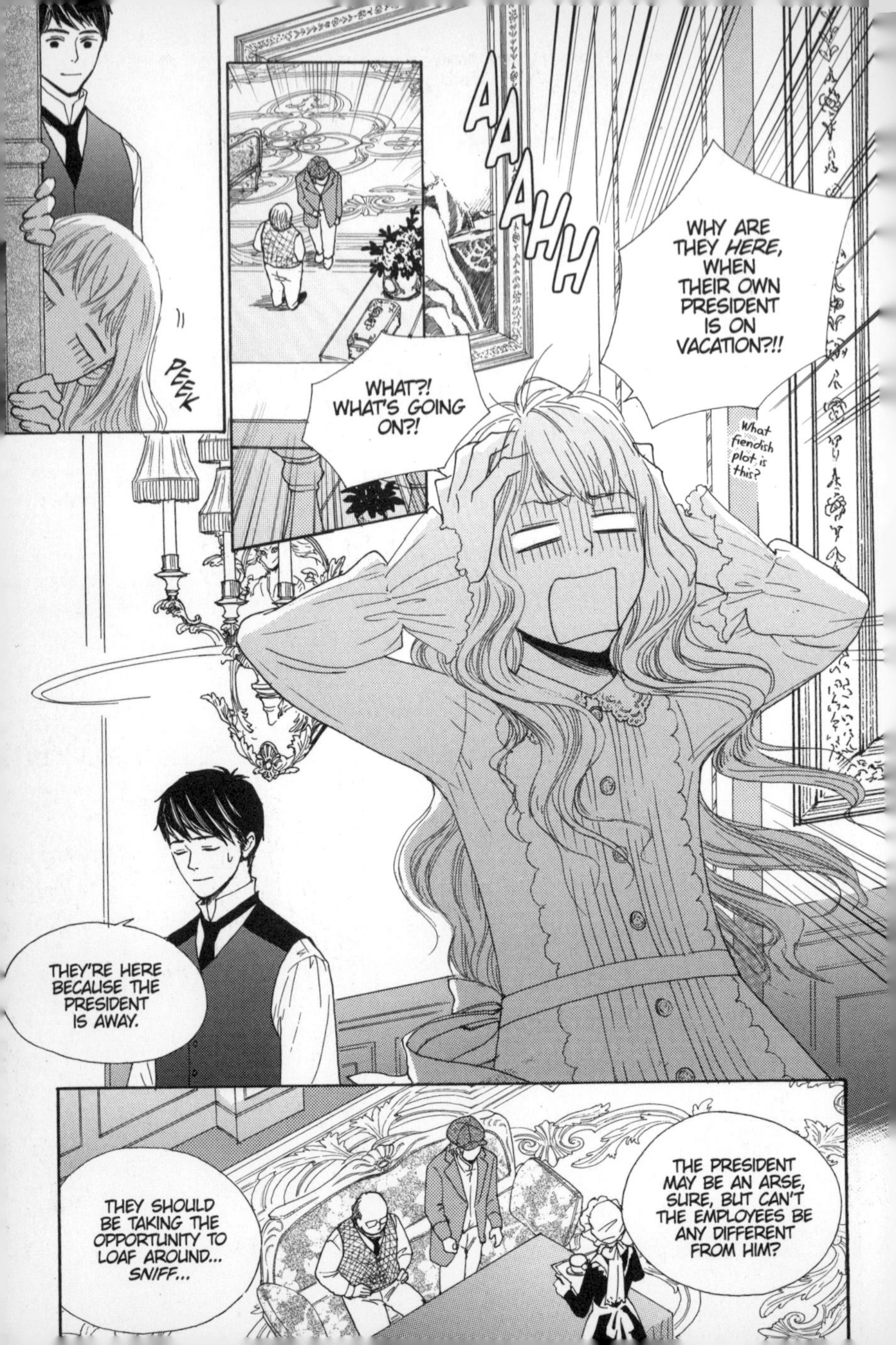
PEEK
WHAT?! WHAT'S GOING ON?!
AAAHHH
WHY ARE THEY HERE, WHEN THEIR OWN PRESIDENT IS ON VACATION?!!
What fiendish plot is this?
THEY'RE HERE BECAUSE THE PRESIDENT IS AWAY.
THEY SHOULD BE TAKING THE OPPORTUNITY TO LOAF AROUND... SNIFF...
THE PRESIDENT MAY BE AN ARSE, SURE, BUT CAN'T THE EMPLOYEES BE ANY DIFFERENT FROM HIM?

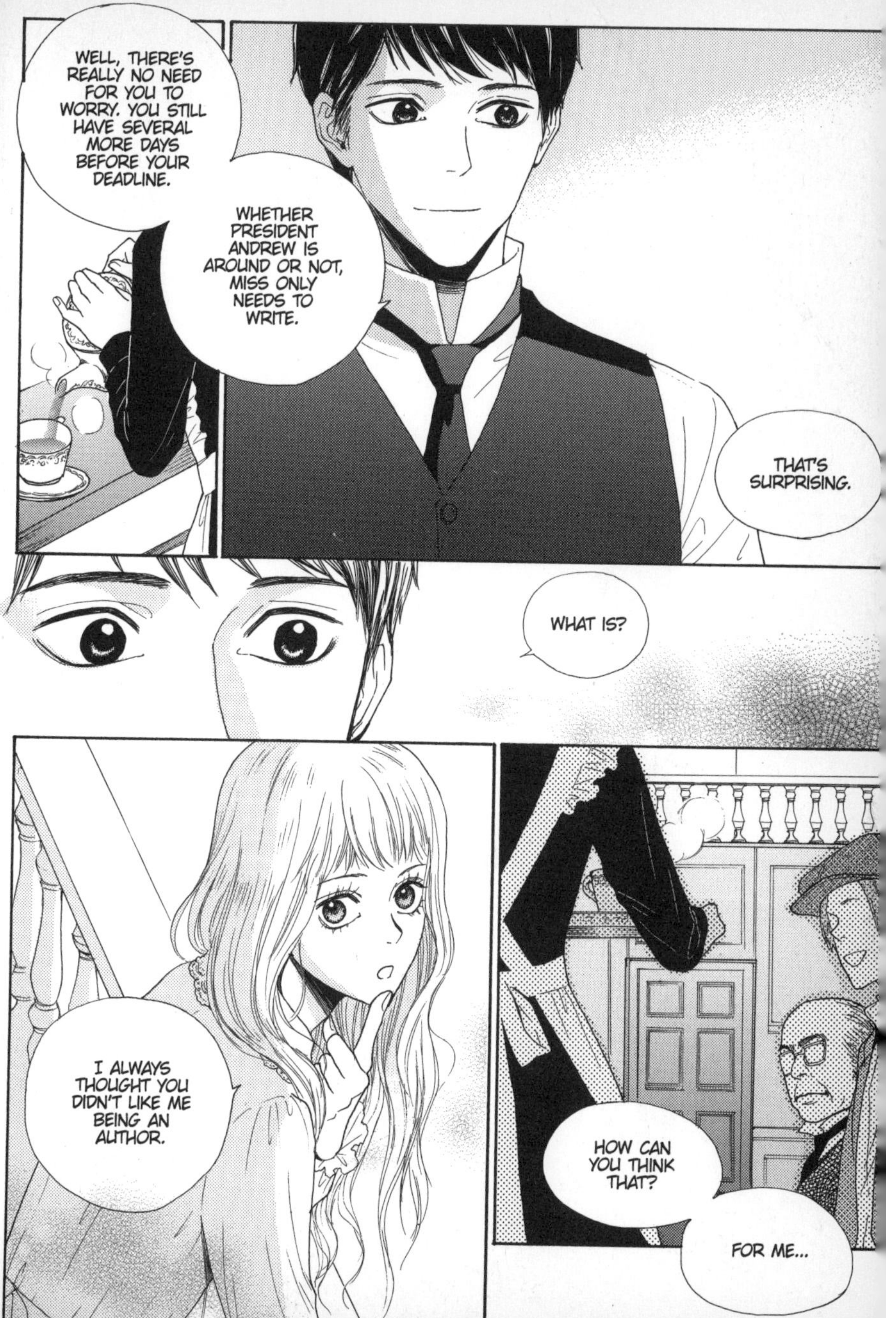
WELL, THERE'S REALLY NO NEED FOR YOU TO WORRY. YOU STILL HAVE SEVERAL MORE DAYS BEFORE YOUR DEADLINE.
WHETHER PRESIDENT ANDREW IS AROUND OR NOT, MISS ONLY NEEDS TO WRITE.
THAT'S SURPRISING.
WHAT IS?
I ALWAYS THOUGHT YOU DIDN'T LIKE ME BEING AN AUTHOR.
HOW CAN YOU THINK THAT?
FOR ME...

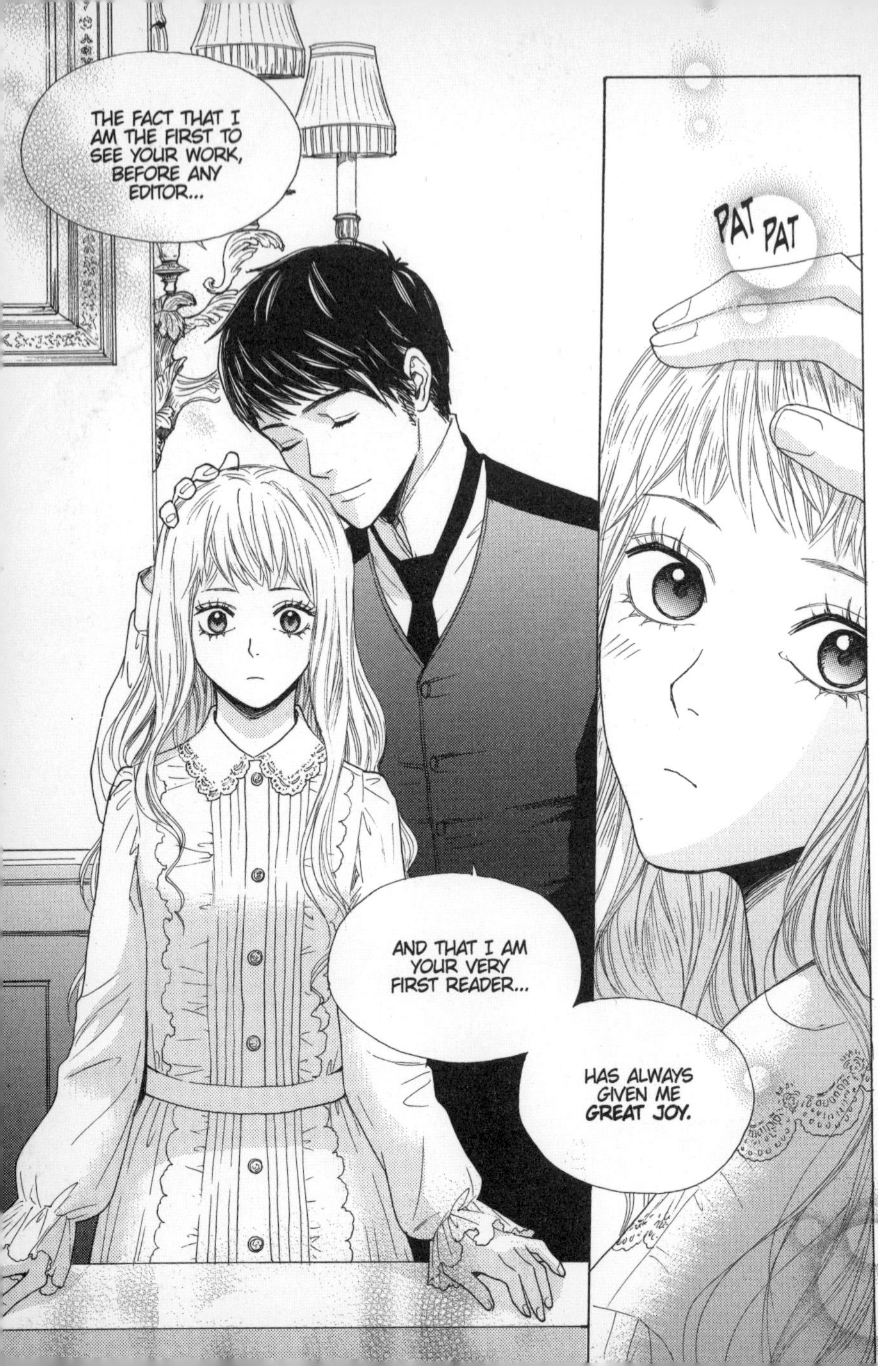
THE FACT THAT I AM THE FIRST TO SEE YOUR WORK, BEFORE ANY EDITOR...
AND THAT I AM YOUR VERY FIRST READER...
PAT PAT
HAS ALWAYS GIVEN ME GREAT JOY.

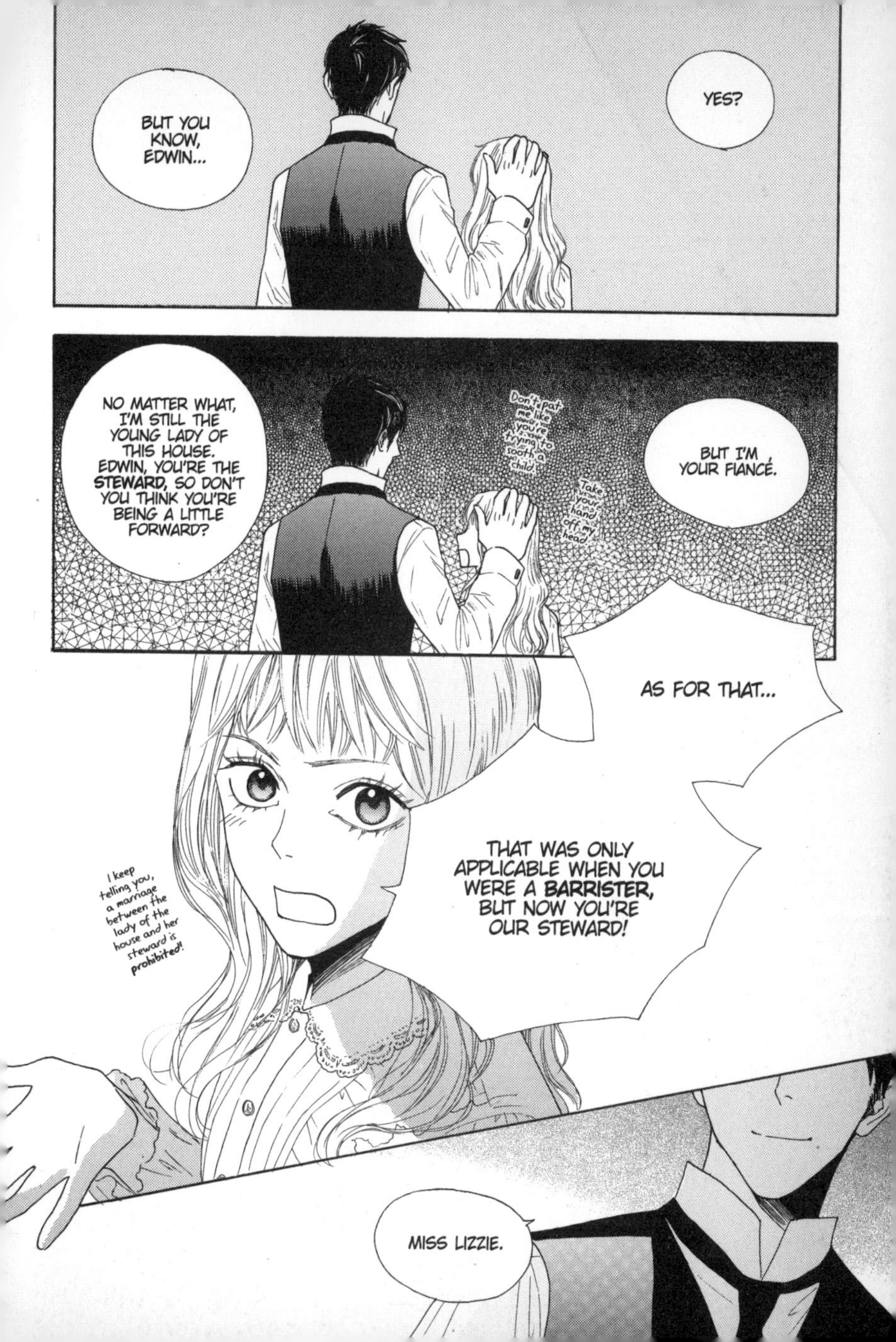
BUT YOU KNOW, EDWIN...
YES?
NO MATTER WHAT, I'M STILL THE YOUNG LADY OF THIS HOUSE. EDWIN, YOU'RE THE STEWARD, SO DON'T YOU THINK YOU'RE BEING A LITTLE FORWARD?
Don't pat me like you're trying to sooth a child.
Take your hand off my head!
BUT I'M YOUR FIANCÉ.
AS FOR THAT...
THAT WAS ONLY APPLICABLE WHEN YOU WERE A BARRISTER, BUT NOW YOU'RE OUR STEWARD!
I keep telling you, a marriage between the lady of the house and her steward is prohibited!
MISS LIZZIE.

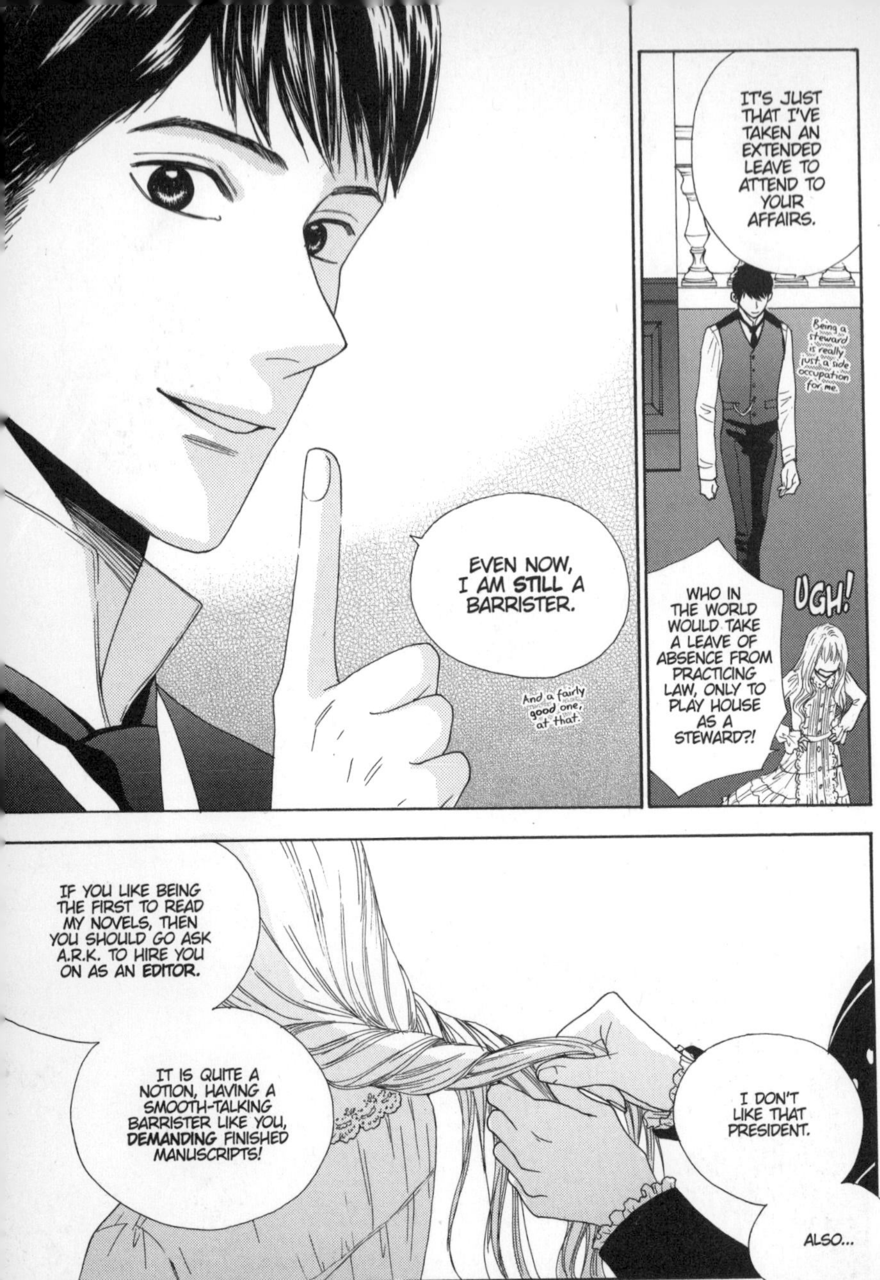
EVEN NOW, I AM STILL A BARRISTER.
And a fairly good one, at that.
IT'S JUST THAT I'VE TAKEN AN EXTENDED LEAVE TO ATTEND TO YOUR AFFAIRS.
Being a steward is really just a side occupation for me.
WHO IN THE WORLD WOULD TAKE A LEAVE OF ABSENCE FROM PRACTICING LAW, ONLY TO PLAY HOUSE AS A STEWARD?!
UGH!
IF YOU LIKE BEING THE FIRST TO READ MY NOVELS, THEN YOU SHOULD GO ASK A.R.K. TO HIRE YOU ON AS AN EDITOR.
IT IS QUITE A NOTION, HAVING A SMOOTH-TALKING BARRISTER LIKE YOU, DEMANDING FINISHED MANUSCRIPTS!
I DON'T LIKE THAT PRESIDENT.
ALSO...

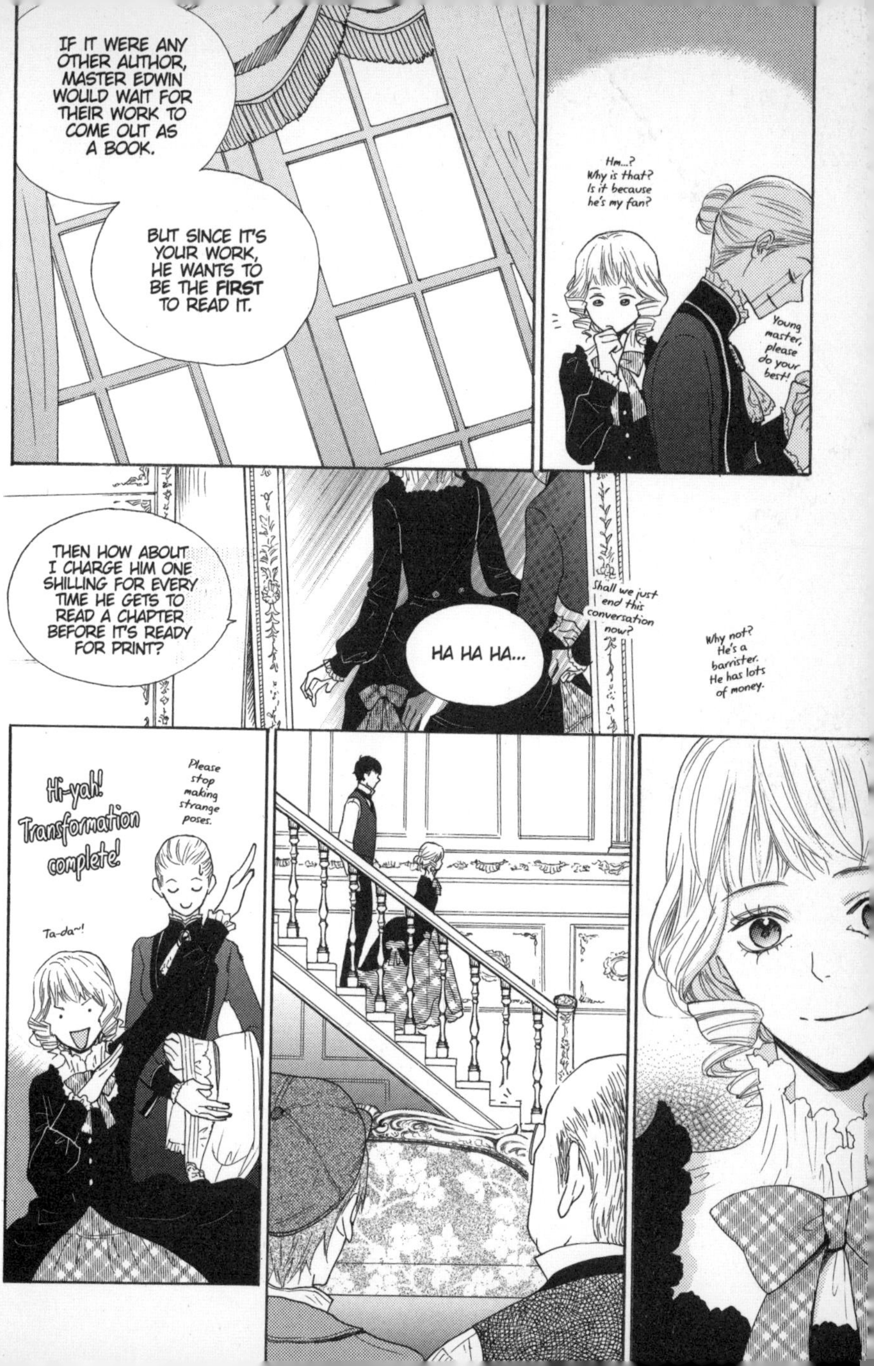
IF IT WERE ANY OTHER AUTHOR, MASTER EDWIN WOULD WAIT FOR THEIR WORK TO COME OUT AS A BOOK.
BUT SINCE IT'S YOUR WORK, HE WANTS TO BE THE FIRST TO READ IT.
Hm...? Why is that? Is it because he's my fan?
Young master, please do your best!
THEN HOW ABOUT I CHARGE HIM ONE SHILLING FOR EVERY TIME HE GETS TO READ A CHAPTER BEFORE IT'S READY FOR PRINT?
Shall we just end this conversation now?
HA HA HA...
Why not? He's a barrister. He has lots of money.
Hi-yah! Transformation complete!
Please stop making strange poses.
Ta-da~!

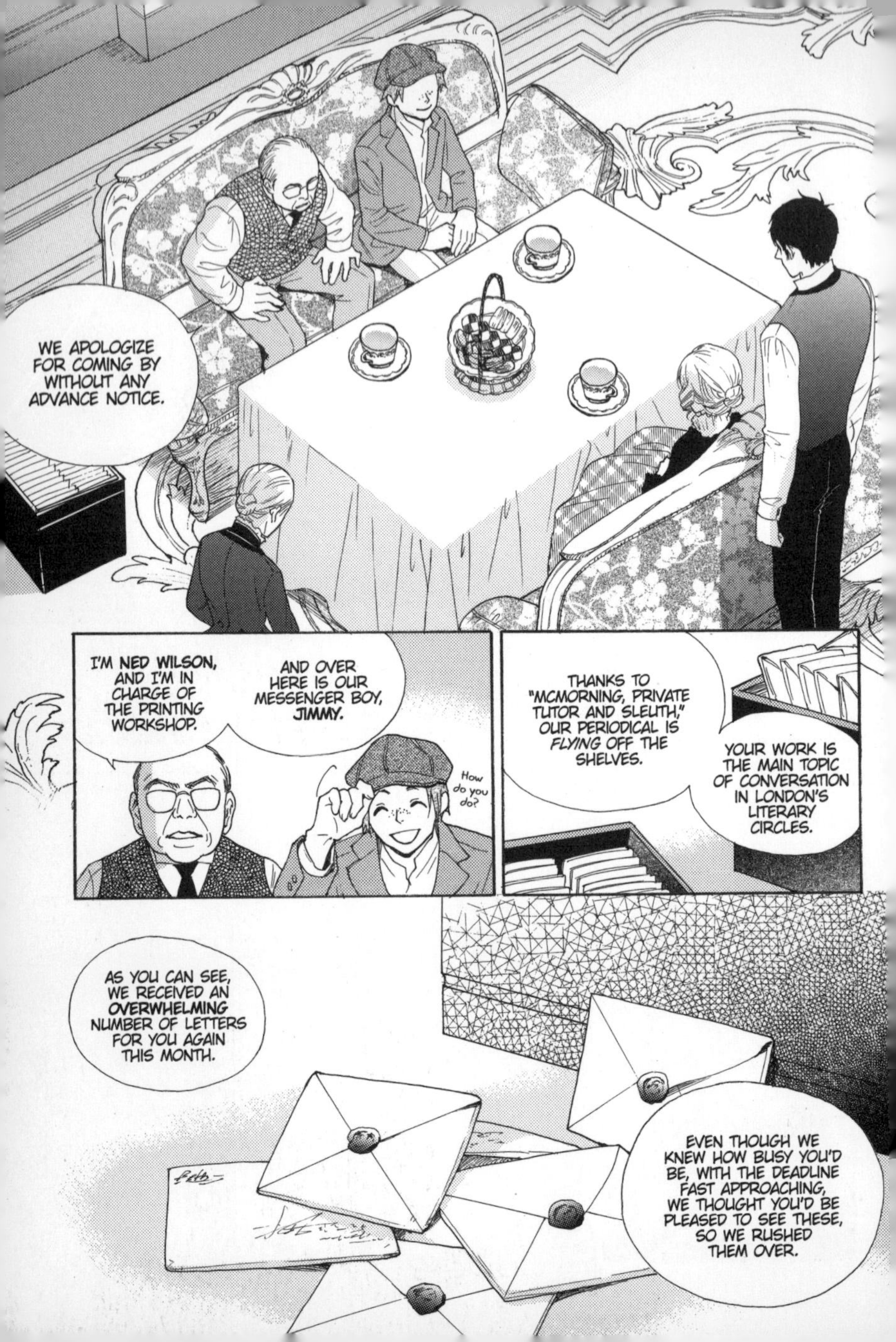
WE APOLOGIZE FOR COMING BY WITHOUT ANY ADVANCE NOTICE.
I'M NED WILSON, AND I'M IN CHARGE OF THE PRINTING WORKSHOP.
AND OVER HERE IS OUR MESSENGER BOY, JIMMY.
How do you do?
THANKS TO "MCMORNING, PRIVATE TUTOR AND SLEUTH," OUR PERIODICAL IS FLYING OFF THE SHELVES.
YOUR WORK IS THE MAIN TOPIC OF CONVERSATION IN LONDON'S LITERARY CIRCLES.
AS YOU CAN SEE, WE RECEIVED AN OVERWHELMING NUMBER OF LETTERS FOR YOU AGAIN THIS MONTH.
EVEN THOUGH WE KNEW HOW BUSY YOU'D BE, WITH THE DEADLINE FAST APPROACHING, WE THOUGHT YOU'D BE PLEASED TO SEE THESE, SO WE RUSHED THEM OVER.

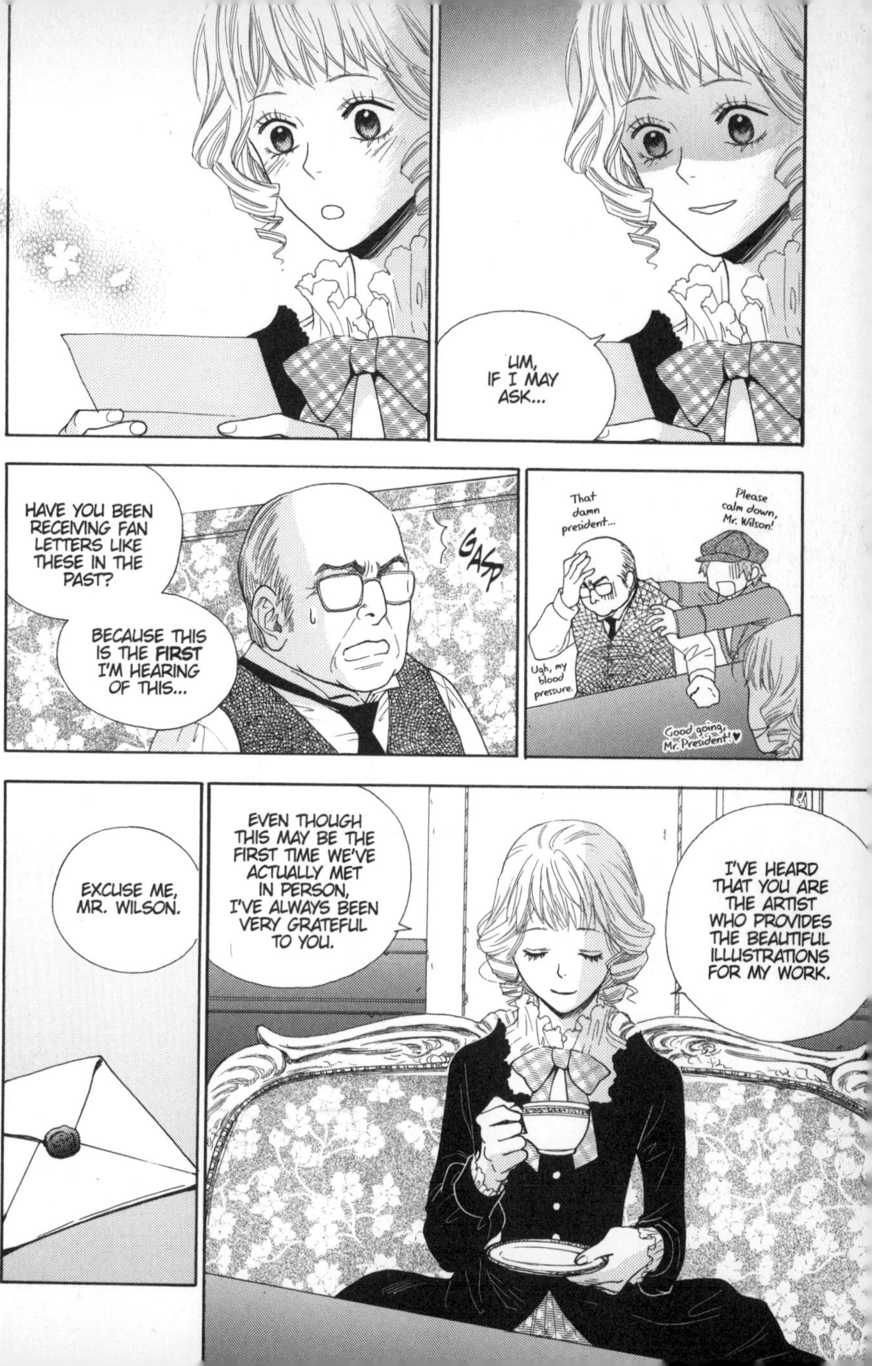
UM, IF I MAY ASK...
HAVE YOU BEEN RECEIVING FAN LETTERS LIKE THESE IN THE PAST?
BECAUSE THIS IS THE FIRST I'M HEARING OF THIS...
GASP
That damn president...
Please calm down, Mr. Wilson!
Ugh, my blood pressure.
Good going, Mr. President! ♥
EXCUSE ME, MR. WILSON.
EVEN THOUGH THIS MAY BE THE FIRST TIME WE'VE ACTUALLY MET IN PERSON, I'VE ALWAYS BEEN VERY GRATEFUL TO YOU.
I'VE HEARD THAT YOU ARE THE ARTIST WHO PROVIDES THE BEAUTIFUL ILLUSTRATIONS FOR MY WORK.

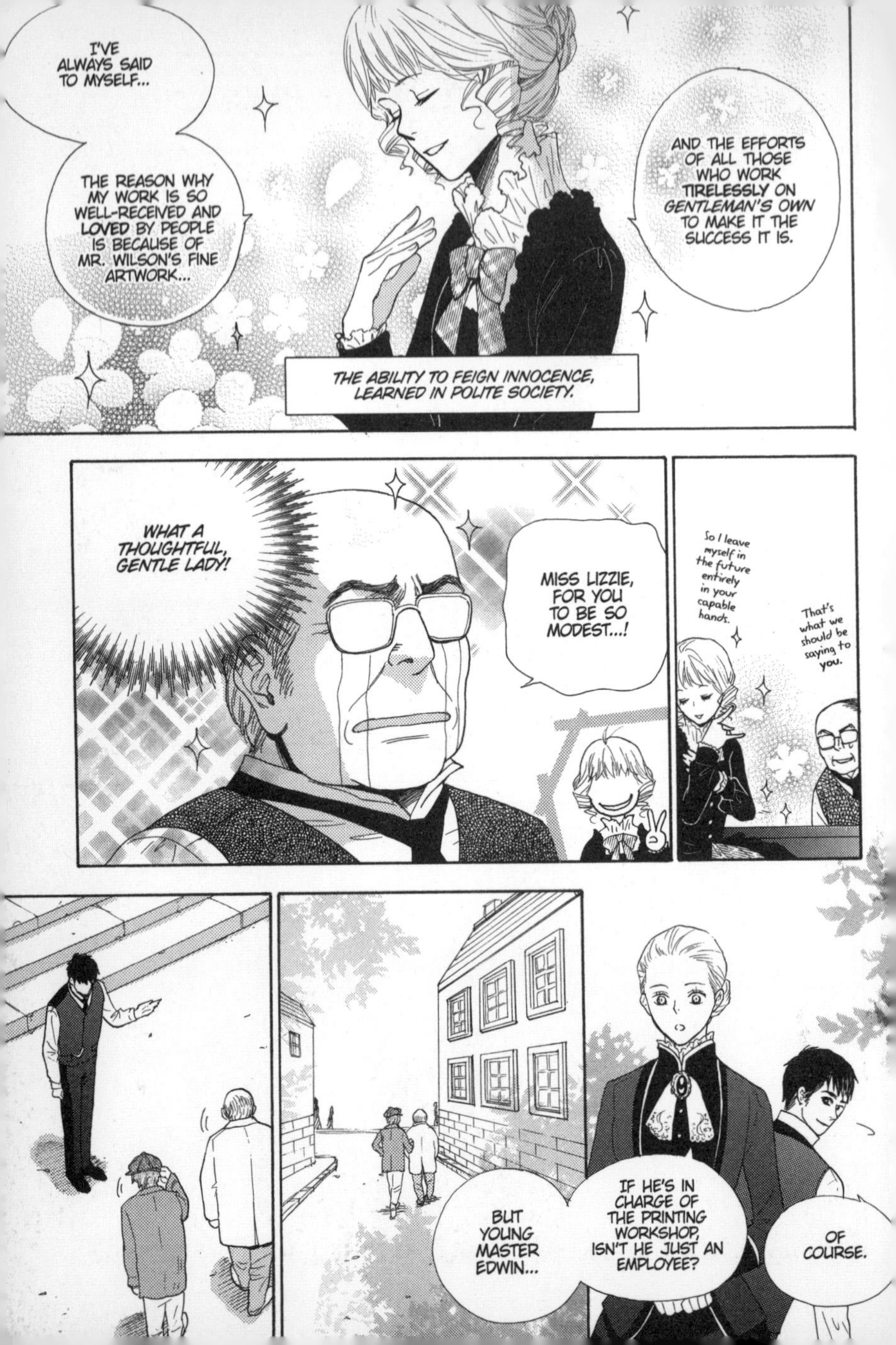

I'VE ALWAYS SAID TO MYSELF...
THE REASON WHY MY WORK IS SO WELL-RECEIVED AND LOVED BY PEOPLE IS BECAUSE OF MR. WILSON'S FINE ARTWORK...
AND THE EFFORTS OF ALL THOSE WHO WORK TIRELESSLY ON GENTLEMAN'S OWN TO MAKE IT THE SUCCESS IT IS.
THE ABILITY TO FEIGN INNOCENCE, LEARNED IN POLITE SOCIETY.
WHAT A THOUGHTFUL, GENTLE LADY!
MISS LIZZIE, FOR YOU TO BE SO MODEST...!
So I leave myself in the future entirely in your capable hands.
That's what we should be saying to you.
BUT YOUNG MASTER EDWIN...
IF HE'S IN CHARGE OF THE PRINTING WORKSHOP, ISN'T HE JUST AN EMPLOYEE?
OF COURSE.

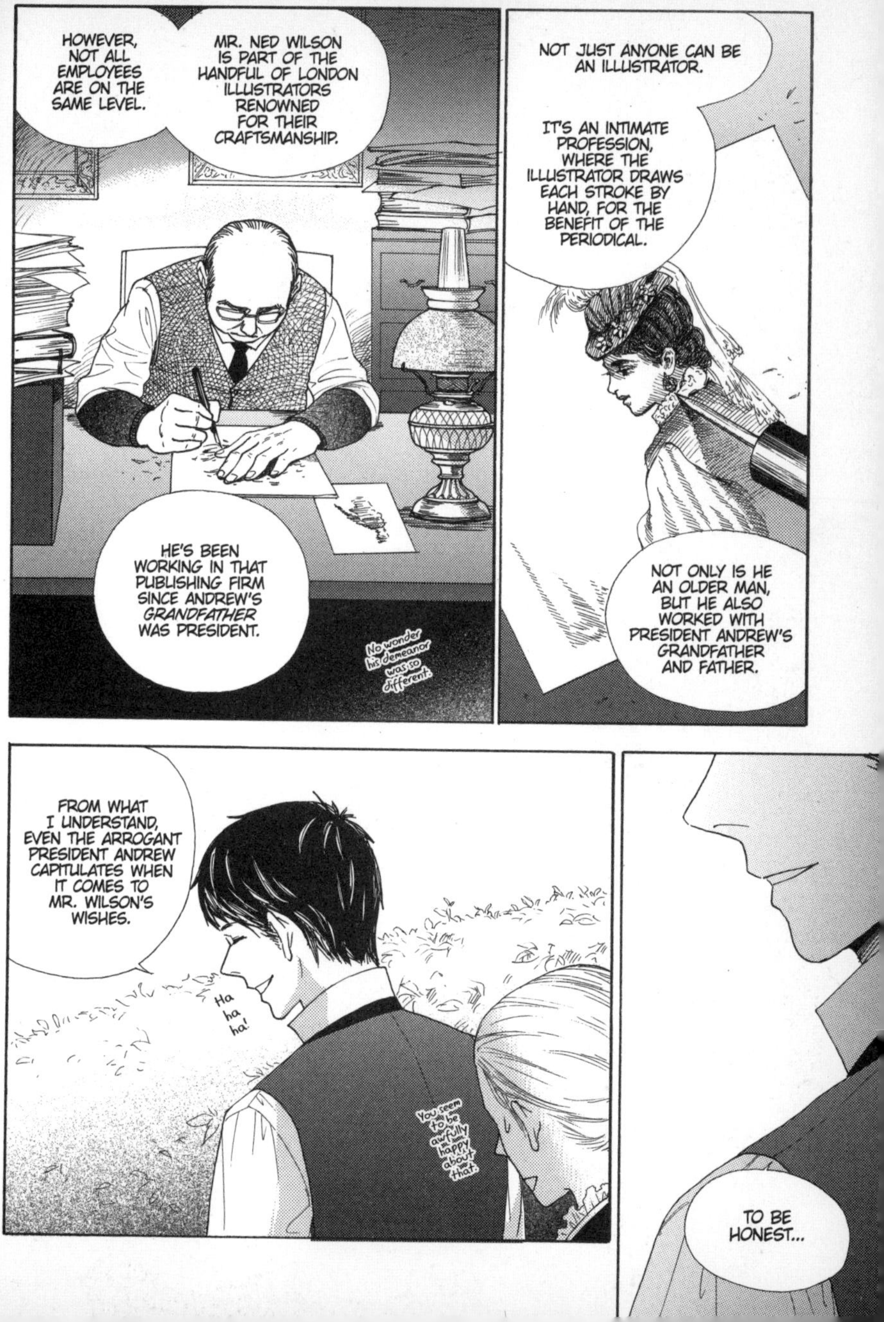
HOWEVER, NOT ALL EMPLOYEES ARE ON THE SAME LEVEL.
MR. NED WILSON IS PART OF THE HANDFUL OF LONDON ILLUSTRATORS RENOWNED FOR THEIR CRAFTSMANSHIP.
HE'S BEEN WORKING IN THAT PUBLISHING FIRM SINCE ANDREW'S *GRANDFATHER* WAS PRESIDENT.
No wonder his demeanor was so different.
NOT JUST ANYONE CAN BE AN ILLUSTRATOR.
IT'S AN INTIMATE PROFESSION, WHERE THE ILLUSTRATOR DRAWS EACH STROKE BY HAND, FOR THE BENEFIT OF THE PERIODICAL.
NOT ONLY IS HE AN OLDER MAN, BUT HE ALSO WORKED WITH PRESIDENT ANDREW'S GRANDFATHER AND FATHER.
FROM WHAT I UNDERSTAND, EVEN THE ARROGANT PRESIDENT ANDREW CAPITULATES WHEN IT COMES TO MR. WILSON'S WISHES.
Ha ha ha!
You seem to be awfully happy about that.
TO BE HONEST...

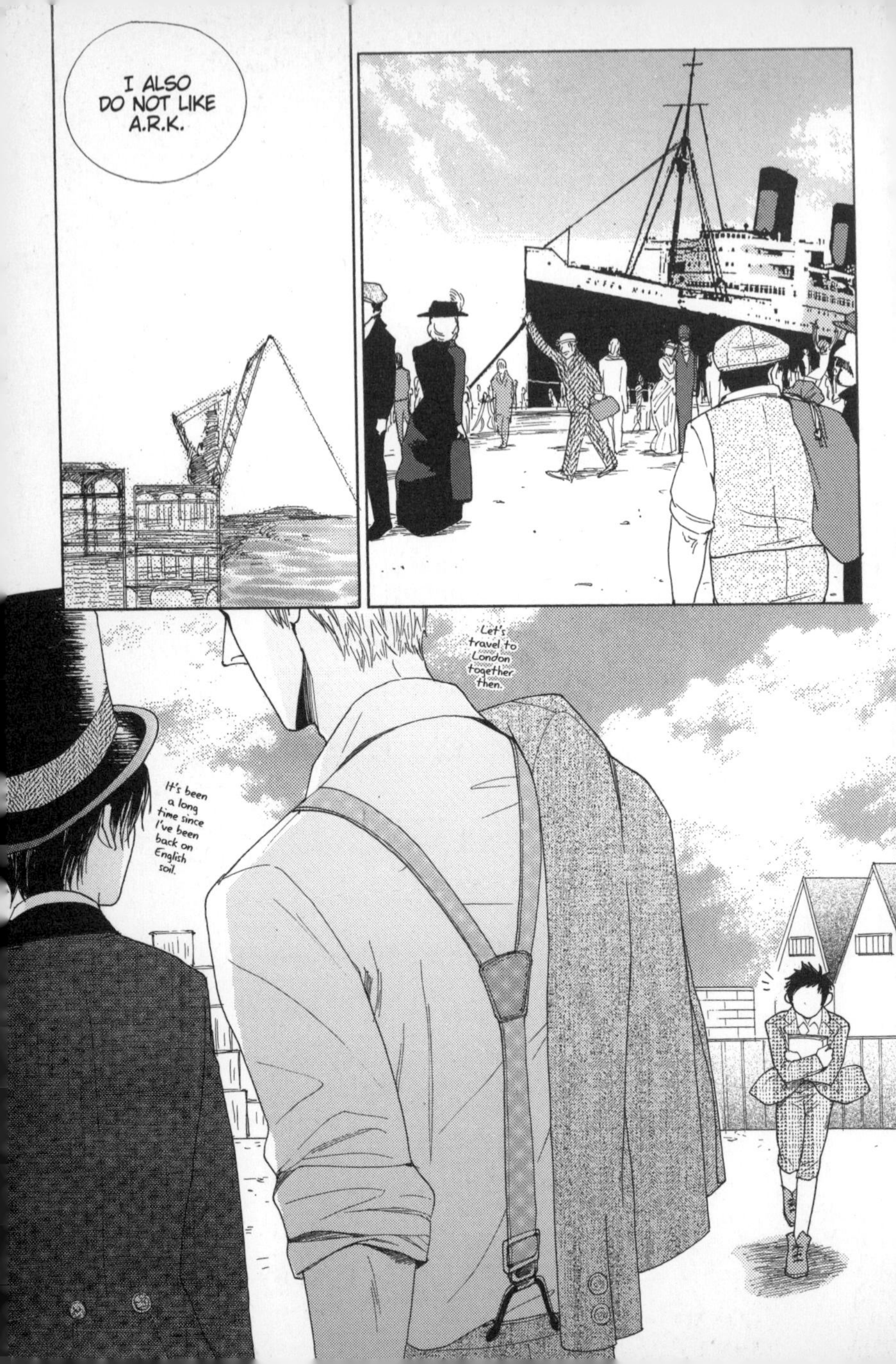
I ALSO DO NOT LIKE A.R.K.
It's been a long time since I've been back on English soil.
Let's travel to London together then.

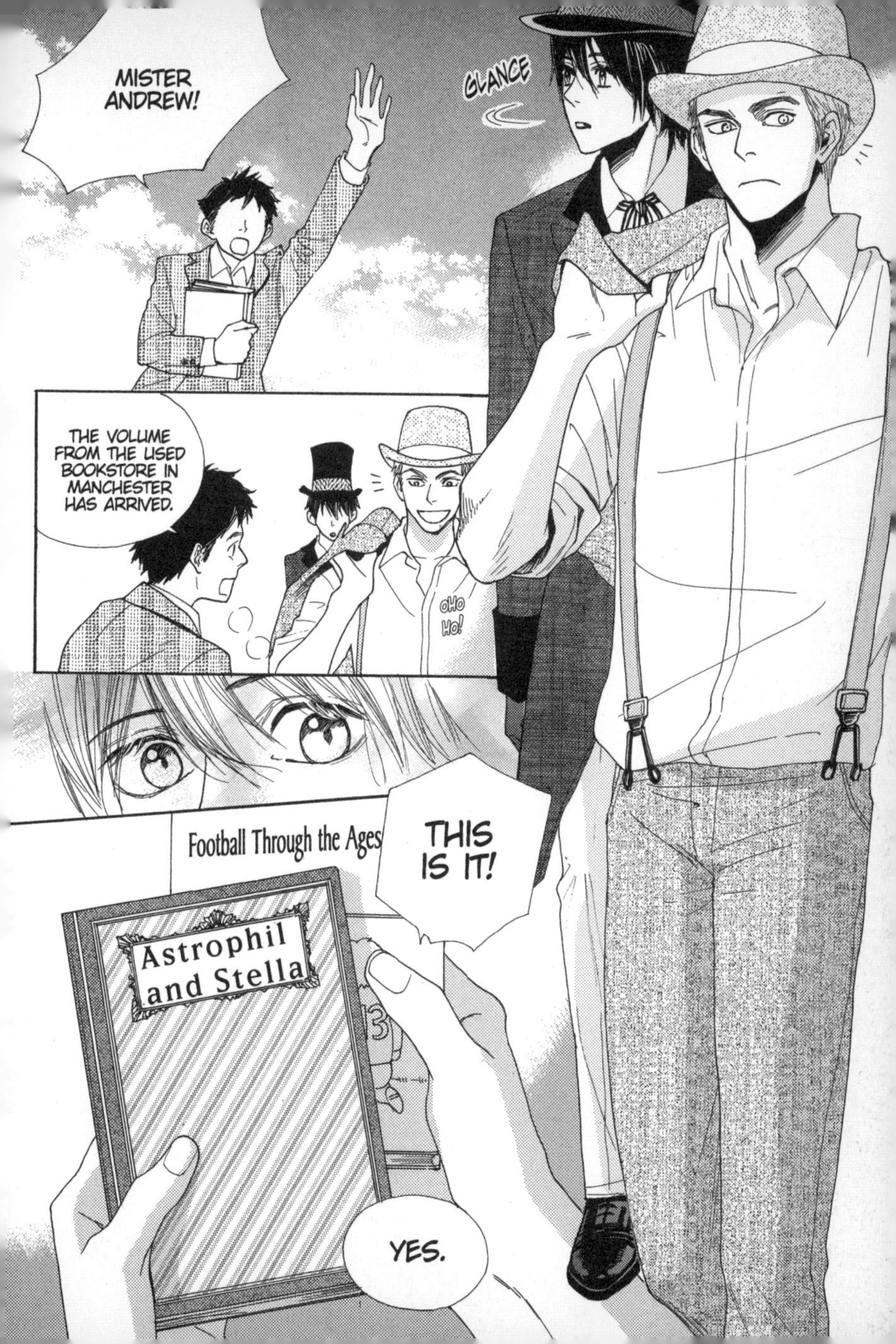
MISTER ANDREW!
GLANCE
THE VOLUME FROM THE USED BOOKSTORE IN MANCHESTER HAS ARRIVED.
OHO HO!
Football Through the Ages
THIS IS IT!
Astrophil and Stella
YES.

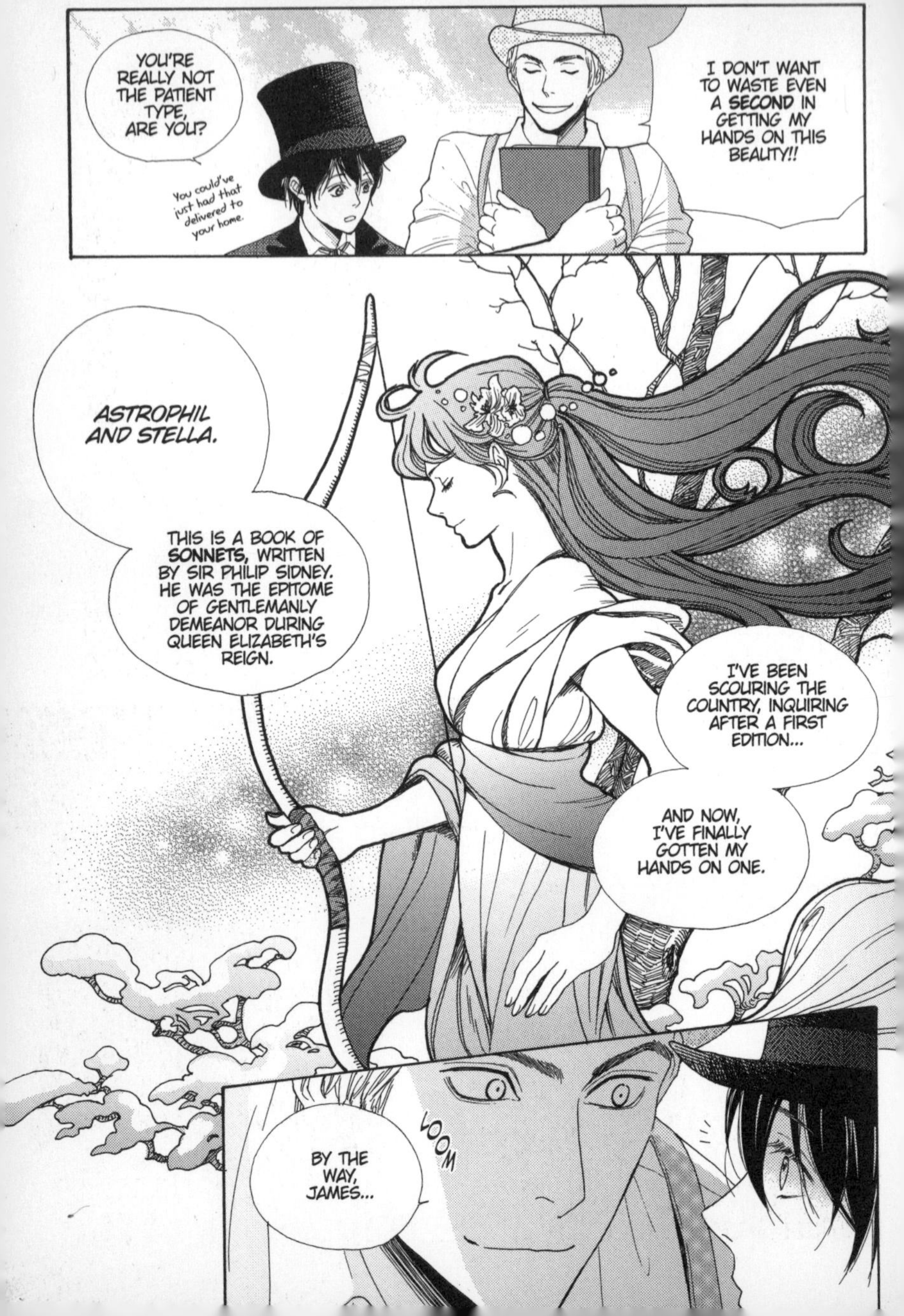
YOU'RE REALLY NOT THE PATIENT TYPE, ARE YOU?
You could've just had that delivered to your home.
I DON'T WANT TO WASTE EVEN A SECOND IN GETTING MY HANDS ON THIS BEAUTY!!
ASTROPHIL AND STELLA.
THIS IS A BOOK OF SONNETS, WRITTEN BY SIR PHILIP SIDNEY. HE WAS THE EPITOME OF GENTLEMANLY DEMEANOR DURING QUEEN ELIZABETH'S REIGN.
I'VE BEEN SCOURING THE COUNTRY, INQUIRING AFTER A FIRST EDITION...
AND NOW, I'VE FINALLY GOTTEN MY HANDS ON ONE.
VOOM
BY THE WAY, JAMES...

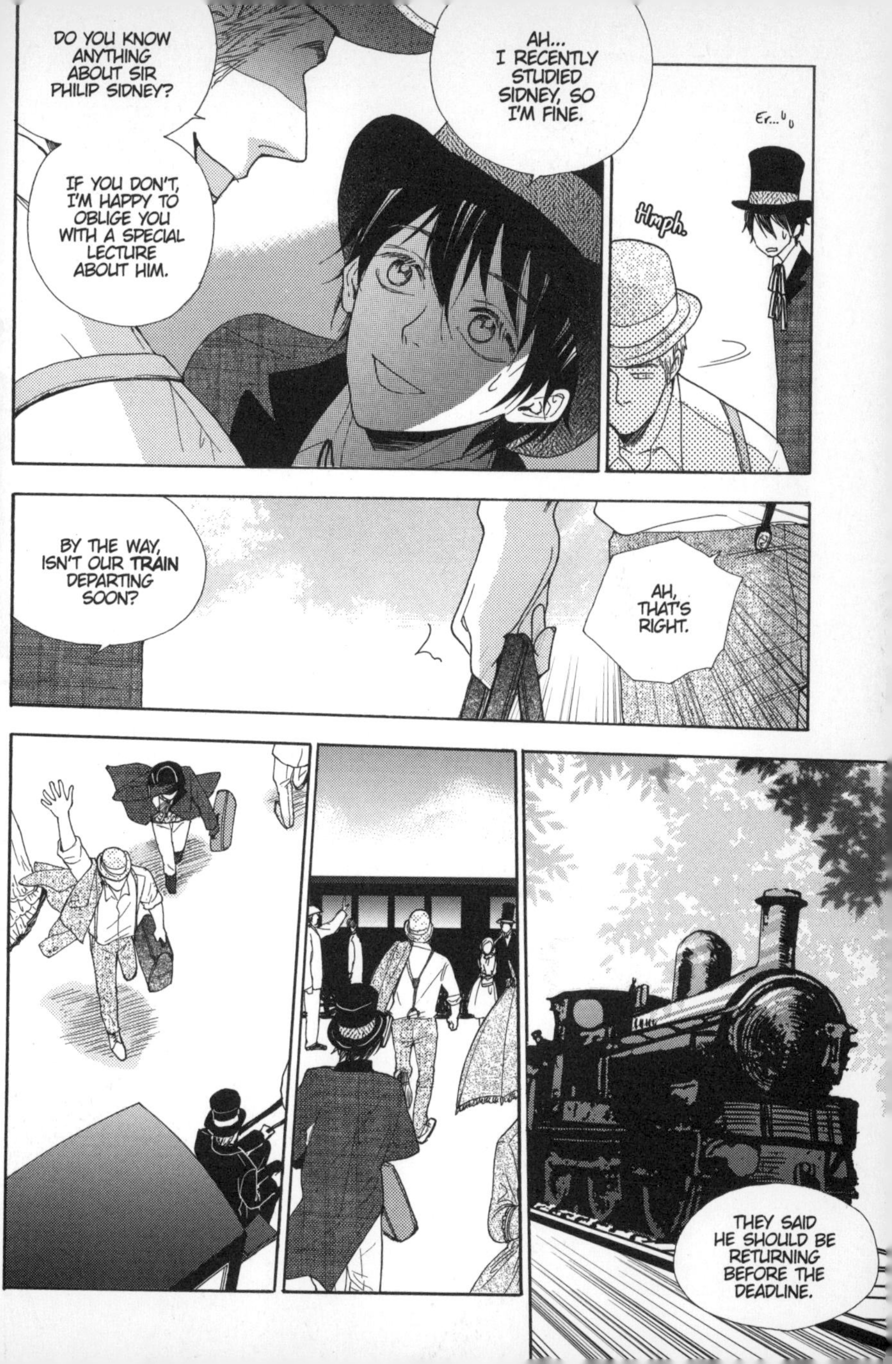
DO YOU KNOW ANYTHING ABOUT SIR PHILIP SIDNEY?
IF YOU DON'T, I'M HAPPY TO OBLIGE YOU WITH A SPECIAL LECTURE ABOUT HIM.
AH... I RECENTLY STUDIED SIDNEY, SO I'M FINE.
Er...
Hmph.
BY THE WAY, ISN'T OUR TRAIN DEPARTING SOON?
AH, THAT'S RIGHT.
THEY SAID HE SHOULD BE RETURNING BEFORE THE DEADLINE.

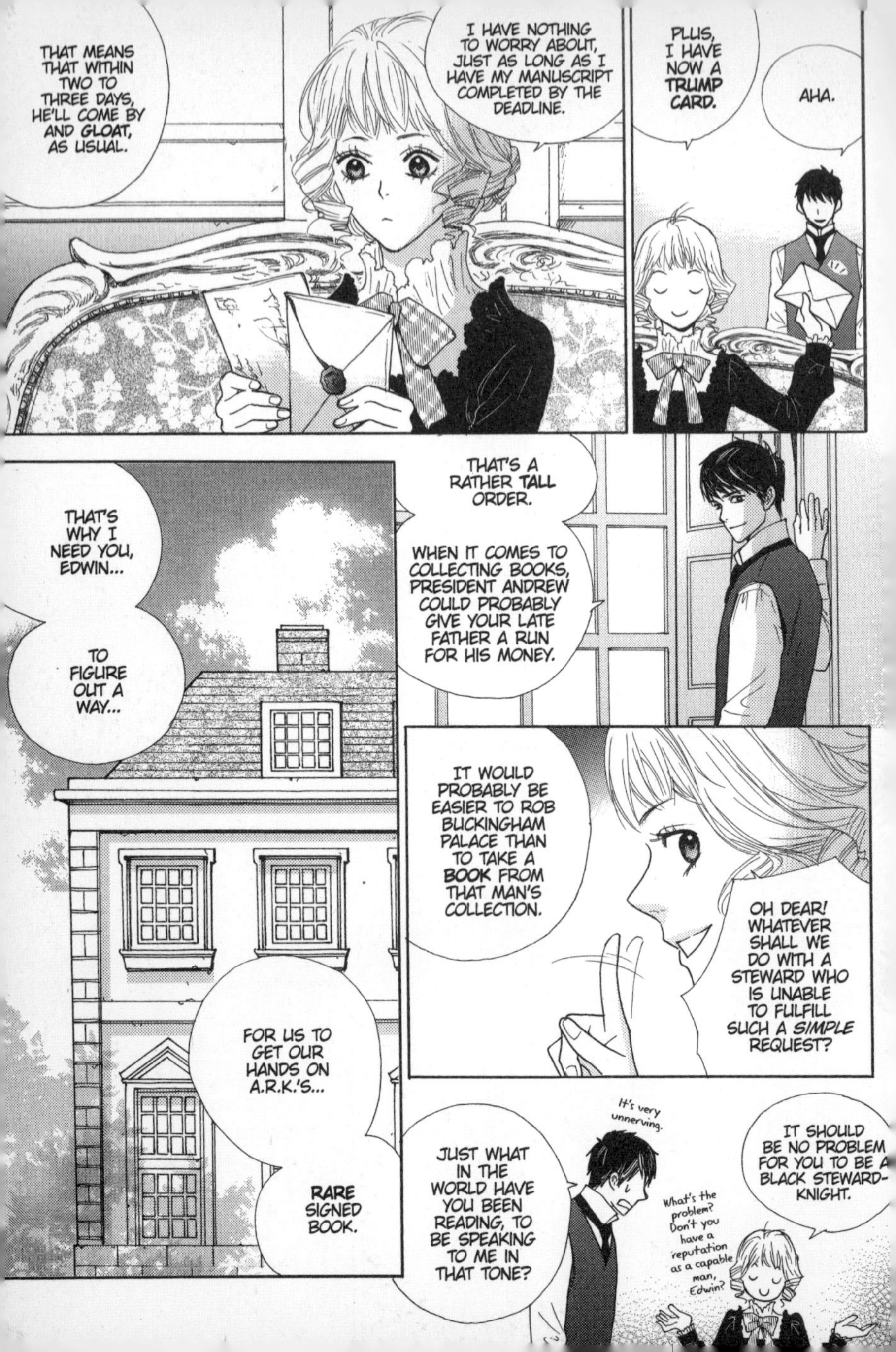

THAT MEANS THAT WITHIN TWO TO THREE DAYS, HE'LL COME BY AND GLOAT, AS USUAL.
I HAVE NOTHING TO WORRY ABOUT, JUST AS LONG AS I HAVE MY MANUSCRIPT COMPLETED BY THE DEADLINE.
PLUS, I HAVE NOW A TRUMP CARD.
AHA.
THAT'S WHY I NEED YOU, EDWIN...
TO FIGURE OUT A WAY...
FOR US TO GET OUR HANDS ON A.R.K.'S...
RARE SIGNED BOOK.
THAT'S A RATHER TALL ORDER.
WHEN IT COMES TO COLLECTING BOOKS, PRESIDENT ANDREW COULD PROBABLY GIVE YOUR LATE FATHER A RUN FOR HIS MONEY.
IT WOULD PROBABLY BE EASIER TO ROB BUCKINGHAM PALACE THAN TO TAKE A BOOK FROM THAT MAN'S COLLECTION.
OH DEAR! WHATEVER SHALL WE DO WITH A STEWARD WHO IS UNABLE TO FULFILL SUCH A SIMPLE REQUEST?
JUST WHAT IN THE WORLD HAVE YOU BEEN READING, TO BE SPEAKING TO ME IN THAT TONE?
It's very unnerving.
IT SHOULD BE NO PROBLEM FOR YOU TO BE A BLACK STEWARD-KNIGHT.
What's the problem? Don't you have a reputation as a capable man, Edwin?

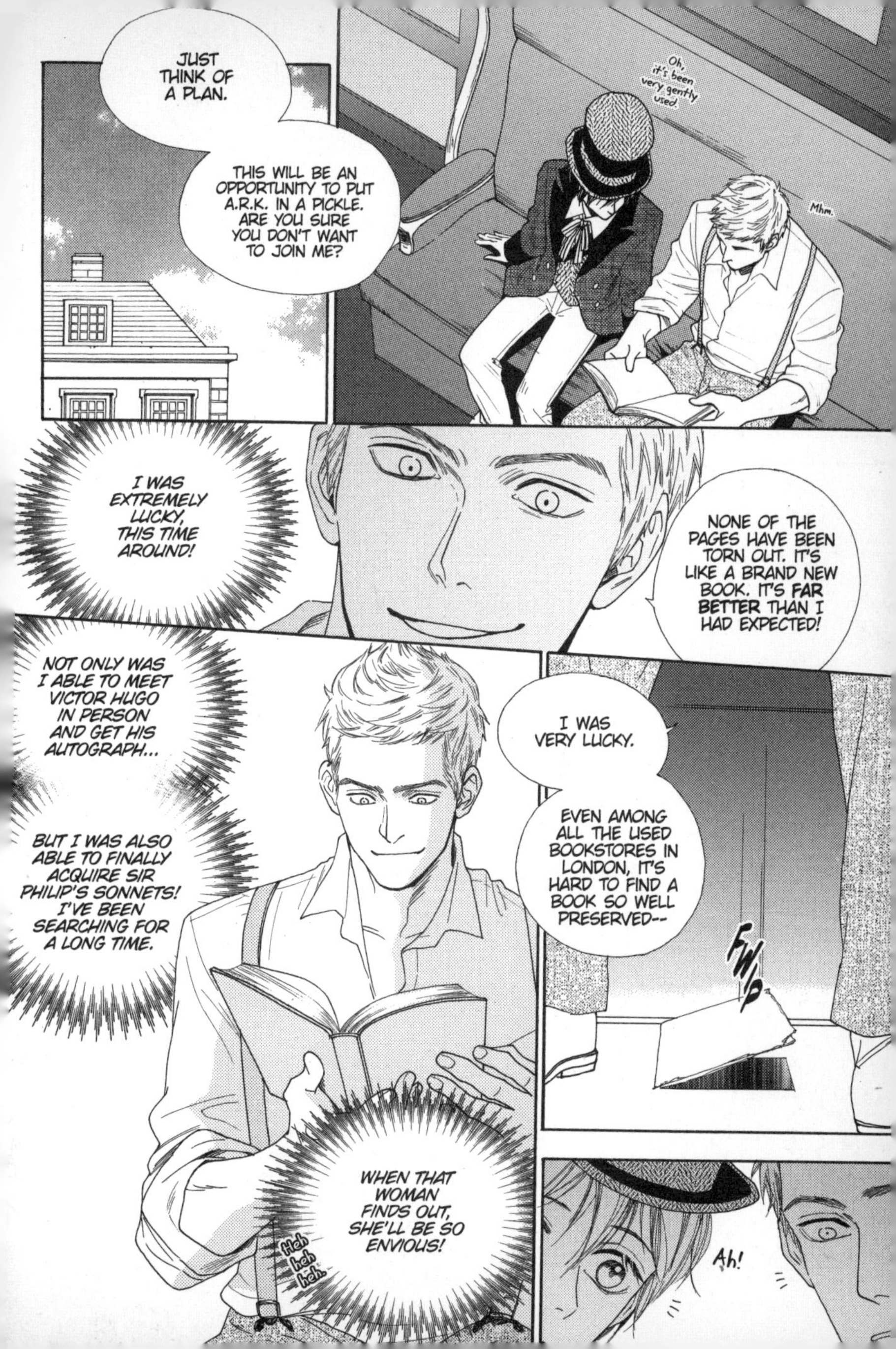
JUST THINK OF A PLAN.
THIS WILL BE AN OPPORTUNITY TO PUT A.R.K. IN A PICKLE. ARE YOU SURE YOU DON'T WANT TO JOIN ME?
Oh, it's been very gently used.
Mhm.
I WAS EXTREMELY LUCKY, THIS TIME AROUND!
NONE OF THE PAGES HAVE BEEN TORN OUT. IT'S LIKE A BRAND NEW BOOK. IT'S **FAR BETTER** THAN I HAD EXPECTED!
NOT ONLY WAS I ABLE TO MEET VICTOR HUGO IN PERSON AND GET HIS AUTOGRAPH...
BUT I WAS ALSO ABLE TO FINALLY ACQUIRE SIR PHILIP'S SONNETS! I'VE BEEN SEARCHING FOR A LONG TIME.
WHEN THAT WOMAN FINDS OUT, SHE'LL BE SO ENVIOUS!
Heh heh heh.
I WAS VERY LUCKY.
EVEN AMONG ALL THE USED BOOKSTORES IN LONDON, IT'S HARD TO FIND A BOOK SO WELL PRESERVED--
FWIP
Ah!

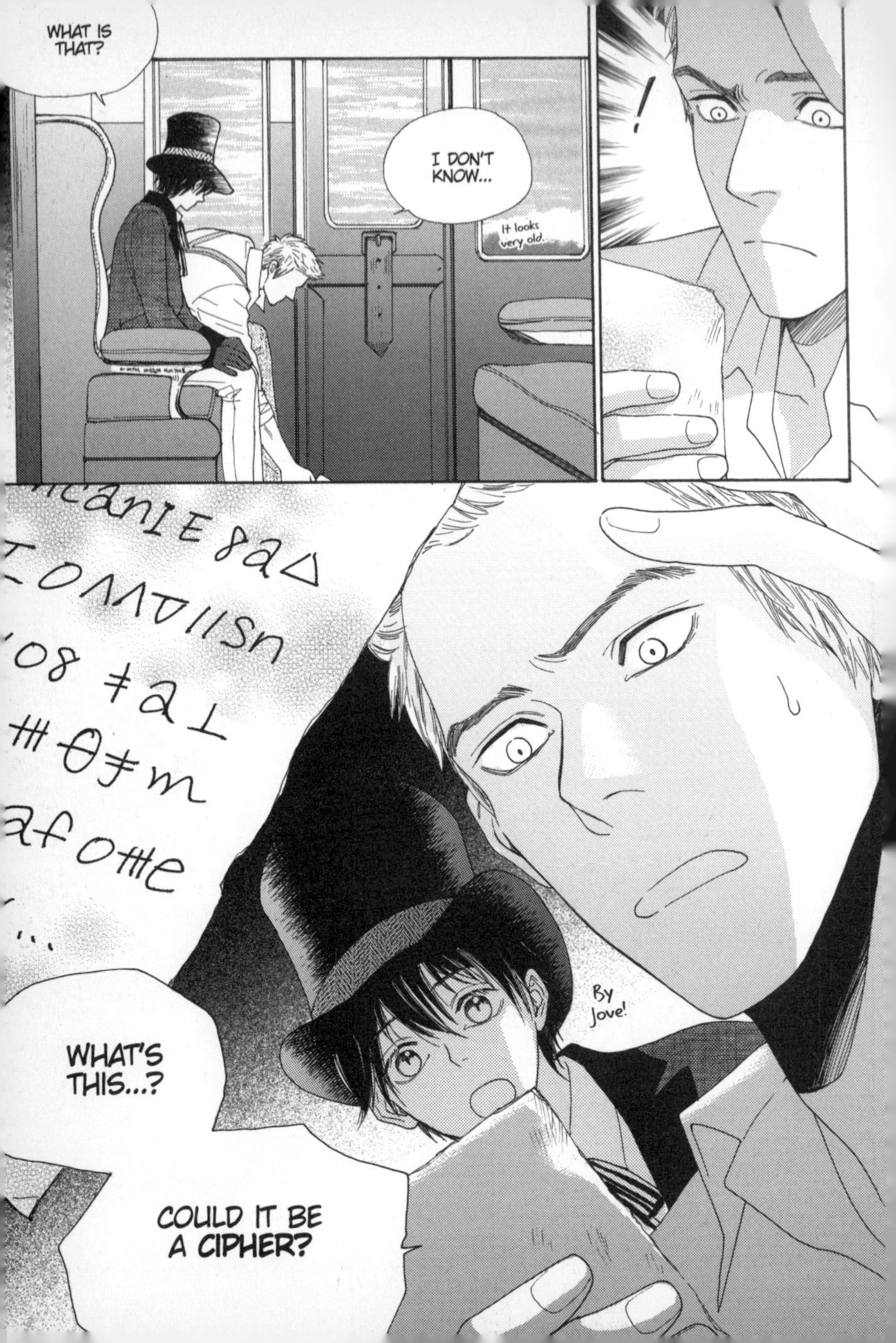
WHAT IS THAT?
I DON'T KNOW...
It looks very old.
!
By Jove!
WHAT'S THIS...?
COULD IT BE A CIPHER?

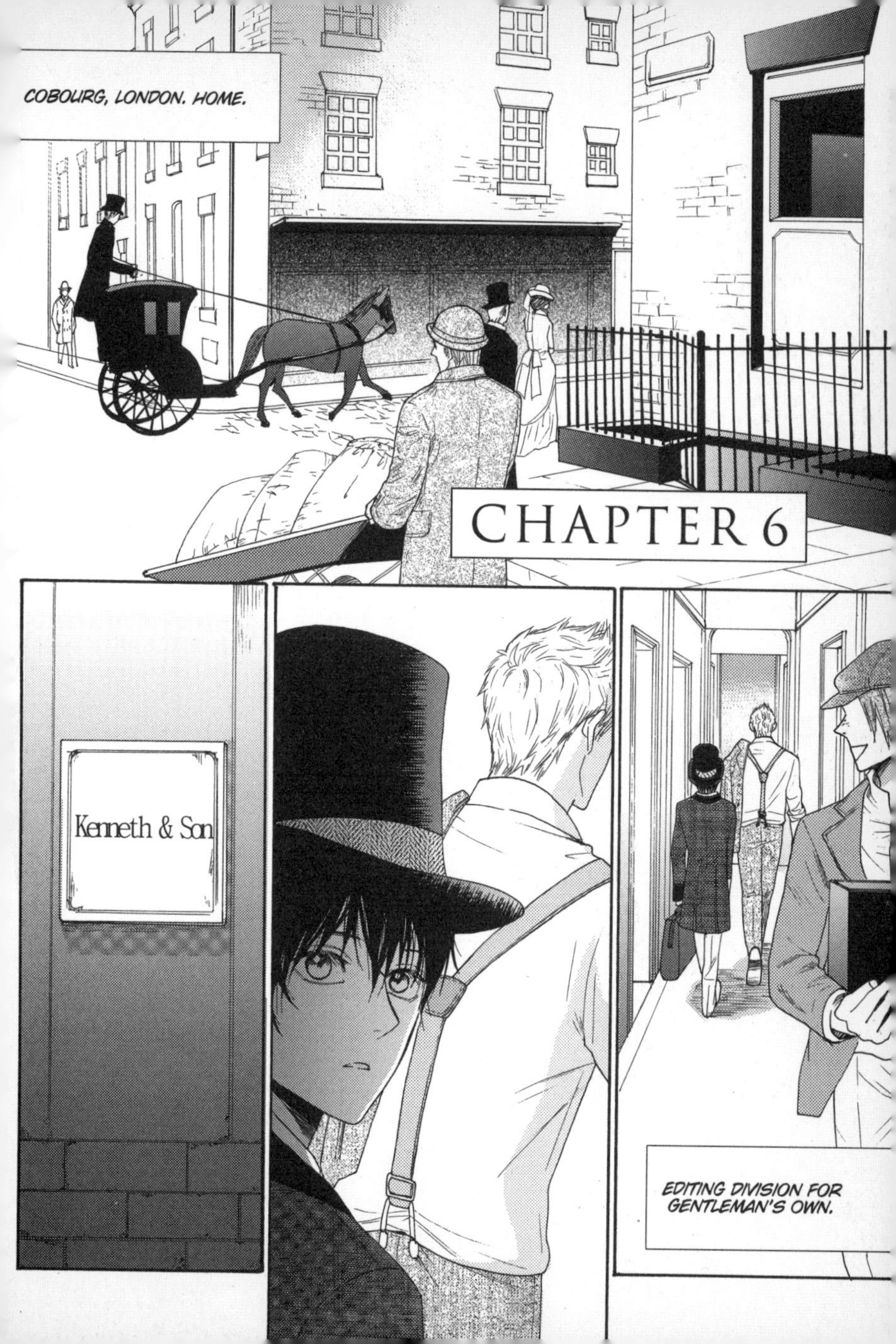
COBOURG, LONDON. HOME.
CHAPTER 6
Kenneth & Son
EDITING DIVISION FOR GENTLEMAN'S OWN.

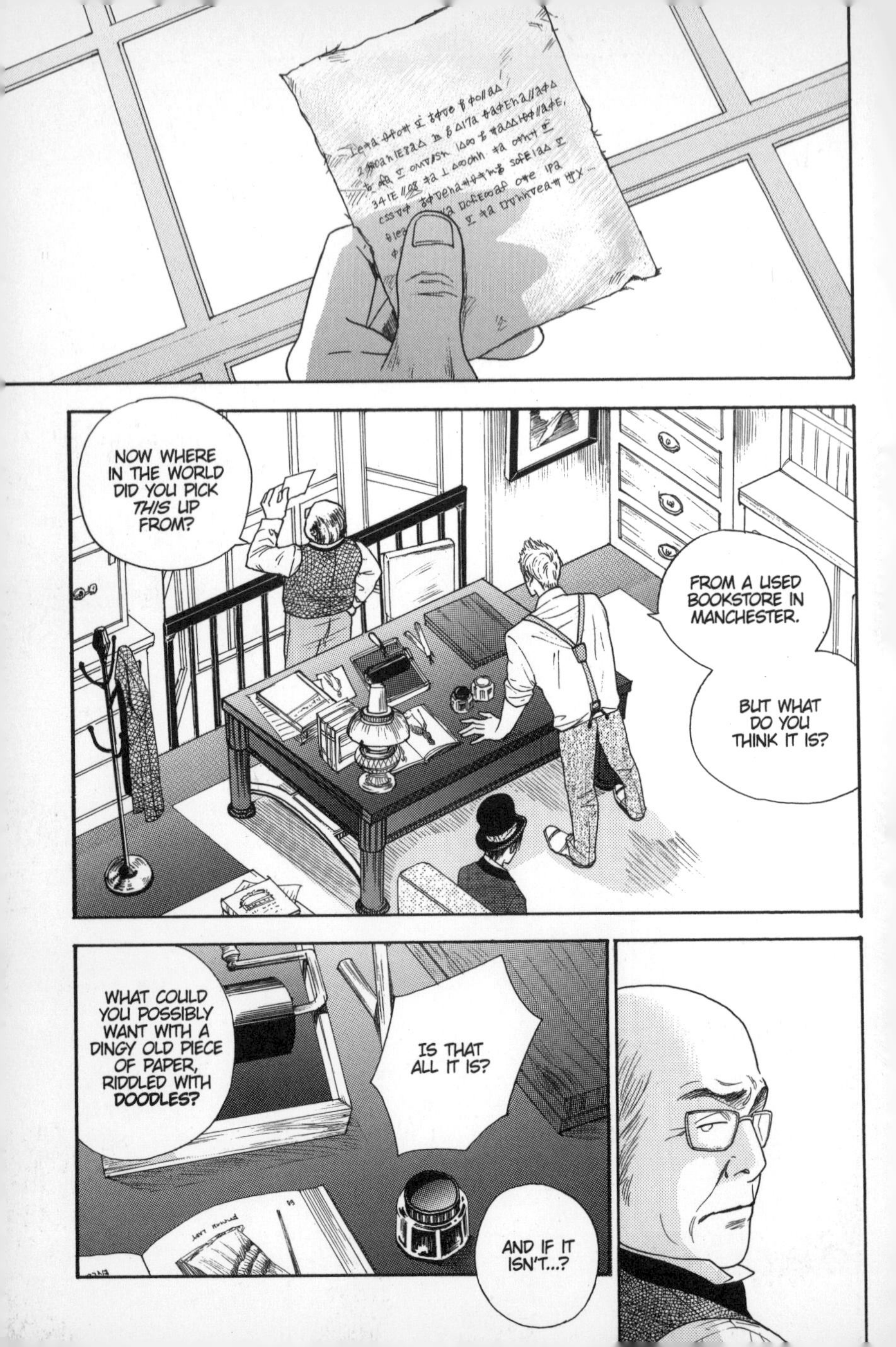
NOW WHERE IN THE WORLD DID YOU PICK *THIS* UP FROM?
FROM A USED BOOKSTORE IN MANCHESTER.
BUT WHAT DO YOU THINK IT IS?
WHAT COULD YOU POSSIBLY WANT WITH A DINGY OLD PIECE OF PAPER, RIDDLED WITH **DOODLES?**
IS THAT ALL IT IS?
AND IF IT ISN'T...?

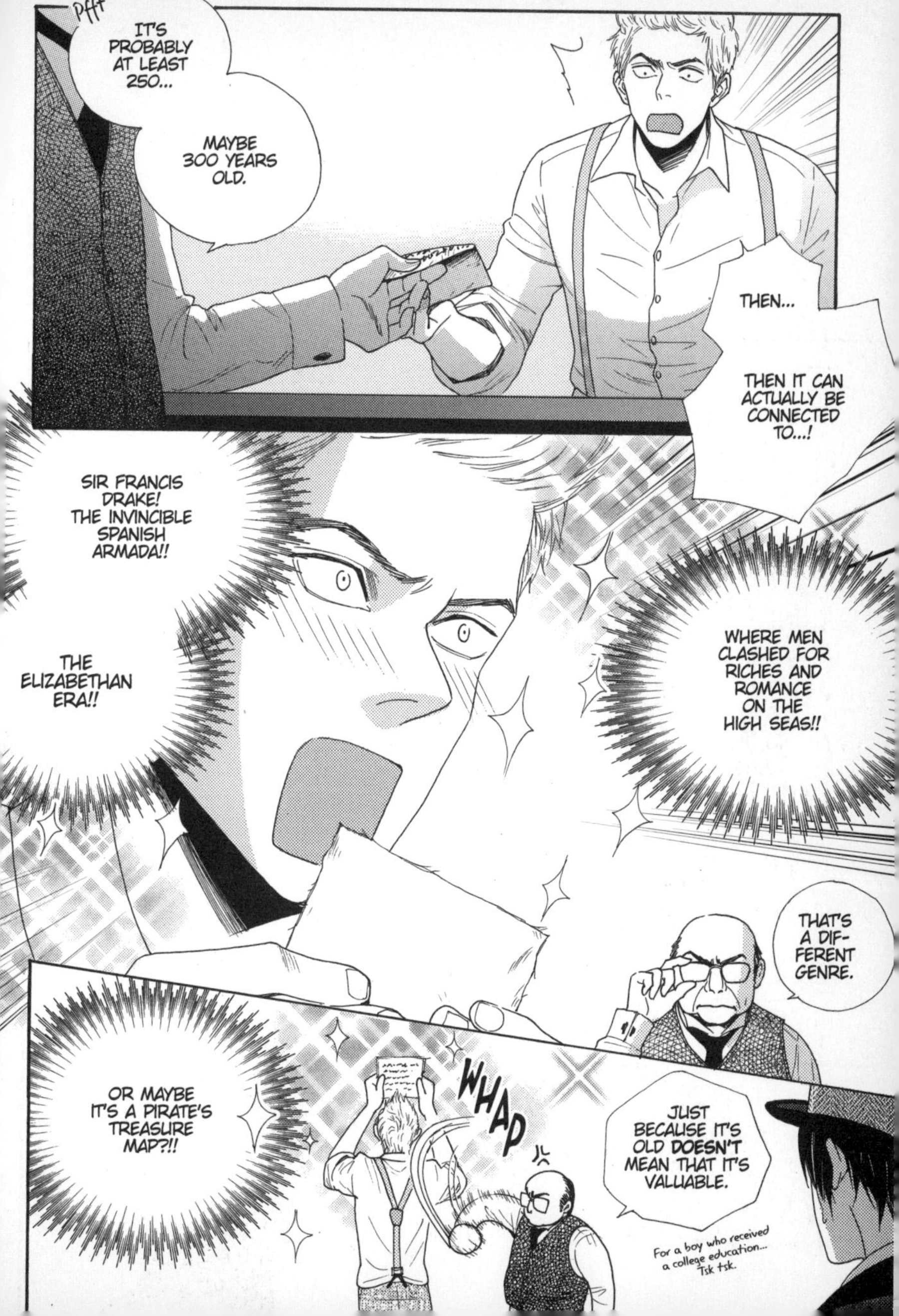
Pfft
IT'S PROBABLY AT LEAST 250...
MAYBE 300 YEARS OLD.
THEN...
THEN IT CAN ACTUALLY BE CONNECTED TO...!
SIR FRANCIS DRAKE! THE INVINCIBLE SPANISH ARMADA!!
THE ELIZABETHAN ERA!!
WHERE MEN CLASHED FOR RICHES AND ROMANCE ON THE HIGH SEAS!!
THAT'S A DIF-FERENT GENRE.
OR MAYBE IT'S A PIRATE'S TREASURE MAP?!!
WHAP
JUST BECAUSE IT'S OLD DOESN'T MEAN THAT IT'S VALUABLE.
For a boy who received a college education... Tsk tsk.

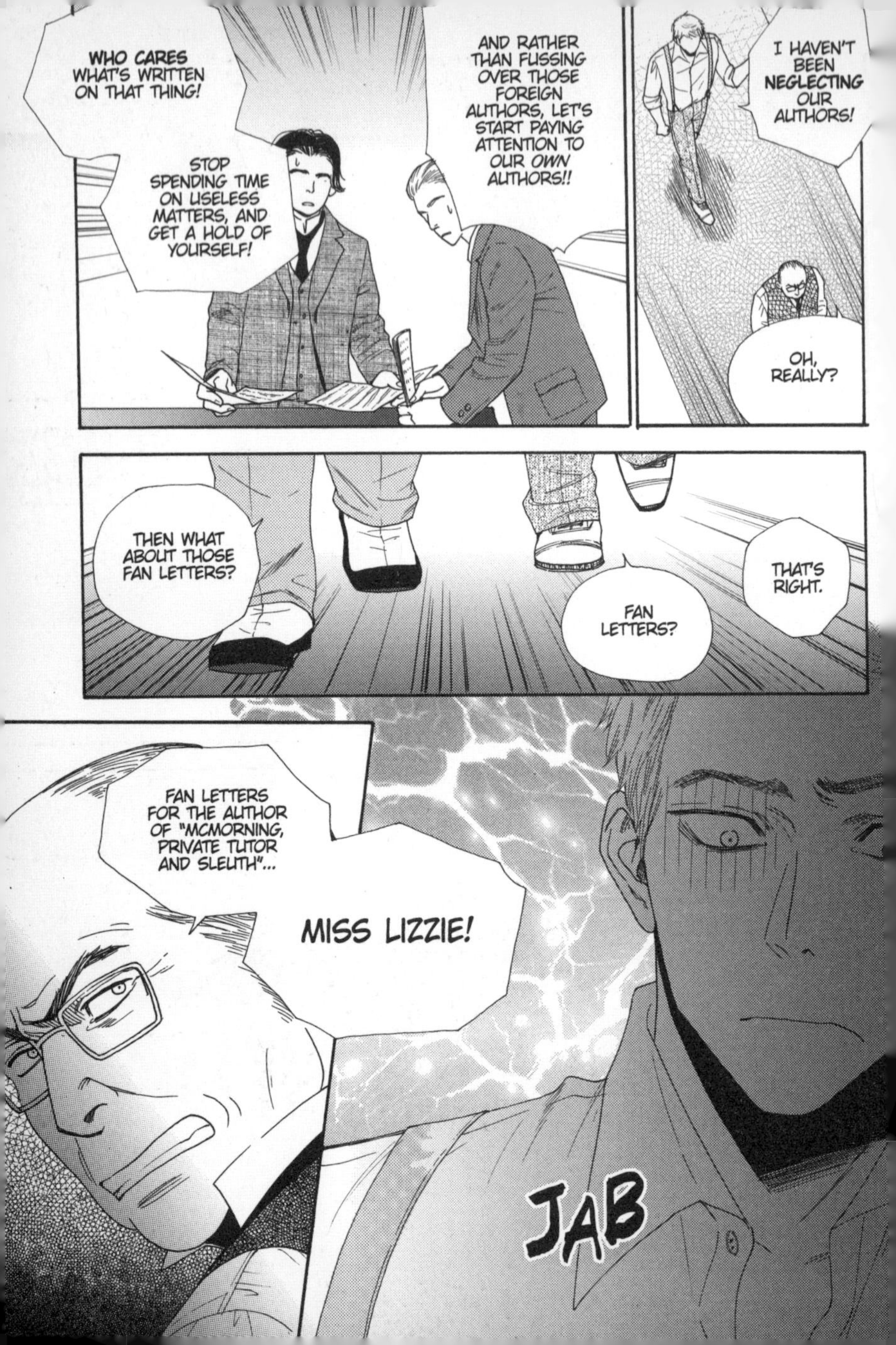
WHO CARES WHAT'S WRITTEN ON THAT THING!
STOP SPENDING TIME ON USELESS MATTERS, AND GET A HOLD OF YOURSELF!
AND RATHER THAN FUSSING OVER THOSE FOREIGN AUTHORS, LET'S START PAYING ATTENTION TO OUR OWN AUTHORS!!
I HAVEN'T BEEN NEGLECTING OUR AUTHORS!
OH, REALLY?
THEN WHAT ABOUT THOSE FAN LETTERS?
FAN LETTERS?
THAT'S RIGHT.
FAN LETTERS FOR THE AUTHOR OF "MCMORNING, PRIVATE TUTOR AND SLEUTH"...
MISS LIZZIE!
JAB

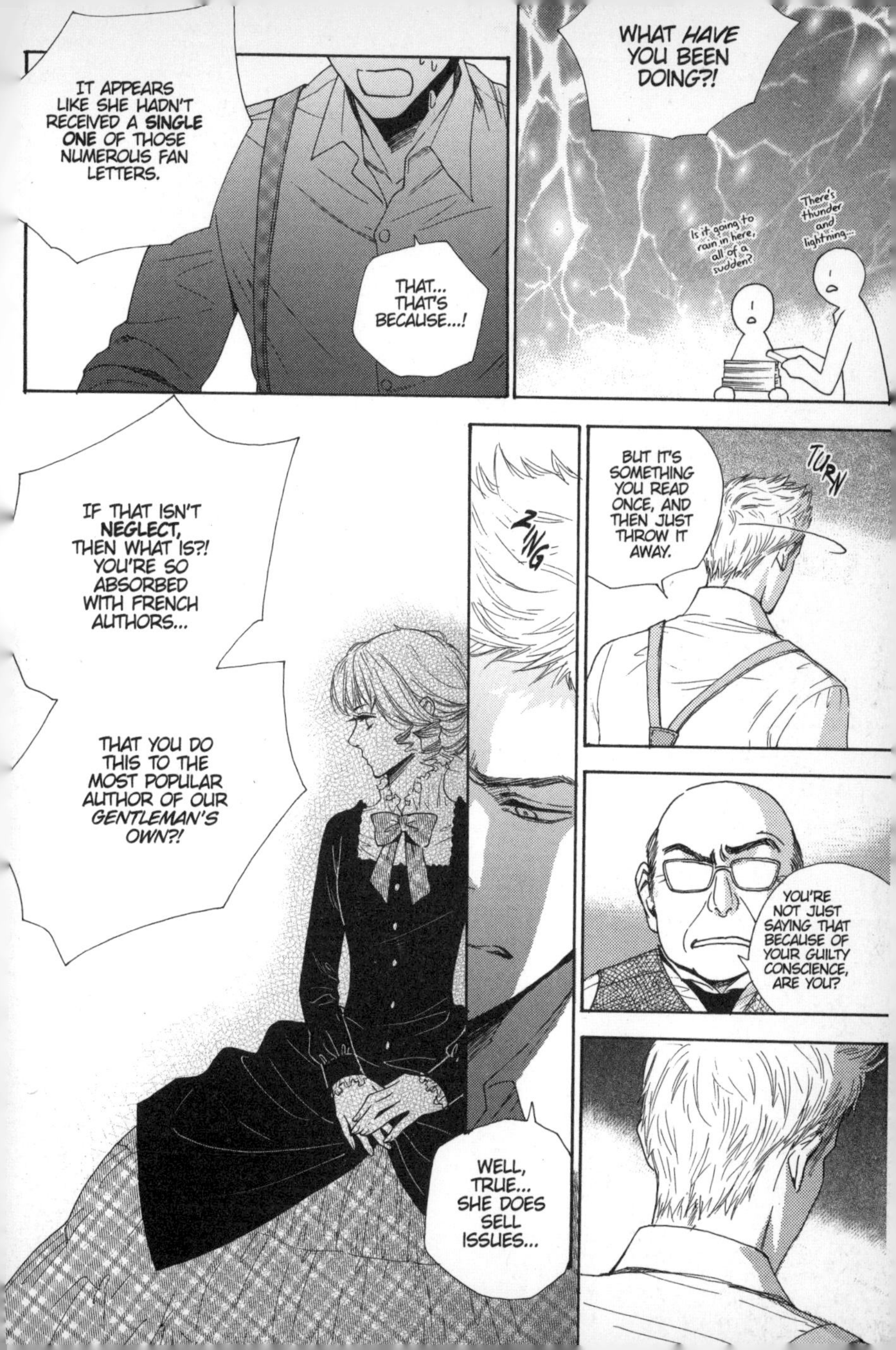
IT APPEARS LIKE SHE HADN'T RECEIVED A **SINGLE ONE** OF THOSE NUMEROUS FAN LETTERS.
THAT... THAT'S BECAUSE...!
WHAT *HAVE* YOU BEEN DOING?!
Is it going to rain in here, all of a sudden?
There's thunder and lightning...
IF THAT ISN'T **NEGLECT**, THEN WHAT IS?! YOU'RE SO ABSORBED WITH FRENCH AUTHORS...
THAT YOU DO THIS TO THE MOST POPULAR AUTHOR OF OUR *GENTLEMAN'S OWN*?!
ZING
WELL, TRUE... SHE DOES SELL ISSUES...
BUT IT'S SOMETHING YOU READ ONCE, AND THEN JUST THROW IT AWAY.
TURN
YOU'RE NOT JUST SAYING THAT BECAUSE OF YOUR GUILTY CONSCIENCE, ARE YOU?

SHE'S A **WOMAN**, AND YET SHE HAS THE **AUDACITY** TO PUT ON AIRS AND ACT LIKE SHE'S THE ONLY ONE WHO HAS GOT HALF A BRAIN!

SHE'S NOT HUMBLE, WILLING TO CONCEDE, OBEDIENT, SO FORTH AND. ETC. NONE OF THE WOMANLY VIRTUES THAT A\WELL-BRED WOMAN **SHOULD** BE CULTIVATING CAN BE FOUND IN THAT "SMART" BRAIN OF HERS!!

WHAT DO YOU MEAN, "GUILTY CONSCIENCE"? IT'S NOTHING LIKE THAT.

I SIMPLY DON'T LIKE HER.

That lady-in-waiting-for-the-bizarre...

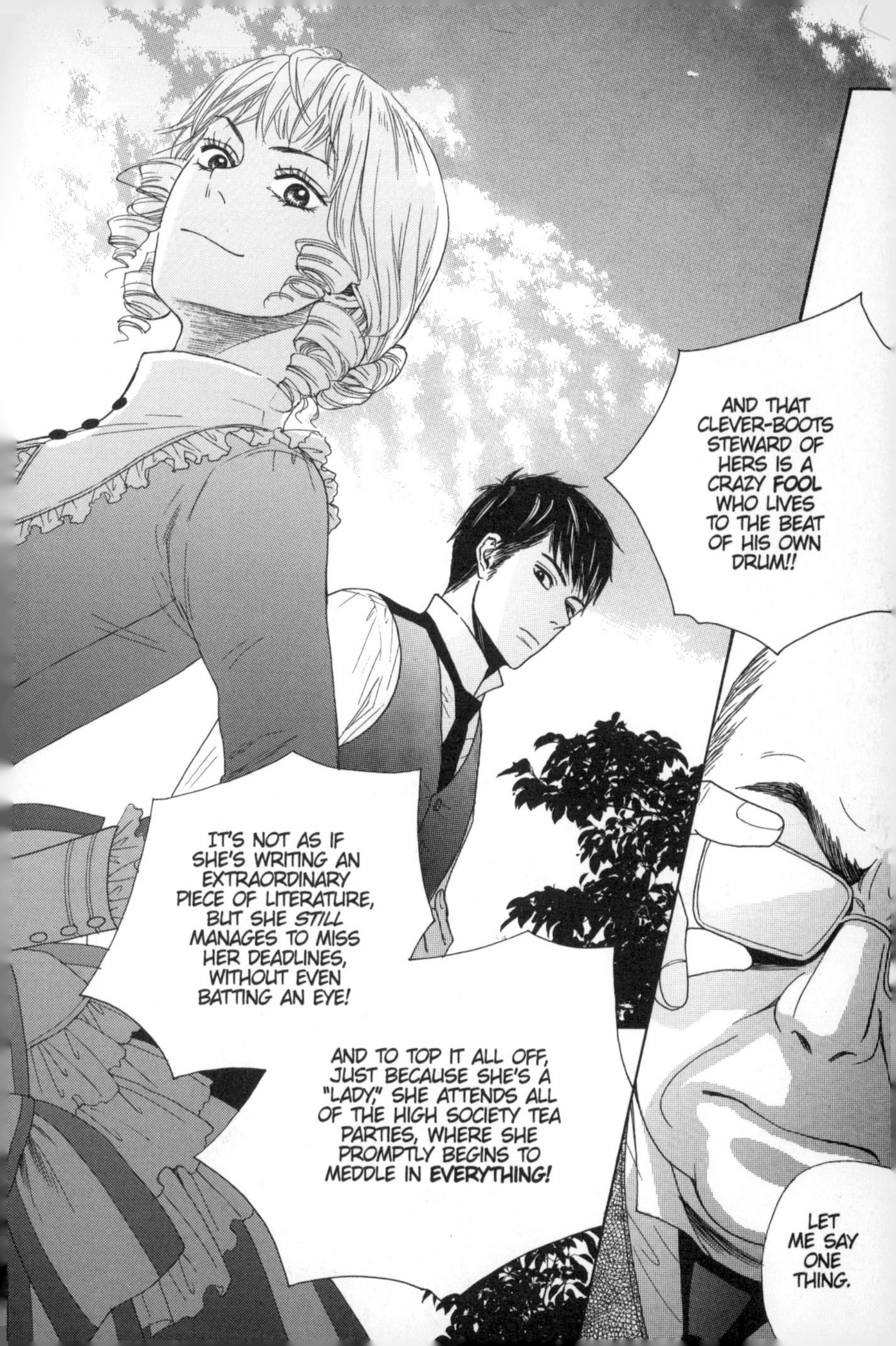
AND THAT CLEVER-BOOTS STEWARD OF HERS IS A CRAZY FOOL WHO LIVES TO THE BEAT OF HIS OWN DRUM!!
IT'S NOT AS IF SHE'S WRITING AN EXTRAORDINARY PIECE OF LITERATURE, BUT SHE STILL MANAGES TO MISS HER DEADLINES, WITHOUT EVEN BATTING AN EYE!
AND TO TOP IT ALL OFF, JUST BECAUSE SHE'S A "LADY," SHE ATTENDS ALL OF THE HIGH SOCIETY TEA PARTIES, WHERE SHE PROMPTLY BEGINS TO MEDDLE IN EVERYTHING!
LET ME SAY ONE THING.

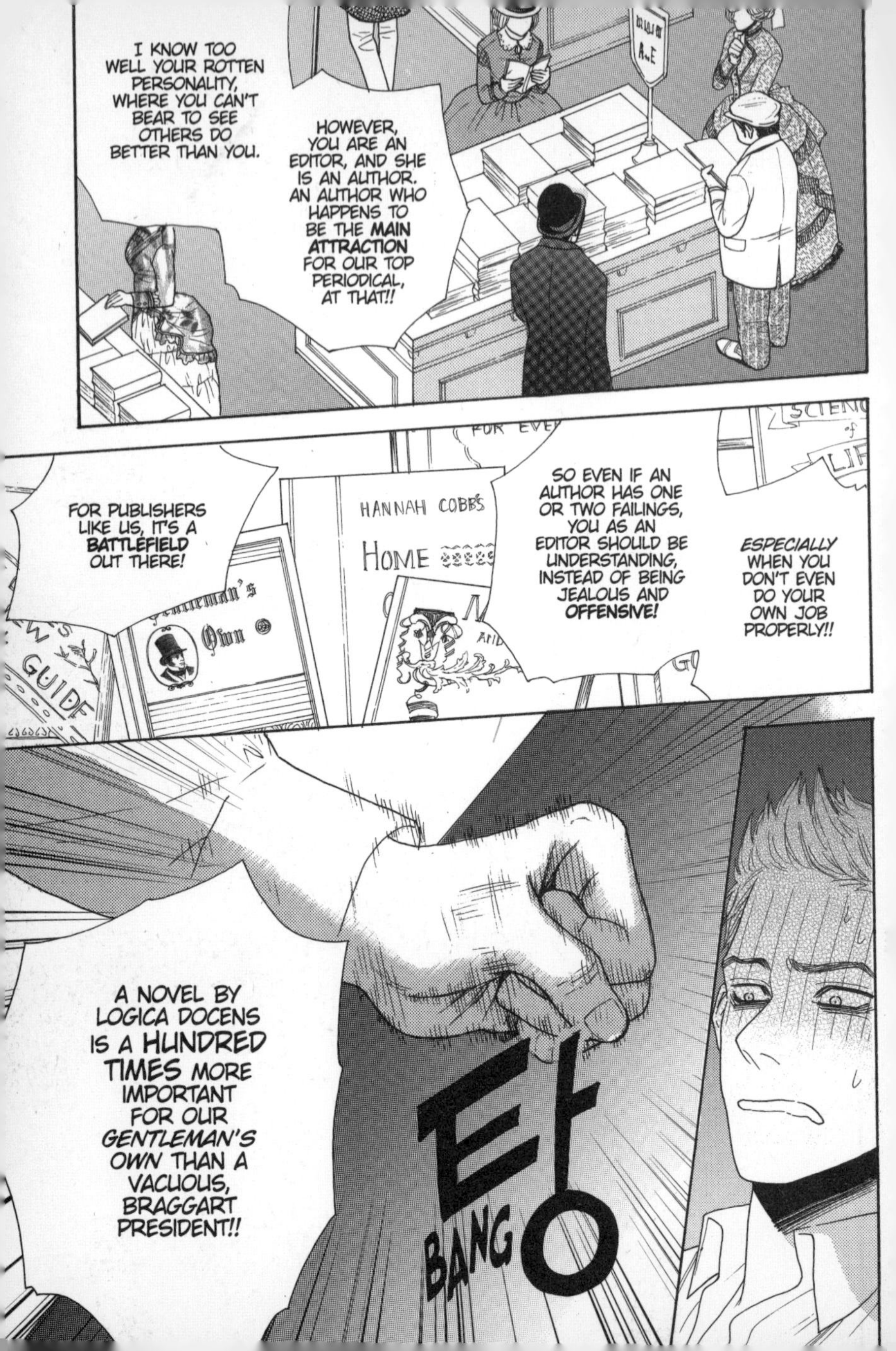
I KNOW TOO WELL YOUR ROTTEN PERSONALITY, WHERE YOU CAN'T BEAR TO SEE OTHERS DO BETTER THAN YOU.
HOWEVER, YOU ARE AN EDITOR, AND SHE IS AN AUTHOR. AN AUTHOR WHO HAPPENS TO BE THE **MAIN ATTRACTION** FOR OUR TOP PERIODICAL, AT THAT!!
FOR PUBLISHERS LIKE US, IT'S A **BATTLEFIELD** OUT THERE!
HANNAH COBB'S
HOME
Gentleman's Own
GUIDE
SO EVEN IF AN AUTHOR HAS ONE OR TWO FAILINGS, YOU AS AN EDITOR SHOULD BE UNDERSTANDING, INSTEAD OF BEING JEALOUS AND **OFFENSIVE!**
ESPECIALLY WHEN YOU DON'T EVEN DO YOUR OWN JOB PROPERLY!!
A NOVEL BY LOGICA DOCENS IS A **HUNDRED TIMES** MORE IMPORTANT FOR OUR *GENTLEMAN'S OWN* THAN A VACUOUS, BRAGGART PRESIDENT!!
BANG

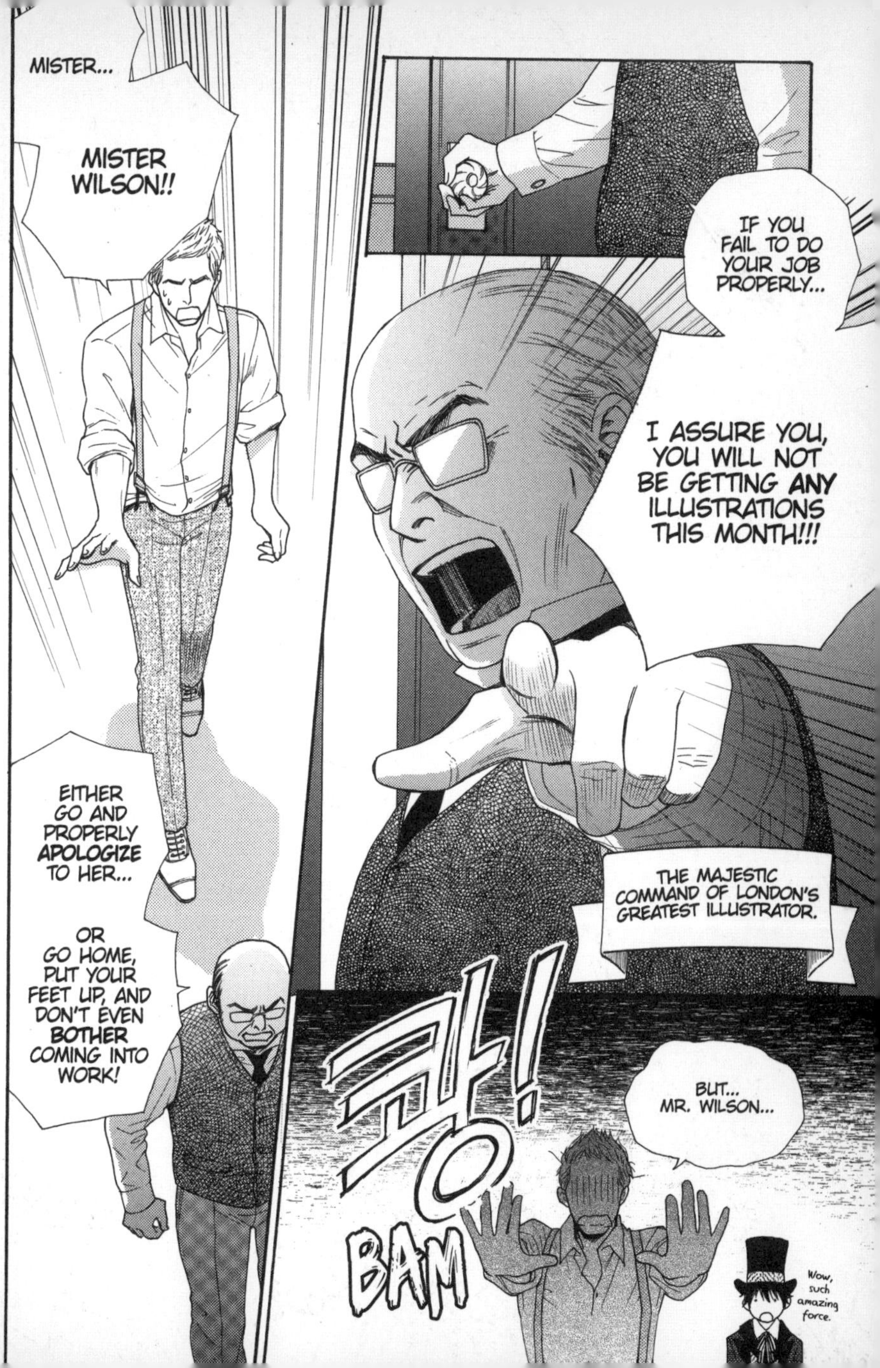

MISTER...
MISTER WILSON!!
EITHER GO AND PROPERLY APOLOGIZE TO HER...
OR GO HOME, PUT YOUR FEET UP, AND DON'T EVEN BOTHER COMING INTO WORK!
IF YOU FAIL TO DO YOUR JOB PROPERLY...
I ASSURE YOU, YOU WILL NOT BE GETTING ANY ILLUSTRATIONS THIS MONTH!!!
THE MAJESTIC COMMAND OF LONDON'S GREATEST ILLUSTRATOR.
쾅!
BAM
BUT... MR. WILSON...
Wow, such amazing force.

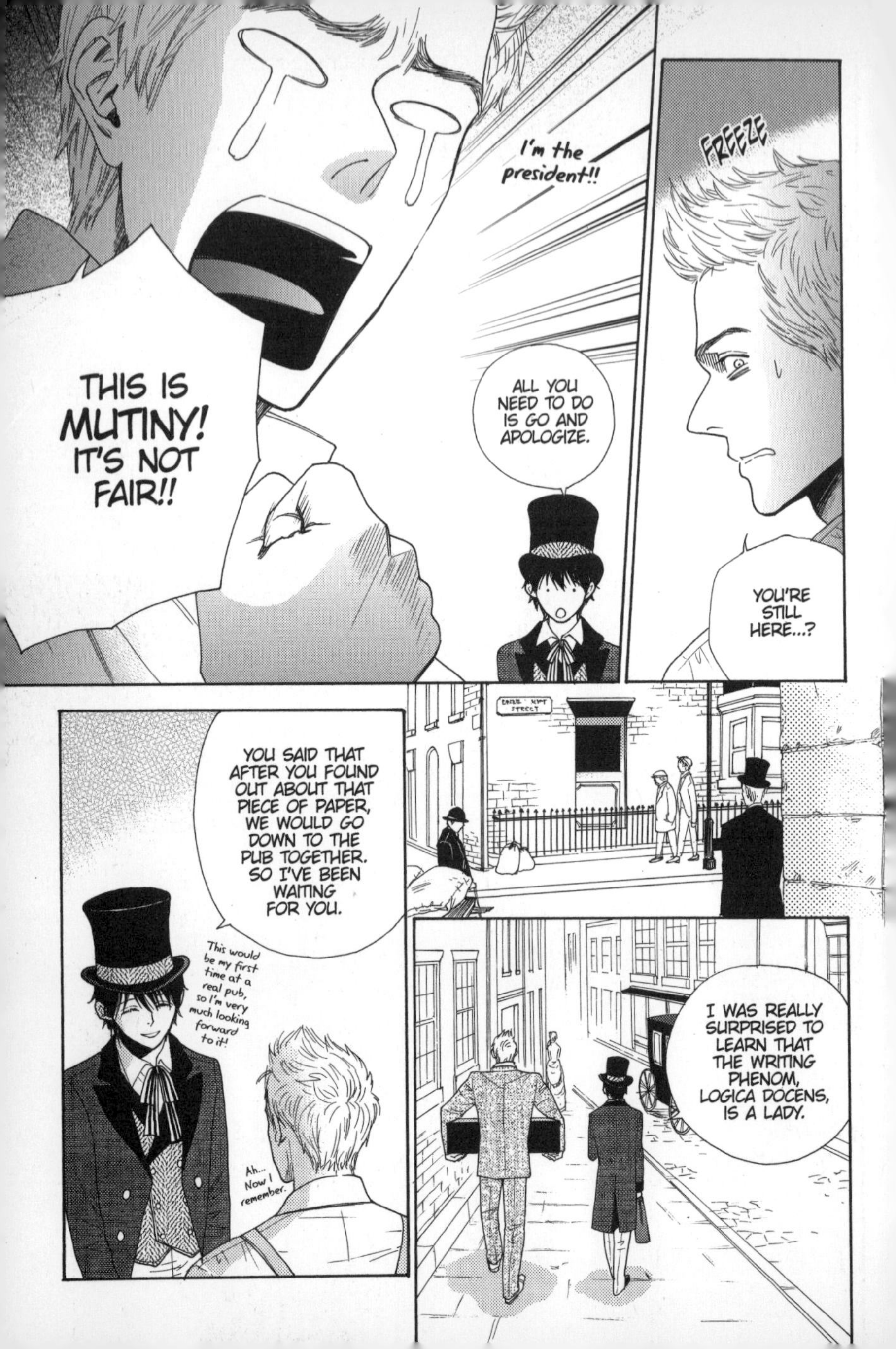
THIS IS MUTINY! IT'S NOT FAIR!!
I'm the president!!
ALL YOU NEED TO DO IS GO AND APOLOGIZE.
FREEZE
YOU'RE STILL HERE...?
YOU SAID THAT AFTER YOU FOUND OUT ABOUT THAT PIECE OF PAPER, WE WOULD GO DOWN TO THE PUB TOGETHER. SO I'VE BEEN WAITING FOR YOU.
This would be my first time at a real pub, so I'm very much looking forward to it!
Ah... Now I remember.
I WAS REALLY SURPRISED TO LEARN THAT THE WRITING PHENOM, LOGICA DOCENS, IS A LADY.

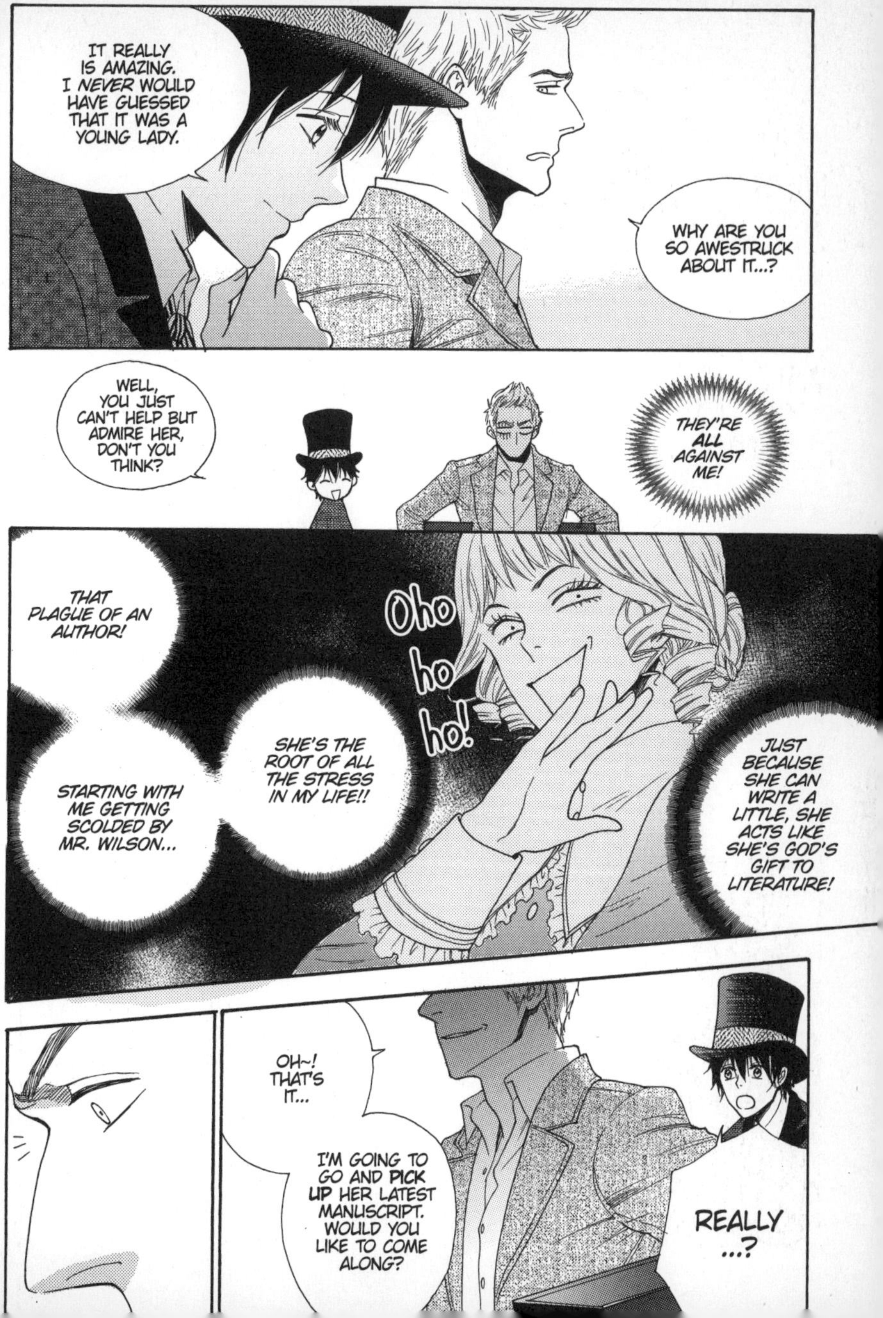
IT REALLY IS AMAZING. I *NEVER* WOULD HAVE GUESSED THAT IT WAS A YOUNG LADY.
WHY ARE YOU SO AWESTRUCK ABOUT IT...?
WELL, YOU JUST CAN'T HELP BUT ADMIRE HER, DON'T YOU THINK?
THEY'RE **ALL** AGAINST ME!
THAT PLAGUE OF AN AUTHOR!
STARTING WITH ME GETTING SCOLDED BY MR. WILSON...
SHE'S THE ROOT OF ALL THE STRESS IN MY LIFE!!
Oho ho ho!
JUST BECAUSE SHE CAN WRITE A LITTLE, SHE ACTS LIKE SHE'S GOD'S GIFT TO LITERATURE!
OH~! THAT'S IT...
I'M GOING TO GO AND **PICK UP** HER LATEST MANUSCRIPT. WOULD YOU LIKE TO COME ALONG?
REALLY ...?

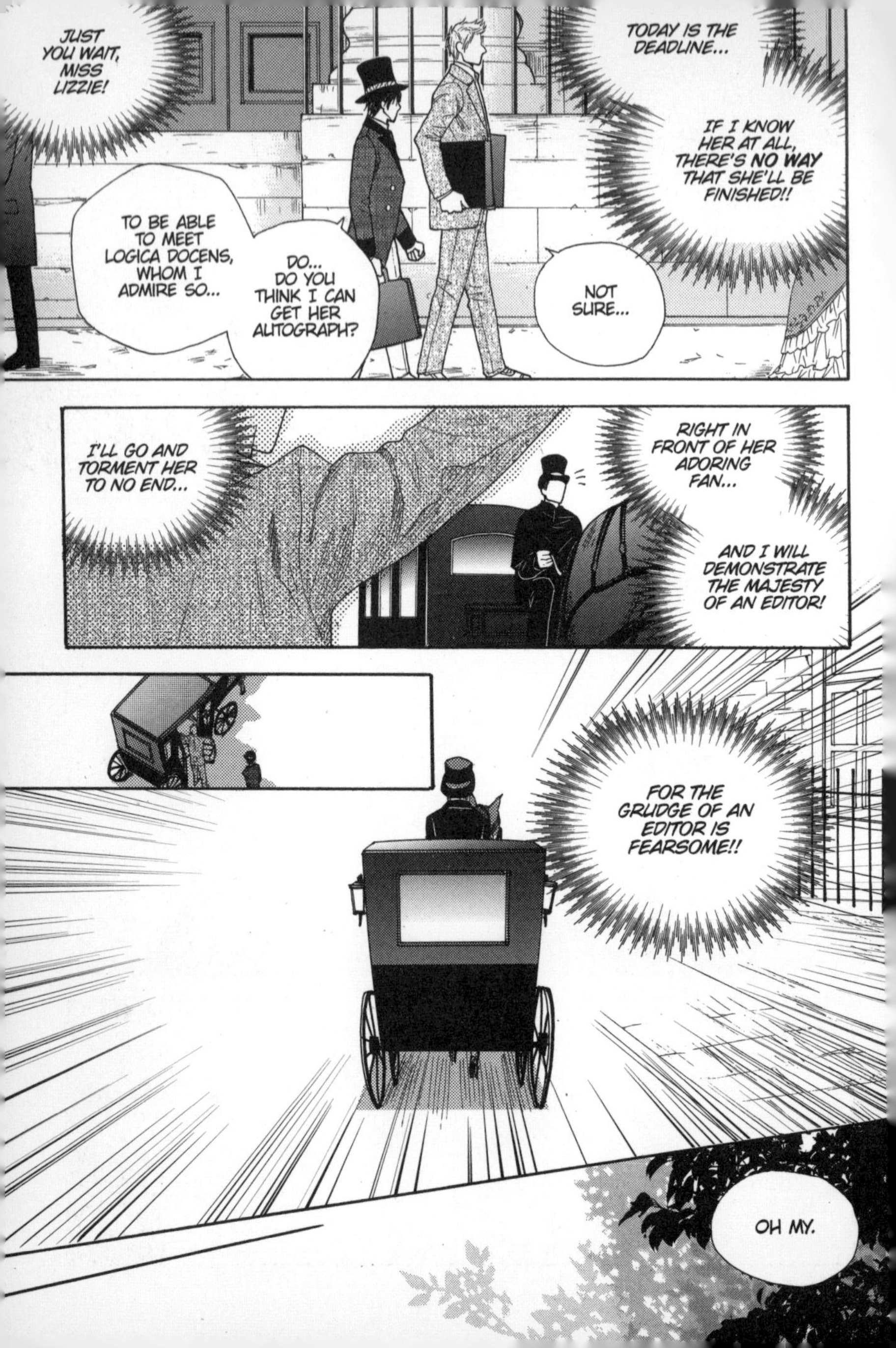

JUST YOU WAIT, MISS LIZZIE!
TO BE ABLE TO MEET LOGICA DOCENS, WHOM I ADMIRE SO...
DO... DO YOU THINK I CAN GET HER AUTOGRAPH?
TODAY IS THE DEADLINE...
IF I KNOW HER AT ALL, THERE'S NO WAY THAT SHE'LL BE FINISHED!!
NOT SURE...
I'LL GO AND TORMENT HER TO NO END...
RIGHT IN FRONT OF HER ADORING FAN...
AND I WILL DEMONSTRATE THE MAJESTY OF AN EDITOR!
FOR THE GRUDGE OF AN EDITOR IS FEARSOME!!
OH MY.

I HEARD YOU HAD GONE TO FRANCE, BUT DID YOU COME TO SEE ME AS SOON AS YOU RETURNED?

OH HO HO HO!

YOU'RE SO ATTENTIVE! ♡

THE MAJESTY OF AN AUTHOR WHO HAS STRICTLY ADHERED TO HER DEADLINE.

HOW CAN THIS BE POSSIBLE?!!

Hee hee hee...

At long last, a manuscript finished by the deadline.

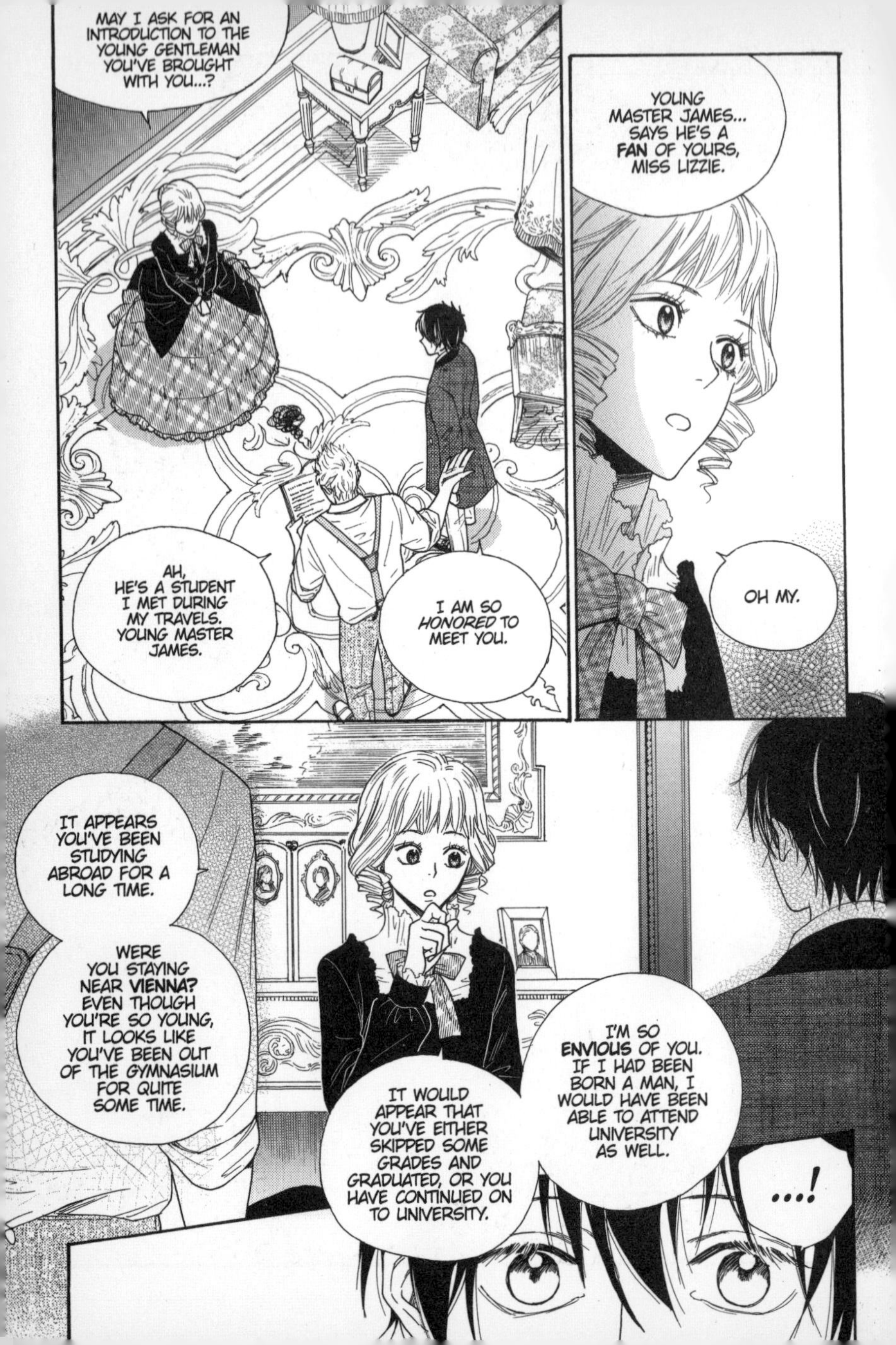
MAY I ASK FOR AN INTRODUCTION TO THE YOUNG GENTLEMAN YOU'VE BROUGHT WITH YOU...?
AH, HE'S A STUDENT I MET DURING MY TRAVELS. YOUNG MASTER JAMES.
I AM SO *HONORED* TO MEET YOU.
YOUNG MASTER JAMES... SAYS HE'S A **FAN** OF YOURS, MISS LIZZIE.
OH MY.
IT APPEARS YOU'VE BEEN STUDYING ABROAD FOR A LONG TIME.
WERE YOU STAYING NEAR **VIENNA?** EVEN THOUGH YOU'RE SO YOUNG, IT LOOKS LIKE YOU'VE BEEN OUT OF THE GYMNASIUM FOR QUITE SOME TIME.
IT WOULD APPEAR THAT YOU'VE EITHER SKIPPED SOME GRADES AND GRADUATED, OR YOU HAVE CONTINUED ON TO UNIVERSITY.
I'M SO **ENVIOUS** OF YOU. IF I HAD BEEN BORN A MAN, I WOULD HAVE BEEN ABLE TO ATTEND UNIVERSITY AS WELL.
...!

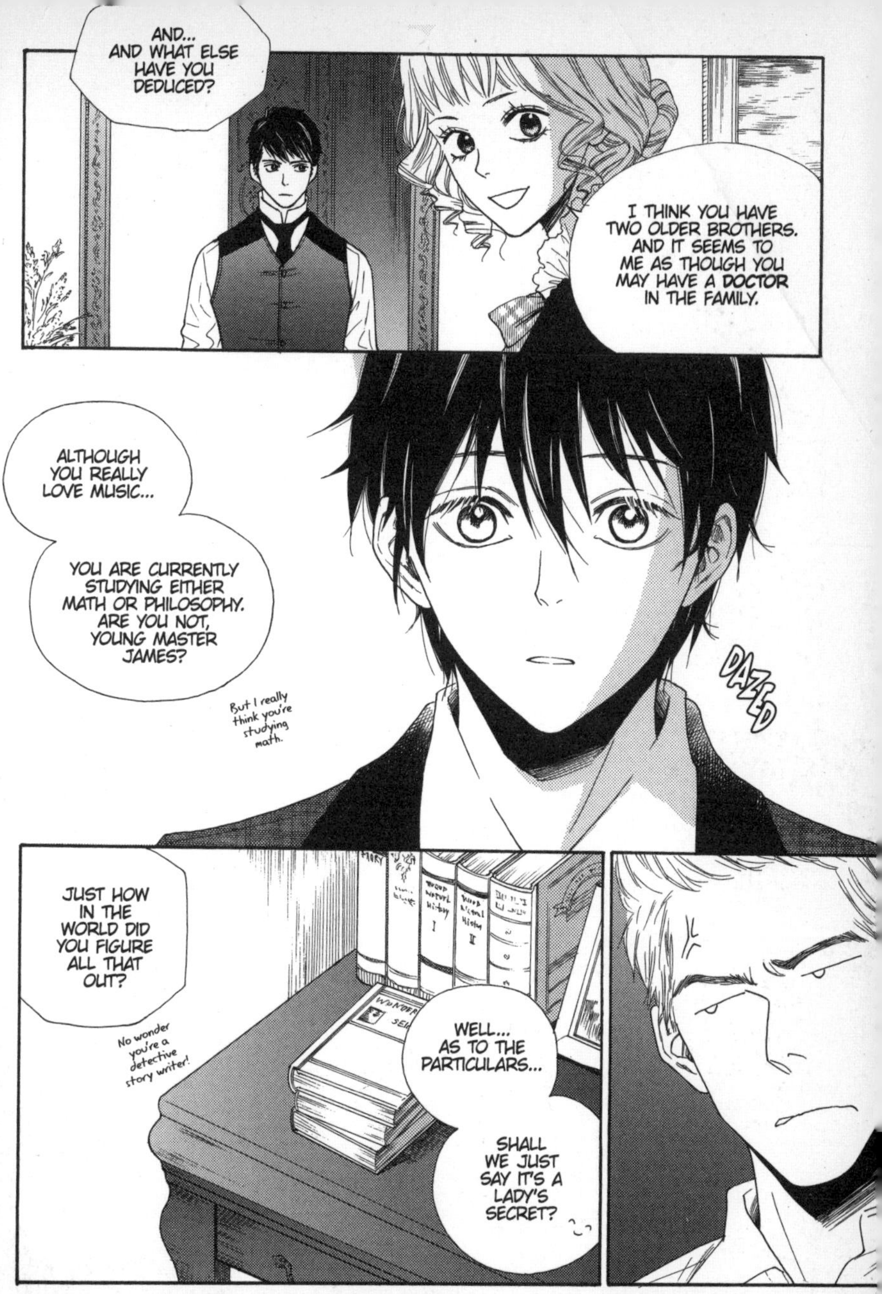
AND... AND WHAT ELSE HAVE YOU DEDUCED?
I THINK YOU HAVE TWO OLDER BROTHERS. AND IT SEEMS TO ME AS THOUGH YOU MAY HAVE A **DOCTOR** IN THE FAMILY.
ALTHOUGH YOU REALLY LOVE MUSIC...
YOU ARE CURRENTLY STUDYING EITHER MATH OR PHILOSOPHY. ARE YOU NOT, YOUNG MASTER JAMES?
But I really think you're studying math.
DAZED
JUST HOW IN THE WORLD DID YOU FIGURE ALL THAT OUT?
No wonder you're a detective story writer!
WELL... AS TO THE PARTICULARS...
SHALL WE JUST SAY IT'S A LADY'S SECRET?

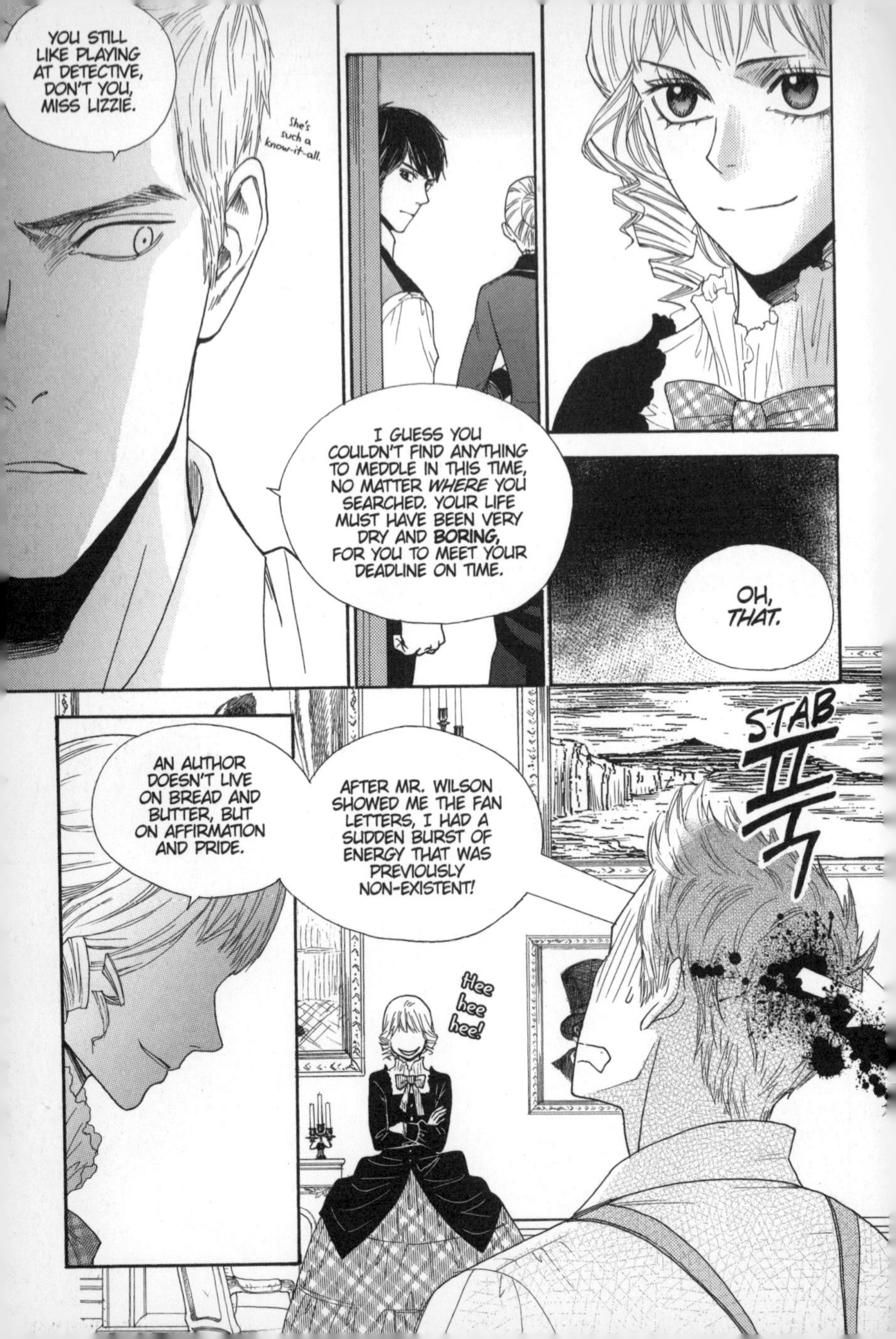
YOU STILL LIKE PLAYING AT DETECTIVE, DON'T YOU, MISS LIZZIE.
She's such a know-it-all.
I GUESS YOU COULDN'T FIND ANYTHING TO MEDDLE IN THIS TIME, NO MATTER *WHERE* YOU SEARCHED. YOUR LIFE MUST HAVE BEEN VERY DRY AND **BORING,** FOR YOU TO MEET YOUR DEADLINE ON TIME.
OH, *THAT.*
AN AUTHOR DOESN'T LIVE ON BREAD AND BUTTER, BUT ON AFFIRMATION AND PRIDE.
AFTER MR. WILSON SHOWED ME THE FAN LETTERS, I HAD A SUDDEN BURST OF ENERGY THAT WAS PREVIOUSLY NON-EXISTENT!
STAB
Hee hee hee!

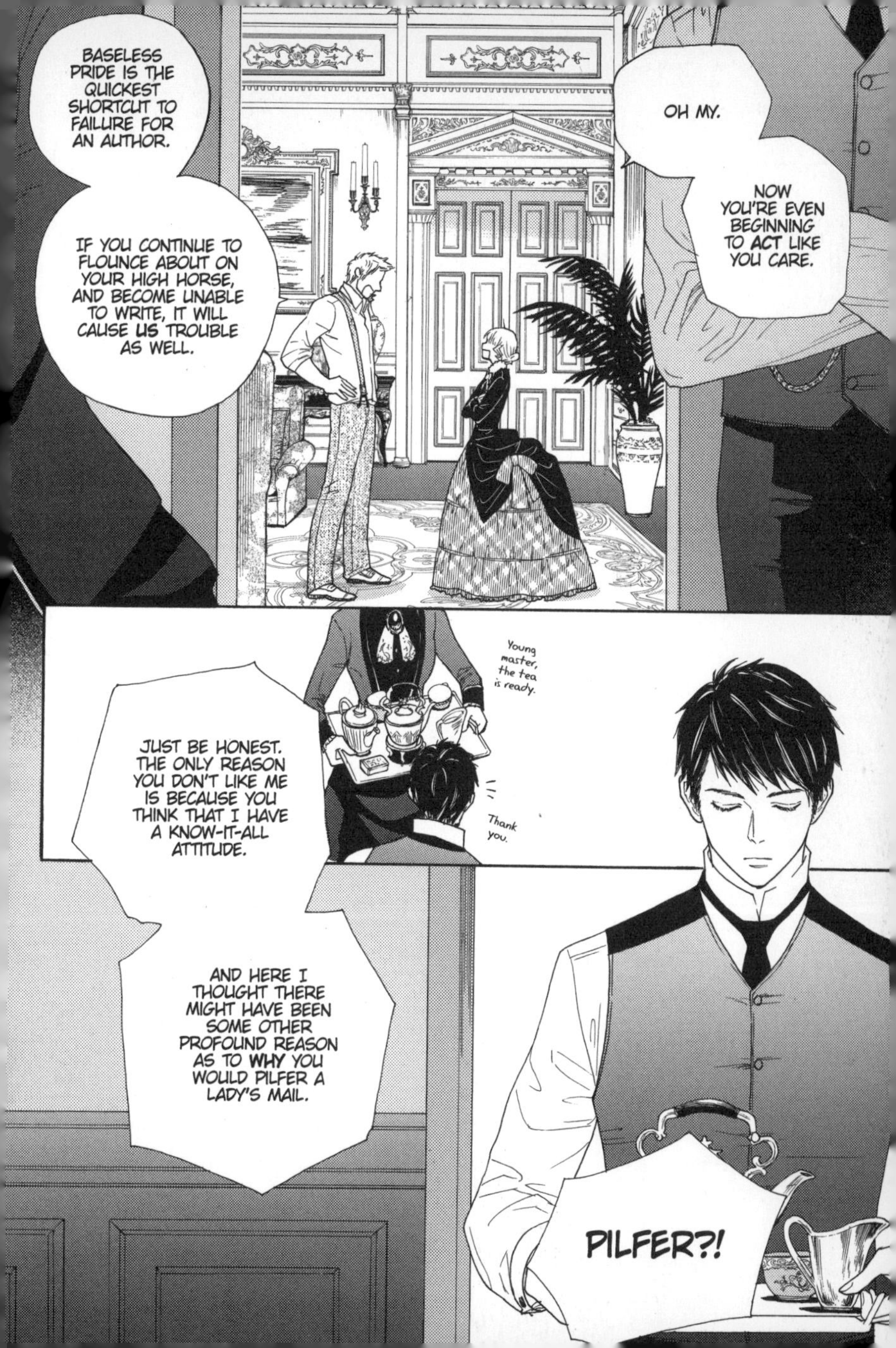
BASELESS PRIDE IS THE QUICKEST SHORTCUT TO FAILURE FOR AN AUTHOR.
IF YOU CONTINUE TO FLOUNCE ABOUT ON YOUR HIGH HORSE, AND BECOME UNABLE TO WRITE, IT WILL CAUSE **US** TROUBLE AS WELL.
OH MY.
NOW YOU'RE EVEN BEGINNING TO **ACT** LIKE YOU CARE.
JUST BE HONEST. THE ONLY REASON YOU DON'T LIKE ME IS BECAUSE YOU THINK THAT I HAVE A KNOW-IT-ALL ATTITUDE.
Young master, the tea is ready.
Thank you.
AND HERE I THOUGHT THERE MIGHT HAVE BEEN SOME OTHER PROFOUND REASON AS TO **WHY** YOU WOULD PILFER A LADY'S MAIL.
PILFER?!

SHALL I INQUIRE WITH THE VARIOUS ESTEEMED **WIVES** OF LONDON'S HIGH SOCIETY?

ASK THEM, WHAT EVER SHALL I **DO** TO THE YOUNG EDITOR OF *GENTLEMAN'S OWN*, WHO PILFERED ALL OF THE LETTERS ADDRESSED TO ME?

ALL MY LETTERS HAVE BEEN ROTTING AWAY IN YOUR STORAGE ROOM. IF THAT ISN'T PILFERING, THEN WHAT IS?

ARE YOU TRYING TO **THREATEN ME** BECAUSE OF SOME WRETCHED LETTERS?

How could you even think that a lady like our Miss would do such a thing as threaten someone?

IMPOSSIBLE.

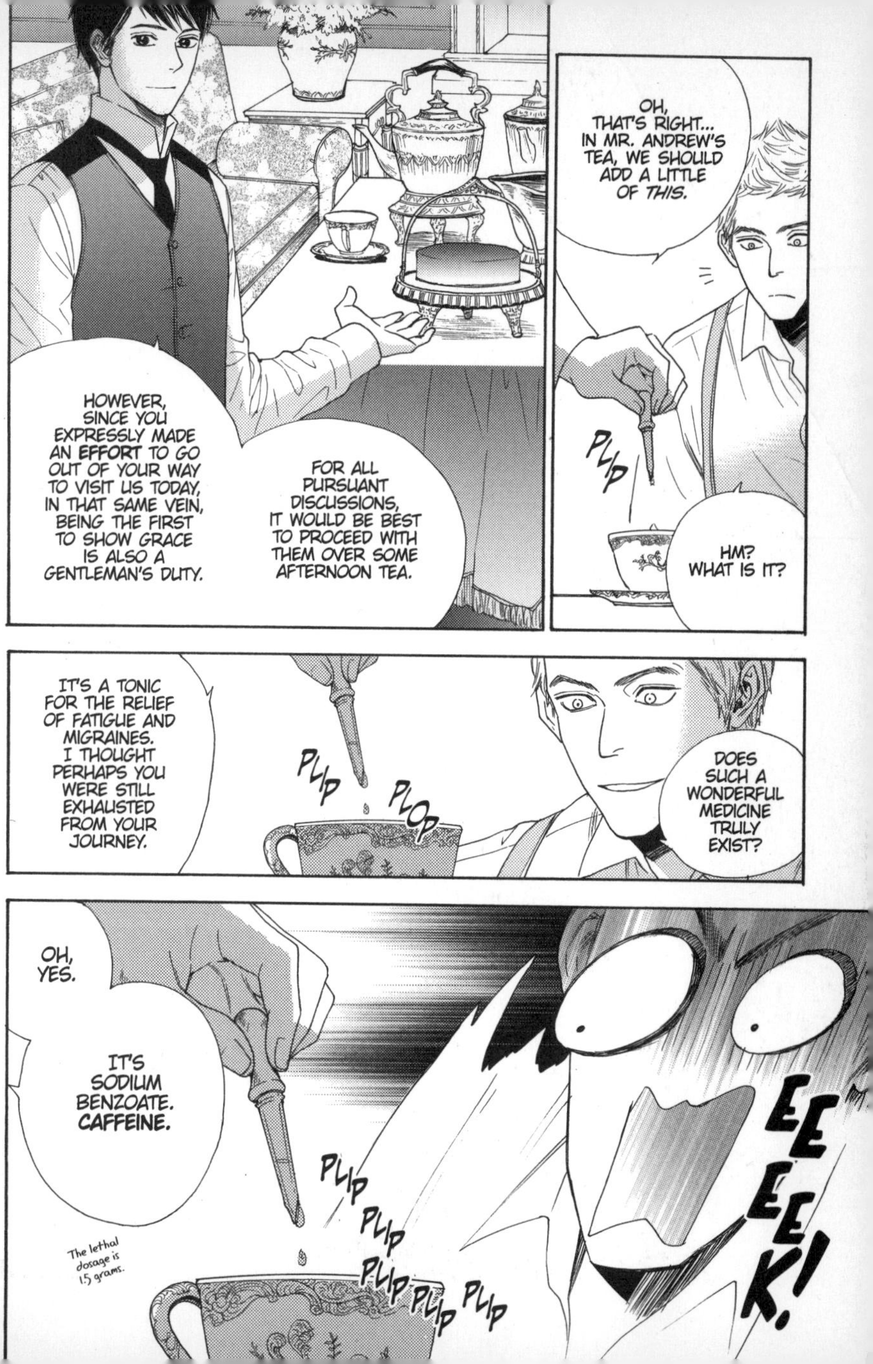
HOWEVER, SINCE YOU EXPRESSLY MADE AN EFFORT TO GO OUT OF YOUR WAY TO VISIT US TODAY, IN THAT SAME VEIN, BEING THE FIRST TO SHOW GRACE IS ALSO A GENTLEMAN'S DUTY.
FOR ALL PURSUANT DISCUSSIONS, IT WOULD BE BEST TO PROCEED WITH THEM OVER SOME AFTERNOON TEA.
OH, THAT'S RIGHT... IN MR. ANDREW'S TEA, WE SHOULD ADD A LITTLE OF THIS.
PLIP
HM? WHAT IS IT?
IT'S A TONIC FOR THE RELIEF OF FATIGUE AND MIGRAINES. I THOUGHT PERHAPS YOU WERE STILL EXHAUSTED FROM YOUR JOURNEY.
PLIP
PLOP
DOES SUCH A WONDERFUL MEDICINE TRULY EXIST?
OH, YES.
IT'S SODIUM BENZOATE. CAFFEINE.
PLIP PLIP PLIP PLIP PLIP
The lethal dosage is 1.5 grams.
EEEEK!

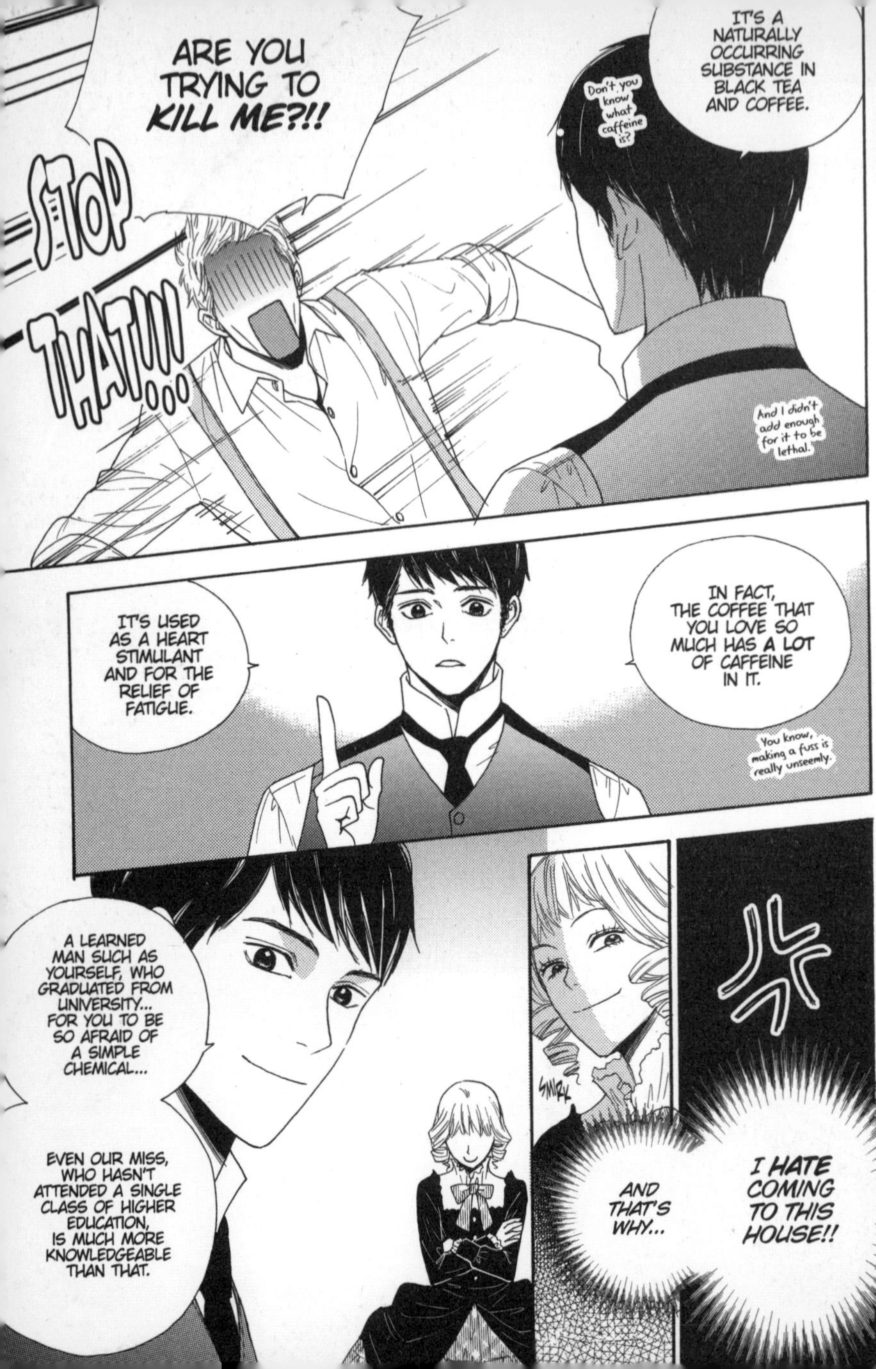
ARE YOU TRYING TO KILL ME?!!
STOP THAT!!!...
IT'S A NATURALLY OCCURRING SUBSTANCE IN BLACK TEA AND COFFEE.
Don't you know what caffeine is?
And I didn't add enough for it to be lethal.
IT'S USED AS A HEART STIMULANT AND FOR THE RELIEF OF FATIGUE.
IN FACT, THE COFFEE THAT YOU LOVE SO MUCH HAS A LOT OF CAFFEINE IN IT.
You know, making a fuss is really unseemly.
A LEARNED MAN SUCH AS YOURSELF, WHO GRADUATED FROM UNIVERSITY... FOR YOU TO BE SO AFRAID OF A SIMPLE CHEMICAL...
EVEN OUR MISS, WHO HASN'T ATTENDED A SINGLE CLASS OF HIGHER EDUCATION, IS MUCH MORE KNOWLEDGEABLE THAN THAT.
SMIRK
AND THAT'S WHY...
I HATE COMING TO THIS HOUSE!!

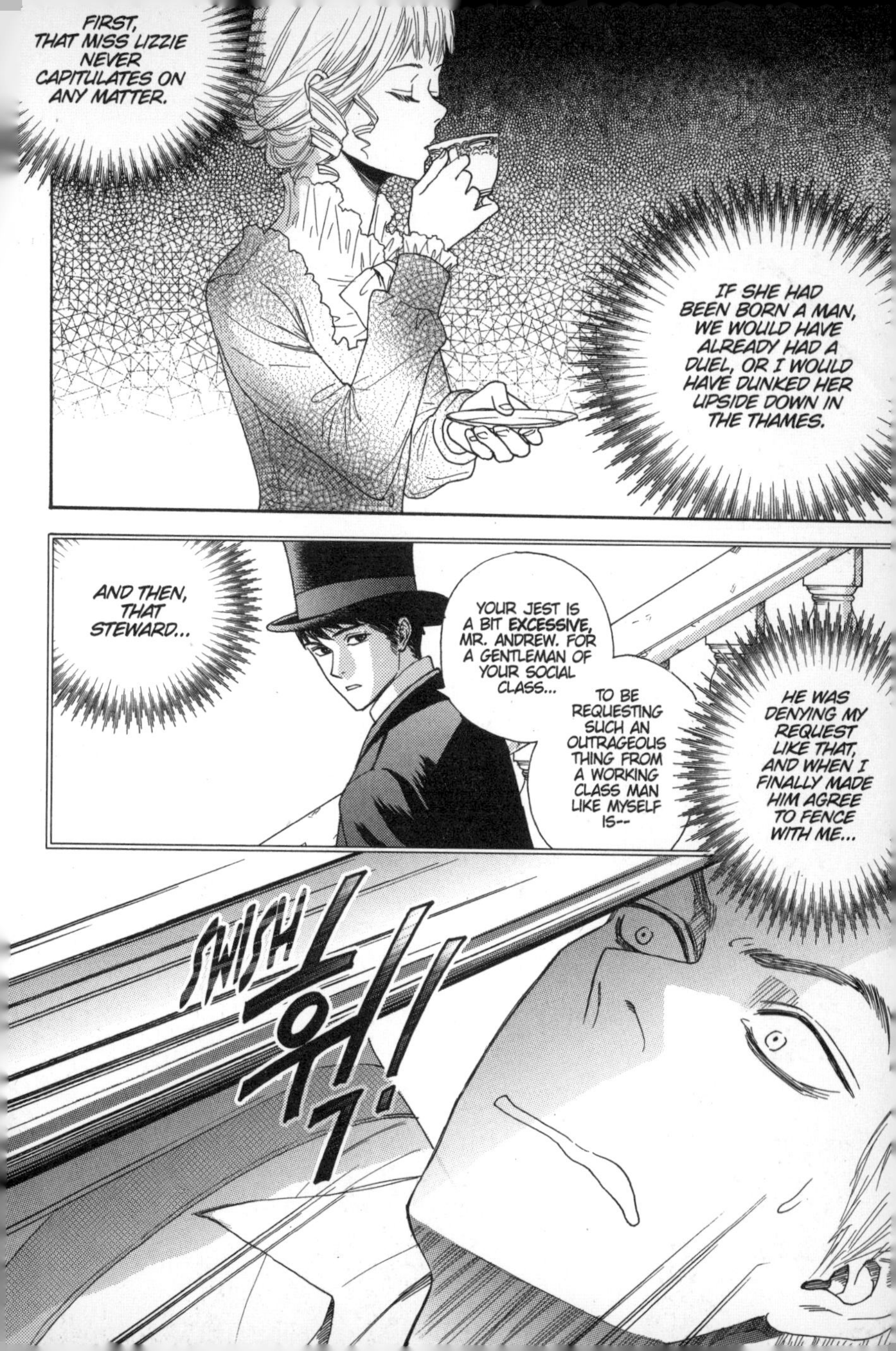
FIRST, THAT MISS LIZZIE NEVER CAPITULATES ON ANY MATTER.
IF SHE HAD BEEN BORN A MAN, WE WOULD HAVE ALREADY HAD A DUEL, OR I WOULD HAVE DUNKED HER UPSIDE DOWN IN THE THAMES.
AND THEN, THAT STEWARD...
YOUR JEST IS A BIT EXCESSIVE, MR. ANDREW. FOR A GENTLEMAN OF YOUR SOCIAL CLASS...
TO BE REQUESTING SUCH AN OUTRAGEOUS THING FROM A WORKING CLASS MAN LIKE MYSELF IS--
HE WAS DENYING MY REQUEST LIKE THAT, AND WHEN I FINALLY MADE HIM AGREE TO FENCE WITH ME...
SWISH

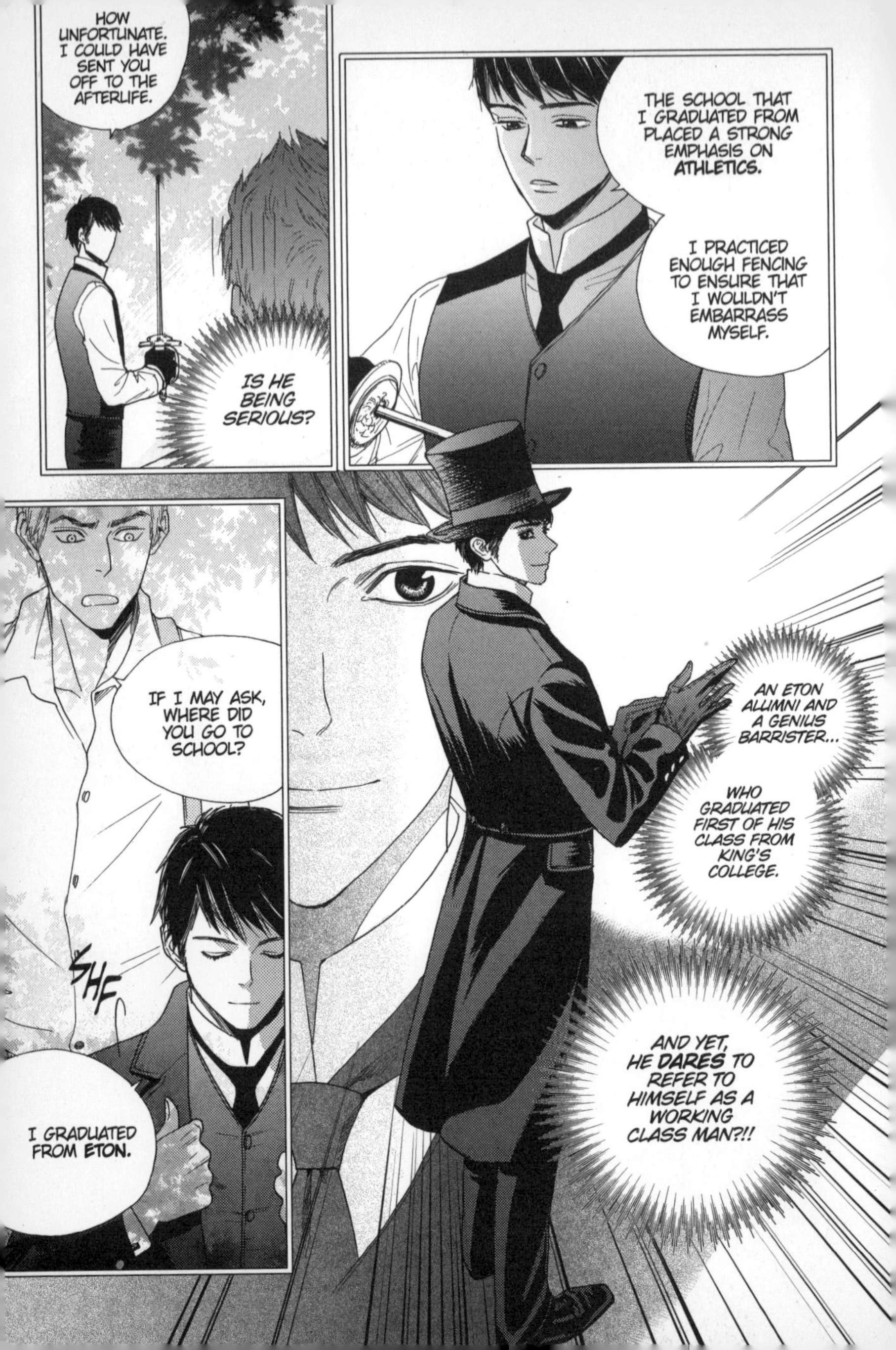
HOW UNFORTUNATE. I COULD HAVE SENT YOU OFF TO THE AFTERLIFE.
IS HE BEING SERIOUS?
THE SCHOOL THAT I GRADUATED FROM PLACED A STRONG EMPHASIS ON ATHLETICS.
I PRACTICED ENOUGH FENCING TO ENSURE THAT I WOULDN'T EMBARRASS MYSELF.
IF I MAY ASK, WHERE DID YOU GO TO SCHOOL?
SHF
I GRADUATED FROM ETON.
AN ETON ALUMNI AND A GENIUS BARRISTER...
WHO GRADUATED FIRST OF HIS CLASS FROM KING'S COLLEGE.
AND YET, HE DARES TO REFER TO HIMSELF AS A WORKING CLASS MAN?!!

I REALLY CAN'T STAND PEOPLE WHO PUT ON AIRS!!

We can tell what he's thinking just by looking at his face, Miss Lizzie.

You're right.

OH, BY THE WAY...

WHY DON'T WE CONSULT MISS LIZZIE ABOUT THAT THING?

Judging from her earlier demonstration, she certainly has a gift for deduction.

TURN

WHAT?! WHAT ARE YOU TALKING ABOUT?!!

"THAT THING"?

OH. MR. ANDREW HAD PURCHASED A **BOOK** FROM A USED BOOKSTORE.

INSIDE OF THE BOOK, WE FOUND AN OLD PIECE OF PAPER WITH A CODED MESSAGE.

WHAT ARE YOU DOING?!!

They say the paper is about 300 years old.

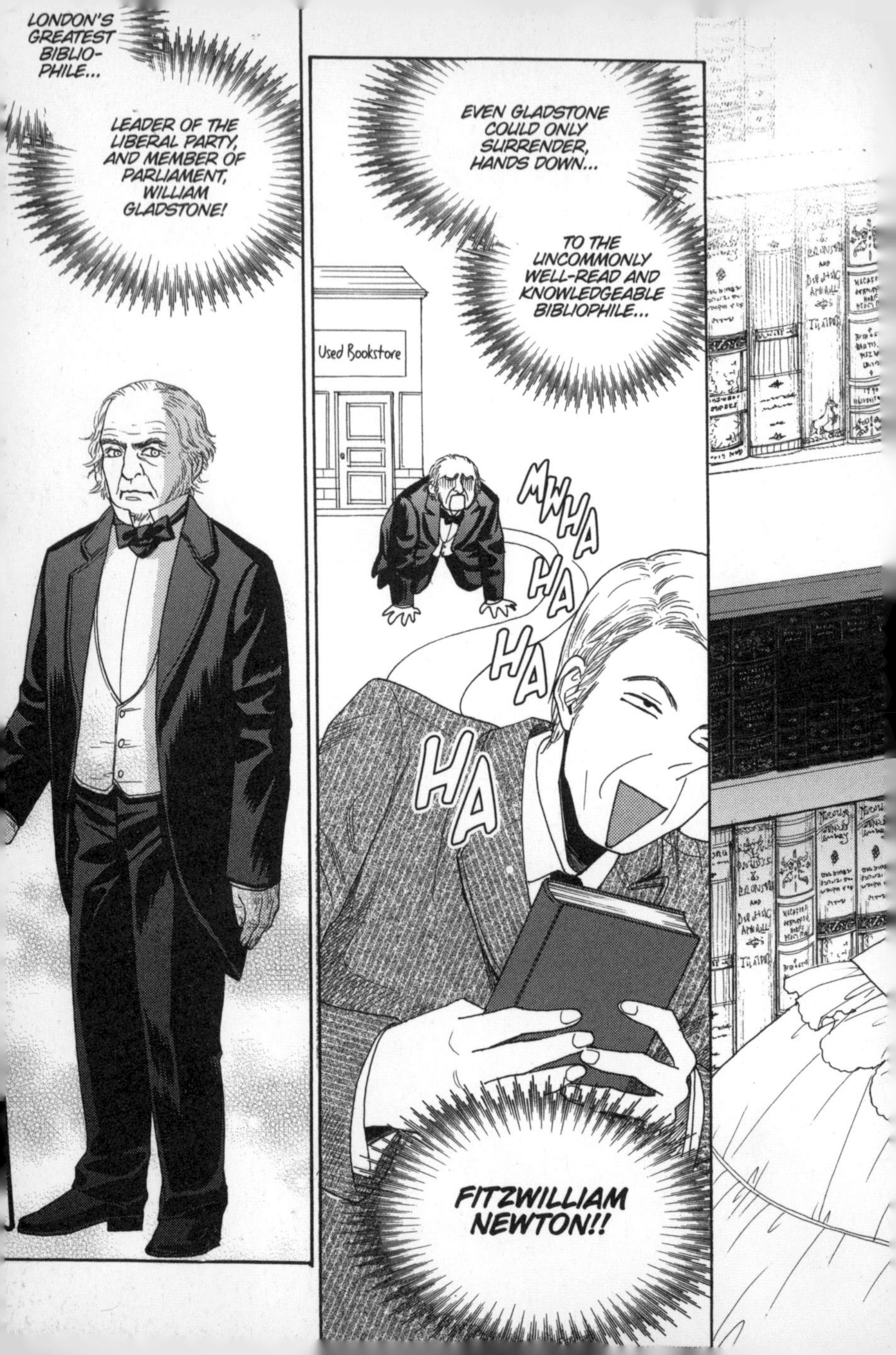
LONDON'S GREATEST BIBLIO-PHILE...
LEADER OF THE LIBERAL PARTY, AND MEMBER OF PARLIAMENT, WILLIAM GLADSTONE!
EVEN GLADSTONE COULD ONLY SURRENDER, HANDS DOWN...
TO THE UNCOMMONLY WELL-READ AND KNOWLEDGEABLE BIBLIOPHILE...
Used Bookstore
MWHA HA HA HA
FITZWILLIAM NEWTON!!

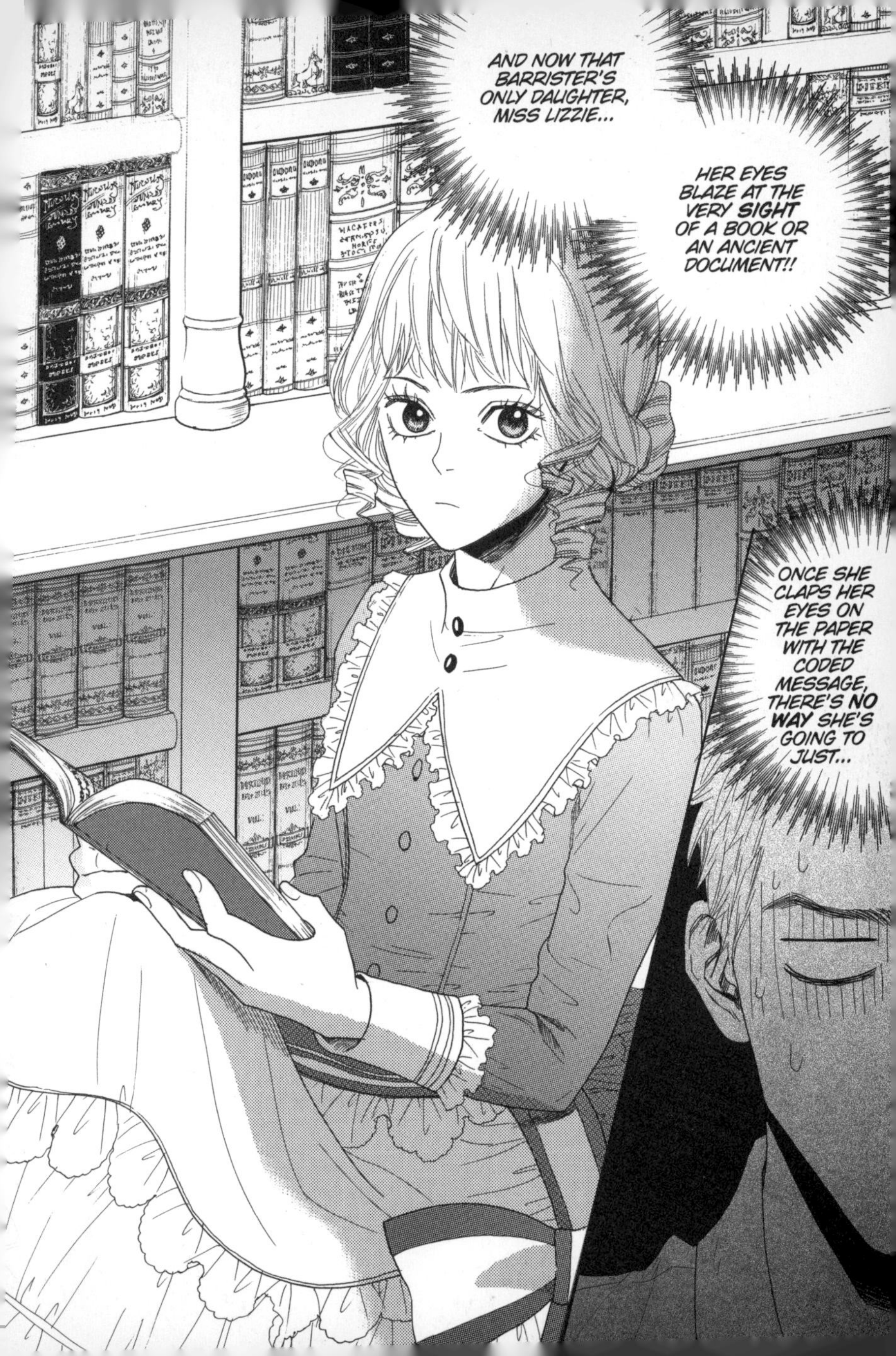
AND NOW THAT BARRISTER'S ONLY DAUGHTER, MISS LIZZIE...
HER EYES BLAZE AT THE VERY **SIGHT** OF A BOOK OR AN ANCIENT DOCUMENT!!
ONCE SHE CLAPS HER EYES ON THE PAPER WITH THE CODED MESSAGE, THERE'S **NO WAY** SHE'S GOING TO JUST...

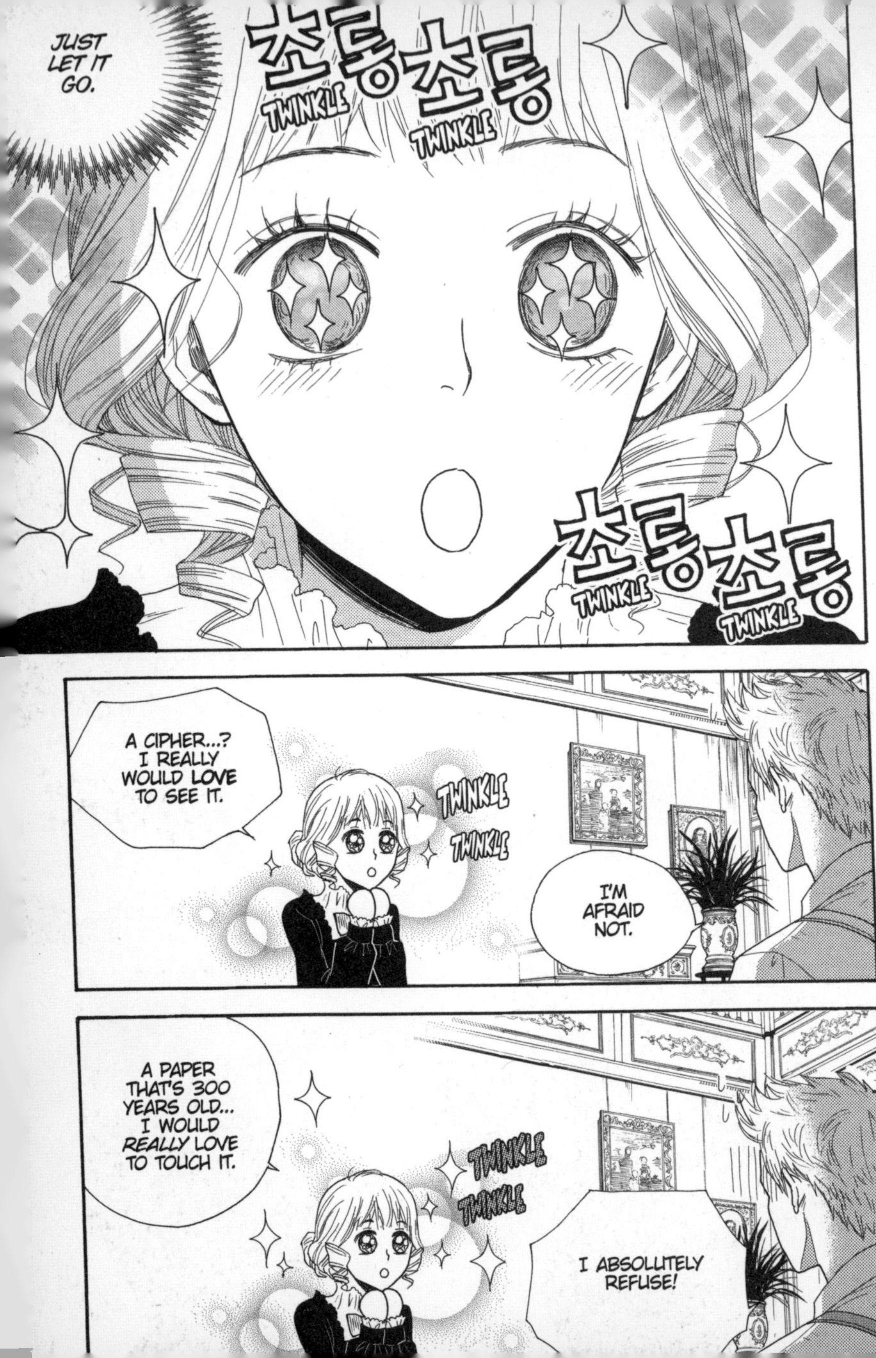
JUST LET IT GO.
초롱초롱
TWINKLE
TWINKLE
초롱초롱
TWINKLE
TWINKLE
A CIPHER...? I REALLY WOULD LOVE TO SEE IT.
TWINKLE
TWINKLE
I'M AFRAID NOT.
A PAPER THAT'S 300 YEARS OLD... I WOULD REALLY LOVE TO TOUCH IT.
TWINKLE
TWINKLE
I ABSOLUTELY REFUSE!

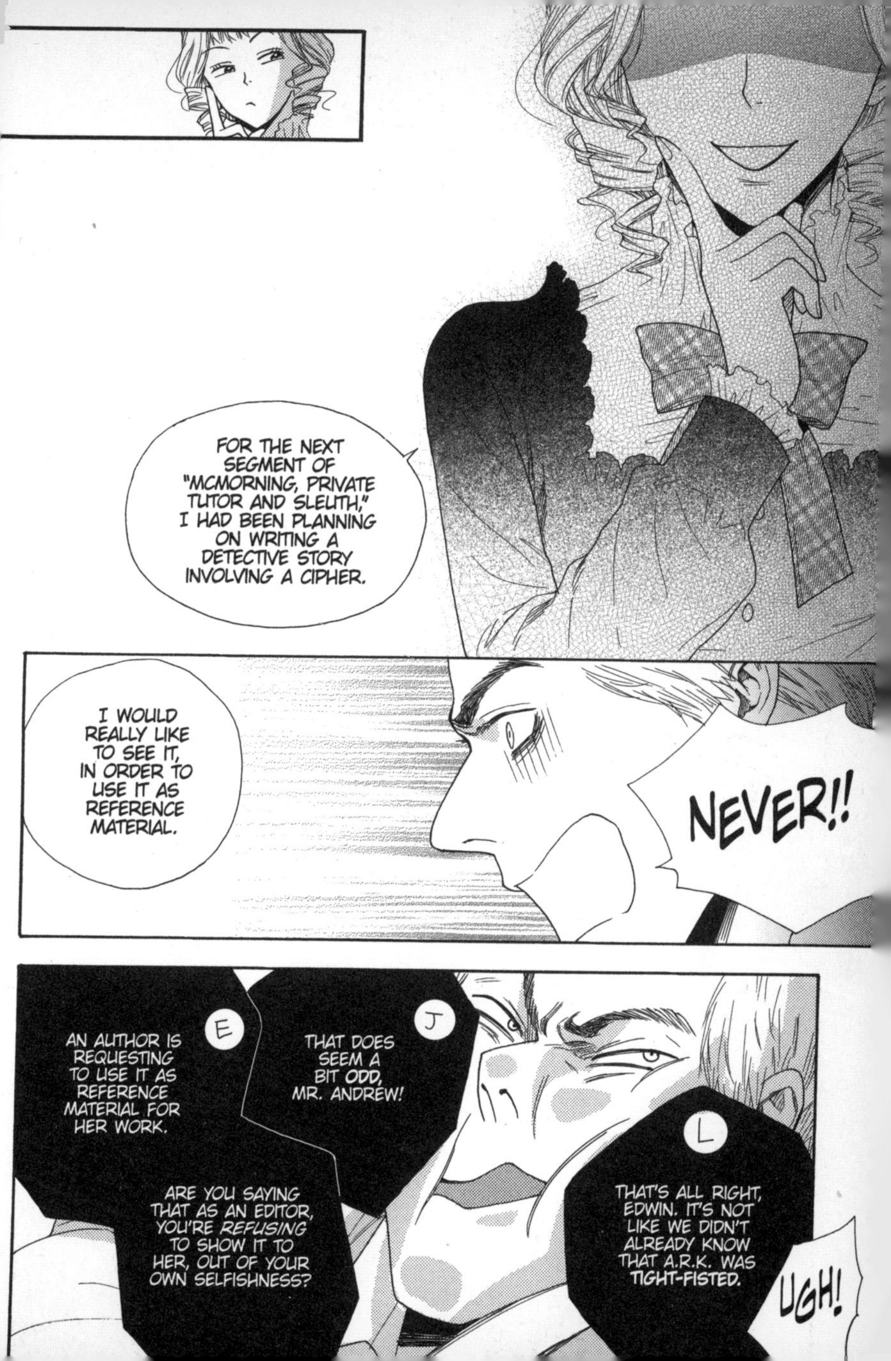
FOR THE NEXT SEGMENT OF "MCMORNING, PRIVATE TUTOR AND SLEUTH," I HAD BEEN PLANNING ON WRITING A DETECTIVE STORY INVOLVING A CIPHER.
I WOULD REALLY LIKE TO SEE IT, IN ORDER TO USE IT AS REFERENCE MATERIAL.
NEVER!!
E
AN AUTHOR IS REQUESTING TO USE IT AS REFERENCE MATERIAL FOR HER WORK.
J
THAT DOES SEEM A BIT ODD, MR. ANDREW!
ARE YOU SAYING THAT AS AN EDITOR, YOU'RE REFUSING TO SHOW IT TO HER, OUT OF YOUR OWN SELFISHNESS?
L
THAT'S ALL RIGHT, EDWIN. IT'S NOT LIKE WE DIDN'T ALREADY KNOW THAT A.R.K. WAS TIGHT-FISTED.
UGH!

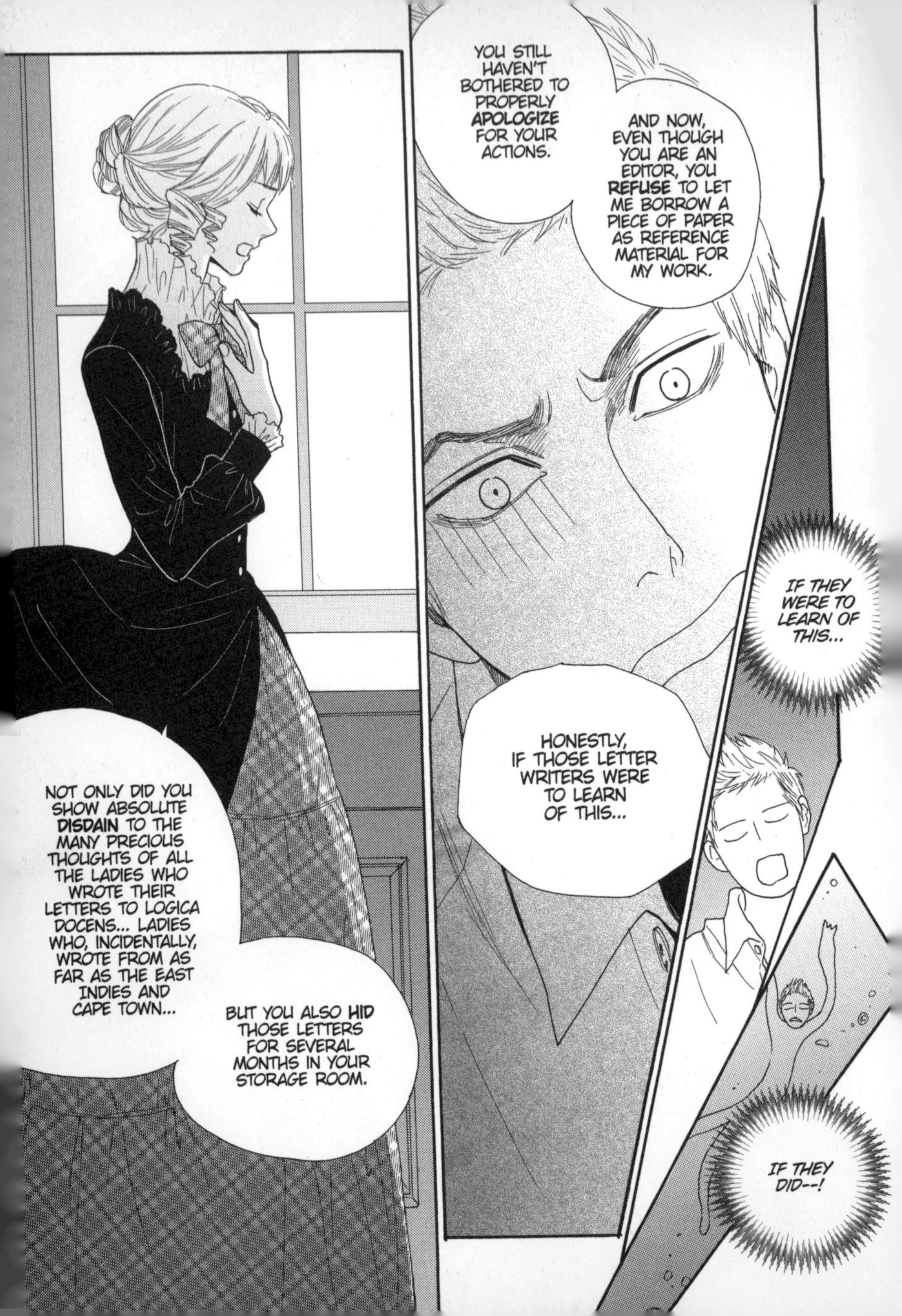
NOT ONLY DID YOU SHOW ABSOLUTE DISDAIN TO THE MANY PRECIOUS THOUGHTS OF ALL THE LADIES WHO WROTE THEIR LETTERS TO LOGICA DOCENS... LADIES WHO, INCIDENTALLY, WROTE FROM AS FAR AS THE EAST INDIES AND CAPE TOWN...
BUT YOU ALSO HID THOSE LETTERS FOR SEVERAL MONTHS IN YOUR STORAGE ROOM.
YOU STILL HAVEN'T BOTHERED TO PROPERLY APOLOGIZE FOR YOUR ACTIONS.
AND NOW, EVEN THOUGH YOU ARE AN EDITOR, YOU REFUSE TO LET ME BORROW A PIECE OF PAPER AS REFERENCE MATERIAL FOR MY WORK.
HONESTLY, IF THOSE LETTER WRITERS WERE TO LEARN OF THIS...
IF THEY WERE TO LEARN OF THIS...
IF THEY DID--!

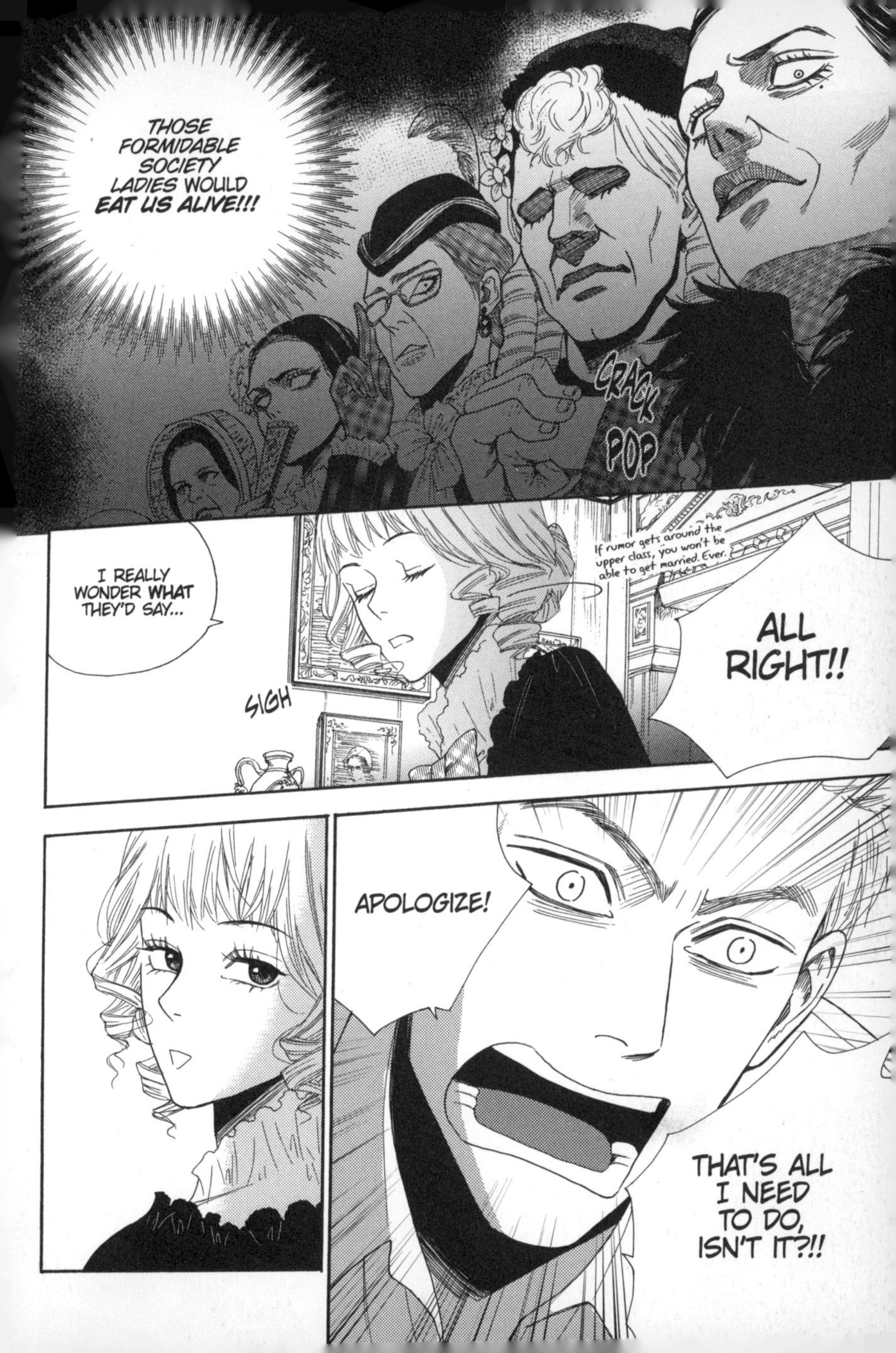
THOSE FORMIDABLE SOCIETY LADIES WOULD EAT US ALIVE!!!
CRACK
POP
I REALLY WONDER WHAT THEY'D SAY...
SIGH
If rumor gets around the upper class, you won't be able to get married. Ever.
ALL RIGHT!!
APOLOGIZE!
THAT'S ALL I NEED TO DO, ISN'T IT?!!

I APOLOGIZE FOR FAILING TO DELIVER YOUR FAN LETTERS ALL THIS TIME.

SINCE IT APPEARS THAT SOME NOMINAL RISING OF YOUR SPIRITS IS HELPFUL IN HAVING YOU SUCCESSFULLY MEET YOUR DEADLINES...

I WILL BE SURE TO COLLECT EACH MONTH'S LETTERS AND BRING THEM TO YOU.

That man will never change.

In what way is that considered an apology?

AS A DEMONSTRATION OF YOUR APOLOGY, I WILL NEED MR. VICTOR HUGO'S SIGNED BOOK, WHICH I AM SURE THAT YOU'VE BROUGHT BACK WITH YOU.

Words without actions are useless.

DON'T JUMP TO CONCLUSIONS!!

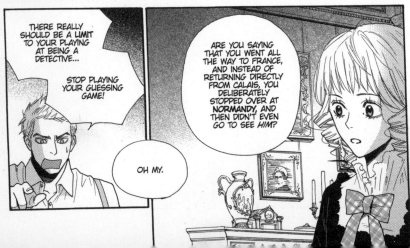

THERE REALLY SHOULD BE A LIMIT TO YOUR PLAYING AT BEING A DETECTIVE...

STOP PLAYING YOUR GUESSING GAME!

OH MY.

ARE YOU SAYING THAT YOU WENT ALL THE WAY TO FRANCE, AND INSTEAD OF RETURNING DIRECTLY FROM CALAIS, YOU DELIBERATELY STOPPED OVER AT NORMANDY, AND THEN DIDN'T EVEN GO TO SEE *HIM*?

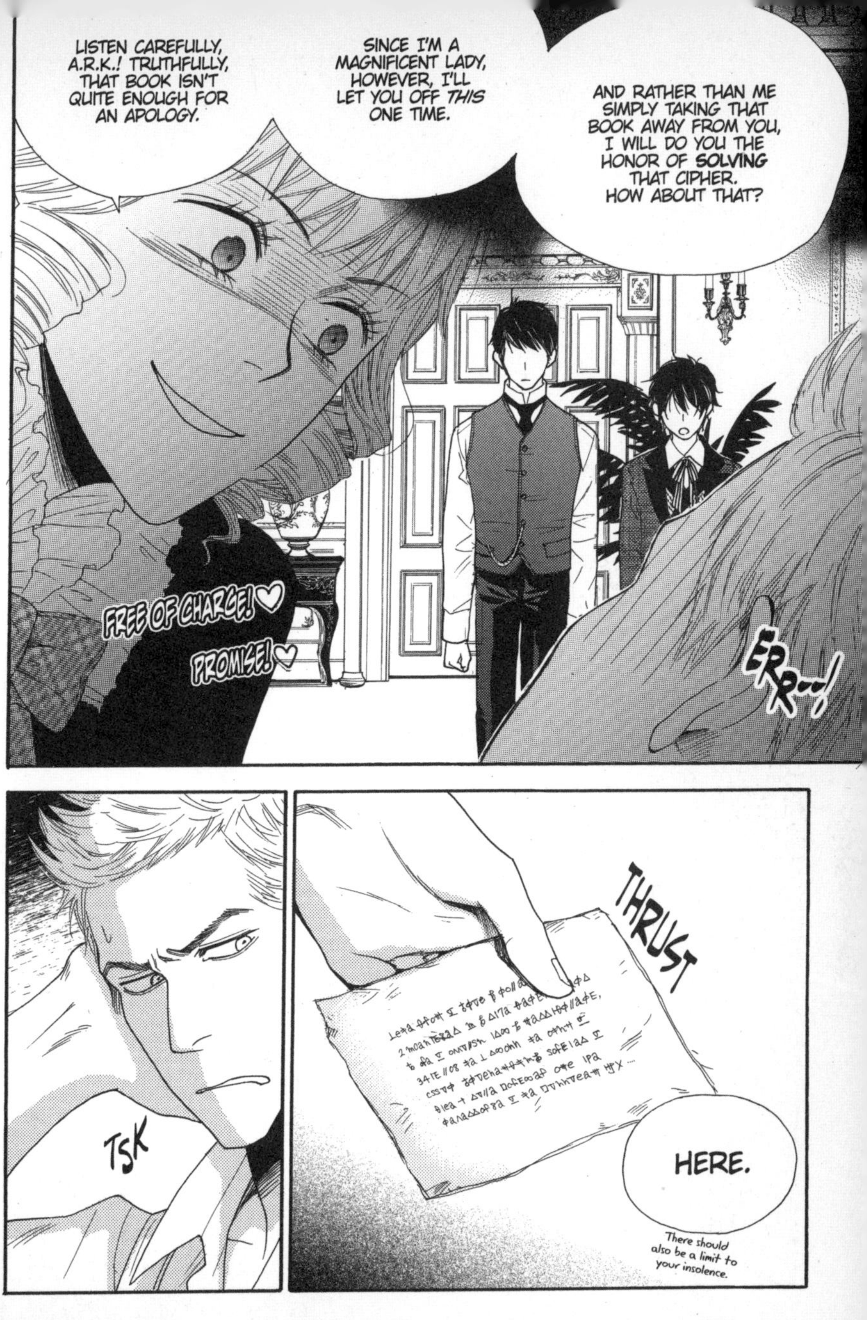
LISTEN CAREFULLY, A.R.K.! TRUTHFULLY, THAT BOOK ISN'T QUITE ENOUGH FOR AN APOLOGY.
SINCE I'M A MAGNIFICENT LADY, HOWEVER, I'LL LET YOU OFF *THIS* ONE TIME.
AND RATHER THAN ME SIMPLY TAKING THAT BOOK AWAY FROM YOU, I WILL DO YOU THE HONOR OF **SOLVING** THAT CIPHER. HOW ABOUT THAT?
FREE OF CHARGE!♡
PROMISE!♡
ERR—!
TSK
THRUST
HERE.
There should also be a limit to your insolence.

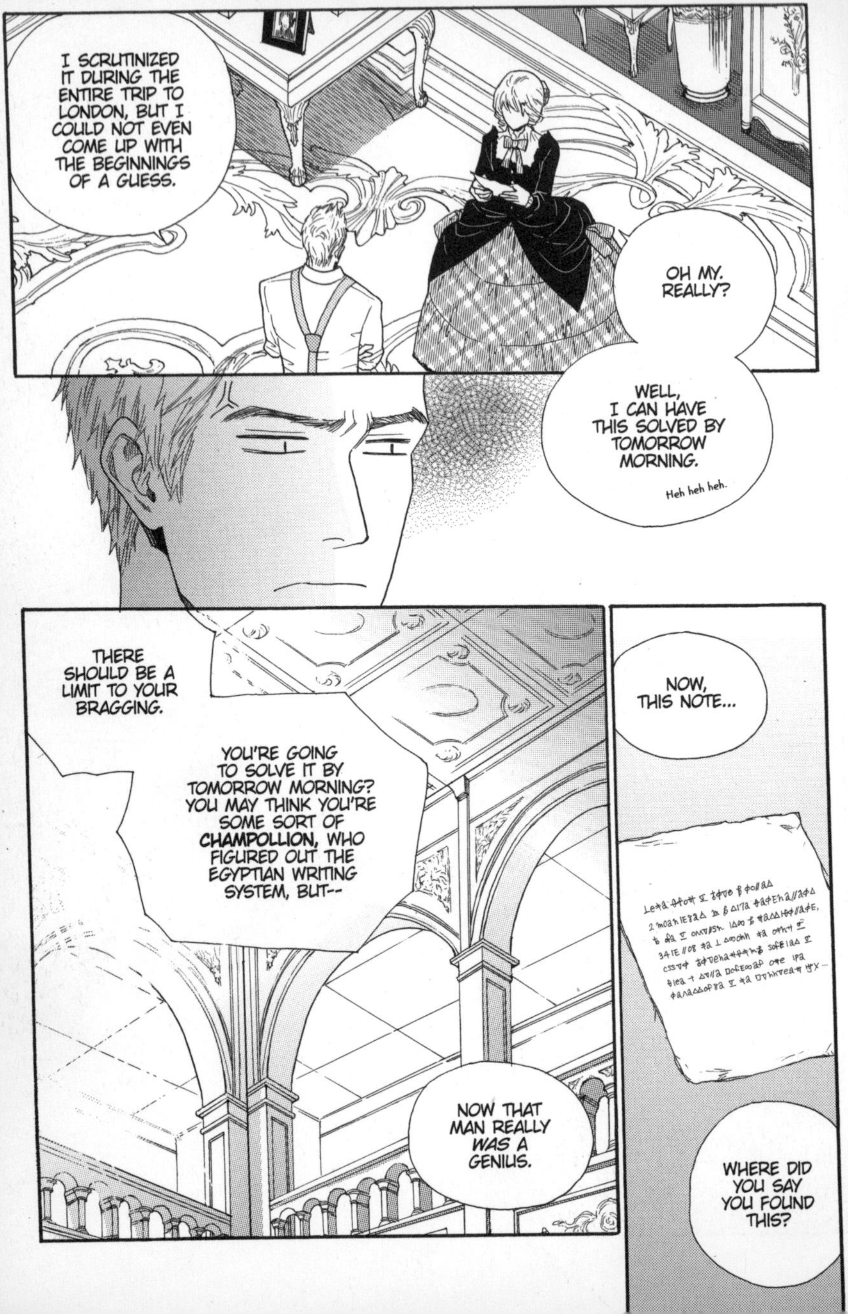
I SCRUTINIZED IT DURING THE ENTIRE TRIP TO LONDON, BUT I COULD NOT EVEN COME UP WITH THE BEGINNINGS OF A GUESS.
OH MY. REALLY?
WELL, I CAN HAVE THIS SOLVED BY TOMORROW MORNING.
Heh heh heh.
THERE SHOULD BE A LIMIT TO YOUR BRAGGING.
YOU'RE GOING TO SOLVE IT BY TOMORROW MORNING? YOU MAY THINK YOU'RE SOME SORT OF **CHAMPOLLION**, WHO FIGURED OUT THE EGYPTIAN WRITING SYSTEM, BUT--
NOW THAT MAN REALLY *WAS* A GENIUS.
NOW, THIS NOTE...
WHERE DID YOU SAY YOU FOUND THIS?

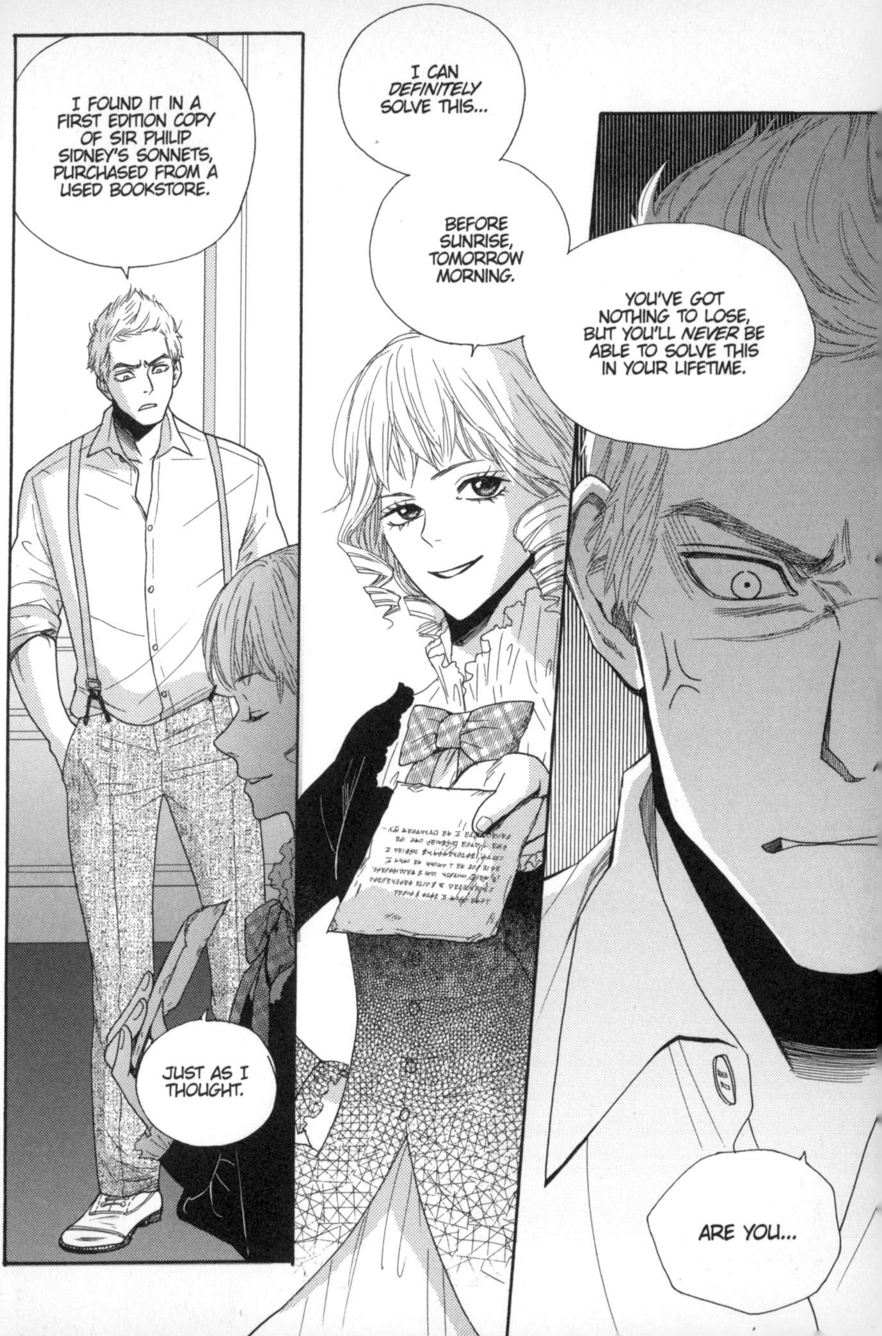
I FOUND IT IN A FIRST EDITION COPY OF SIR PHILIP SIDNEY'S SONNETS, PURCHASED FROM A USED BOOKSTORE.
JUST AS I THOUGHT.
I CAN *DEFINITELY* SOLVE THIS...
BEFORE SUNRISE, TOMORROW MORNING.
YOU'VE GOT NOTHING TO LOSE, BUT YOU'LL *NEVER* BE ABLE TO SOLVE THIS IN YOUR LIFETIME.
ARE YOU...

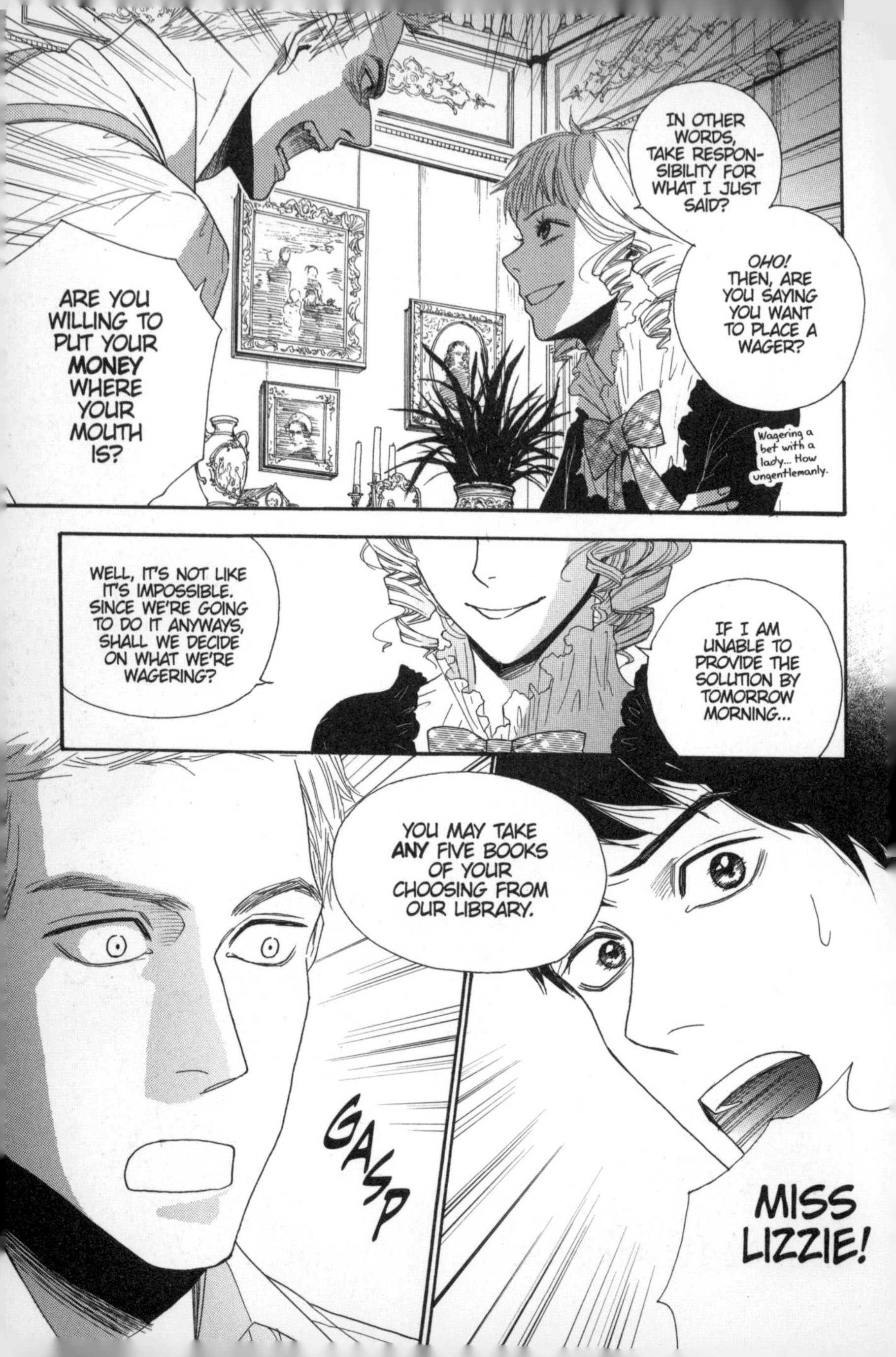
ARE YOU WILLING TO PUT YOUR MONEY WHERE YOUR MOUTH IS?
IN OTHER WORDS, TAKE RESPON-SIBILITY FOR WHAT I JUST SAID?
OHO! THEN, ARE YOU SAYING YOU WANT TO PLACE A WAGER?
Wagering a bet with a lady... How ungentlemanly.
WELL, IT'S NOT LIKE IT'S IMPOSSIBLE. SINCE WE'RE GOING TO DO IT ANYWAYS, SHALL WE DECIDE ON WHAT WE'RE WAGERING?
IF I AM UNABLE TO PROVIDE THE SOLUTION BY TOMORROW MORNING...
YOU MAY TAKE ANY FIVE BOOKS OF YOUR CHOOSING FROM OUR LIBRARY.
GASP
MISS LIZZIE!

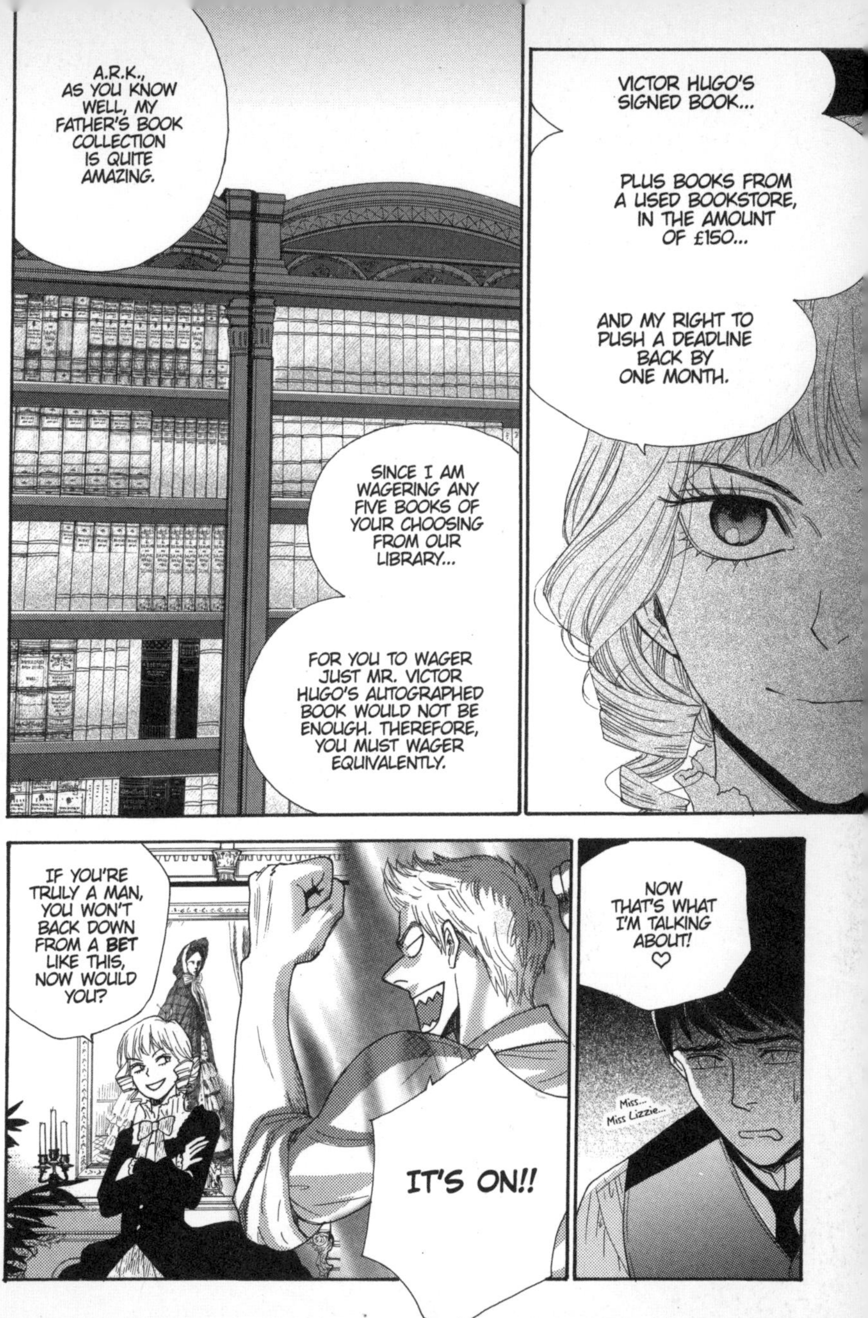
A.R.K., AS YOU KNOW WELL, MY FATHER'S BOOK COLLECTION IS QUITE AMAZING.
SINCE I AM WAGERING ANY FIVE BOOKS OF YOUR CHOOSING FROM OUR LIBRARY...
FOR YOU TO WAGER JUST MR. VICTOR HUGO'S AUTOGRAPHED BOOK WOULD NOT BE ENOUGH. THEREFORE, YOU MUST WAGER EQUIVALENTLY.
VICTOR HUGO'S SIGNED BOOK...
PLUS BOOKS FROM A USED BOOKSTORE, IN THE AMOUNT OF £150...
AND MY RIGHT TO PUSH A DEADLINE BACK BY ONE MONTH.
IF YOU'RE TRULY A MAN, YOU WON'T BACK DOWN FROM A BET LIKE THIS, NOW WOULD YOU?
IT'S ON!!
NOW THAT'S WHAT I'M TALKING ABOUT! ♡
Miss... Miss Lizzie...

WHILE WE'RE AT IT, SHALL WE WRITE UP A CONTRACT?
AS IT JUST SO HAPPENS, OUR STEWARD MOONLIGHTS AS AN ATTORNEY.
FINE!
Oh, the steward is also a barrister?
FALTER
WHAT MADNESS IS THIS?
THERE ARE THINGS YOU CAN AND CANNOT BET WITH! I CAN'T BELIEVE SHE'S WAGERING MEMENTOS OF THE LATE MASTER!!
HOW COULD SHE DO SUCH A THING?!!
This household's steward is truly amazing!
DOOOOM

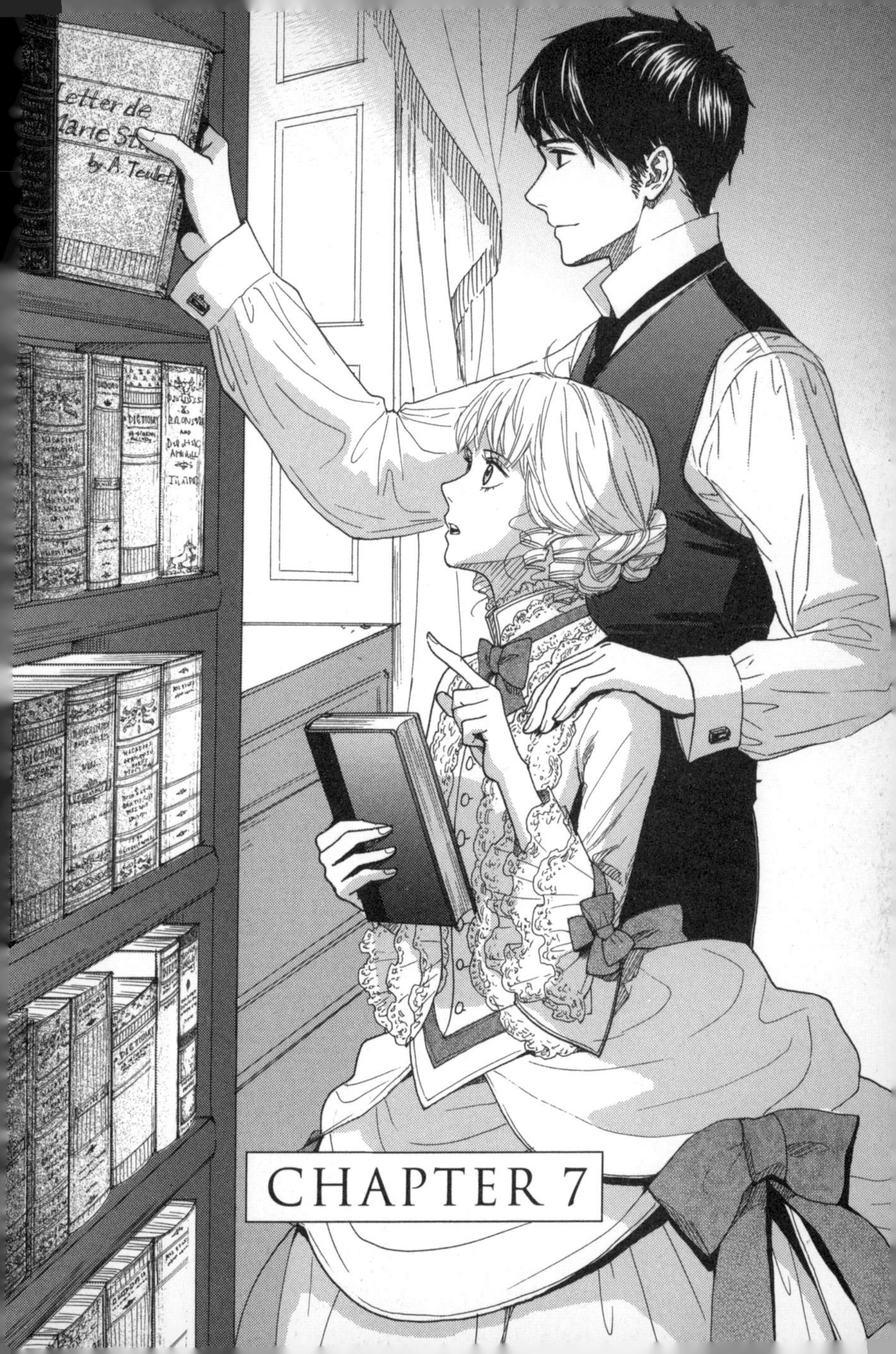
by A. Teulet

CHAPTER 7

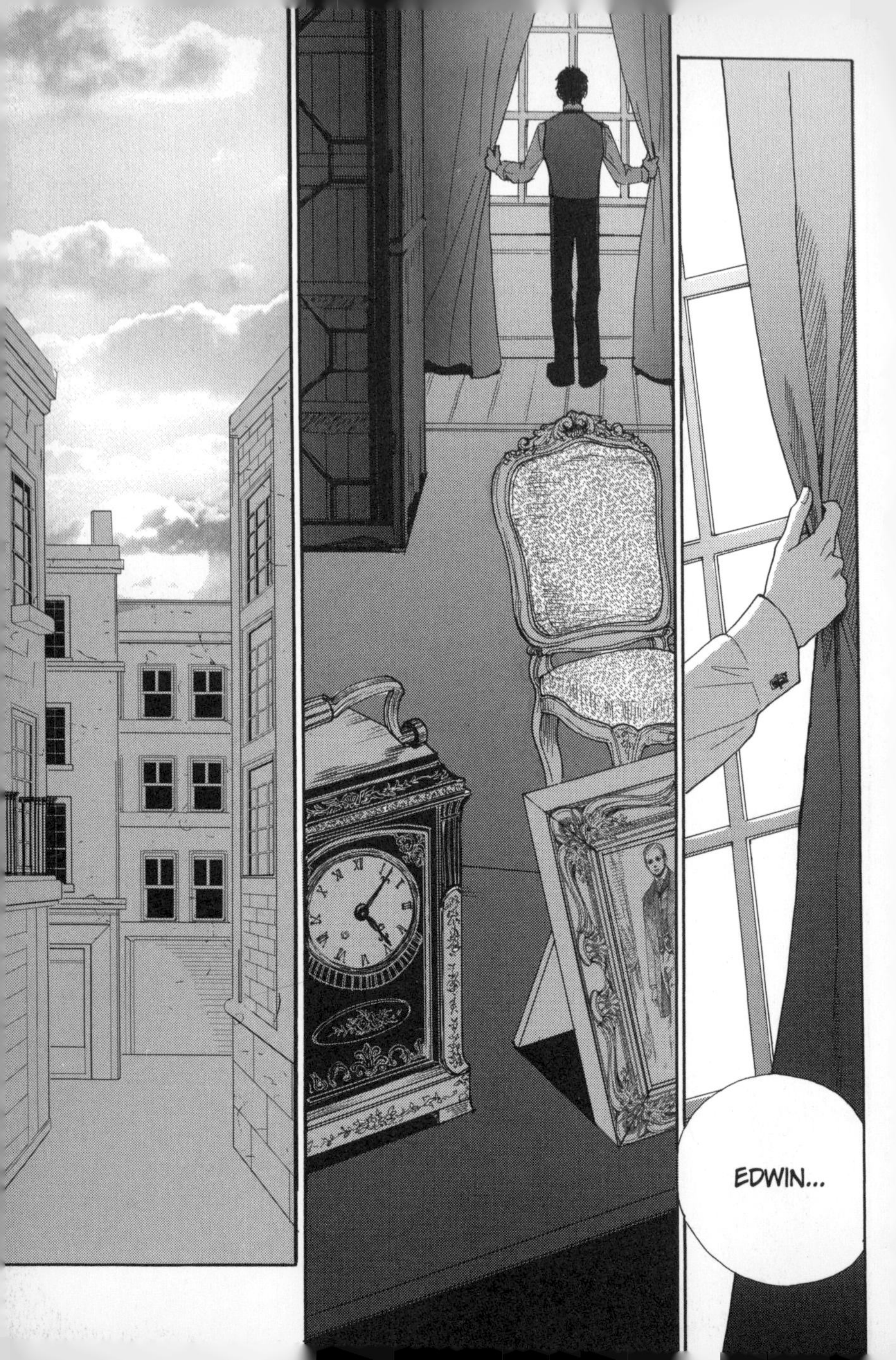
EDWIN...

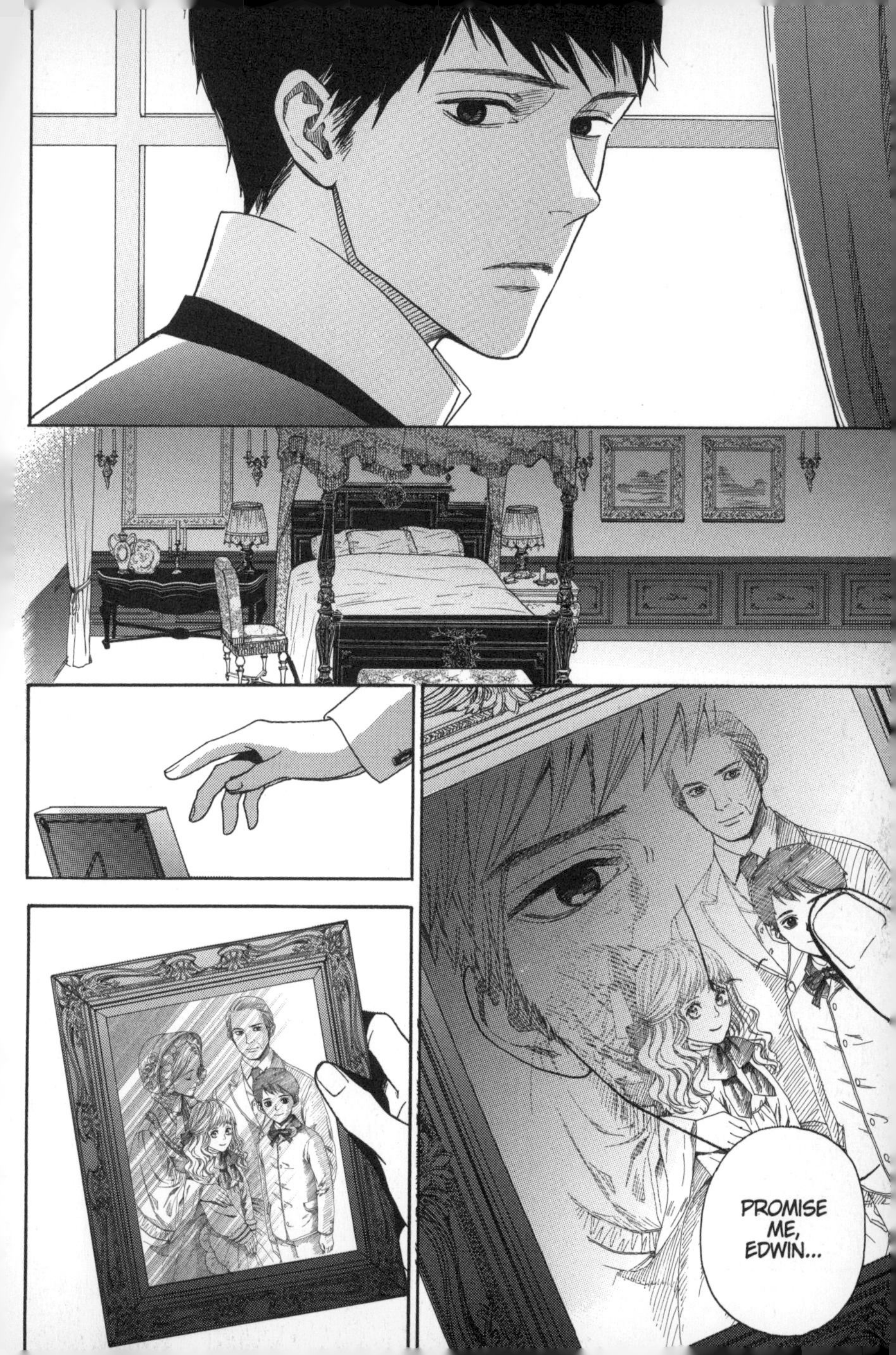
PROMISE ME, EDWIN...

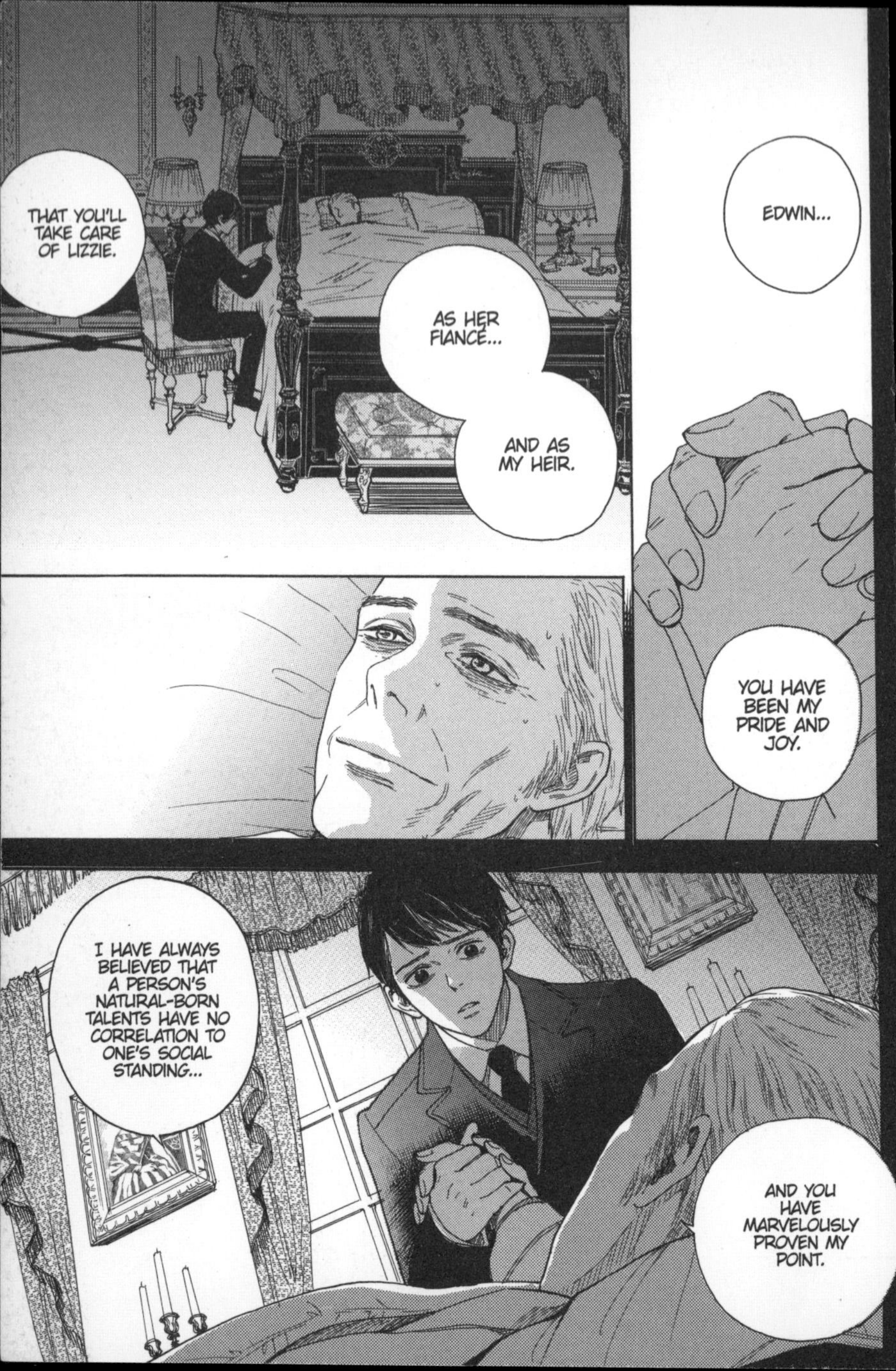
THAT YOU'LL TAKE CARE OF LIZZIE.
AS HER FIANCÉ...
AND AS MY HEIR.
EDWIN...
YOU HAVE BEEN MY PRIDE AND JOY.
I HAVE ALWAYS BELIEVED THAT A PERSON'S NATURAL-BORN TALENTS HAVE NO CORRELATION TO ONE'S SOCIAL STANDING...
AND YOU HAVE MARVELOUSLY PROVEN MY POINT.

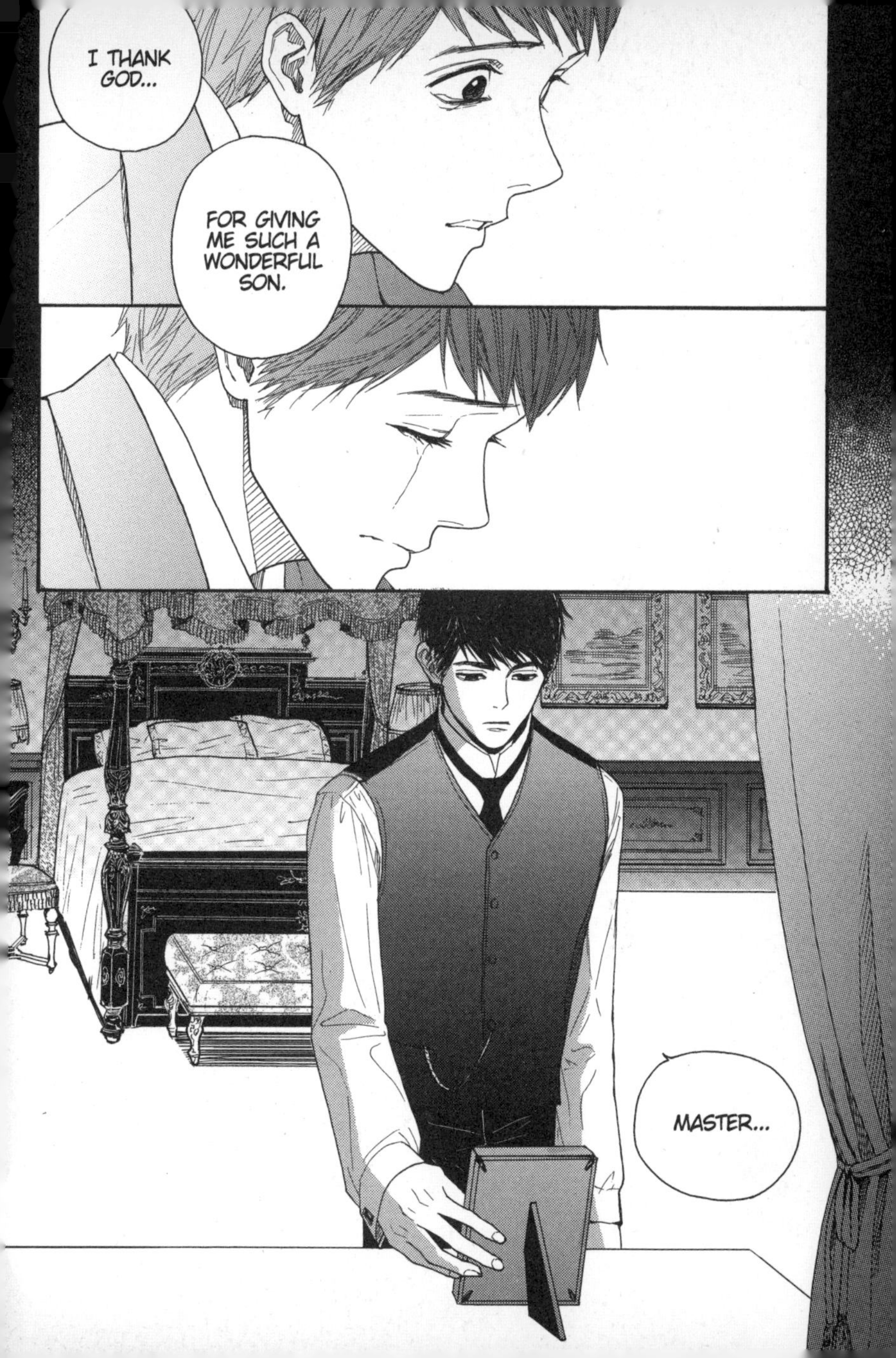
I THANK GOD...
FOR GIVING ME SUCH A WONDERFUL SON.
MASTER...

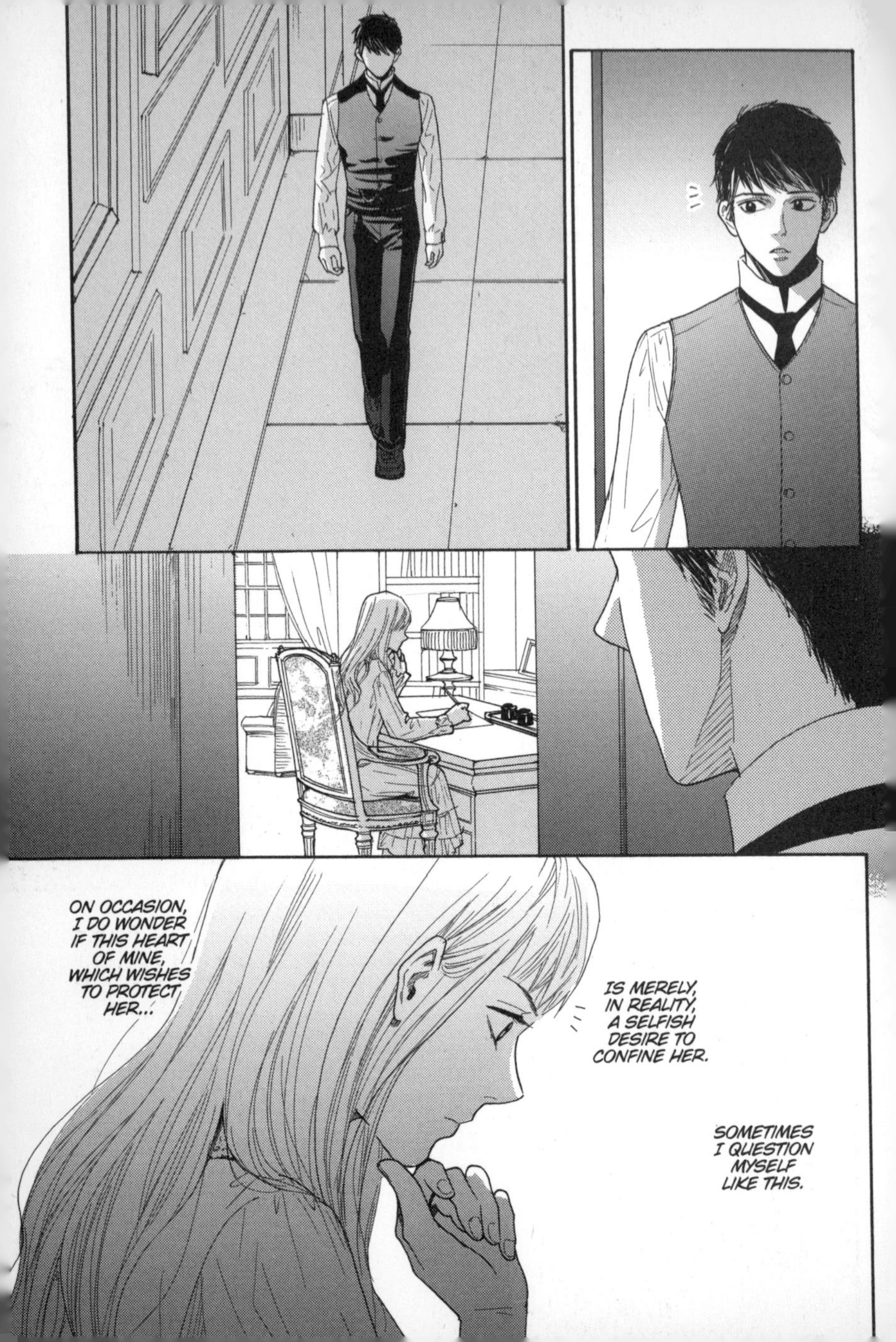
ON OCCASION, I DO WONDER IF THIS HEART OF MINE, WHICH WISHES TO PROTECT HER...
IS MERELY, IN REALITY, A SELFISH DESIRE TO CONFINE HER.
SOMETIMES I QUESTION MYSELF LIKE THIS.

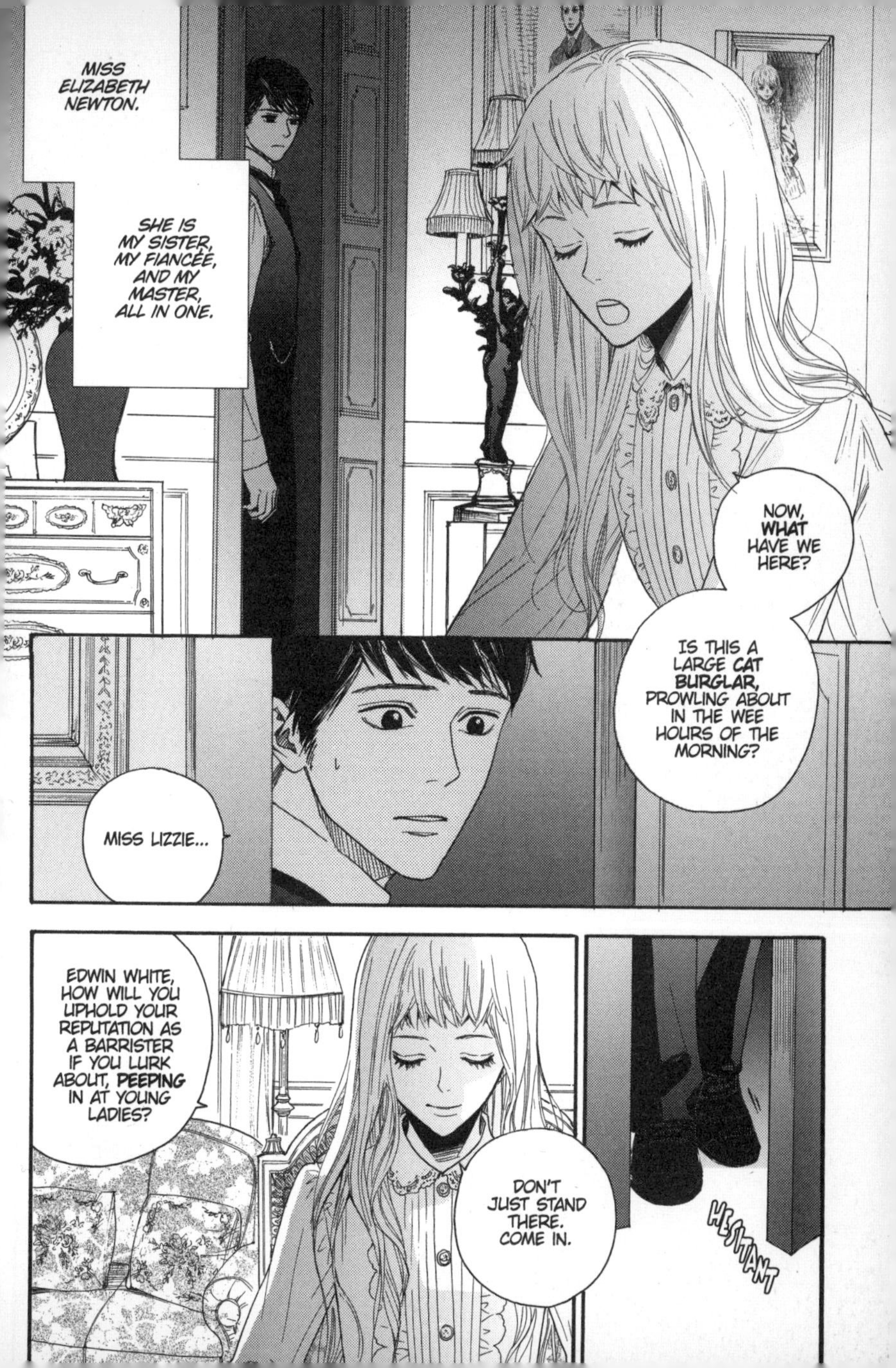
MISS ELIZABETH NEWTON.
SHE IS MY SISTER, MY FIANCÉE, AND MY MASTER, ALL IN ONE.
NOW, WHAT HAVE WE HERE?
IS THIS A LARGE CAT BURGLAR, PROWLING ABOUT IN THE WEE HOURS OF THE MORNING?
MISS LIZZIE...
EDWIN WHITE, HOW WILL YOU UPHOLD YOUR REPUTATION AS A BARRISTER IF YOU LURK ABOUT, PEEPING IN AT YOUNG LADIES?
DON'T JUST STAND THERE. COME IN.
HESITANT

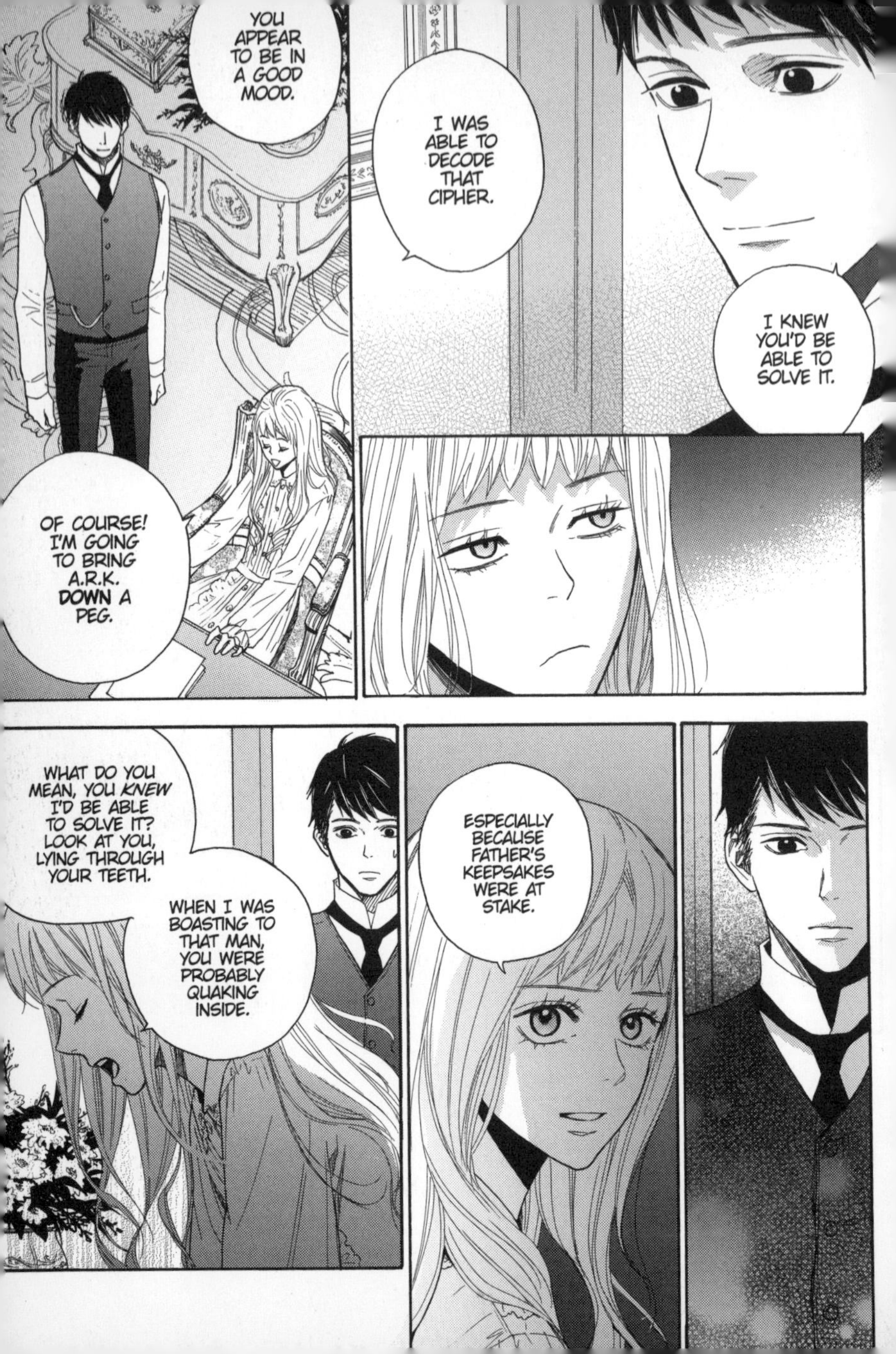
YOU APPEAR TO BE IN A GOOD MOOD.
OF COURSE! I'M GOING TO BRING A.R.K. DOWN A PEG.
I WAS ABLE TO DECODE THAT CIPHER.
I KNEW YOU'D BE ABLE TO SOLVE IT.
WHAT DO YOU MEAN, YOU *KNEW* I'D BE ABLE TO SOLVE IT? LOOK AT YOU, LYING THROUGH YOUR TEETH.
WHEN I WAS BOASTING TO THAT MAN, YOU WERE PROBABLY QUAKING INSIDE.
ESPECIALLY BECAUSE FATHER'S KEEPSAKES WERE AT STAKE.

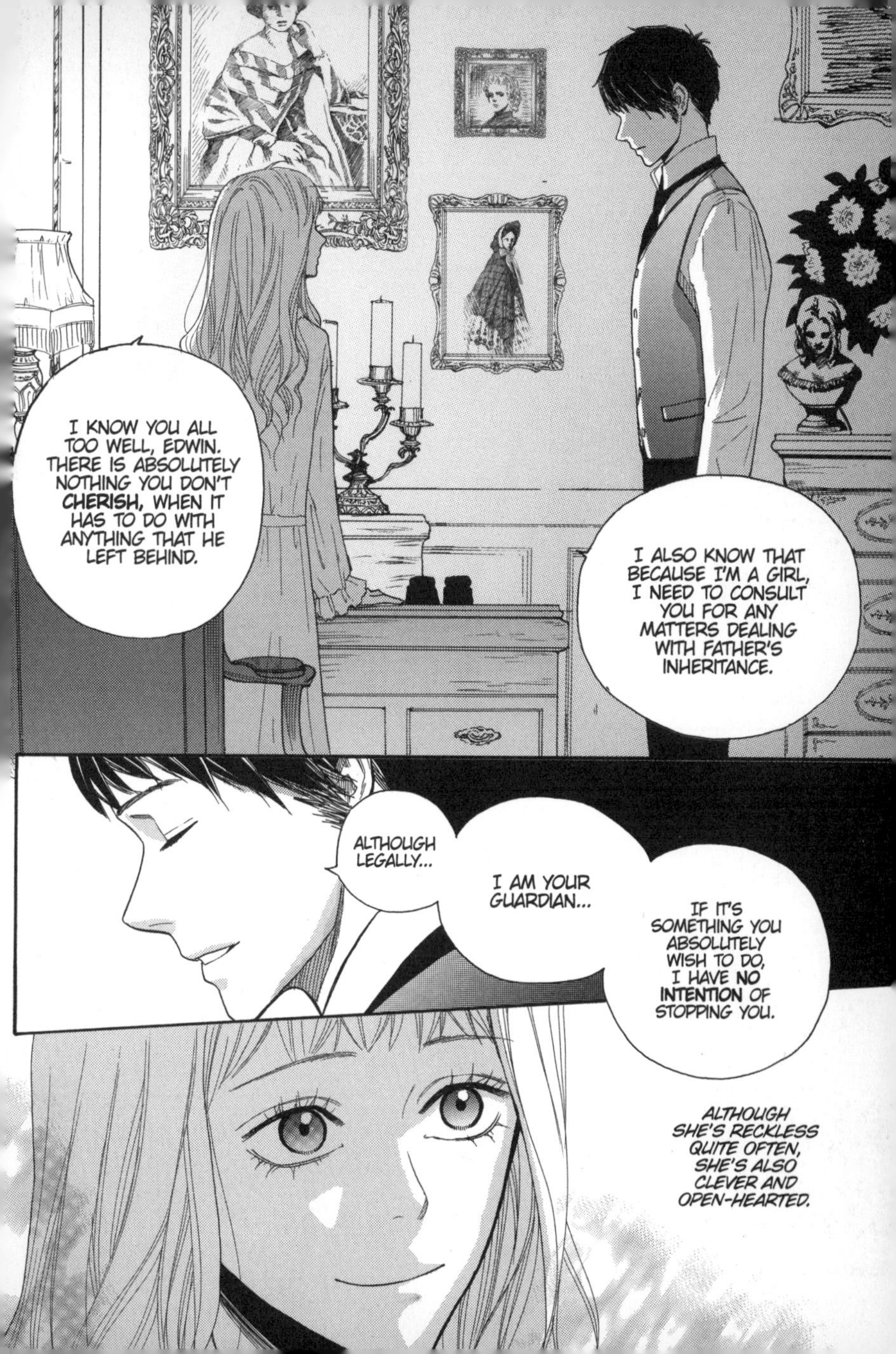
I KNOW YOU ALL TOO WELL, EDWIN. THERE IS ABSOLUTELY NOTHING YOU DON'T **CHERISH,** WHEN IT HAS TO DO WITH ANYTHING THAT HE LEFT BEHIND.
I ALSO KNOW THAT BECAUSE I'M A GIRL, I NEED TO CONSULT YOU FOR ANY MATTERS DEALING WITH FATHER'S INHERITANCE.
ALTHOUGH LEGALLY...
I AM YOUR GUARDIAN...
IF IT'S SOMETHING YOU ABSOLUTELY WISH TO DO, I HAVE **NO INTENTION** OF STOPPING YOU.
ALTHOUGH SHE'S RECKLESS QUITE OFTEN, SHE'S ALSO CLEVER AND OPEN-HEARTED.

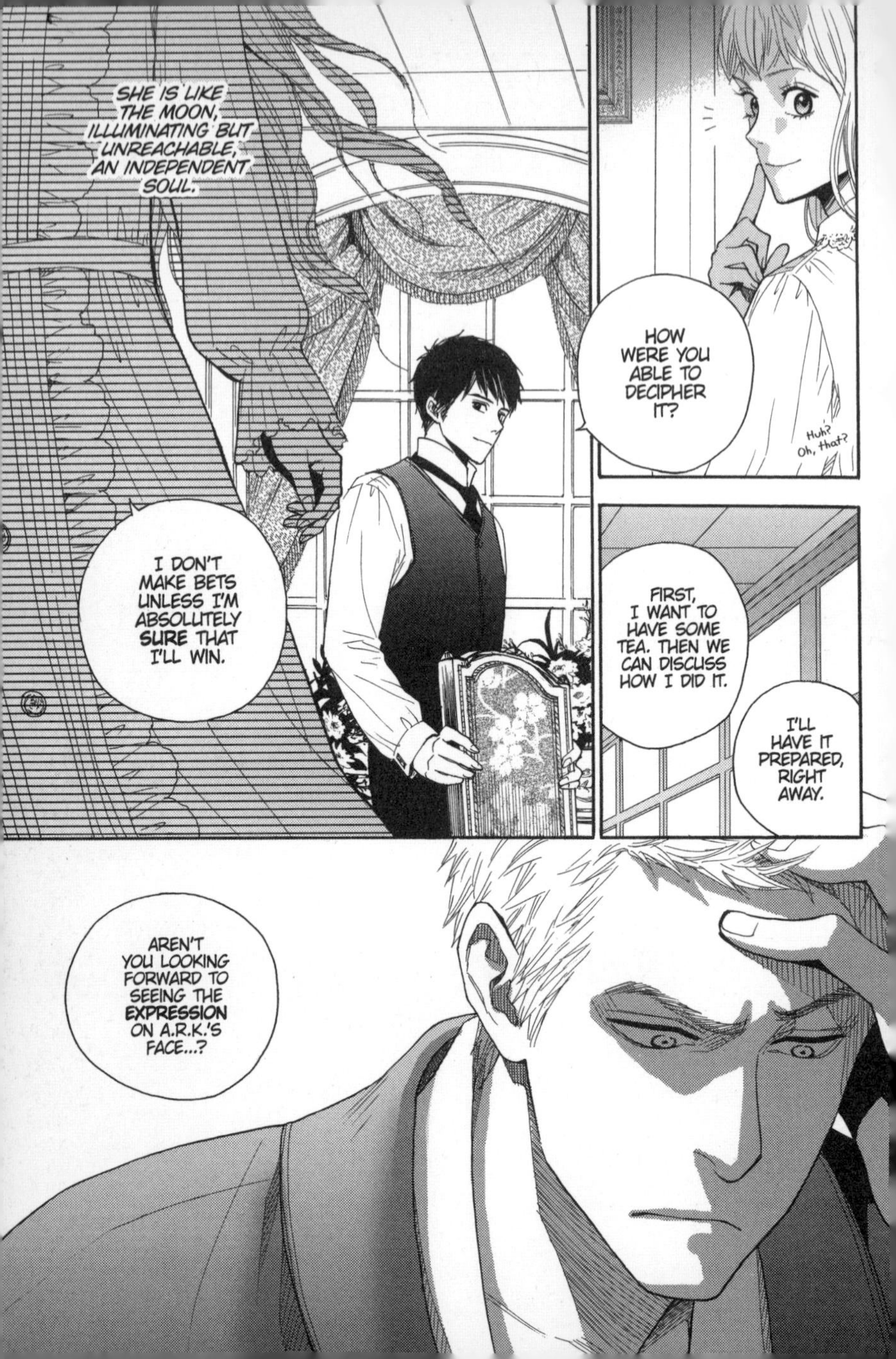
SHE IS LIKE THE MOON, ILLUMINATING BUT UNREACHABLE, AN INDEPENDENT SOUL.
I DON'T MAKE BETS UNLESS I'M ABSOLUTELY **SURE** THAT I'LL WIN.
HOW WERE YOU ABLE TO DECIPHER IT?
Huh? Oh, that?
FIRST, I WANT TO HAVE SOME TEA. THEN WE CAN DISCUSS HOW I DID IT.
I'LL HAVE IT PREPARED, RIGHT AWAY.
AREN'T YOU LOOKING FORWARD TO SEEING THE **EXPRESSION** ON A.R.K.'S FACE...?

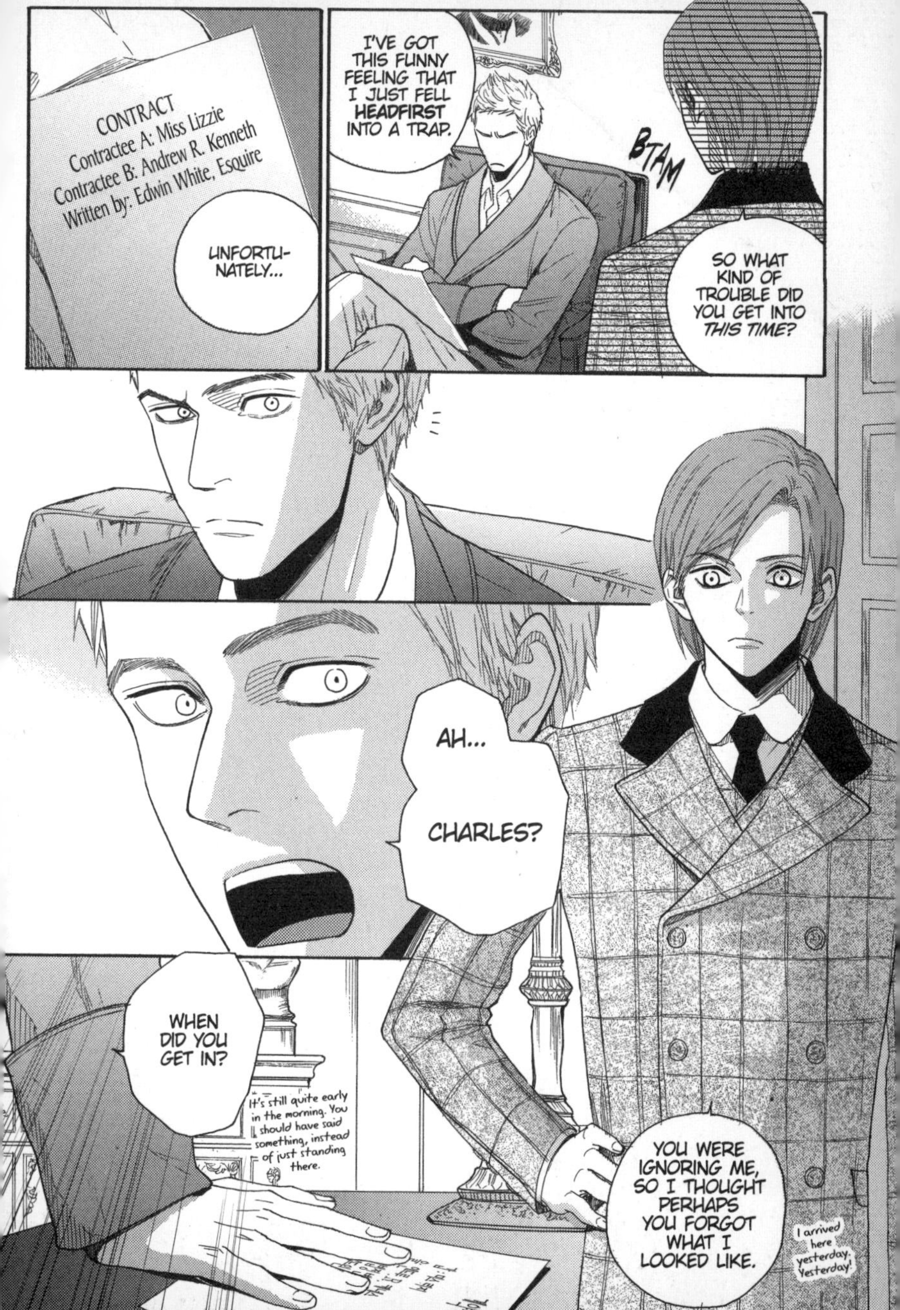
CONTRACT
Contractee A: Miss Lizzie
Contractee B: Andrew R. Kenneth
Written by: Edwin White, Esquire
UNFORTU-NATELY...
I'VE GOT THIS FUNNY FEELING THAT I JUST FELL **HEADFIRST** INTO A TRAP.
BTAM
SO WHAT KIND OF TROUBLE DID YOU GET INTO *THIS TIME?*
AH...
CHARLES?
WHEN DID YOU GET IN?
It's still quite early in the morning. You should have said something, instead of just standing there.
YOU WERE IGNORING ME, SO I THOUGHT PERHAPS YOU FORGOT WHAT I LOOKED LIKE.
I arrived here yesterday. Yesterday!

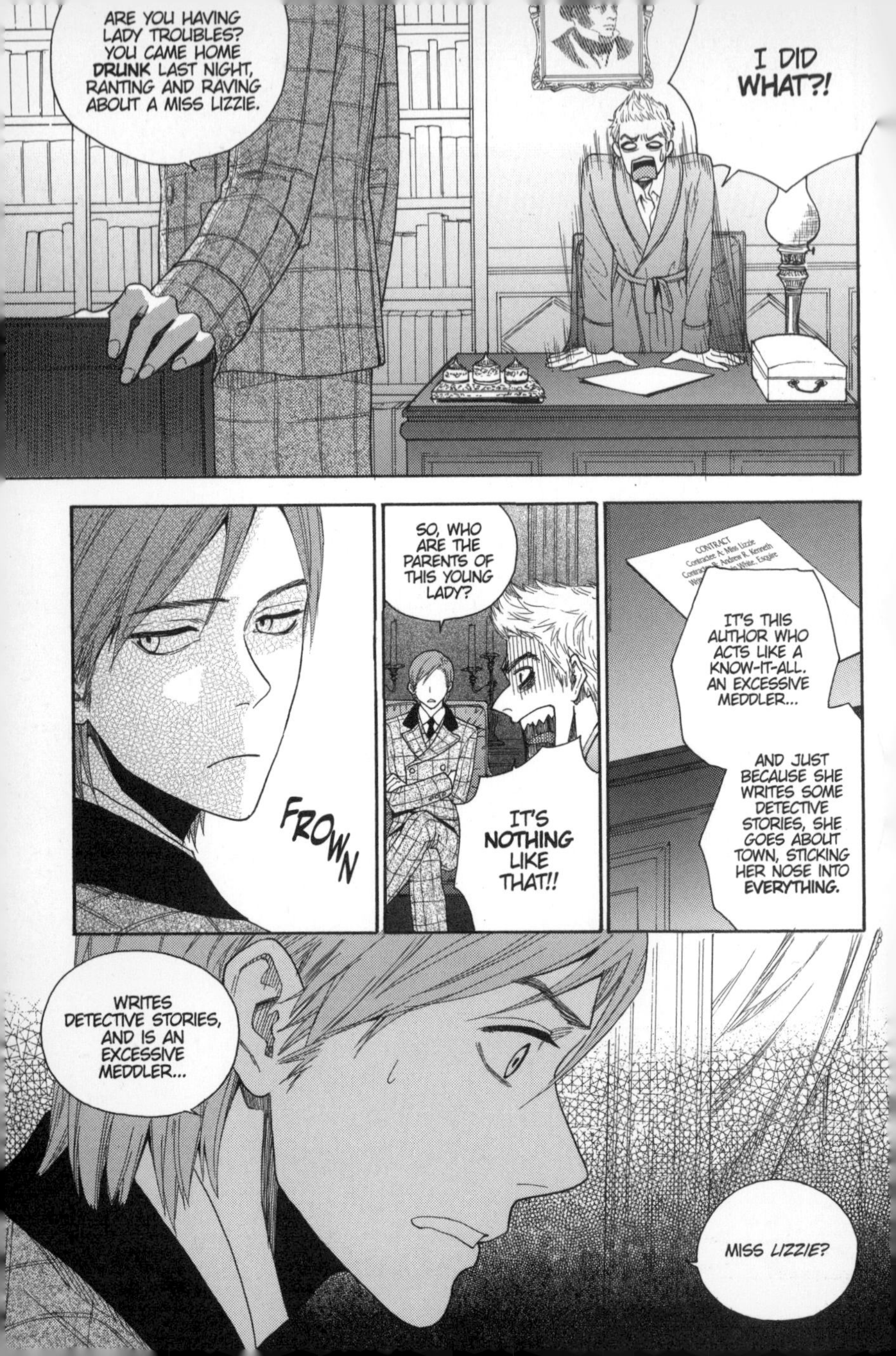

ARE YOU HAVING LADY TROUBLES? YOU CAME HOME DRUNK LAST NIGHT, RANTING AND RAVING ABOUT A MISS LIZZIE.
I DID WHAT?!
FROWN
SO, WHO ARE THE PARENTS OF THIS YOUNG LADY?
IT'S NOTHING LIKE THAT!!
CONTRACT
Contractee A: Miss Lizzie
Andrew R. Kenneth
White, Esquire
IT'S THIS AUTHOR WHO ACTS LIKE A KNOW-IT-ALL. AN EXCESSIVE MEDDLER...
AND JUST BECAUSE SHE WRITES SOME DETECTIVE STORIES, SHE GOES ABOUT TOWN, STICKING HER NOSE INTO EVERYTHING.
WRITES DETECTIVE STORIES, AND IS AN EXCESSIVE MEDDLER...
MISS LIZZIE?

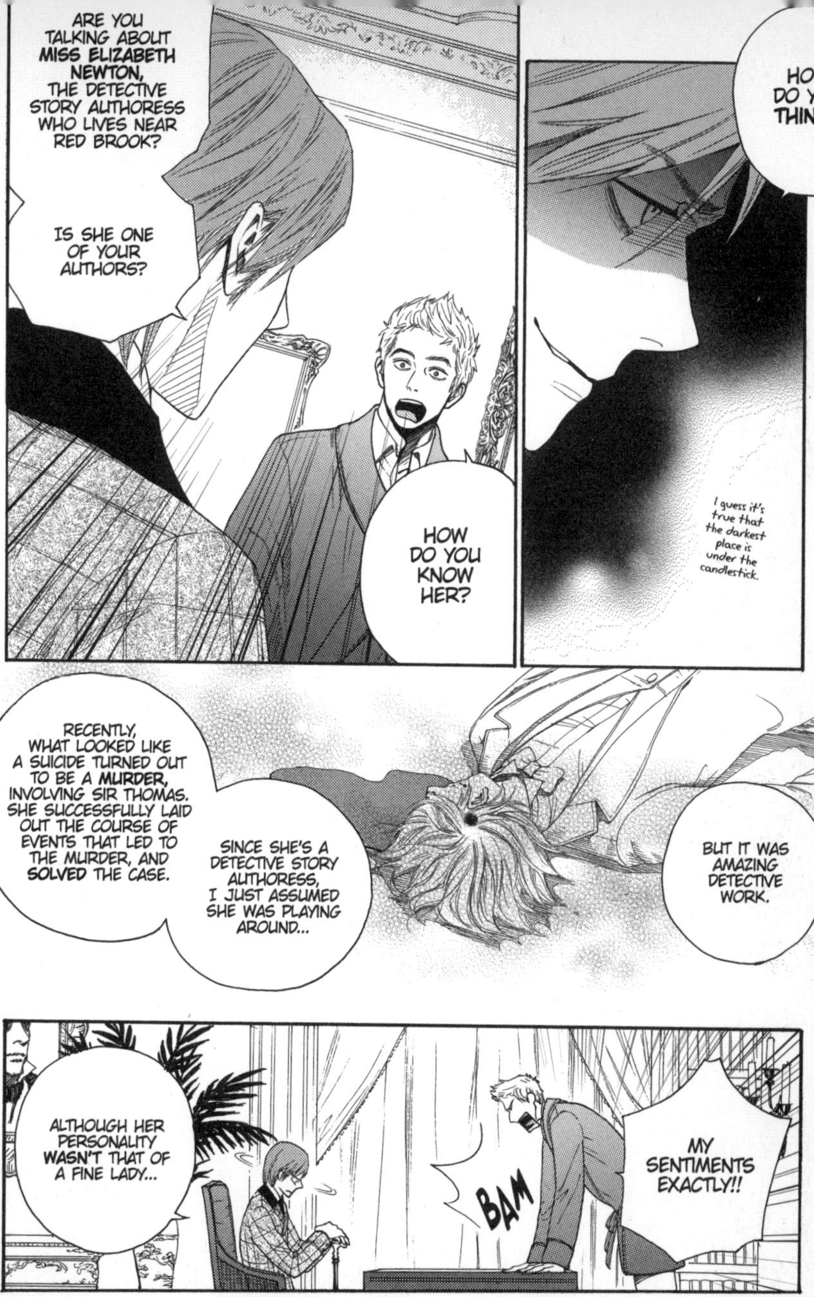
ARE YOU TALKING ABOUT MISS ELIZABETH NEWTON, THE DETECTIVE STORY AUTHORESS WHO LIVES NEAR RED BROOK?
IS SHE ONE OF YOUR AUTHORS?
HOW DO YOU KNOW HER?
HOW DO YOU THINK?
I guess it's true that the darkest place is under the candlestick.
RECENTLY, WHAT LOOKED LIKE A SUICIDE TURNED OUT TO BE A MURDER, INVOLVING SIR THOMAS. SHE SUCCESSFULLY LAID OUT THE COURSE OF EVENTS THAT LED TO THE MURDER, AND SOLVED THE CASE.
SINCE SHE'S A DETECTIVE STORY AUTHORESS, I JUST ASSUMED SHE WAS PLAYING AROUND...
BUT IT WAS AMAZING DETECTIVE WORK.
ALTHOUGH HER PERSONALITY WASN'T THAT OF A FINE LADY...
BAM
MY SENTIMENTS EXACTLY!!

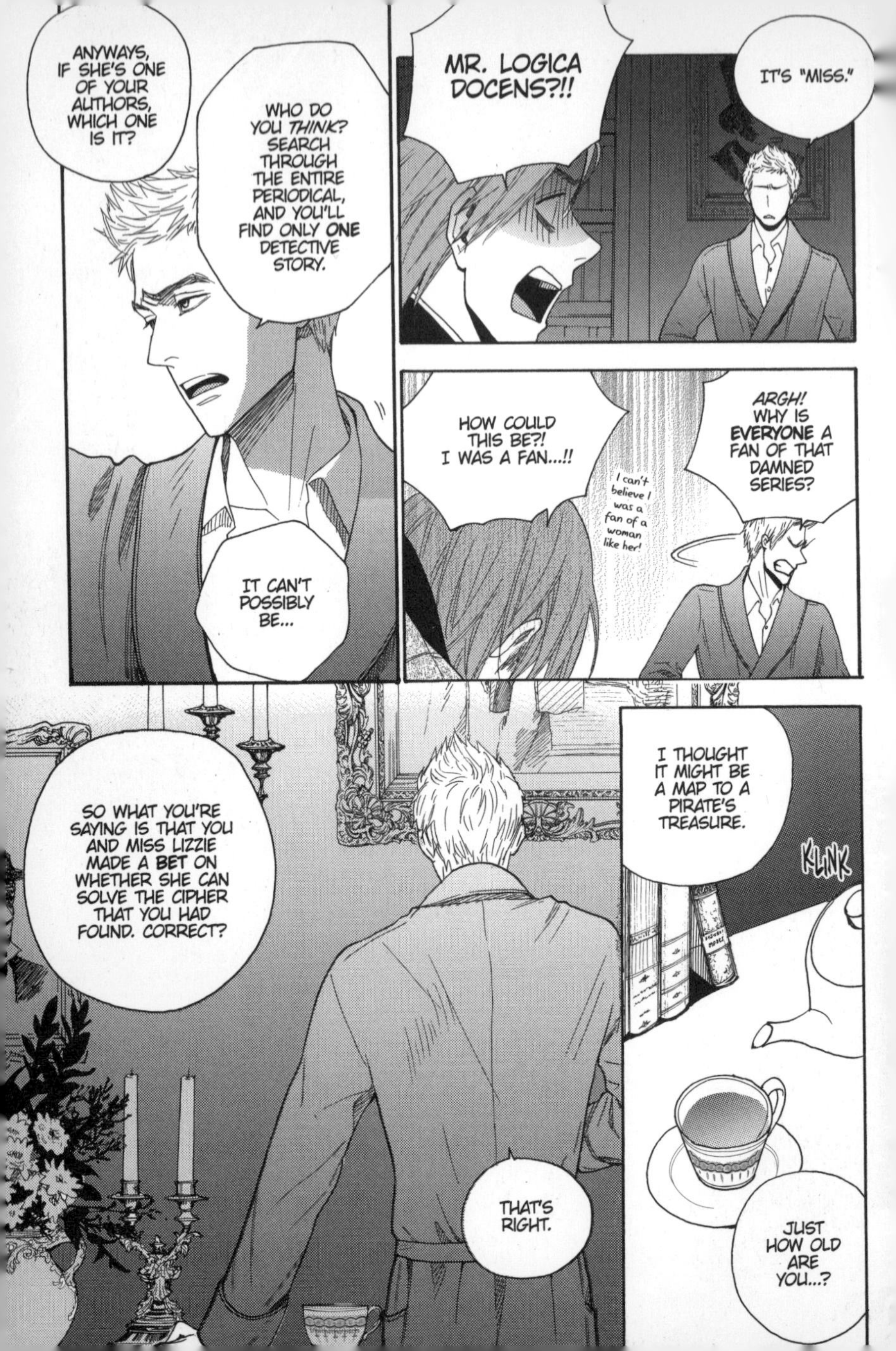
ANYWAYS, IF SHE'S ONE OF YOUR AUTHORS, WHICH ONE IS IT?
WHO DO YOU *THINK?* SEARCH THROUGH THE ENTIRE PERIODICAL, AND YOU'LL FIND ONLY **ONE** DETECTIVE STORY.
IT CAN'T POSSIBLY BE...
MR. LOGICA DOCENS?!!
IT'S "MISS."
HOW COULD THIS BE?! I WAS A FAN...!!
I can't believe I was a fan of a woman like her!
ARGH! WHY IS **EVERYONE** A FAN OF THAT DAMNED SERIES?
SO WHAT YOU'RE SAYING IS THAT YOU AND MISS LIZZIE MADE A **BET** ON WHETHER SHE CAN SOLVE THE CIPHER THAT YOU HAD FOUND. CORRECT?
THAT'S RIGHT.
I THOUGHT IT MIGHT BE A MAP TO A PIRATE'S TREASURE.
K-LINK
JUST HOW OLD ARE YOU...?

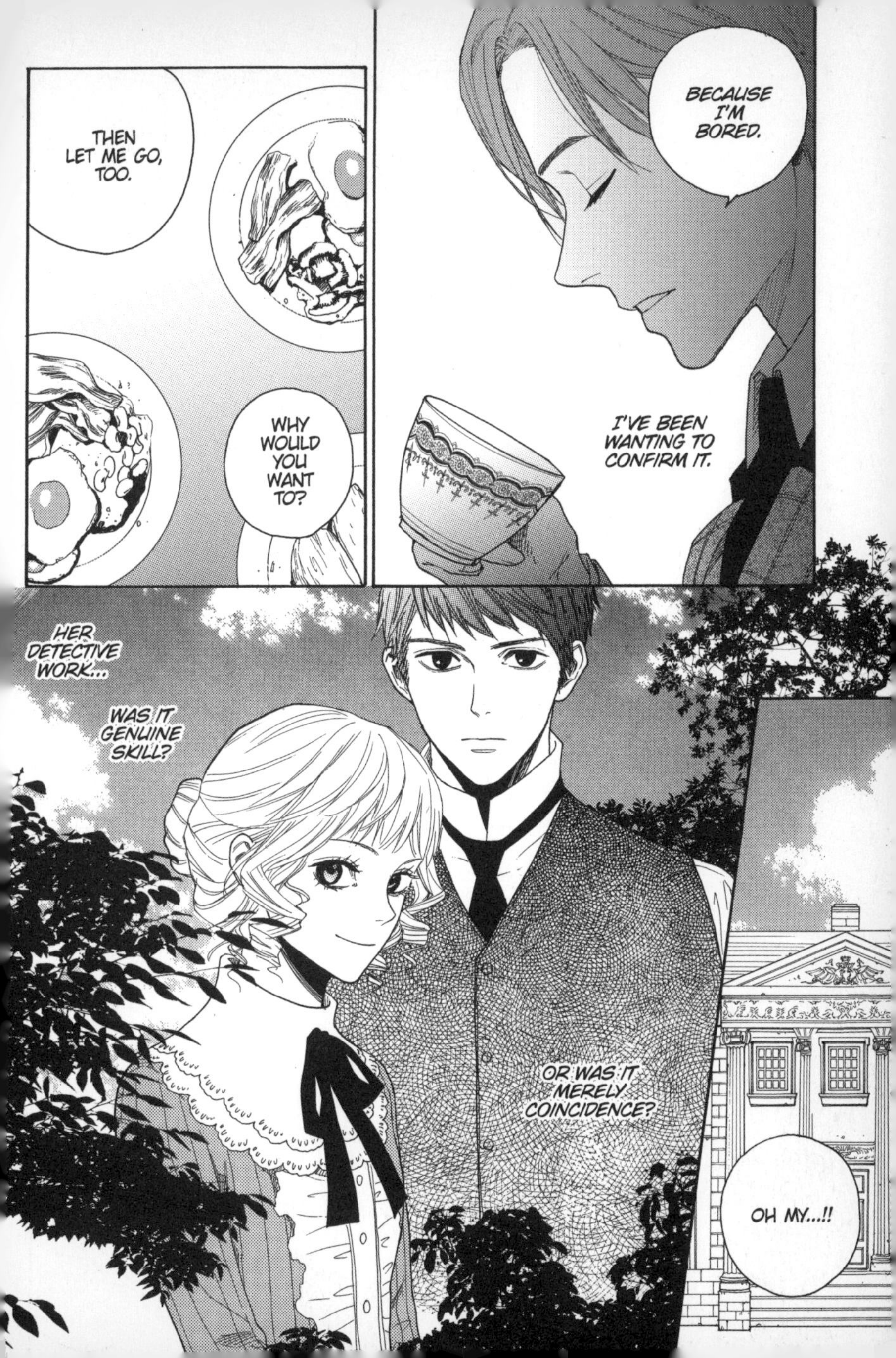
THEN LET ME GO, TOO.
WHY WOULD YOU WANT TO?
BECAUSE I'M BORED.
I'VE BEEN WANTING TO CONFIRM IT.
HER DETECTIVE WORK...
WAS IT GENUINE SKILL?
OR WAS IT MERELY COINCIDENCE?
OH MY...!!

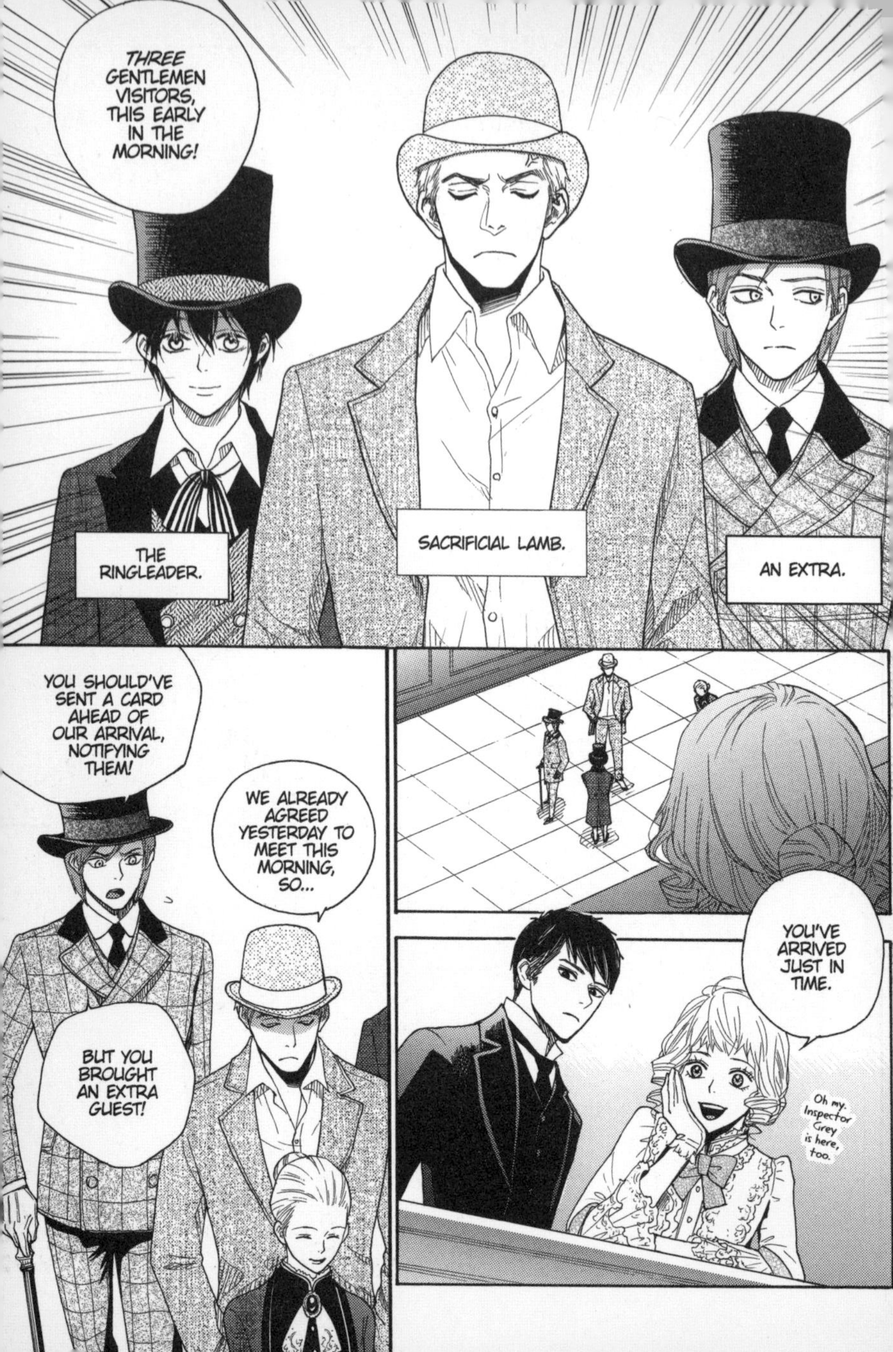
THREE GENTLEMEN VISITORS, THIS EARLY IN THE MORNING!
THE RINGLEADER.
SACRIFICIAL LAMB.
AN EXTRA.
YOU SHOULD'VE SENT A CARD AHEAD OF OUR ARRIVAL, NOTIFYING THEM!
WE ALREADY AGREED YESTERDAY TO MEET THIS MORNING, SO...
BUT YOU BROUGHT AN EXTRA GUEST!
YOU'VE ARRIVED JUST IN TIME.
Oh my. Inspector Grey is here, too.

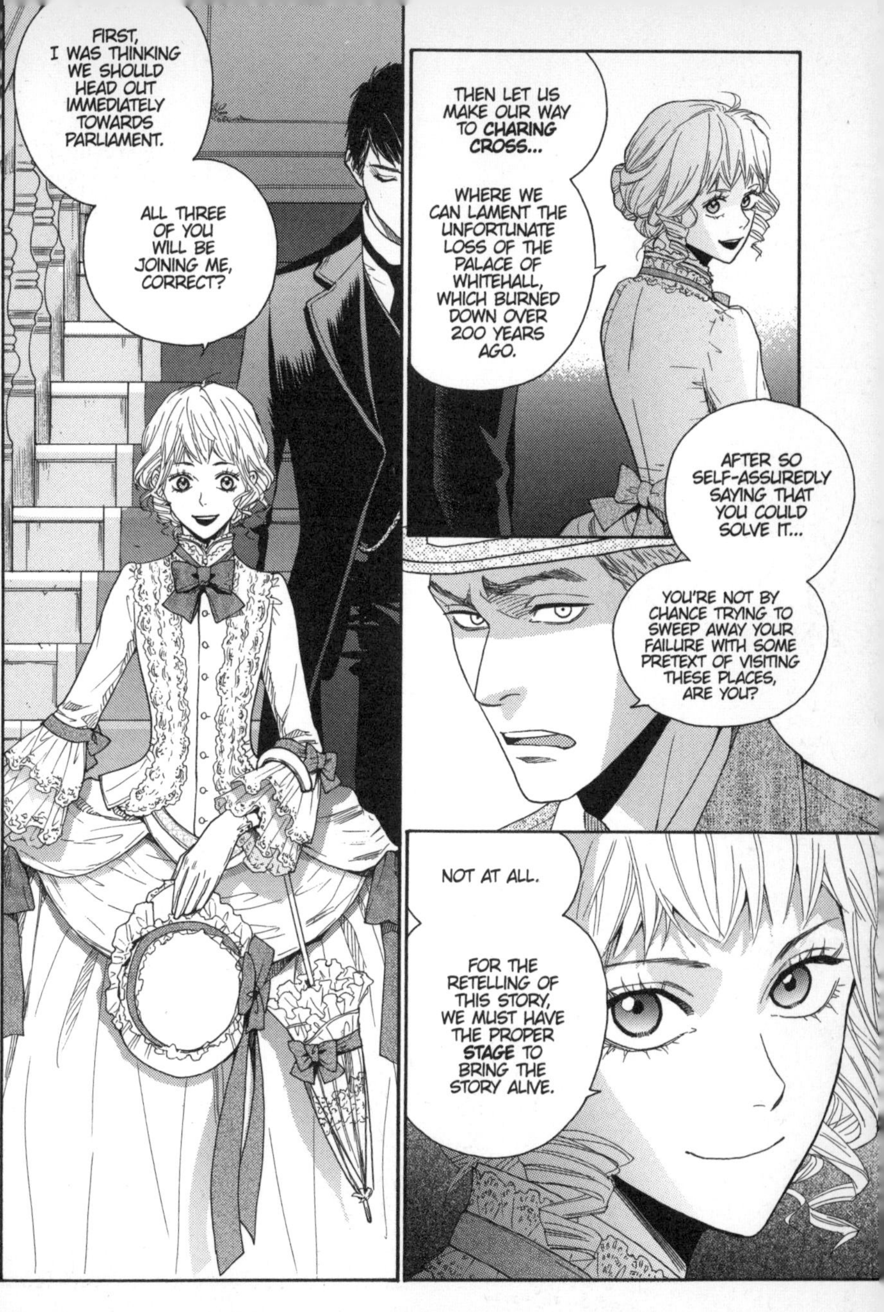
FIRST, I WAS THINKING WE SHOULD HEAD OUT IMMEDIATELY TOWARDS PARLIAMENT.
ALL THREE OF YOU WILL BE JOINING ME, CORRECT?
THEN LET US MAKE OUR WAY TO **CHARING CROSS...**
WHERE WE CAN LAMENT THE UNFORTUNATE LOSS OF THE PALACE OF WHITEHALL, WHICH BURNED DOWN OVER 200 YEARS AGO.
AFTER SO SELF-ASSUREDLY SAYING THAT YOU COULD SOLVE IT...
YOU'RE NOT BY CHANCE TRYING TO SWEEP AWAY YOUR FAILURE WITH SOME PRETEXT OF VISITING THESE PLACES, ARE YOU?
NOT AT ALL.
FOR THE RETELLING OF THIS STORY, WE MUST HAVE THE PROPER **STAGE** TO BRING THE STORY ALIVE.

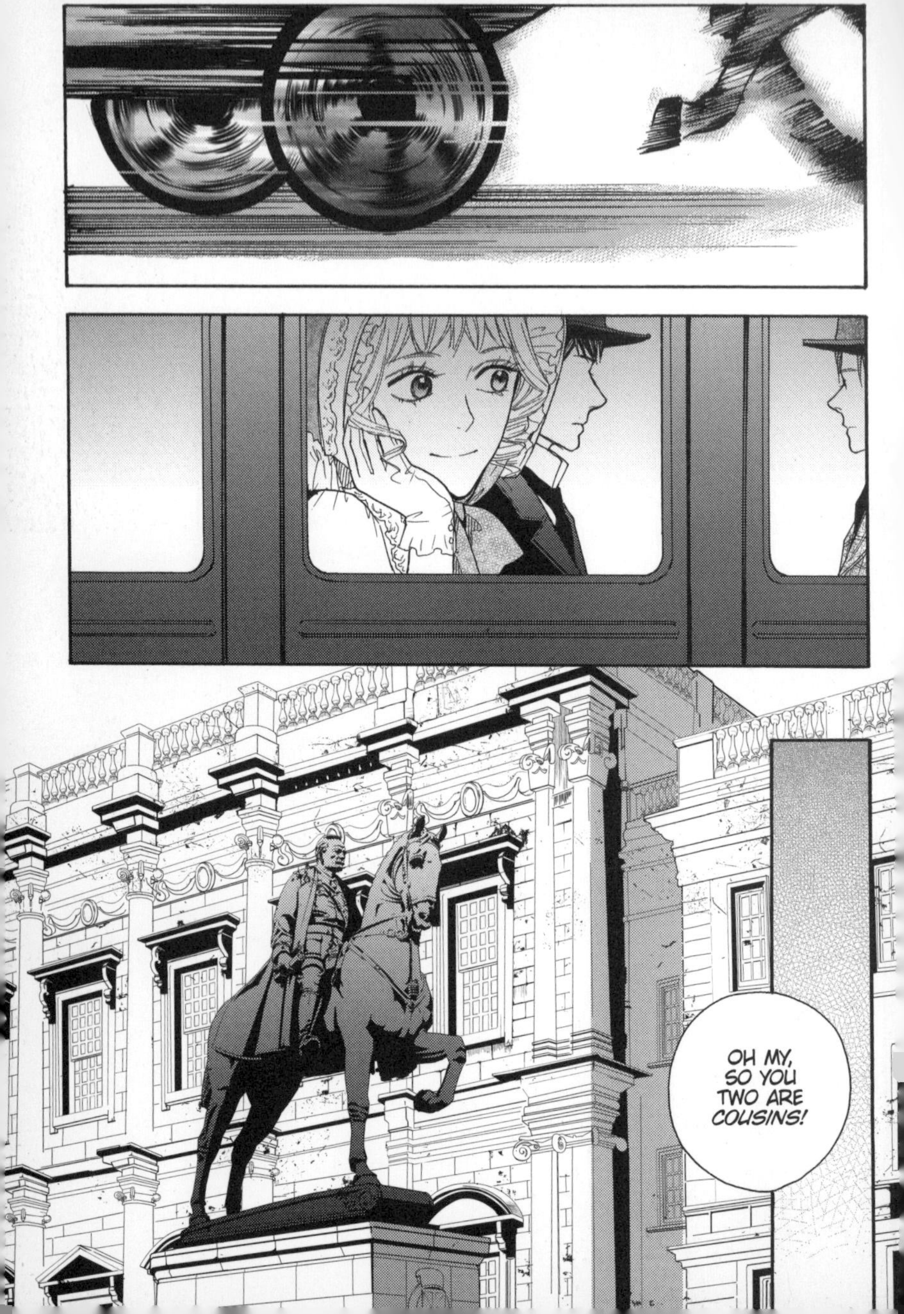
OH MY, SO YOU TWO ARE COUSINS!

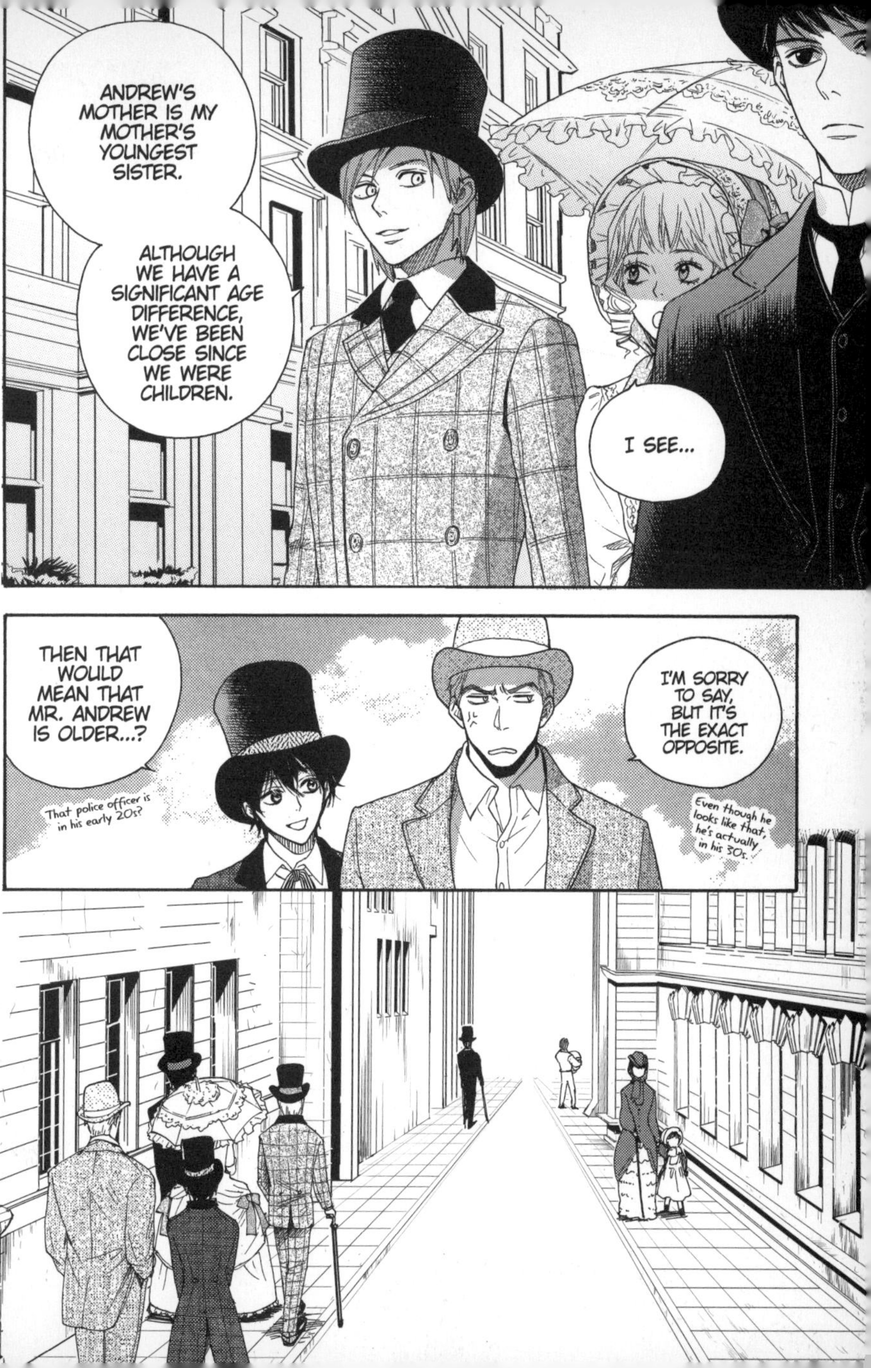
ANDREW'S MOTHER IS MY MOTHER'S YOUNGEST SISTER.
ALTHOUGH WE HAVE A SIGNIFICANT AGE DIFFERENCE, WE'VE BEEN CLOSE SINCE WE WERE CHILDREN.
I SEE...
THEN THAT WOULD MEAN THAT MR. ANDREW IS OLDER...?
That police officer is in his early 20s?
I'M SORRY TO SAY, BUT IT'S THE EXACT OPPOSITE.
Even though he looks like that, he's actually in his 30s.

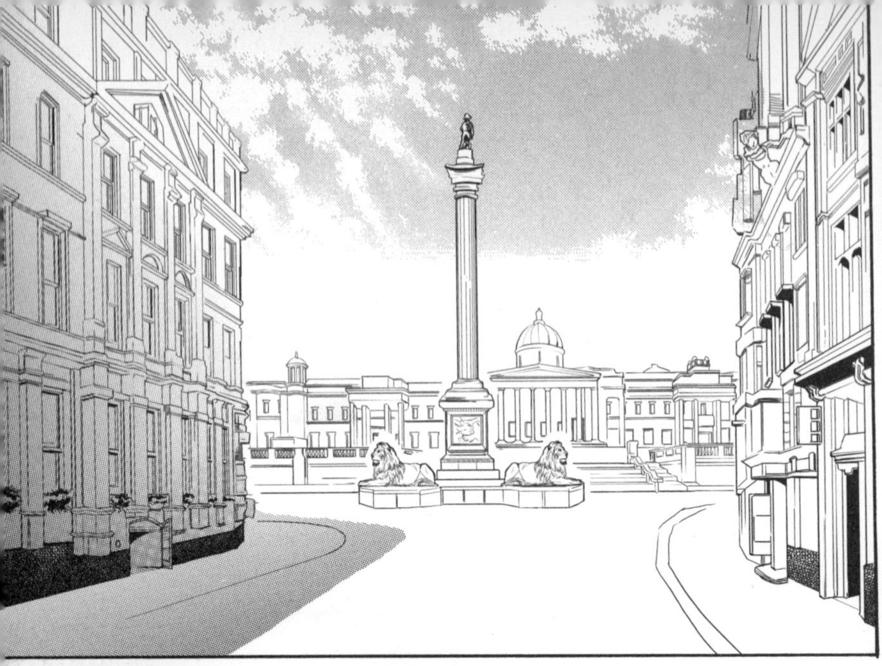

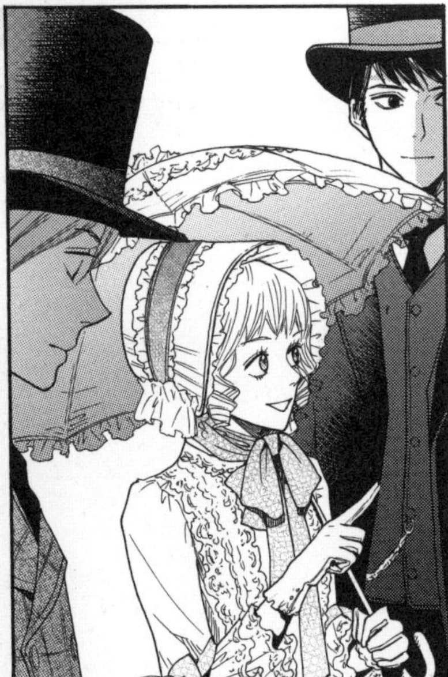

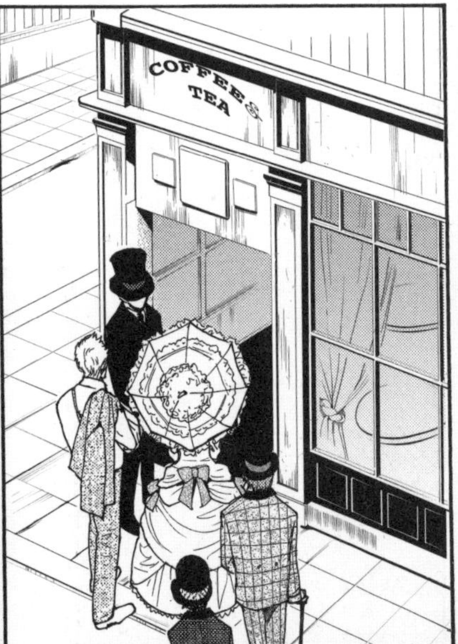
COFFEE & TEA

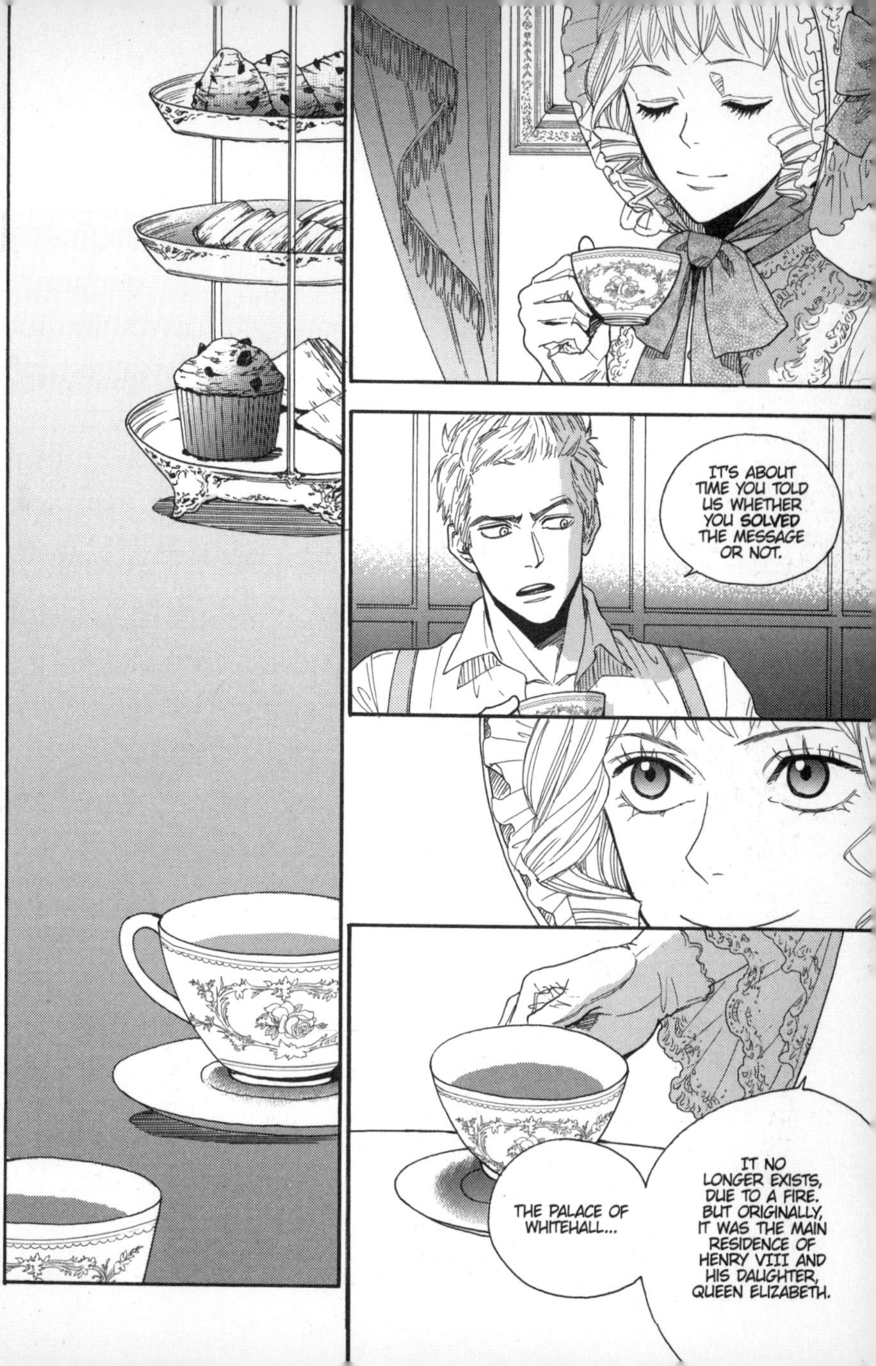
IT'S ABOUT TIME YOU TOLD US WHETHER YOU SOLVED THE MESSAGE OR NOT.
THE PALACE OF WHITEHALL...
IT NO LONGER EXISTS, DUE TO A FIRE. BUT ORIGINALLY, IT WAS THE MAIN RESIDENCE OF HENRY VIII AND HIS DAUGHTER, QUEEN ELIZABETH.

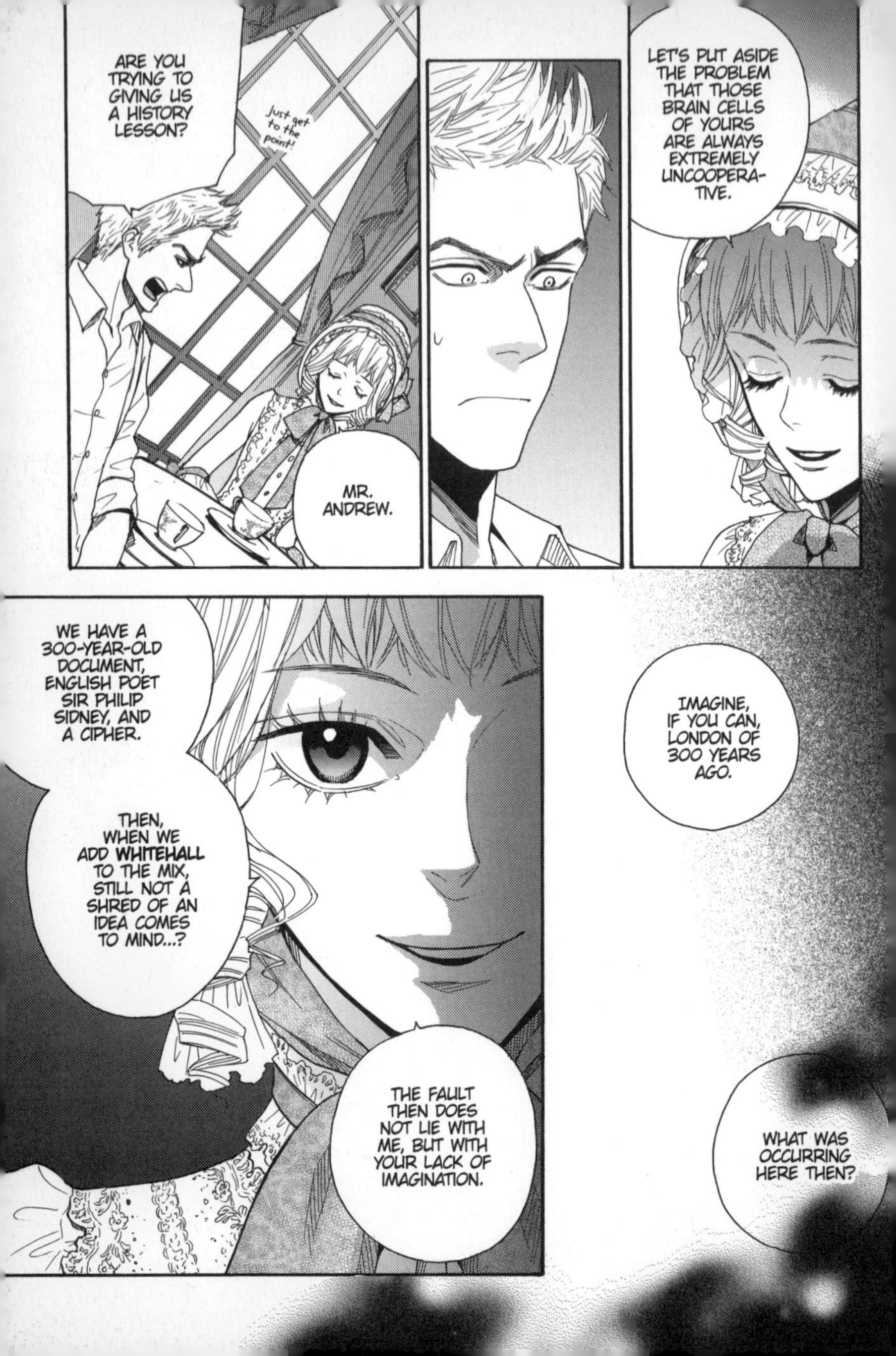
ARE YOU TRYING TO GIVING US A HISTORY LESSON?
Just get to the point!
MR. ANDREW.
LET'S PUT ASIDE THE PROBLEM THAT THOSE BRAIN CELLS OF YOURS ARE ALWAYS EXTREMELY UNCOOPERA-TIVE.
WE HAVE A 300-YEAR-OLD DOCUMENT, ENGLISH POET SIR PHILIP SIDNEY, AND A CIPHER.
THEN, WHEN WE ADD **WHITEHALL** TO THE MIX, STILL NOT A SHRED OF AN IDEA COMES TO MIND...?
THE FAULT THEN DOES NOT LIE WITH ME, BUT WITH YOUR LACK OF IMAGINATION.
IMAGINE, IF YOU CAN, LONDON OF 300 YEARS AGO.
WHAT WAS OCCURRING HERE THEN?

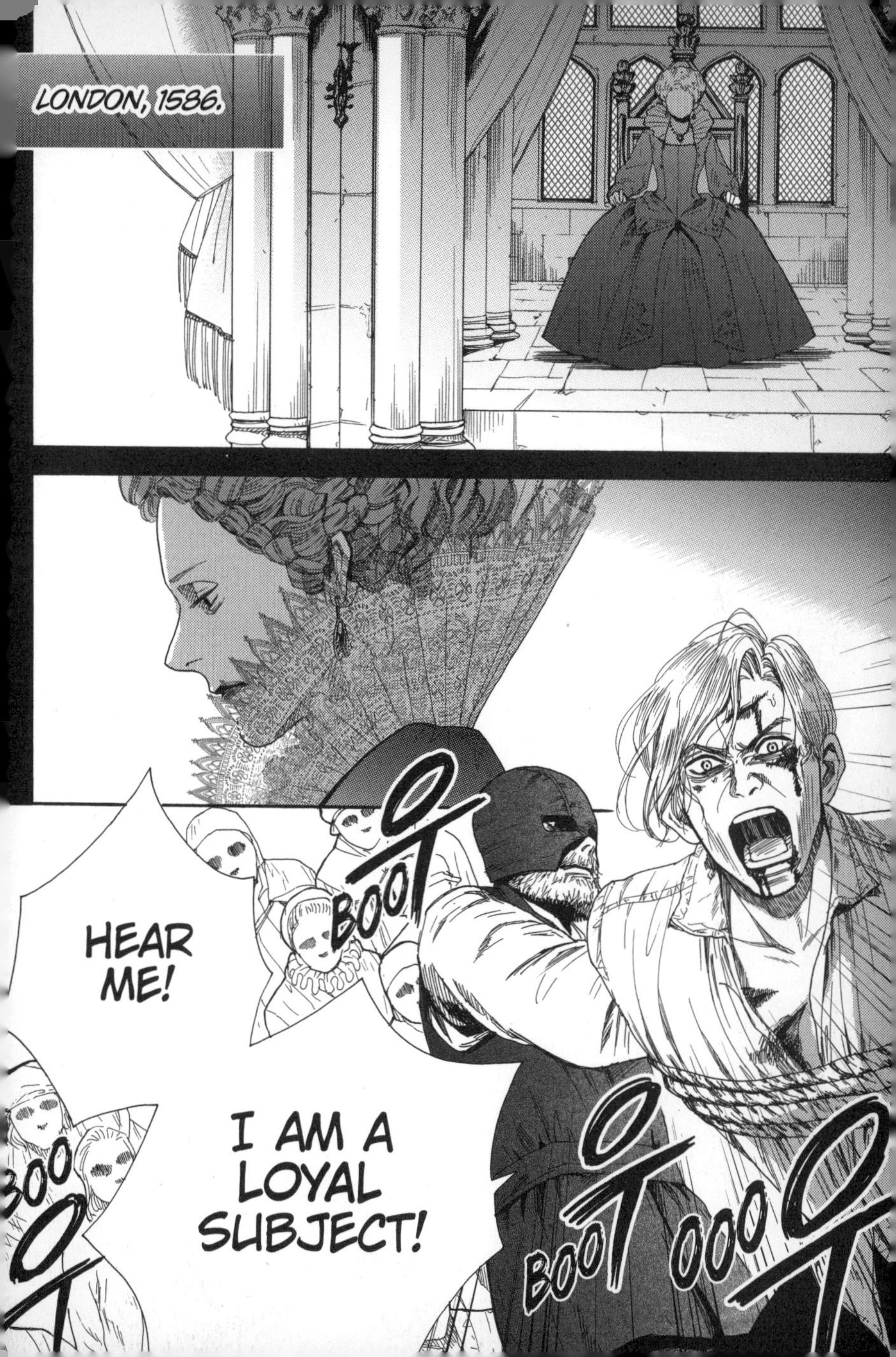
LONDON, 1586.
HEAR ME!
BOOO
BOOO
I AM A LOYAL SUBJECT!
BOOOOOO

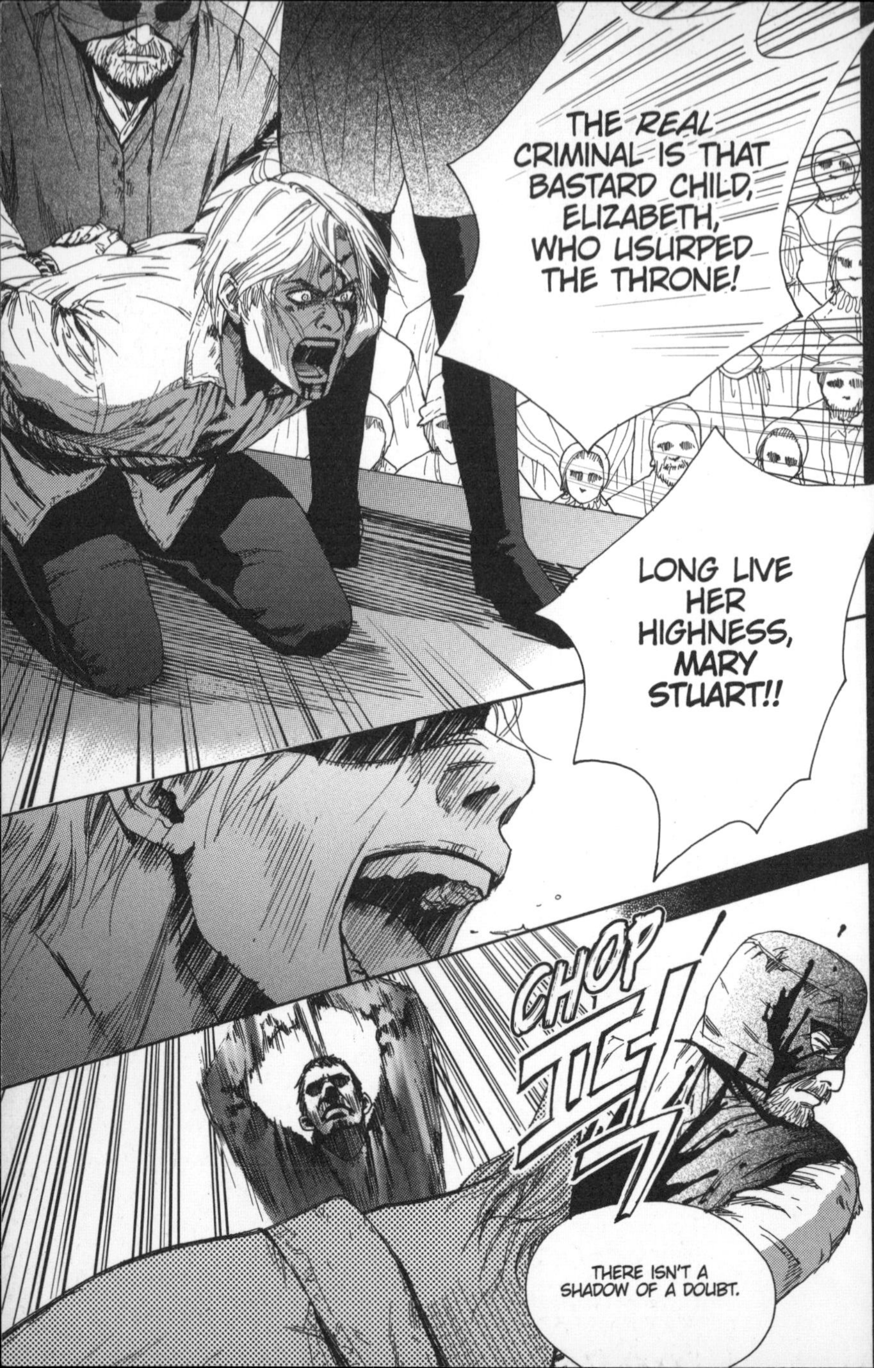
THE REAL CRIMINAL IS THAT BASTARD CHILD, ELIZABETH, WHO USURPED THE THRONE!
LONG LIVE HER HIGHNESS, MARY STUART!!
CHOP
THERE ISN'T A SHADOW OF A DOUBT.

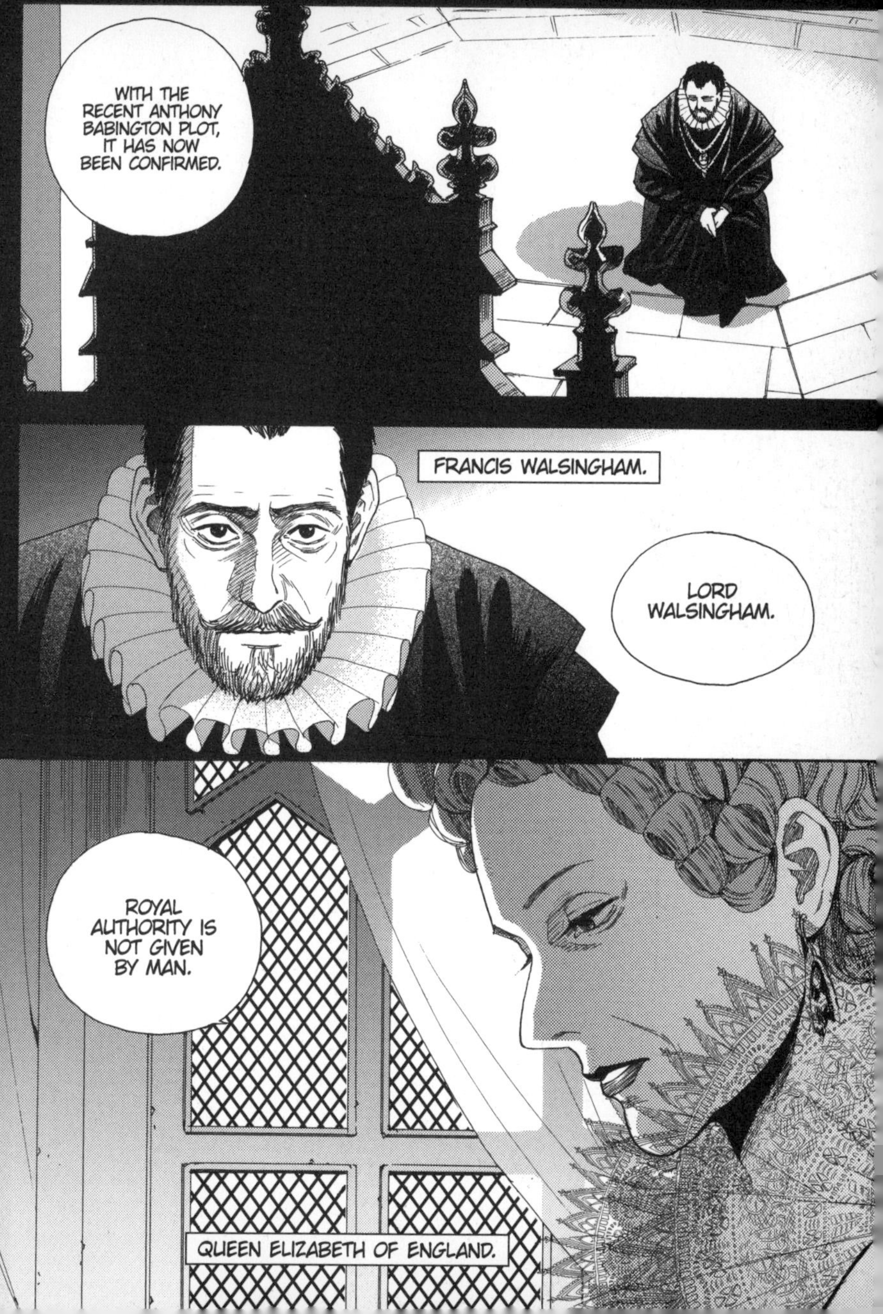
WITH THE RECENT ANTHONY BABINGTON PLOT, IT HAS NOW BEEN CONFIRMED.
FRANCIS WALSINGHAM.
LORD WALSINGHAM.
ROYAL AUTHORITY IS NOT GIVEN BY MAN.
QUEEN ELIZABETH OF ENGLAND.

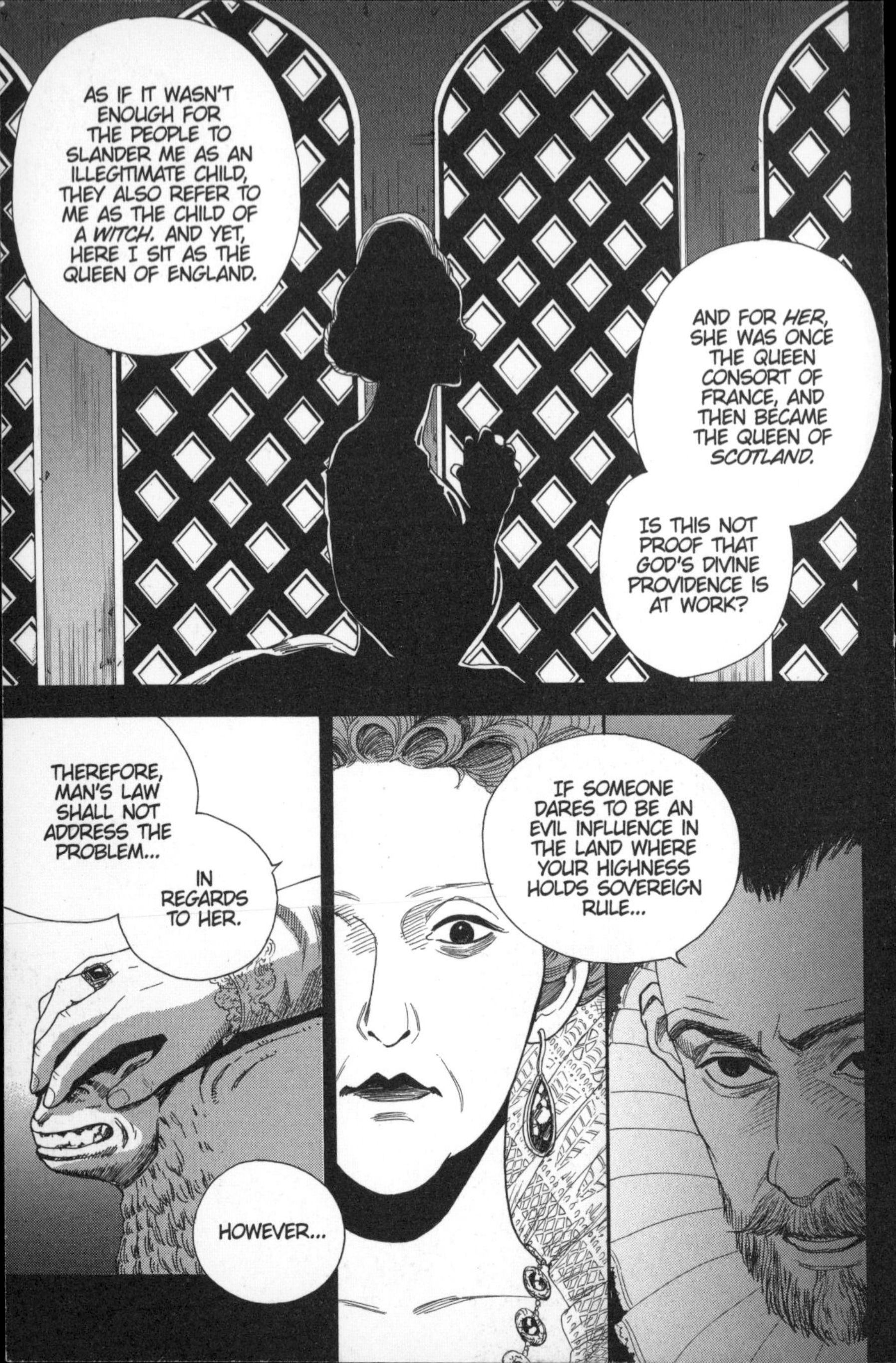
AS IF IT WASN'T ENOUGH FOR THE PEOPLE TO SLANDER ME AS AN ILLEGITIMATE CHILD, THEY ALSO REFER TO ME AS THE CHILD OF A *WITCH*. AND YET, HERE I SIT AS THE QUEEN OF ENGLAND.
AND FOR *HER*, SHE WAS ONCE THE QUEEN CONSORT OF FRANCE, AND THEN BECAME THE QUEEN OF *SCOTLAND*.
IS THIS NOT PROOF THAT GOD'S DIVINE PROVIDENCE IS AT WORK?
THEREFORE, MAN'S LAW SHALL NOT ADDRESS THE PROBLEM...
IN REGARDS TO HER.
HOWEVER...
IF SOMEONE DARES TO BE AN EVIL INFLUENCE IN THE LAND WHERE YOUR HIGHNESS HOLDS SOVEREIGN RULE...

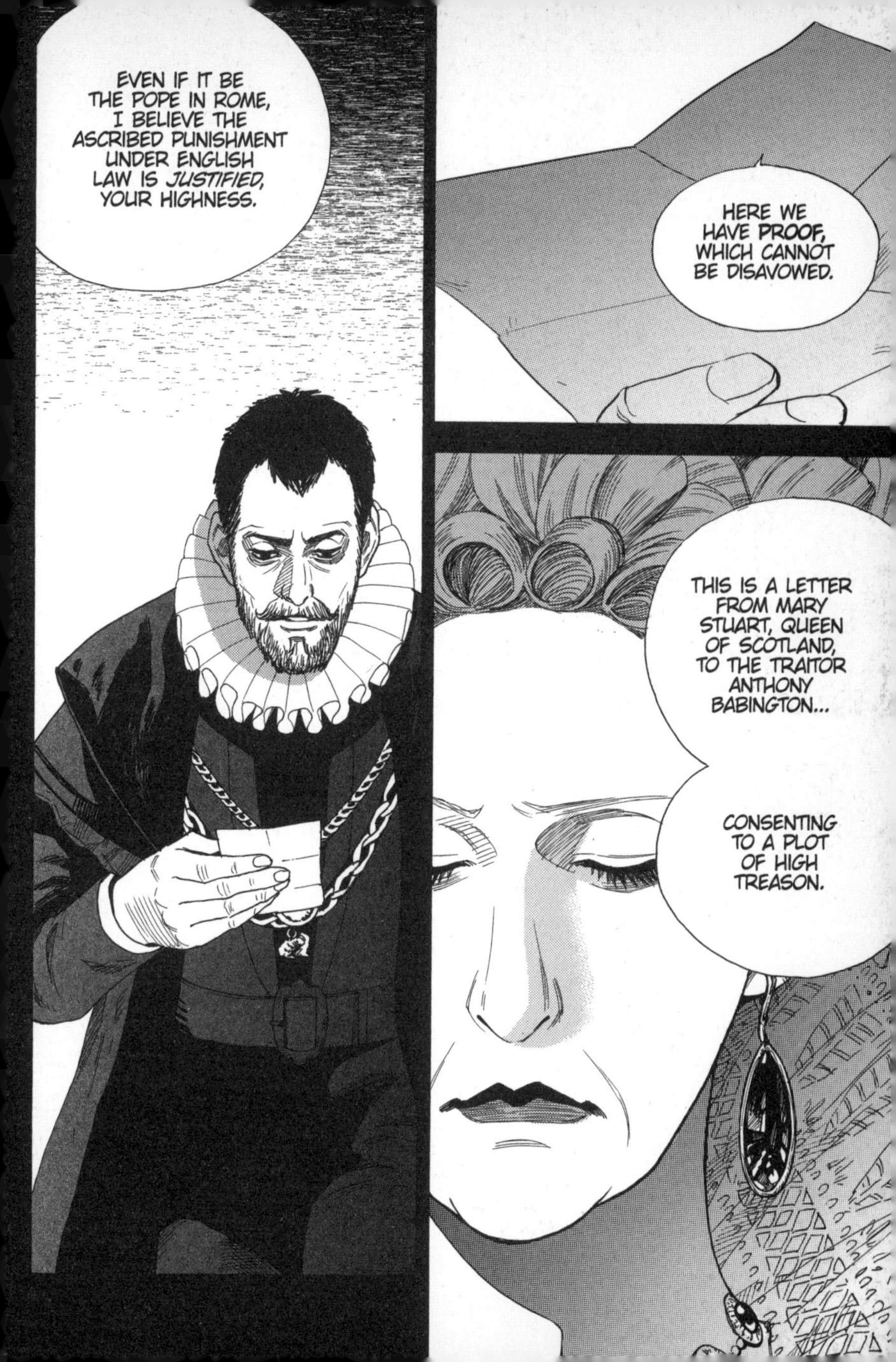
EVEN IF IT BE THE POPE IN ROME, I BELIEVE THE ASCRIBED PUNISHMENT UNDER ENGLISH LAW IS *JUSTIFIED*, YOUR HIGHNESS.
HERE WE HAVE **PROOF**, WHICH CANNOT BE DISAVOWED.
THIS IS A LETTER FROM MARY STUART, QUEEN OF SCOTLAND, TO THE TRAITOR ANTHONY BABINGTON...
CONSENTING TO A PLOT OF HIGH TREASON.

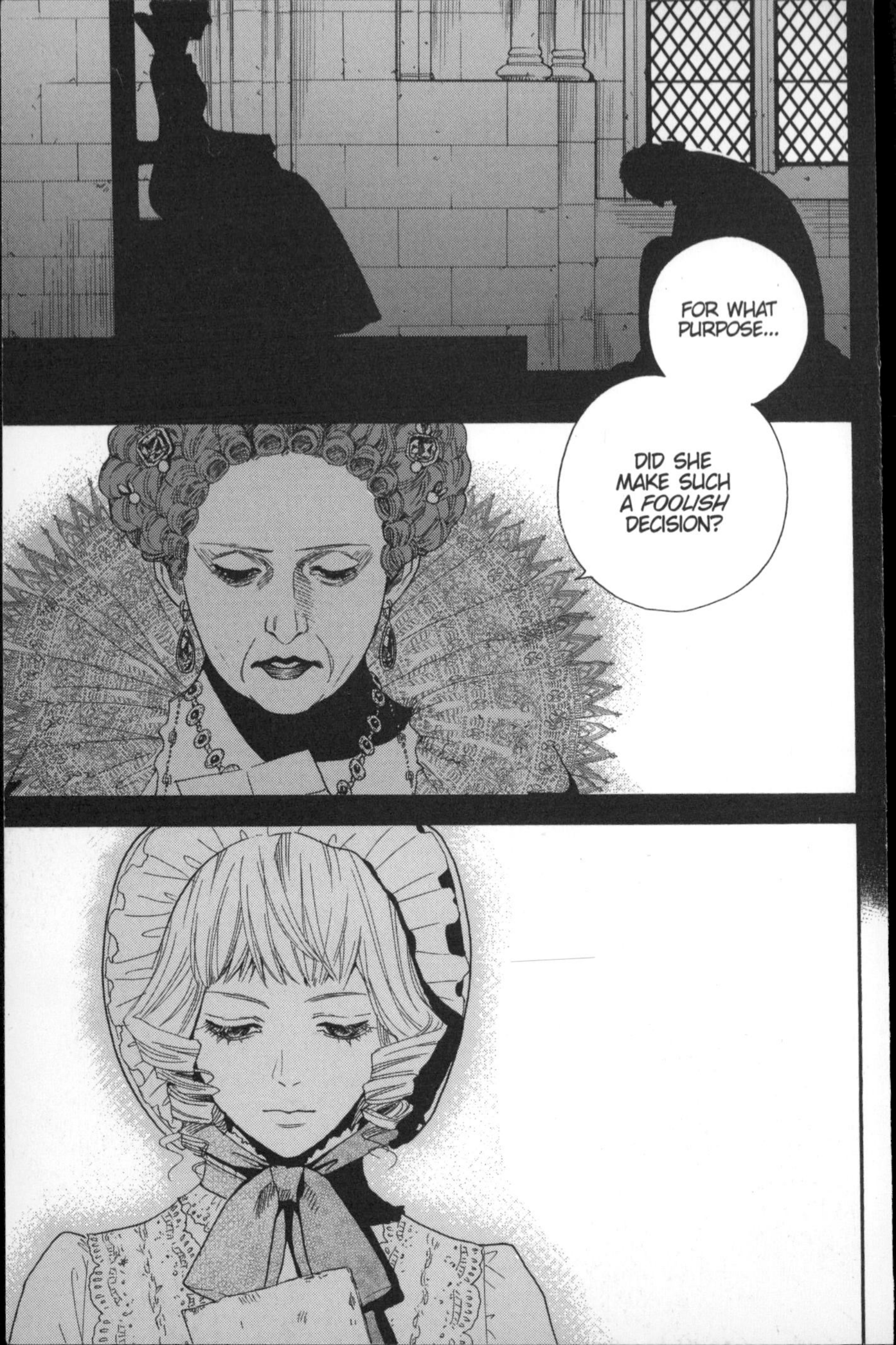
FOR WHAT PURPOSE...
DID SHE MAKE SUCH A *FOOLISH* DECISION?

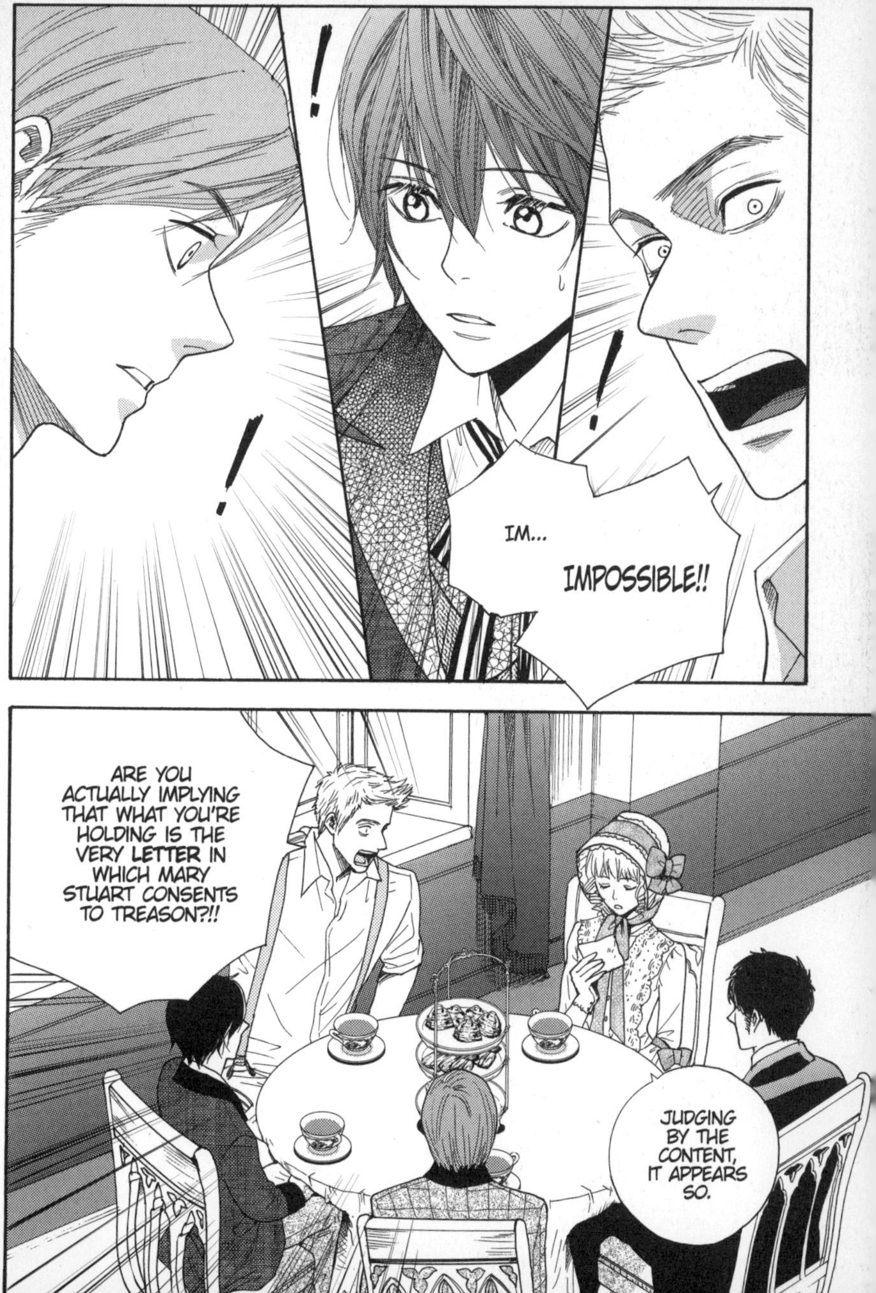
IM...
IMPOSSIBLE!!
ARE YOU ACTUALLY IMPLYING THAT WHAT YOU'RE HOLDING IS THE VERY LETTER IN WHICH MARY STUART CONSENTS TO TREASON?!!
JUDGING BY THE CONTENT, IT APPEARS SO.

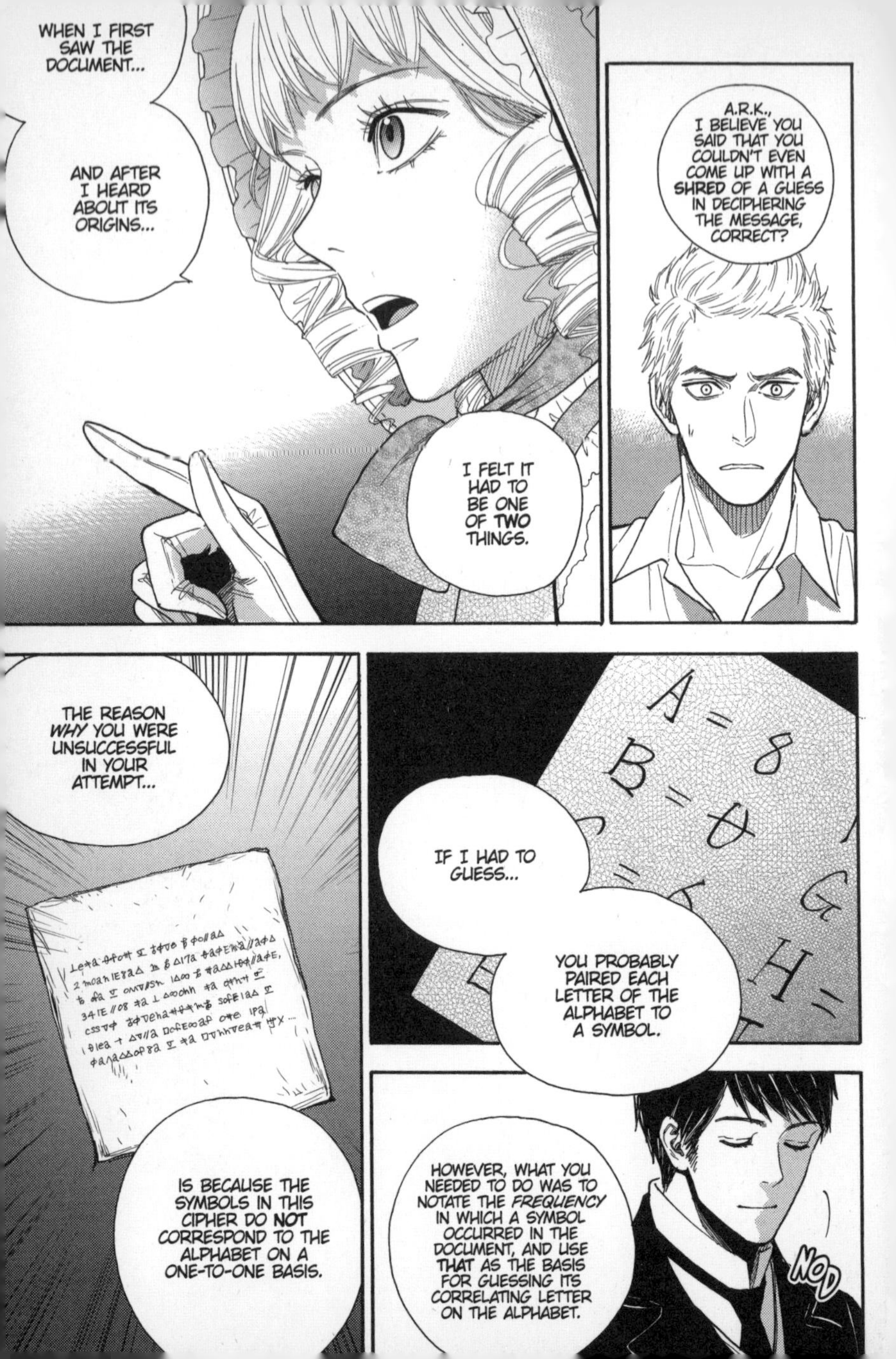
WHEN I FIRST SAW THE DOCUMENT...
AND AFTER I HEARD ABOUT ITS ORIGINS...
I FELT IT HAD TO BE ONE OF TWO THINGS.
A.R.K., I BELIEVE YOU SAID THAT YOU COULDN'T EVEN COME UP WITH A SHRED OF A GUESS IN DECIPHERING THE MESSAGE, CORRECT?
THE REASON WHY YOU WERE UNSUCCESSFUL IN YOUR ATTEMPT...
IS BECAUSE THE SYMBOLS IN THIS CIPHER DO NOT CORRESPOND TO THE ALPHABET ON A ONE-TO-ONE BASIS.
IF I HAD TO GUESS...
YOU PROBABLY PAIRED EACH LETTER OF THE ALPHABET TO A SYMBOL.
HOWEVER, WHAT YOU NEEDED TO DO WAS TO NOTATE THE FREQUENCY IN WHICH A SYMBOL OCCURRED IN THE DOCUMENT, AND USE THAT AS THE BASIS FOR GUESSING ITS CORRELATING LETTER ON THE ALPHABET.
NOD

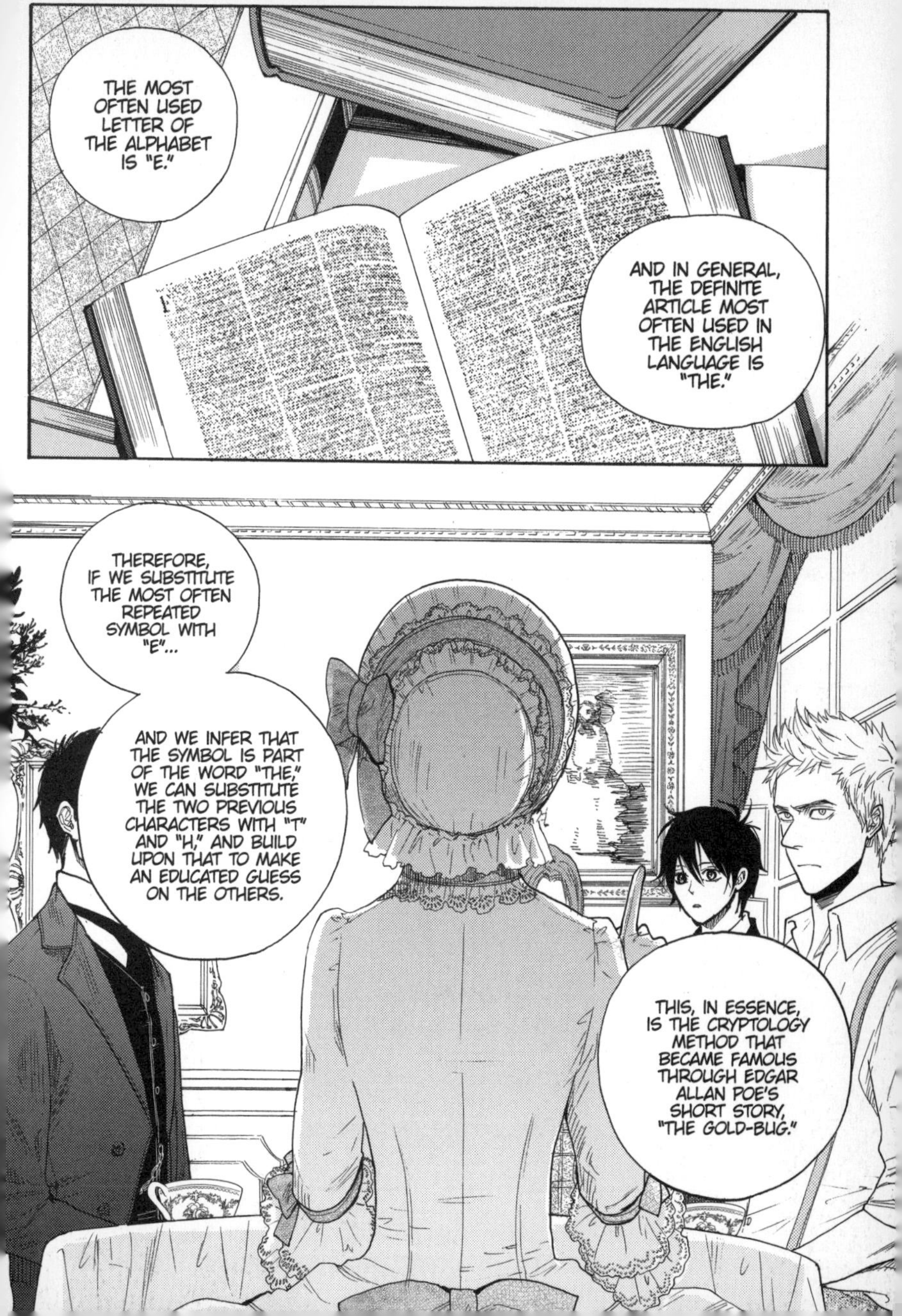
THE MOST OFTEN USED LETTER OF THE ALPHABET IS "E."
AND IN GENERAL, THE DEFINITE ARTICLE MOST OFTEN USED IN THE ENGLISH LANGUAGE IS "THE."
THEREFORE, IF WE SUBSTITUTE THE MOST OFTEN REPEATED SYMBOL WITH "E"...
AND WE INFER THAT THE SYMBOL IS PART OF THE WORD "THE," WE CAN SUBSTITUTE THE TWO PREVIOUS CHARACTERS WITH "T" AND "H," AND BUILD UPON THAT TO MAKE AN EDUCATED GUESS ON THE OTHERS.
THIS, IN ESSENCE, IS THE CRYPTOLOGY METHOD THAT BECAME FAMOUS THROUGH EDGAR ALLAN POE'S SHORT STORY, "THE GOLD-BUG."

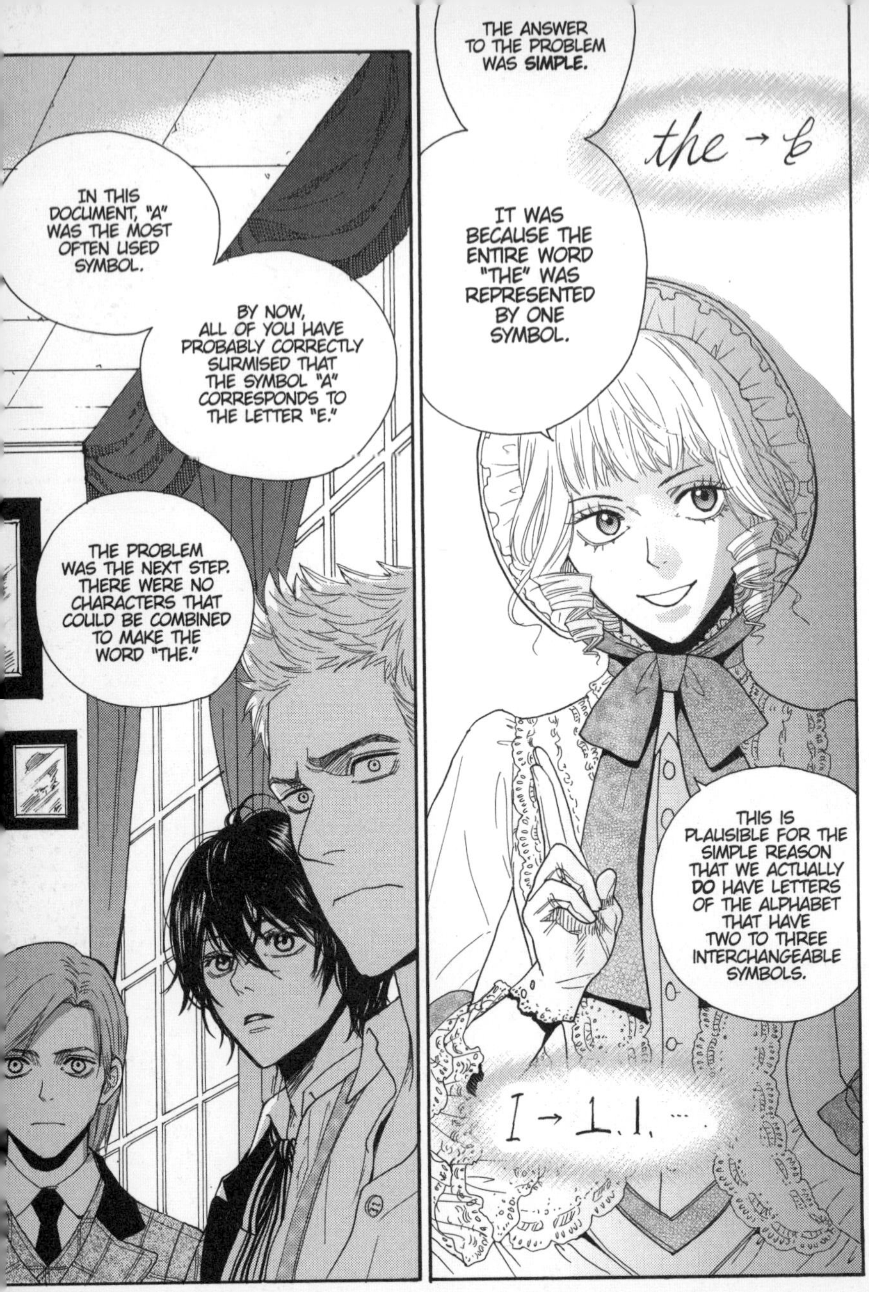
IN THIS DOCUMENT, "A" WAS THE MOST OFTEN USED SYMBOL.
BY NOW, ALL OF YOU HAVE PROBABLY CORRECTLY SURMISED THAT THE SYMBOL "A" CORRESPONDS TO THE LETTER "E."
THE PROBLEM WAS THE NEXT STEP. THERE WERE NO CHARACTERS THAT COULD BE COMBINED TO MAKE THE WORD "THE."
THE ANSWER TO THE PROBLEM WAS **SIMPLE.**
the → ℓ
IT WAS BECAUSE THE ENTIRE WORD "THE" WAS REPRESENTED BY ONE SYMBOL.
THIS IS PLAUSIBLE FOR THE SIMPLE REASON THAT WE ACTUALLY DO HAVE LETTERS OF THE ALPHABET THAT HAVE TWO TO THREE INTERCHANGEABLE SYMBOLS.
I → 1. l, ...

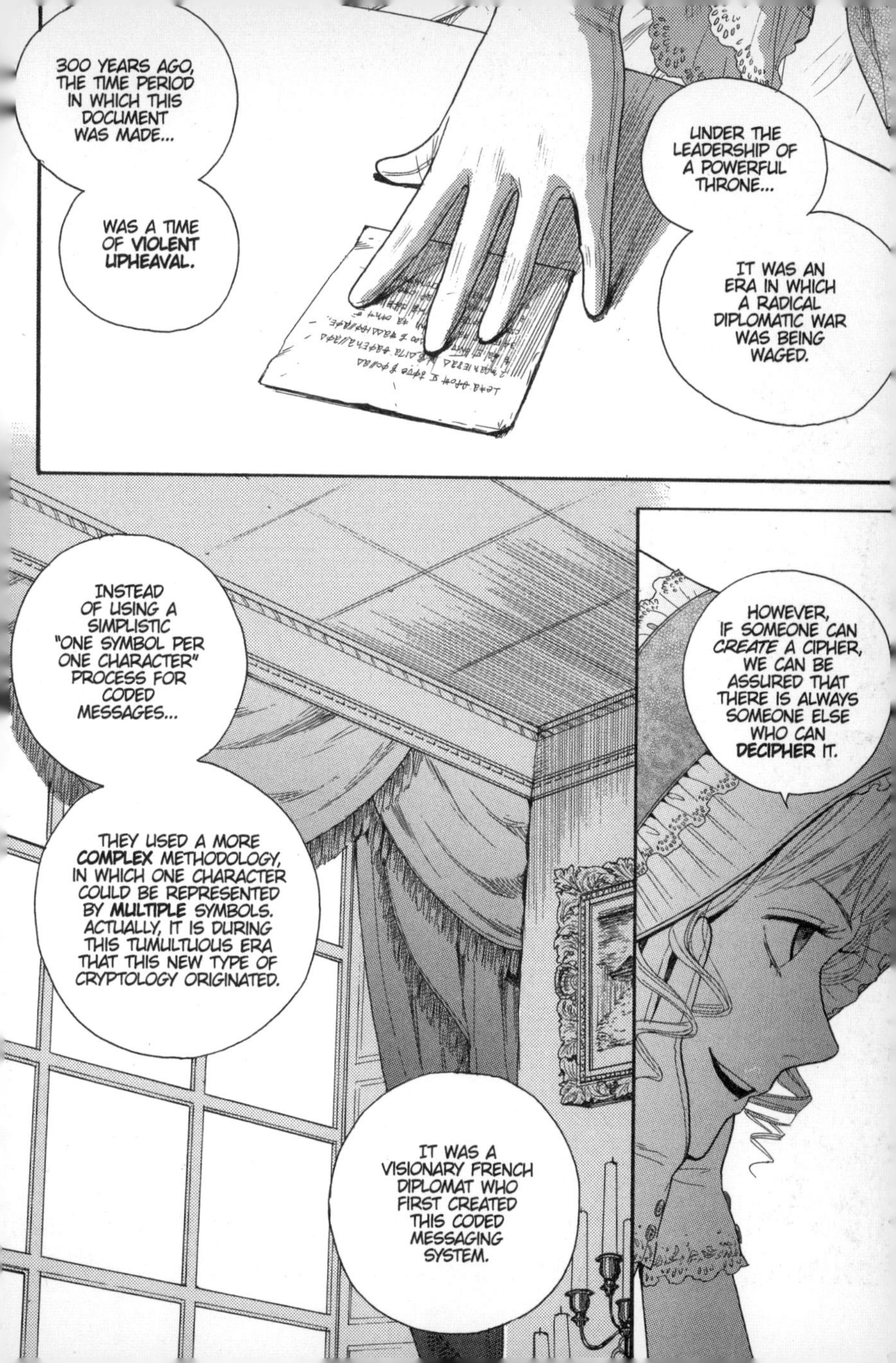
300 YEARS AGO, THE TIME PERIOD IN WHICH THIS DOCUMENT WAS MADE...
WAS A TIME OF **VIOLENT UPHEAVAL.**
UNDER THE LEADERSHIP OF A POWERFUL THRONE...
IT WAS AN ERA IN WHICH A RADICAL DIPLOMATIC WAR WAS BEING WAGED.
INSTEAD OF USING A SIMPLISTIC "ONE SYMBOL PER ONE CHARACTER" PROCESS FOR CODED MESSAGES...
THEY USED A MORE **COMPLEX** METHODOLOGY, IN WHICH ONE CHARACTER COULD BE REPRESENTED BY **MULTIPLE** SYMBOLS. ACTUALLY, IT IS DURING THIS TUMULTUOUS ERA THAT THIS NEW TYPE OF CRYPTOLOGY ORIGINATED.
IT WAS A VISIONARY FRENCH DIPLOMAT WHO FIRST CREATED THIS CODED MESSAGING SYSTEM.
HOWEVER, IF SOMEONE CAN *CREATE* A CIPHER, WE CAN BE ASSURED THAT THERE IS ALWAYS SOMEONE ELSE WHO CAN **DECIPHER** IT.

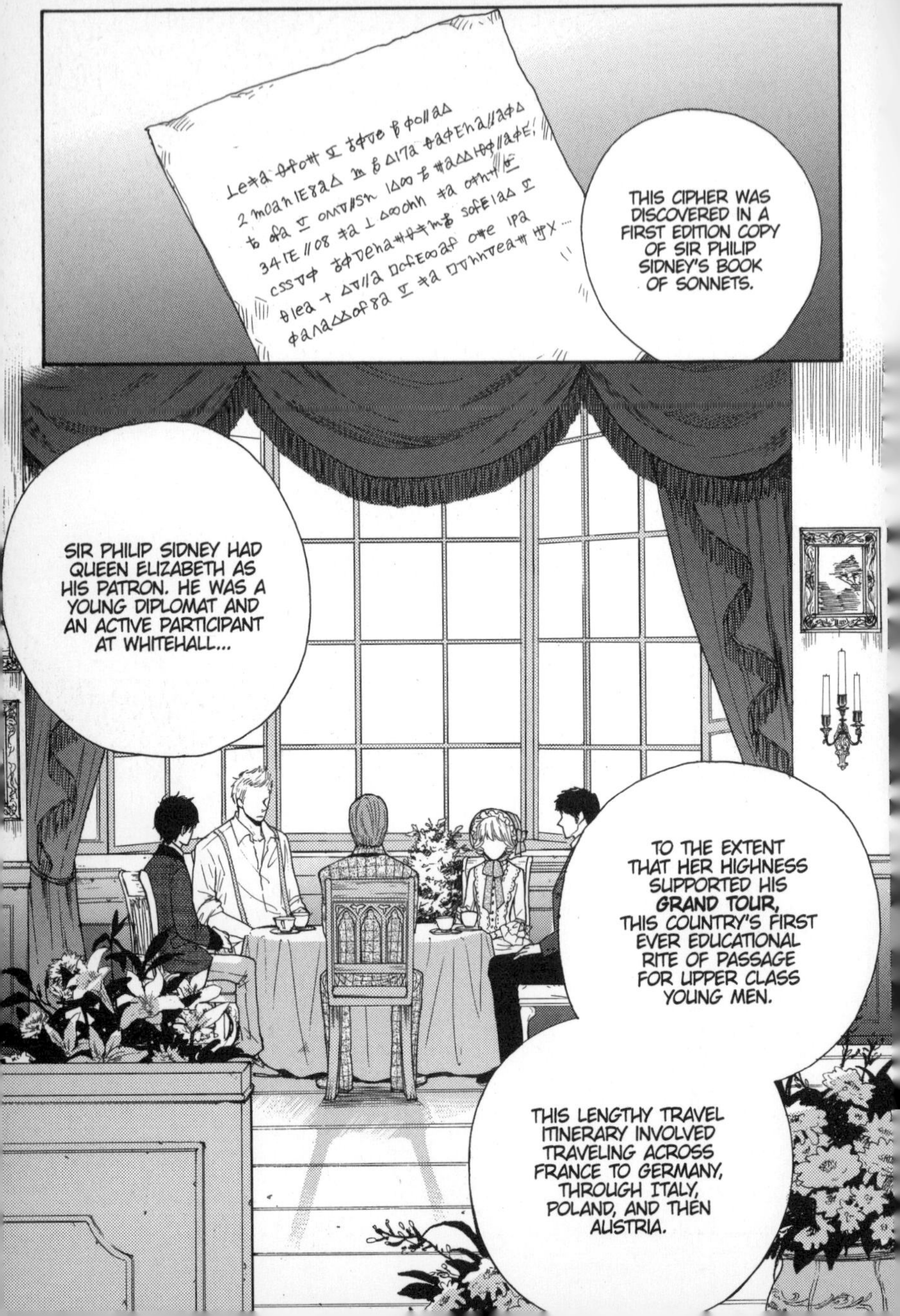
THIS CIPHER WAS DISCOVERED IN A FIRST EDITION COPY OF SIR PHILIP SIDNEY'S BOOK OF SONNETS.
SIR PHILIP SIDNEY HAD QUEEN ELIZABETH AS HIS PATRON. HE WAS A YOUNG DIPLOMAT AND AN ACTIVE PARTICIPANT AT WHITEHALL...
TO THE EXTENT THAT HER HIGHNESS SUPPORTED HIS **GRAND TOUR,** THIS COUNTRY'S FIRST EVER EDUCATIONAL RITE OF PASSAGE FOR UPPER CLASS YOUNG MEN.
THIS LENGTHY TRAVEL ITINERARY INVOLVED TRAVELING ACROSS FRANCE TO GERMANY, THROUGH ITALY, POLAND, AND THEN AUSTRIA.

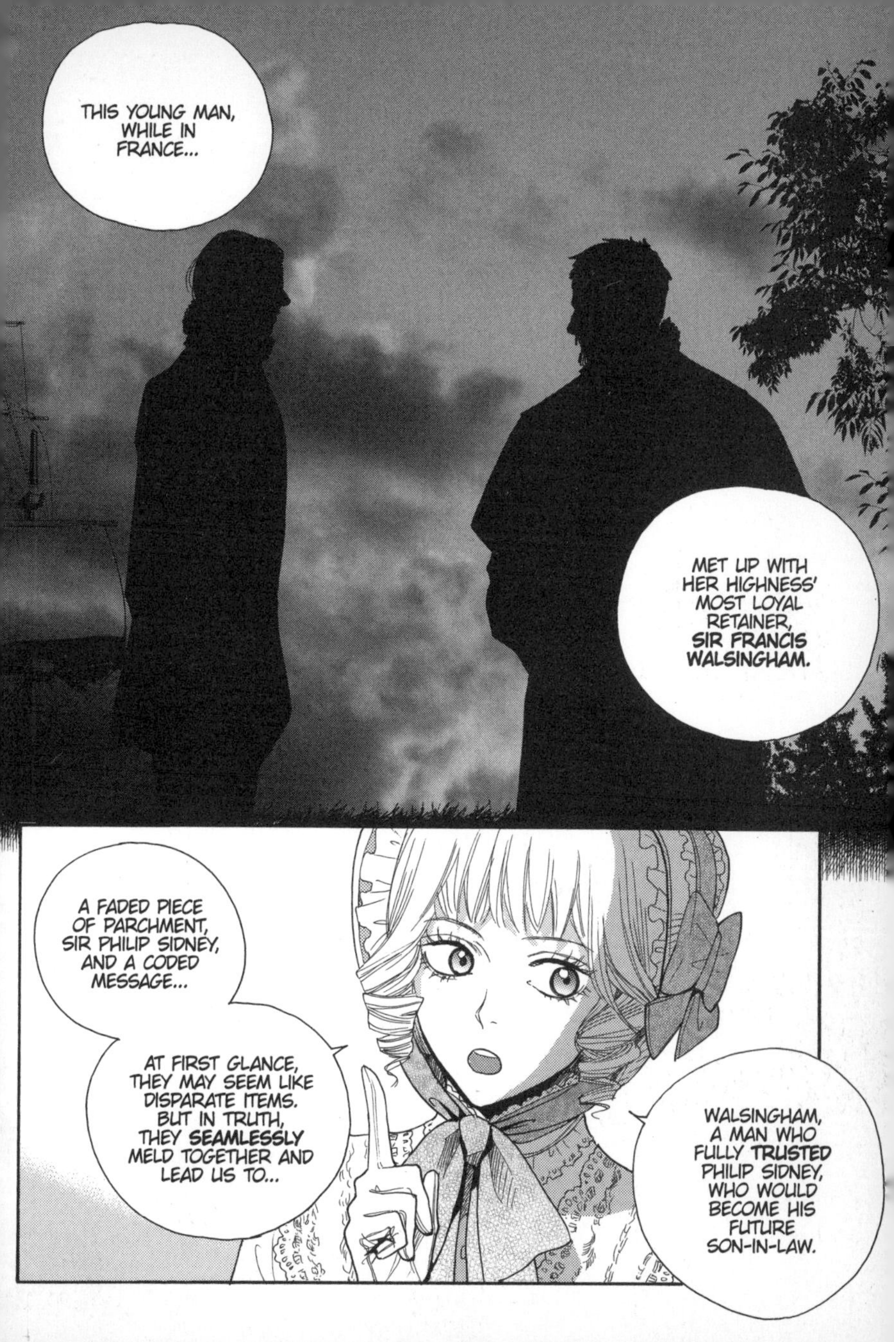
THIS YOUNG MAN, WHILE IN FRANCE...
MET UP WITH HER HIGHNESS' MOST LOYAL RETAINER, **SIR FRANCIS WALSINGHAM.**
A FADED PIECE OF PARCHMENT, SIR PHILIP SIDNEY, AND A CODED MESSAGE...
AT FIRST GLANCE, THEY MAY SEEM LIKE DISPARATE ITEMS. BUT IN TRUTH, THEY **SEAMLESSLY** MELD TOGETHER AND LEAD US TO...
WALSINGHAM, A MAN WHO FULLY **TRUSTED** PHILIP SIDNEY, WHO WOULD BECOME HIS FUTURE SON-IN-LAW.

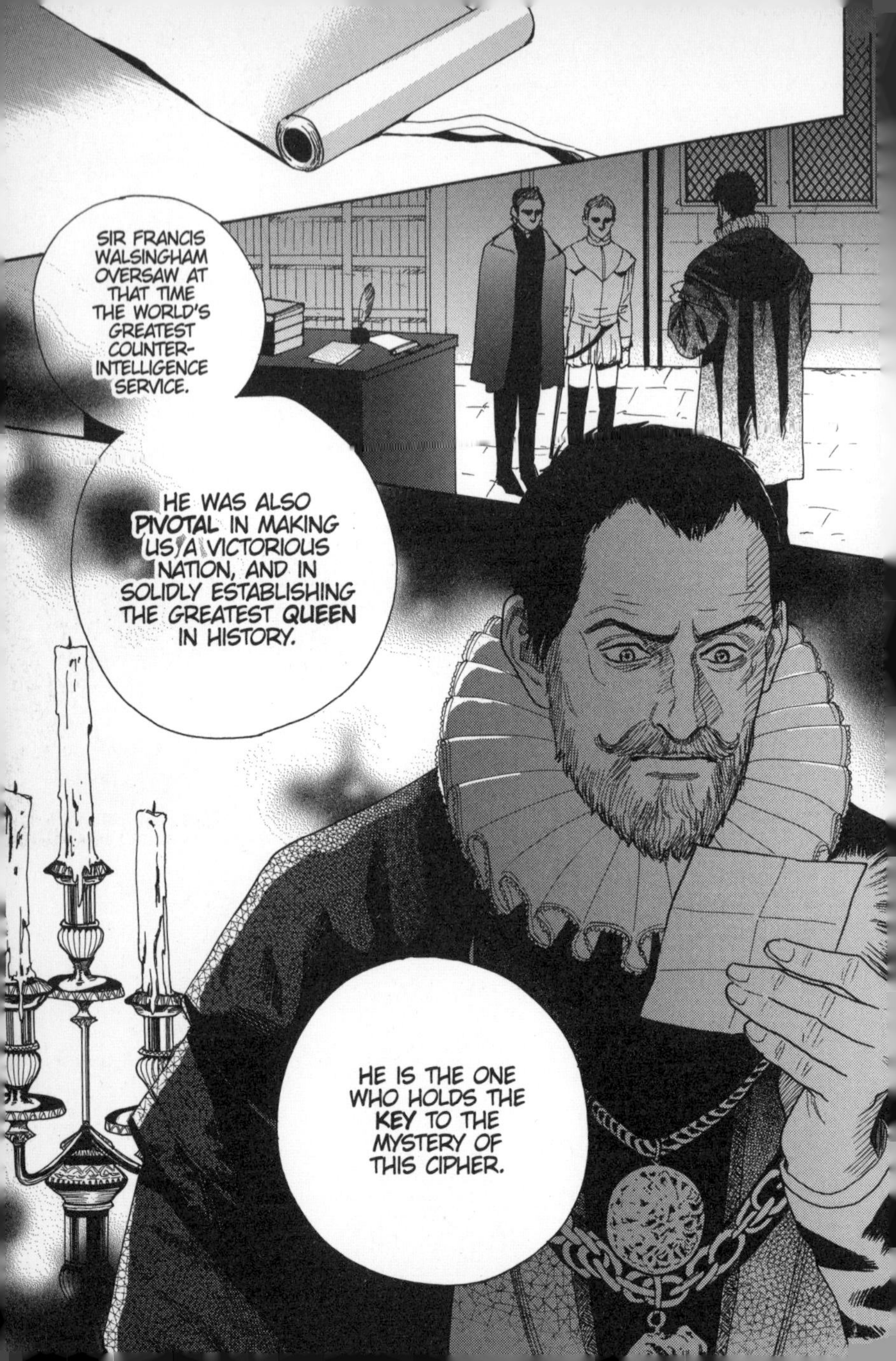
SIR FRANCIS WALSINGHAM OVERSAW AT THAT TIME THE WORLD'S GREATEST COUNTER-INTELLIGENCE SERVICE.
HE WAS ALSO PIVOTAL IN MAKING US A VICTORIOUS NATION, AND IN SOLIDLY ESTABLISHING THE GREATEST QUEEN IN HISTORY.
HE IS THE ONE WHO HOLDS THE KEY TO THE MYSTERY OF THIS CIPHER.

CHAPTER 8

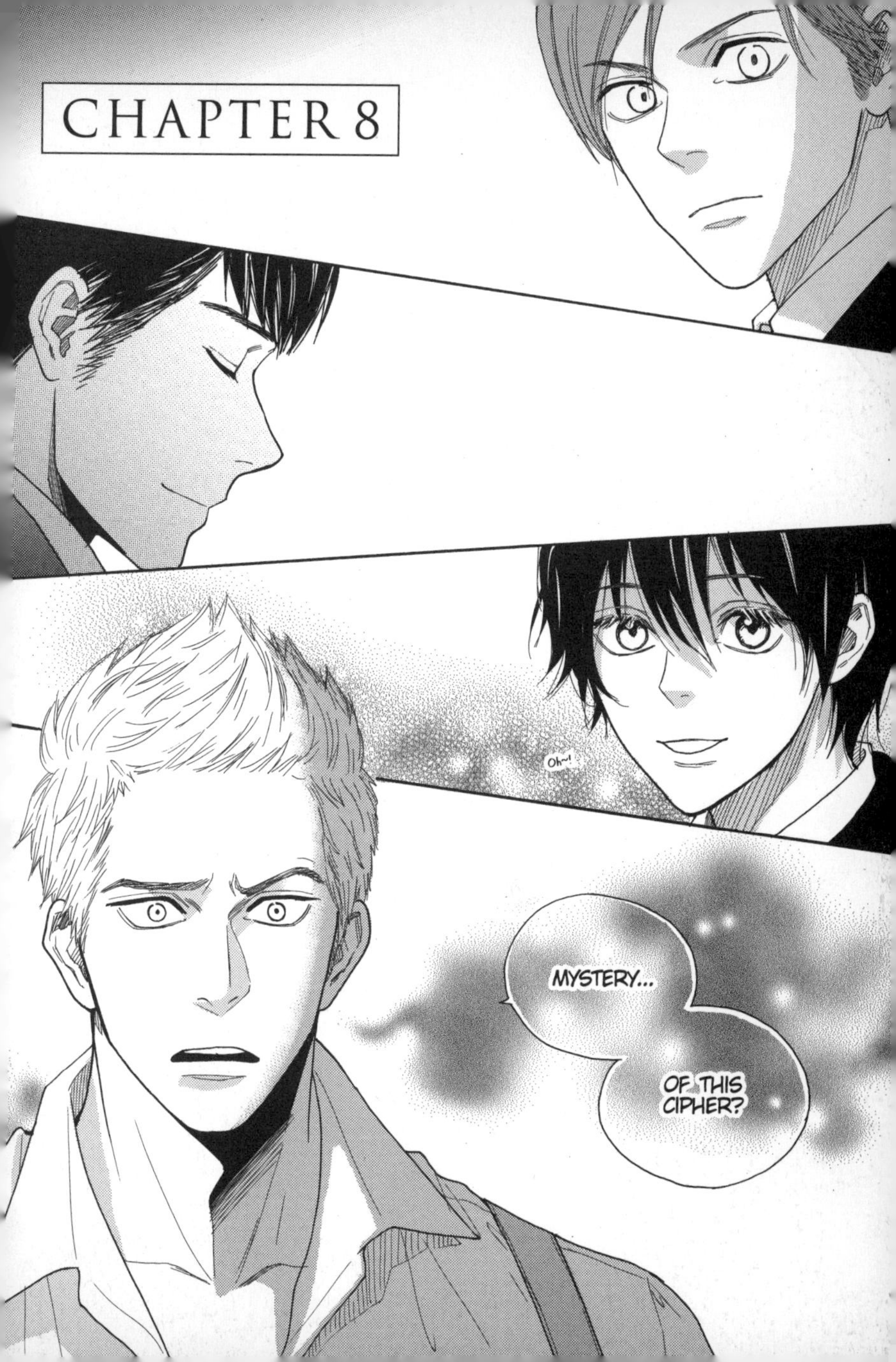
Oh~!
MYSTERY...
OF THIS CIPHER?

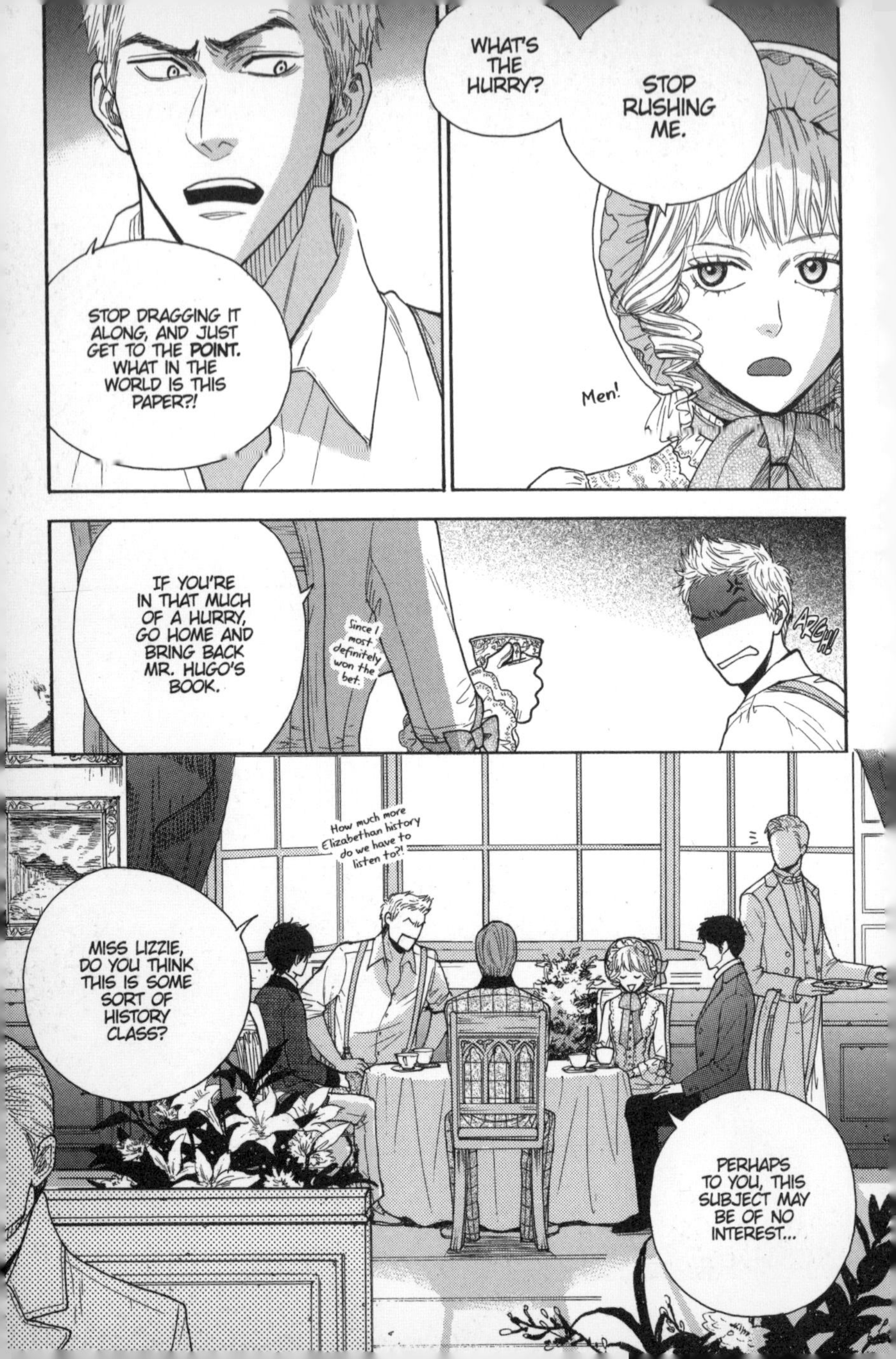
STOP DRAGGING IT ALONG, AND JUST GET TO THE POINT. WHAT IN THE WORLD IS THIS PAPER?!
WHAT'S THE HURRY?
STOP RUSHING ME.
Men!
IF YOU'RE IN THAT MUCH OF A HURRY, GO HOME AND BRING BACK MR. HUGO'S BOOK.
Since I most definitely won the bet.
ARGH!!
How much more Elizabethan history do we have to listen to?!
MISS LIZZIE, DO YOU THINK THIS IS SOME SORT OF HISTORY CLASS?
PERHAPS TO YOU, THIS SUBJECT MAY BE OF NO INTEREST...

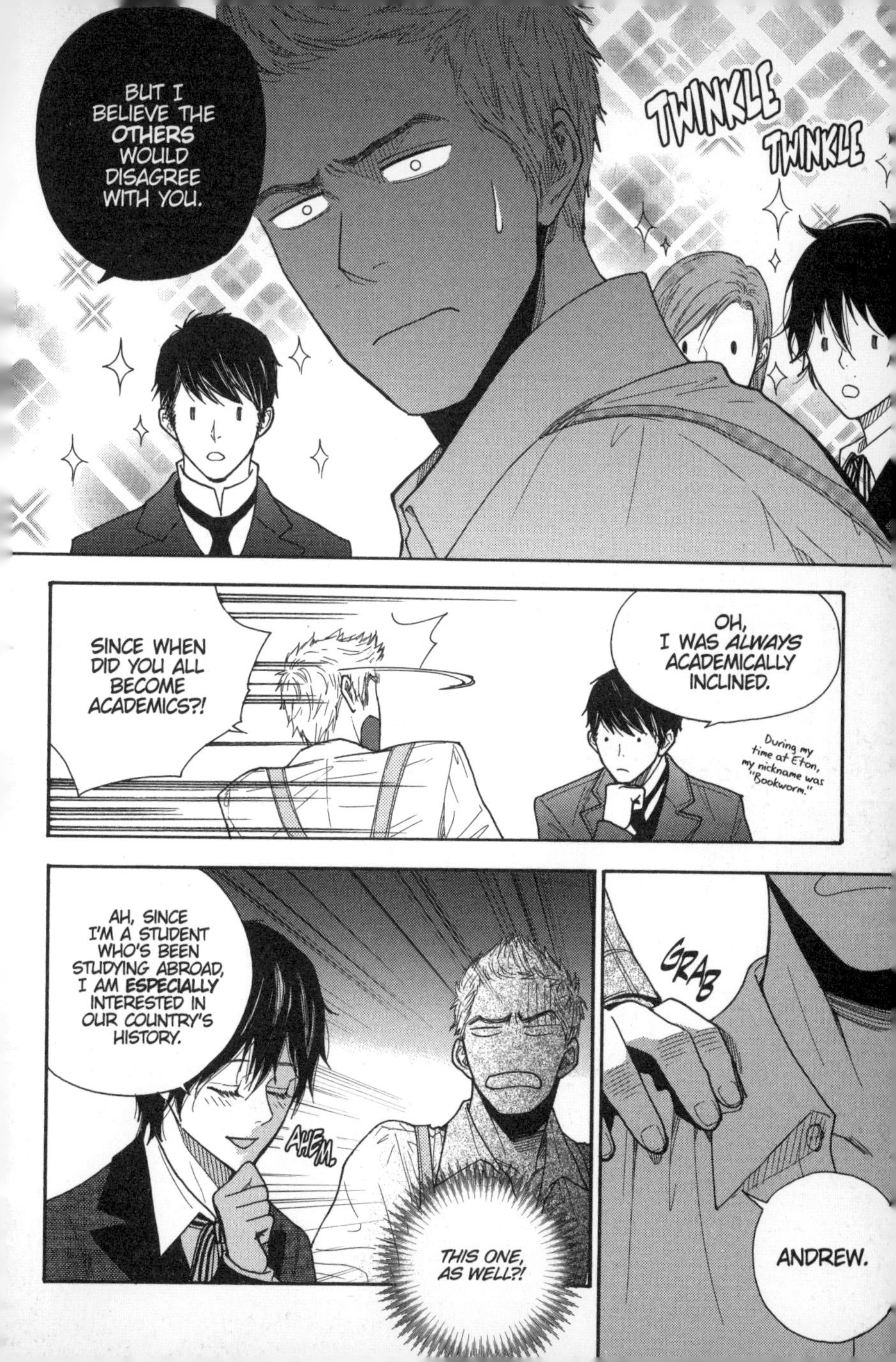
BUT I BELIEVE THE OTHERS WOULD DISAGREE WITH YOU.
TWINKLE
TWINKLE
SINCE WHEN DID YOU ALL BECOME ACADEMICS?!
OH, I WAS ALWAYS ACADEMICALLY INCLINED.
During my time at Eton, my nickname was "Bookworm."
AH, SINCE I'M A STUDENT WHO'S BEEN STUDYING ABROAD, I AM ESPECIALLY INTERESTED IN OUR COUNTRY'S HISTORY.
AHEM.
THIS ONE, AS WELL?!
GRAB
ANDREW.

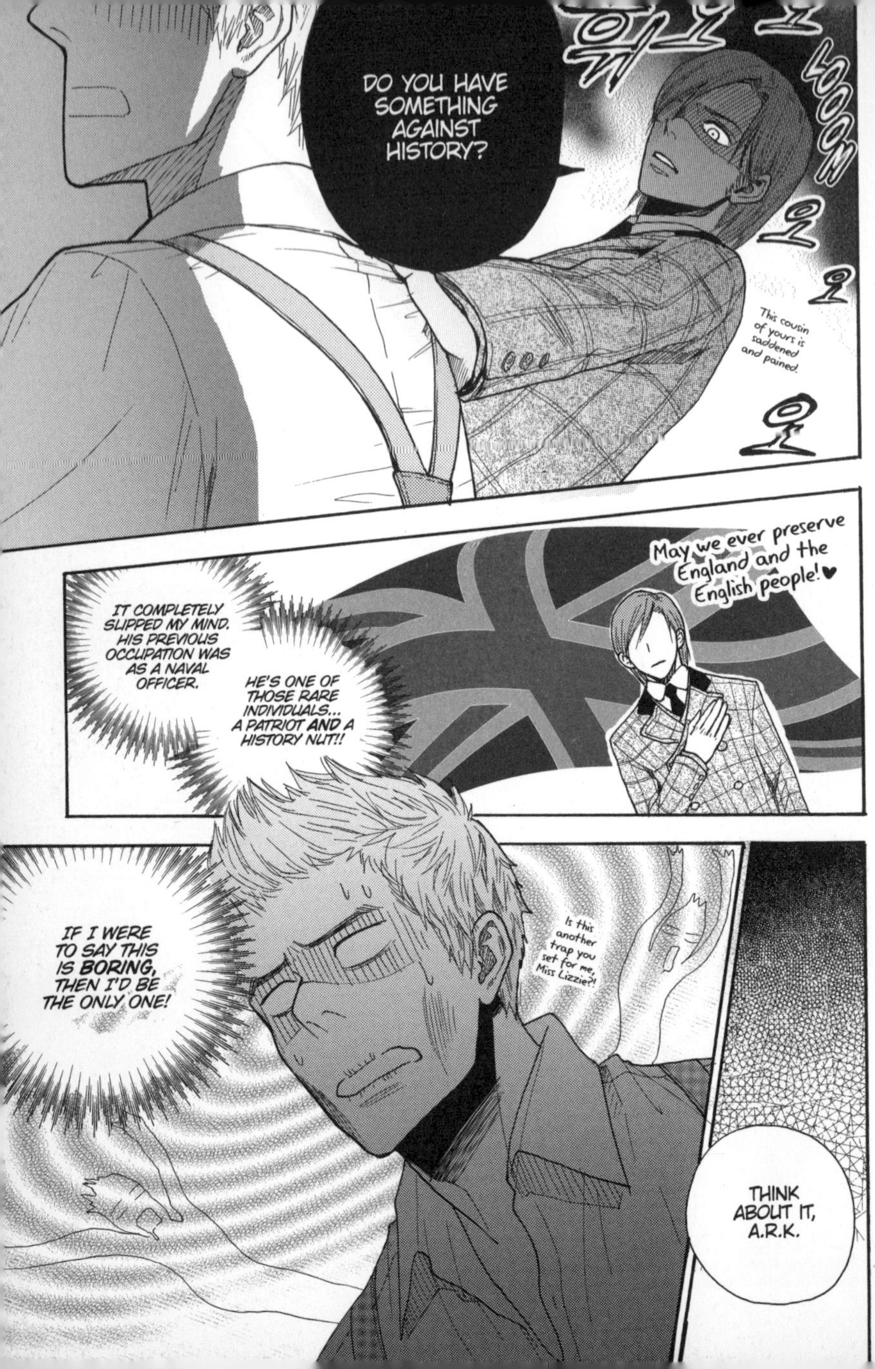
DO YOU HAVE SOMETHING AGAINST HISTORY?
This cousin of yours is saddened and pained.
IT COMPLETELY SLIPPED MY MIND. HIS PREVIOUS OCCUPATION WAS AS A NAVAL OFFICER.
HE'S ONE OF THOSE RARE INDIVIDUALS... A PATRIOT **AND** A HISTORY NUT!!
May we ever preserve England and the English people! ♥
IF I WERE TO SAY THIS IS **BORING**, THEN I'D BE THE ONLY ONE!
Is this another trap you set for me, Miss Lizzie?!
THINK ABOUT IT, A.R.K.

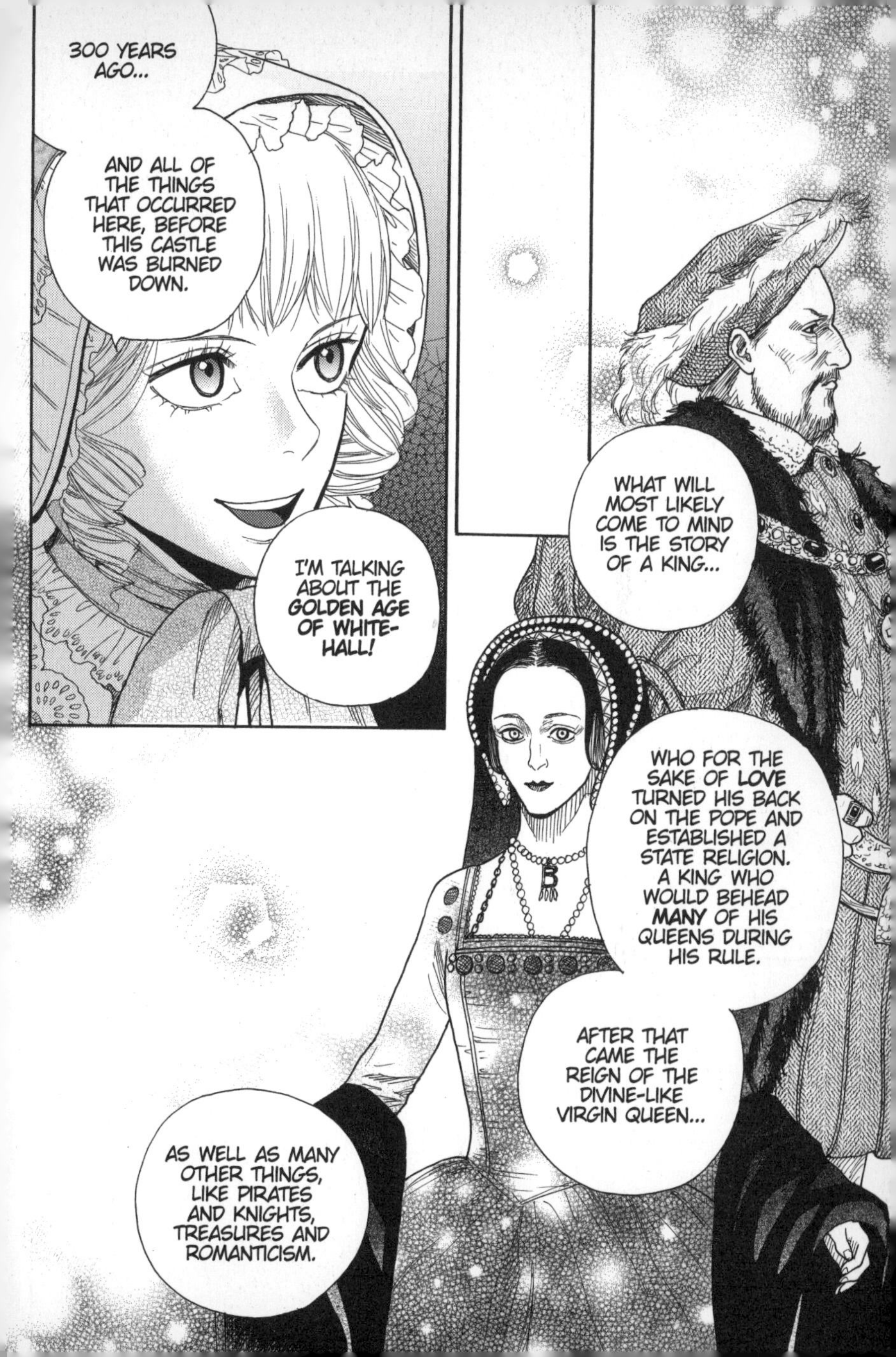
300 YEARS AGO...
AND ALL OF THE THINGS THAT OCCURRED HERE, BEFORE THIS CASTLE WAS BURNED DOWN.
I'M TALKING ABOUT THE **GOLDEN AGE OF WHITE-HALL!**
WHAT WILL MOST LIKELY COME TO MIND IS THE STORY OF A KING...
WHO FOR THE SAKE OF **LOVE** TURNED HIS BACK ON THE POPE AND ESTABLISHED A STATE RELIGION. A KING WHO WOULD BEHEAD **MANY** OF HIS QUEENS DURING HIS RULE.
AFTER THAT CAME THE REIGN OF THE DIVINE-LIKE VIRGIN QUEEN...
AS WELL AS MANY OTHER THINGS, LIKE PIRATES AND KNIGHTS, TREASURES AND ROMANTICISM.

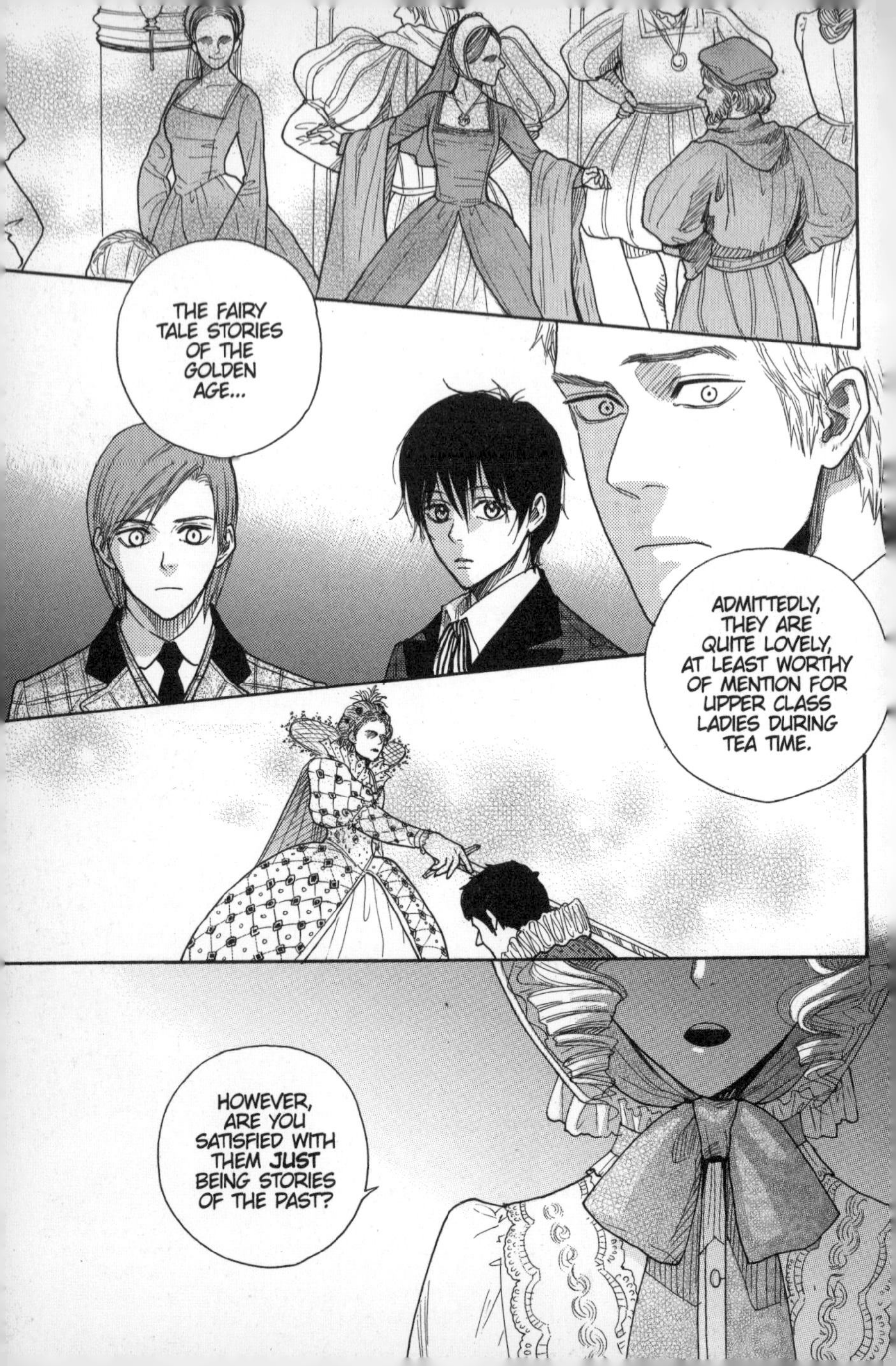
THE FAIRY TALE STORIES OF THE GOLDEN AGE...
ADMITTEDLY, THEY ARE QUITE LOVELY, AT LEAST WORTHY OF MENTION FOR UPPER CLASS LADIES DURING TEA TIME.
HOWEVER, ARE YOU SATISFIED WITH THEM JUST BEING STORIES OF THE PAST?

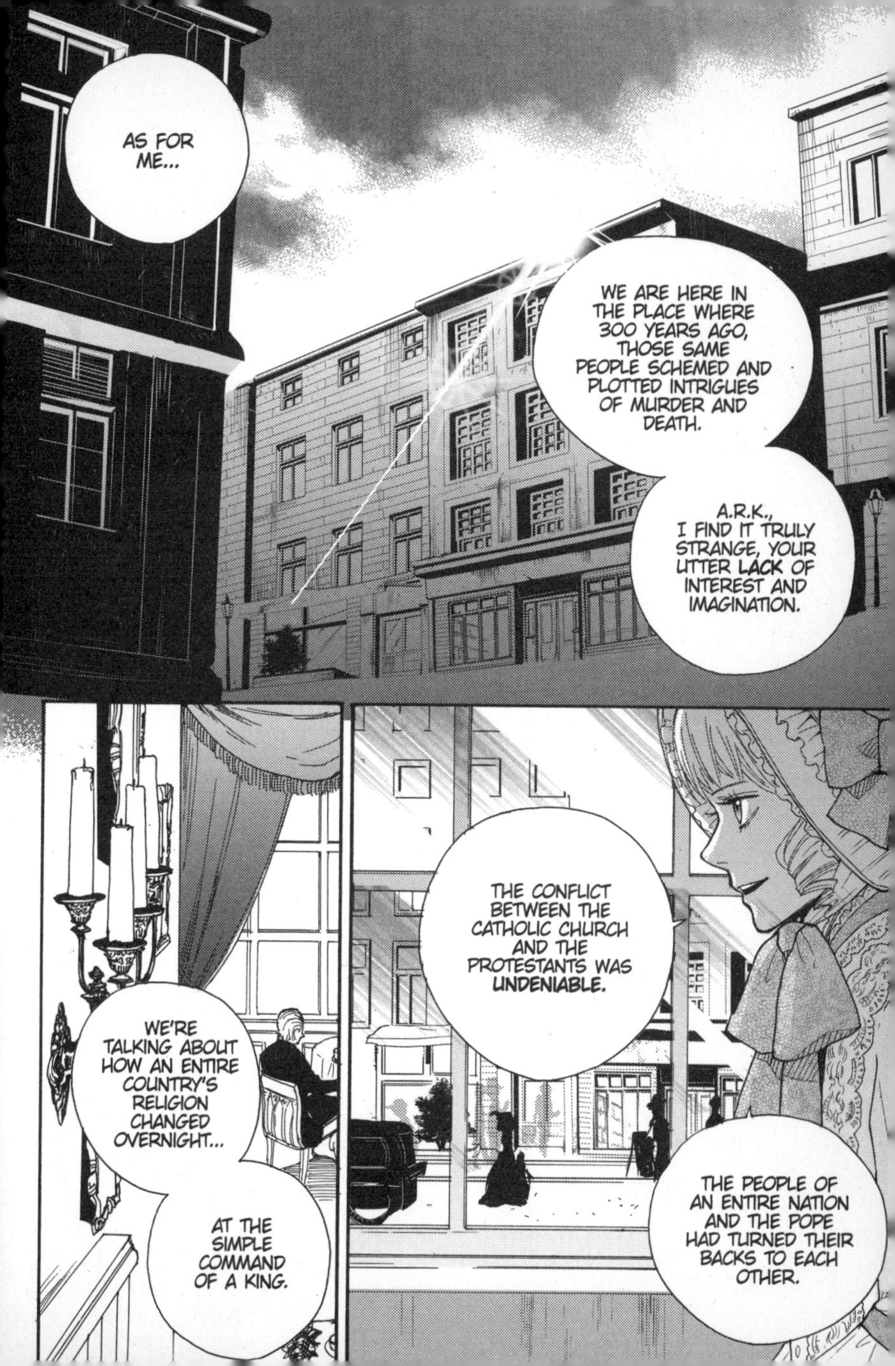
AS FOR ME...
WE ARE HERE IN THE PLACE WHERE 300 YEARS AGO, THOSE SAME PEOPLE SCHEMED AND PLOTTED INTRIGUES OF MURDER AND DEATH.
A.R.K., I FIND IT TRULY STRANGE, YOUR UTTER **LACK** OF INTEREST AND IMAGINATION.
WE'RE TALKING ABOUT HOW AN ENTIRE COUNTRY'S RELIGION CHANGED OVERNIGHT...
AT THE SIMPLE COMMAND OF A KING.
THE CONFLICT BETWEEN THE CATHOLIC CHURCH AND THE PROTESTANTS WAS **UNDENIABLE.**
THE PEOPLE OF AN ENTIRE NATION AND THE POPE HAD TURNED THEIR BACKS TO EACH OTHER.

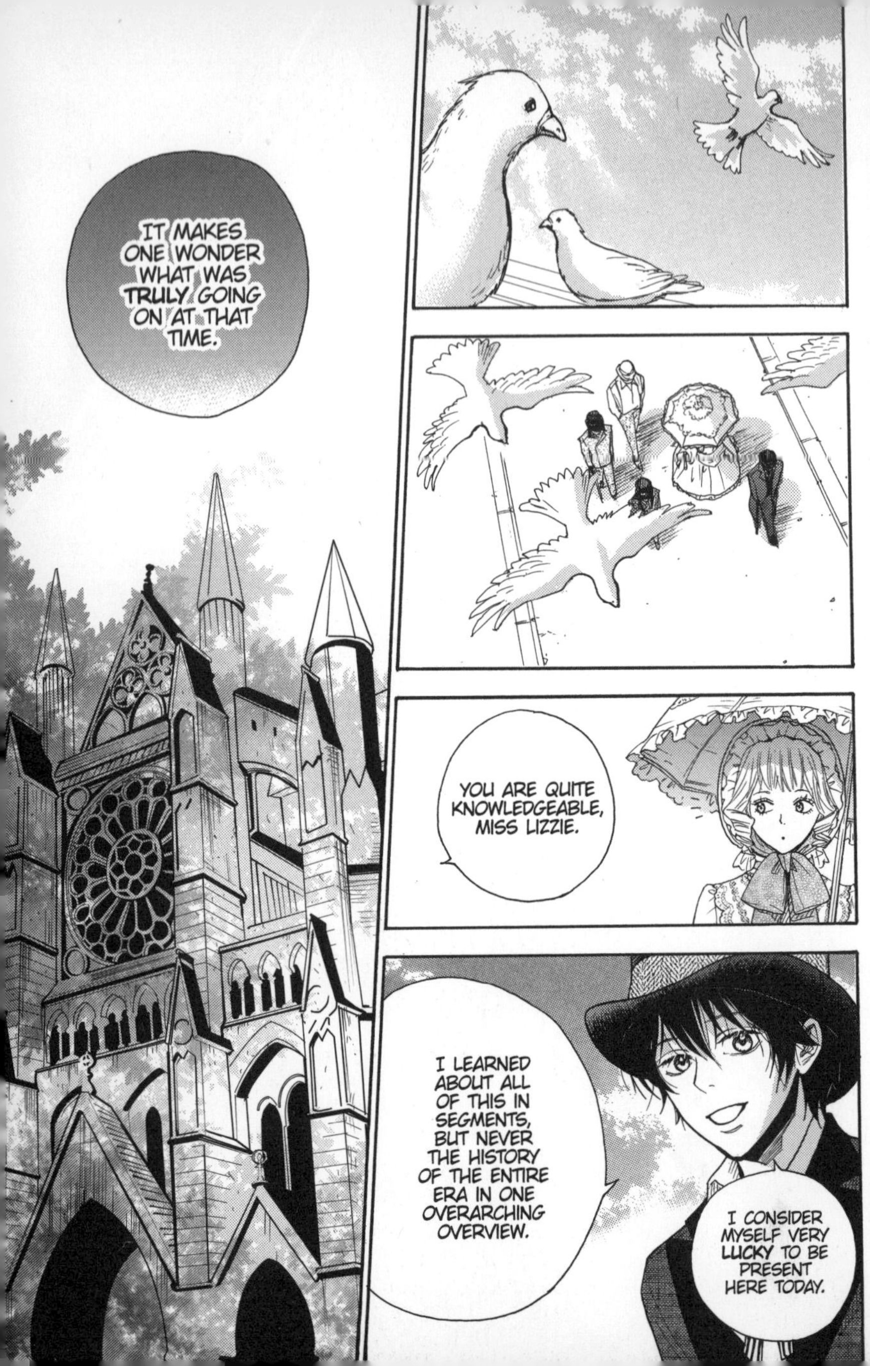
IT MAKES ONE WONDER WHAT WAS TRULY GOING ON AT THAT TIME.
YOU ARE QUITE KNOWLEDGEABLE, MISS LIZZIE.
I LEARNED ABOUT ALL OF THIS IN SEGMENTS, BUT NEVER THE HISTORY OF THE ENTIRE ERA IN ONE OVERARCHING OVERVIEW.
I CONSIDER MYSELF VERY LUCKY TO BE PRESENT HERE TODAY.

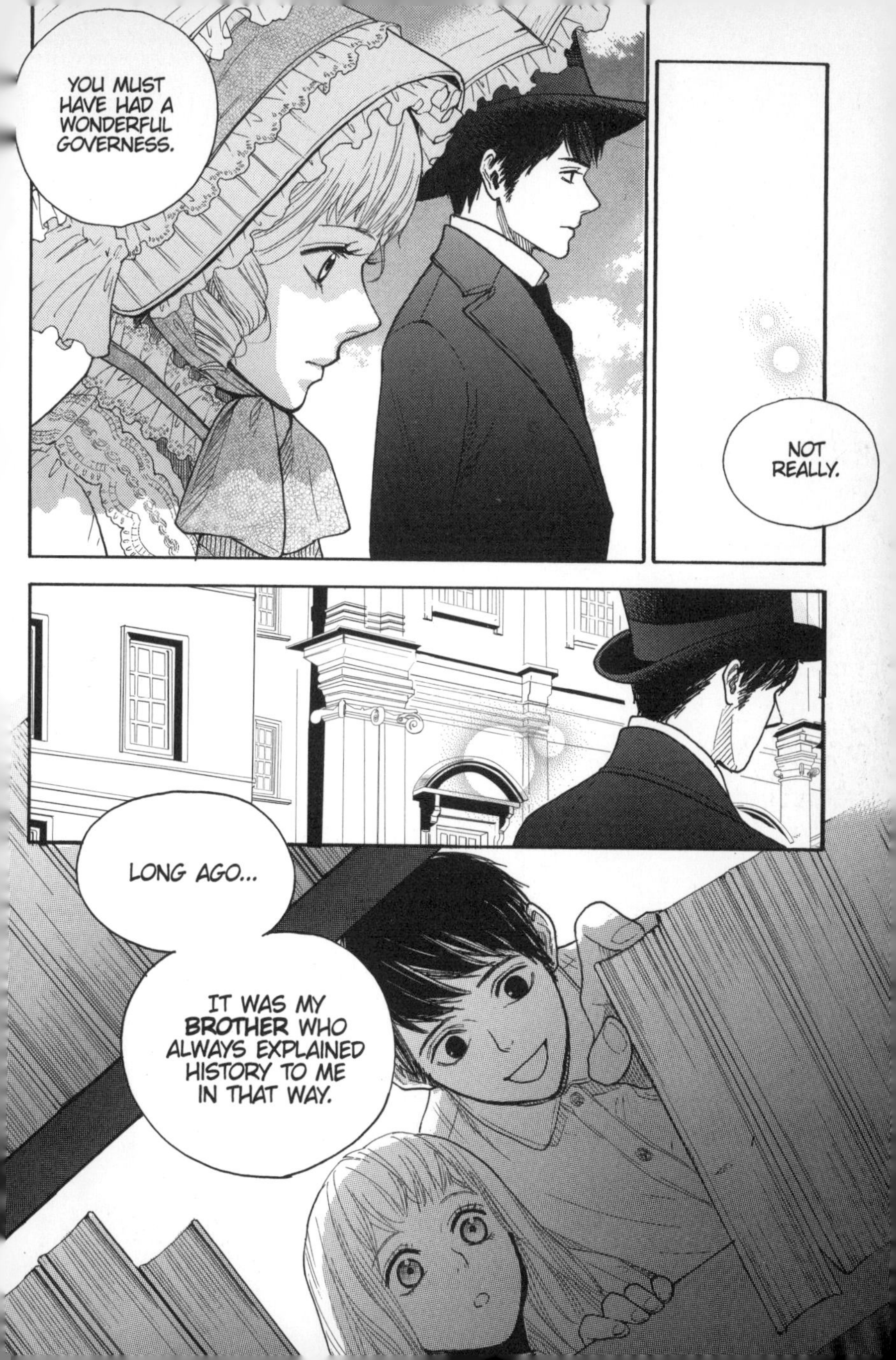
YOU MUST HAVE HAD A WONDERFUL GOVERNESS.
NOT REALLY.
LONG AGO...
IT WAS MY BROTHER WHO ALWAYS EXPLAINED HISTORY TO ME IN THAT WAY.

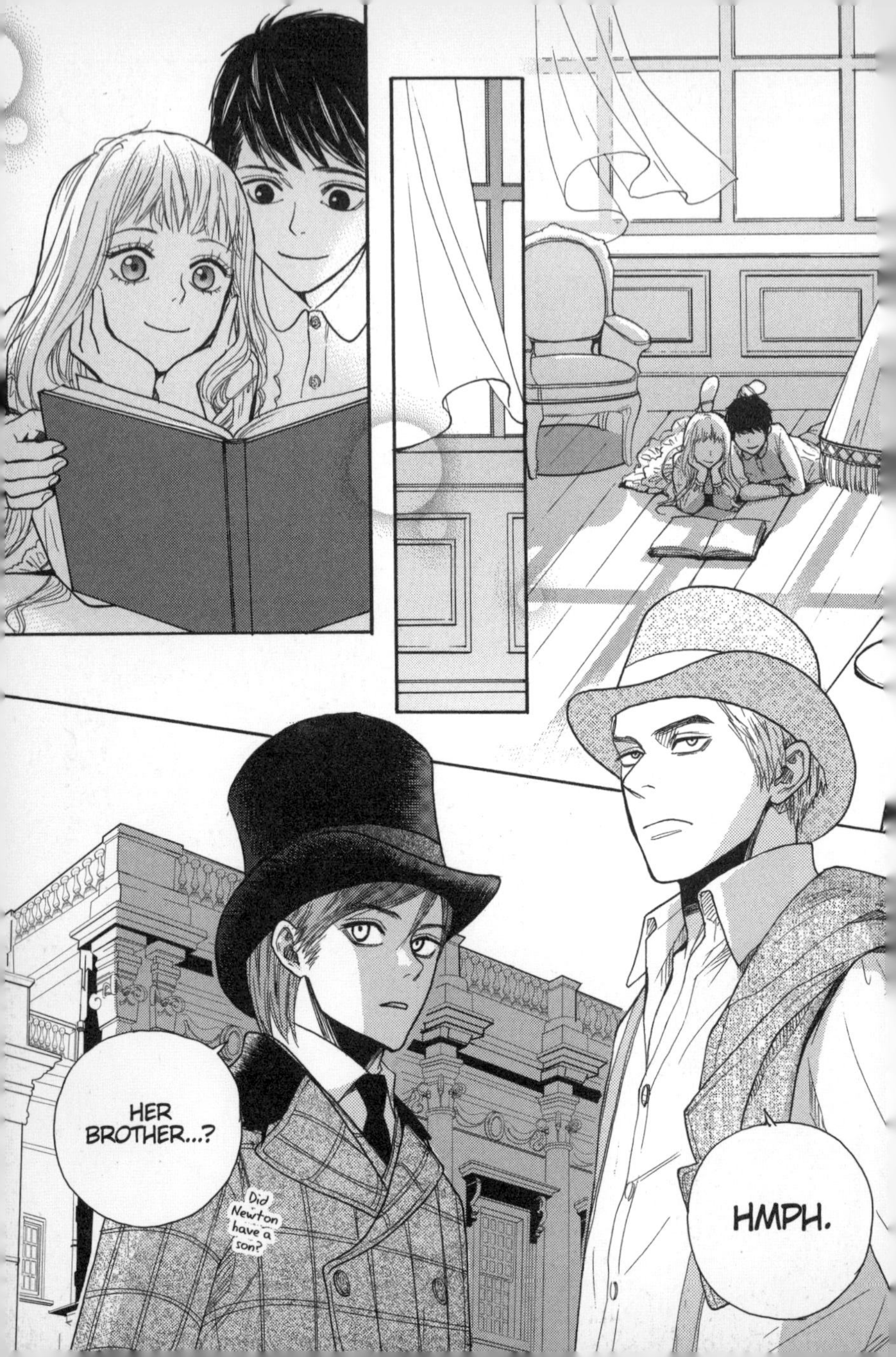
HER BROTHER...?
Did Newton have a son?
HMPH.

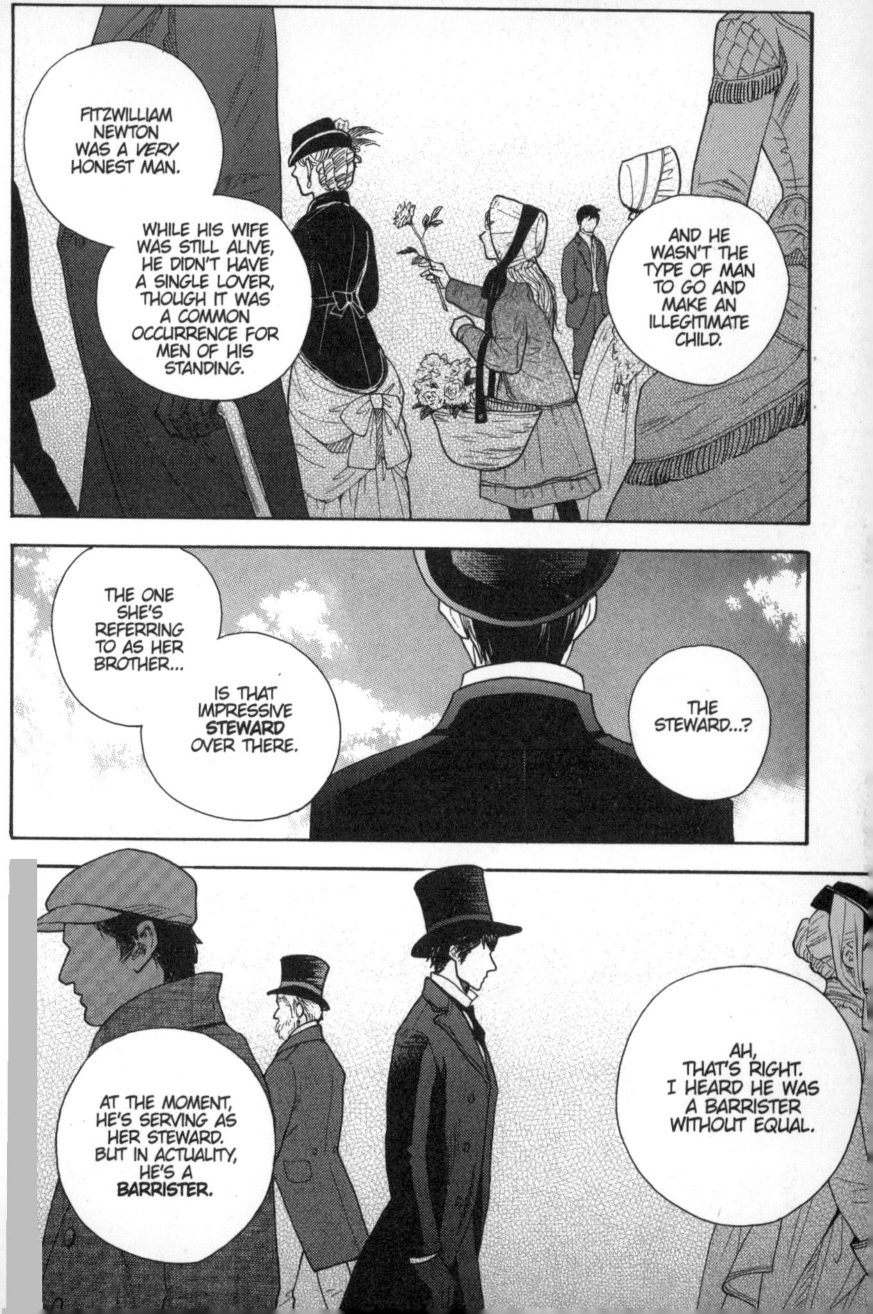

FITZWILLIAM NEWTON WAS A *VERY* HONEST MAN.
WHILE HIS WIFE WAS STILL ALIVE, HE DIDN'T HAVE A SINGLE LOVER, THOUGH IT WAS A COMMON OCCURRENCE FOR MEN OF HIS STANDING.
AND HE WASN'T THE TYPE OF MAN TO GO AND MAKE AN ILLEGITIMATE CHILD.
THE ONE SHE'S REFERRING TO AS HER BROTHER...
IS THAT IMPRESSIVE **STEWARD** OVER THERE.
THE STEWARD...?
AT THE MOMENT, HE'S SERVING AS HER STEWARD. BUT IN ACTUALITY, HE'S A **BARRISTER.**
AH, THAT'S RIGHT. I HEARD HE WAS A BARRISTER WITHOUT EQUAL.

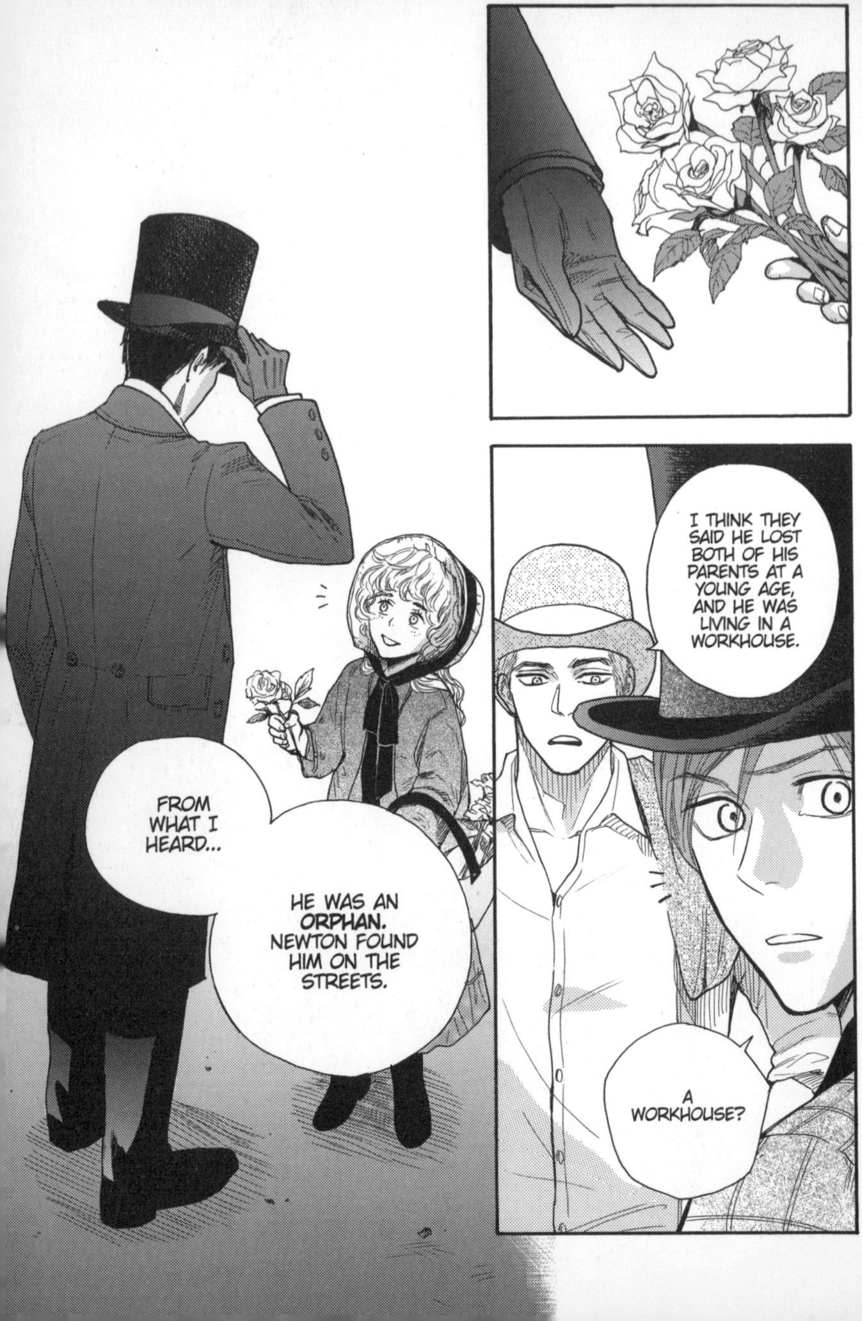
FROM WHAT I HEARD...
HE WAS AN **ORPHAN.** NEWTON FOUND HIM ON THE STREETS.
I THINK THEY SAID HE LOST BOTH OF HIS PARENTS AT A YOUNG AGE, AND HE WAS LIVING IN A WORKHOUSE.
A WORKHOUSE?

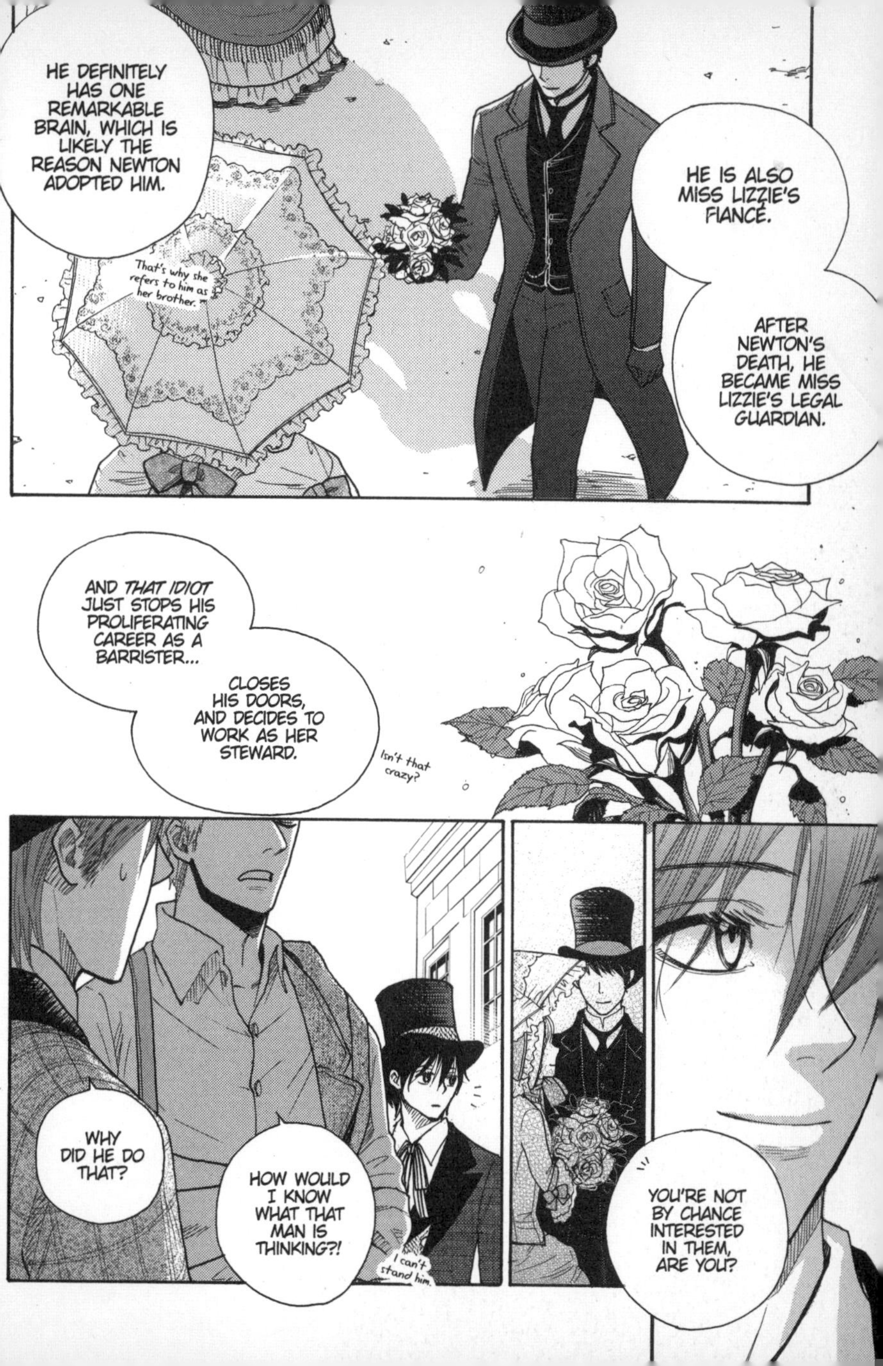
HE DEFINITELY HAS ONE REMARKABLE BRAIN, WHICH IS LIKELY THE REASON NEWTON ADOPTED HIM.
That's why she refers to him as her brother.
HE IS ALSO MISS LIZZIE'S FIANCÉ.
AFTER NEWTON'S DEATH, HE BECAME MISS LIZZIE'S LEGAL GUARDIAN.
AND THAT IDIOT JUST STOPS HIS PROLIFERATING CAREER AS A BARRISTER...
CLOSES HIS DOORS, AND DECIDES TO WORK AS HER STEWARD.
Isn't that crazy?
WHY DID HE DO THAT?
HOW WOULD I KNOW WHAT THAT MAN IS THINKING?!
I can't stand him.
YOU'RE NOT BY CHANCE INTERESTED IN THEM, ARE YOU?

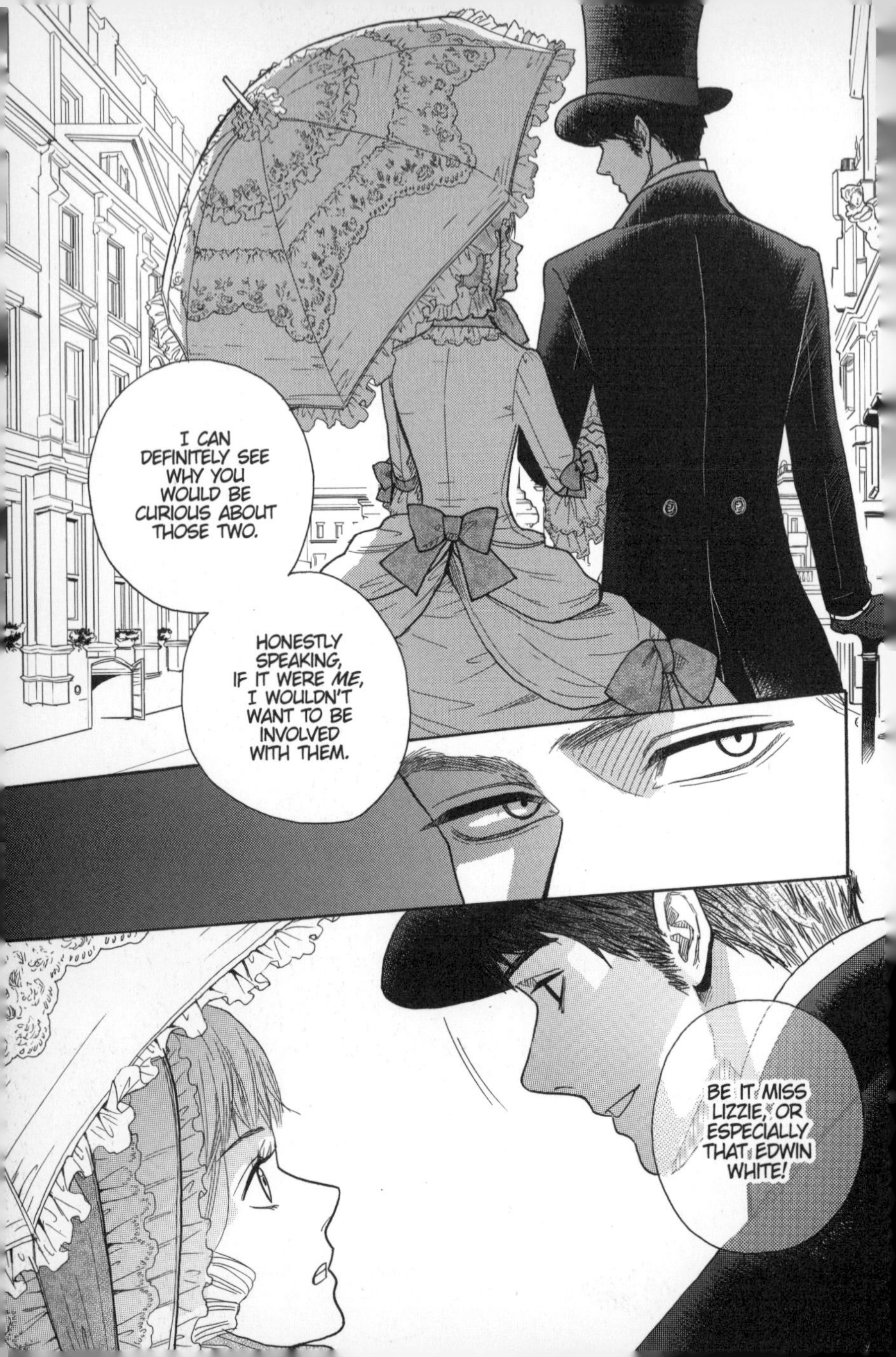
I CAN DEFINITELY SEE WHY YOU WOULD BE CURIOUS ABOUT THOSE TWO.
HONESTLY SPEAKING, IF IT WERE *ME*, I WOULDN'T WANT TO BE INVOLVED WITH THEM.
BE IT MISS LIZZIE, OR ESPECIALLY THAT EDWIN WHITE!

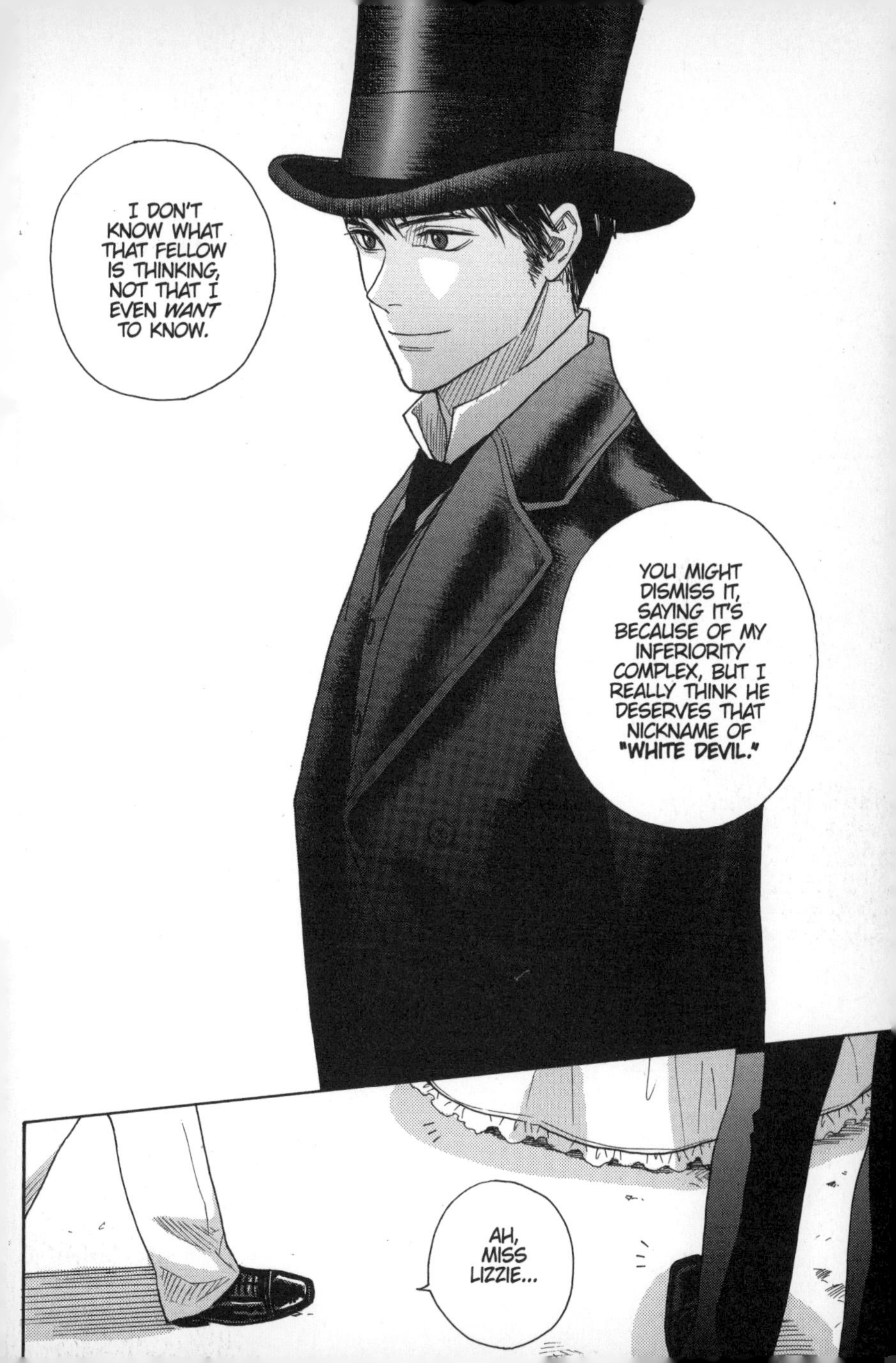
I DON'T KNOW WHAT THAT FELLOW IS THINKING, NOT THAT I EVEN *WANT* TO KNOW.
YOU MIGHT DISMISS IT, SAYING IT'S BECAUSE OF MY INFERIORITY COMPLEX, BUT I REALLY THINK HE DESERVES THAT NICKNAME OF **"WHITE DEVIL."**
AH, MISS LIZZIE...

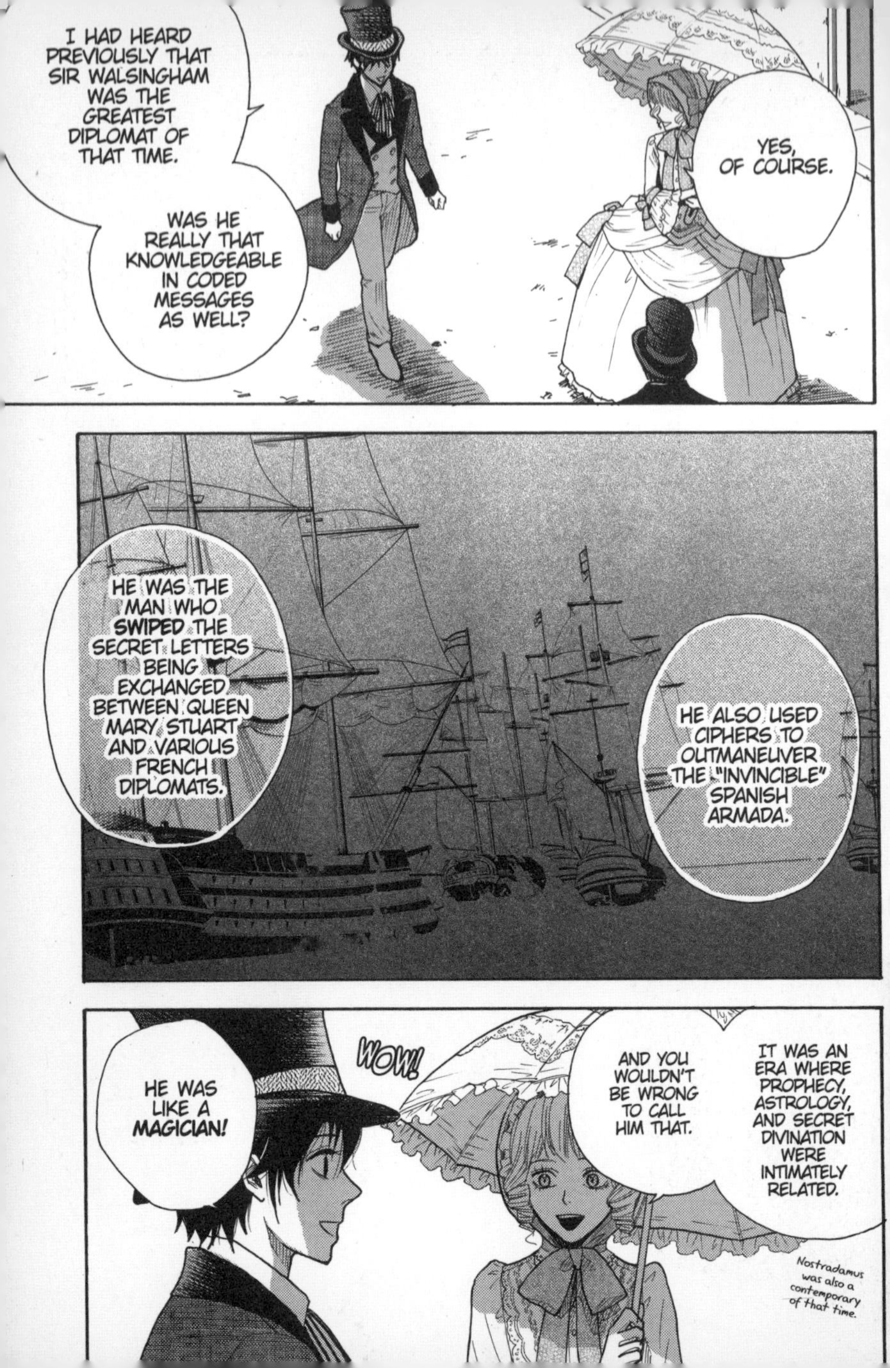
I HAD HEARD PREVIOUSLY THAT SIR WALSINGHAM WAS THE GREATEST DIPLOMAT OF THAT TIME.
WAS HE REALLY THAT KNOWLEDGEABLE IN CODED MESSAGES AS WELL?
YES, OF COURSE.
HE WAS THE MAN WHO **SWIPED** THE SECRET LETTERS BEING EXCHANGED BETWEEN QUEEN MARY STUART AND VARIOUS FRENCH DIPLOMATS.
HE ALSO USED CIPHERS TO OUTMANEUVER THE "INVINCIBLE" SPANISH ARMADA.
HE WAS LIKE A **MAGICIAN!**
WOW!
AND YOU WOULDN'T BE WRONG TO CALL HIM THAT.
IT WAS AN ERA WHERE PROPHECY, ASTROLOGY, AND SECRET DIVINATION WERE INTIMATELY RELATED.
Nostradamus was also a contemporary of that time.

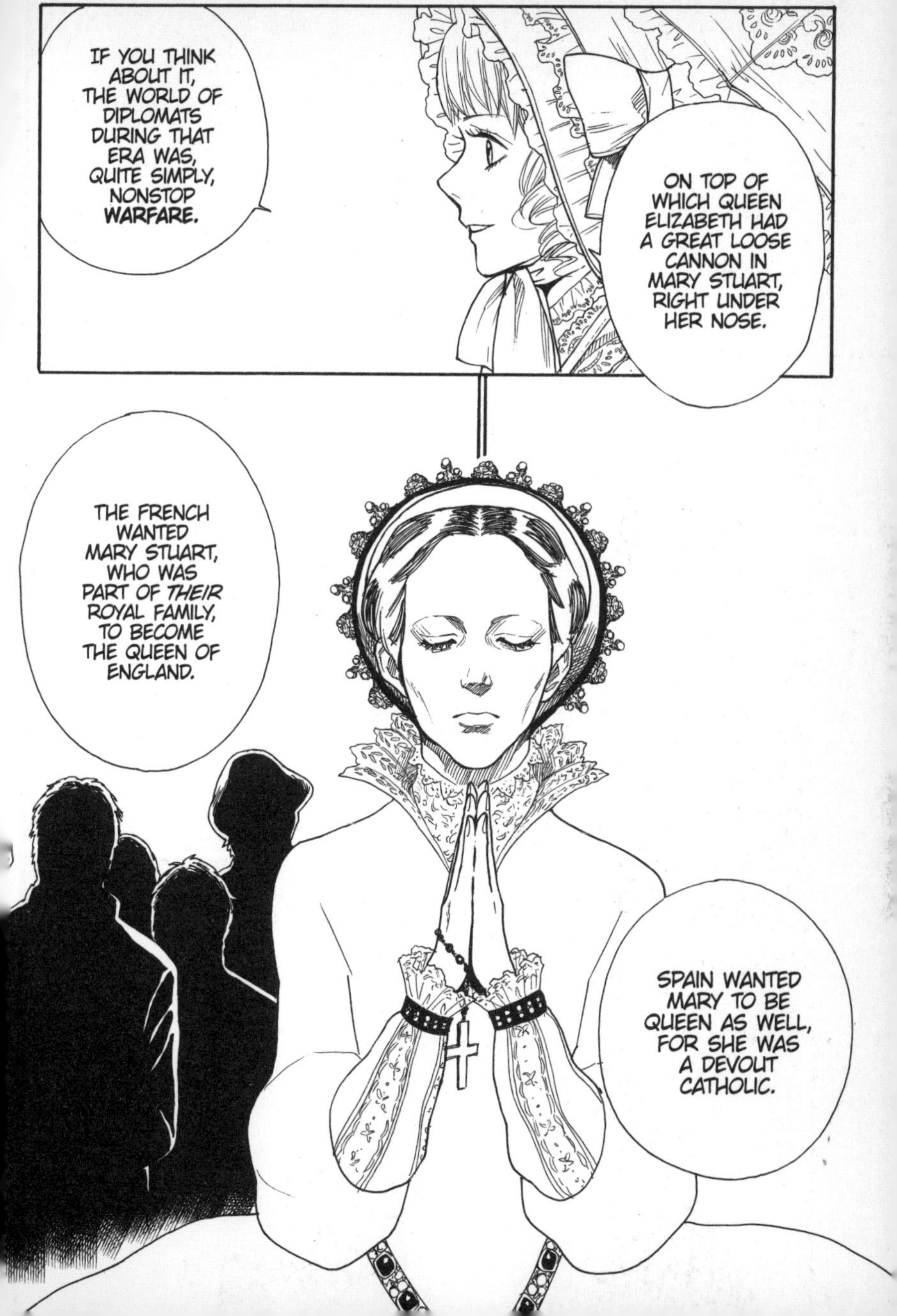
IF YOU THINK ABOUT IT, THE WORLD OF DIPLOMATS DURING THAT ERA WAS, QUITE SIMPLY, NONSTOP **WARFARE.**
ON TOP OF WHICH QUEEN ELIZABETH HAD A GREAT LOOSE CANNON IN MARY STUART, RIGHT UNDER HER NOSE.
THE FRENCH WANTED MARY STUART, WHO WAS PART OF *THEIR* ROYAL FAMILY, TO BECOME THE QUEEN OF ENGLAND.
SPAIN WANTED MARY TO BE QUEEN AS WELL, FOR SHE WAS A DEVOUT CATHOLIC.

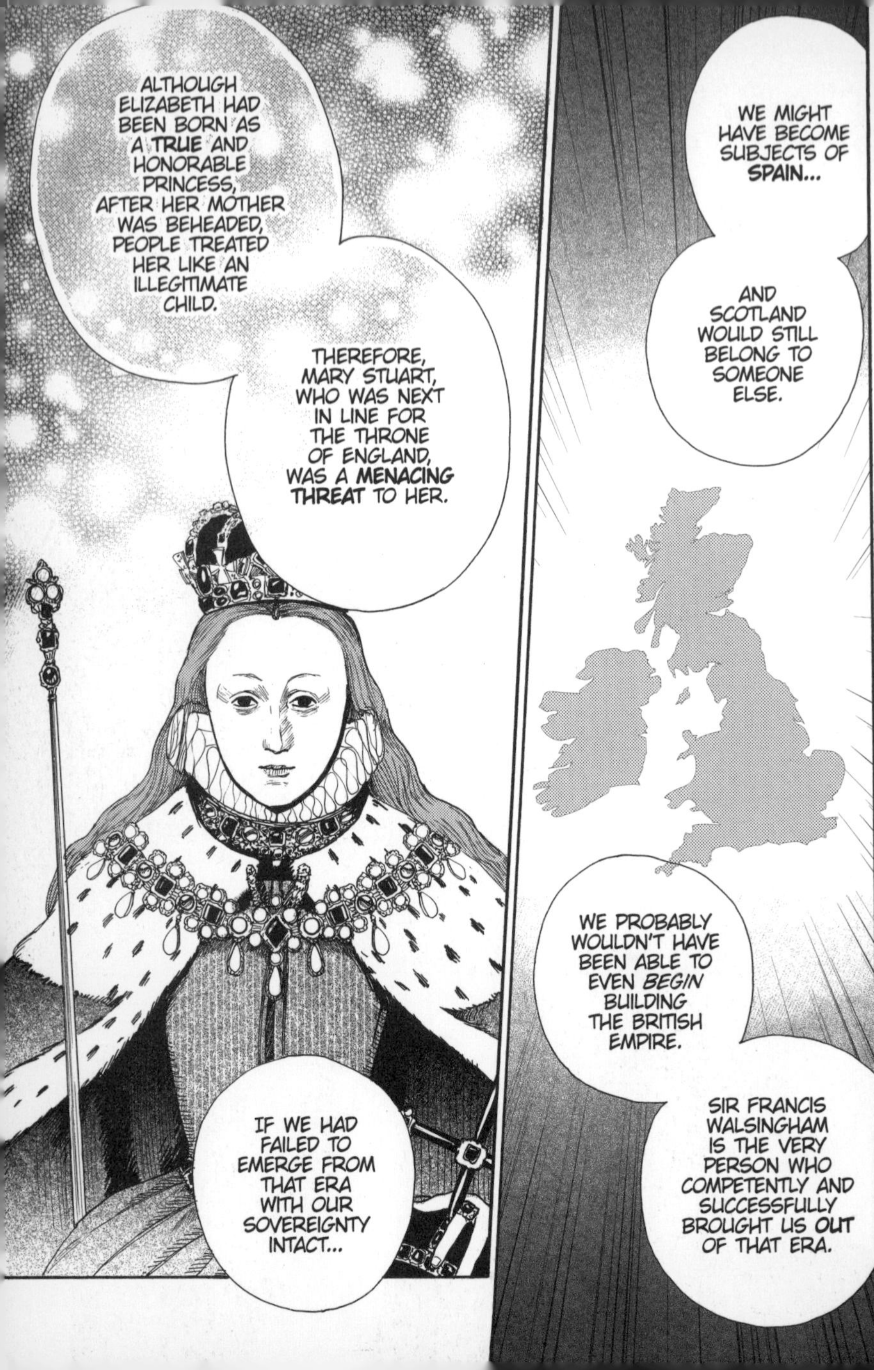
ALTHOUGH ELIZABETH HAD BEEN BORN AS A **TRUE** AND HONORABLE PRINCESS, AFTER HER MOTHER WAS BEHEADED, PEOPLE TREATED HER LIKE AN ILLEGITIMATE CHILD.
THEREFORE, MARY STUART, WHO WAS NEXT IN LINE FOR THE THRONE OF ENGLAND, WAS A **MENACING THREAT** TO HER.
IF WE HAD FAILED TO EMERGE FROM THAT ERA WITH OUR SOVEREIGNTY INTACT...
WE MIGHT HAVE BECOME SUBJECTS OF **SPAIN...**
AND SCOTLAND WOULD STILL BELONG TO SOMEONE ELSE.
WE PROBABLY WOULDN'T HAVE BEEN ABLE TO EVEN *BEGIN* BUILDING THE BRITISH EMPIRE.
SIR FRANCIS WALSINGHAM IS THE VERY PERSON WHO COMPETENTLY AND SUCCESSFULLY BROUGHT US **OUT** OF THAT ERA.

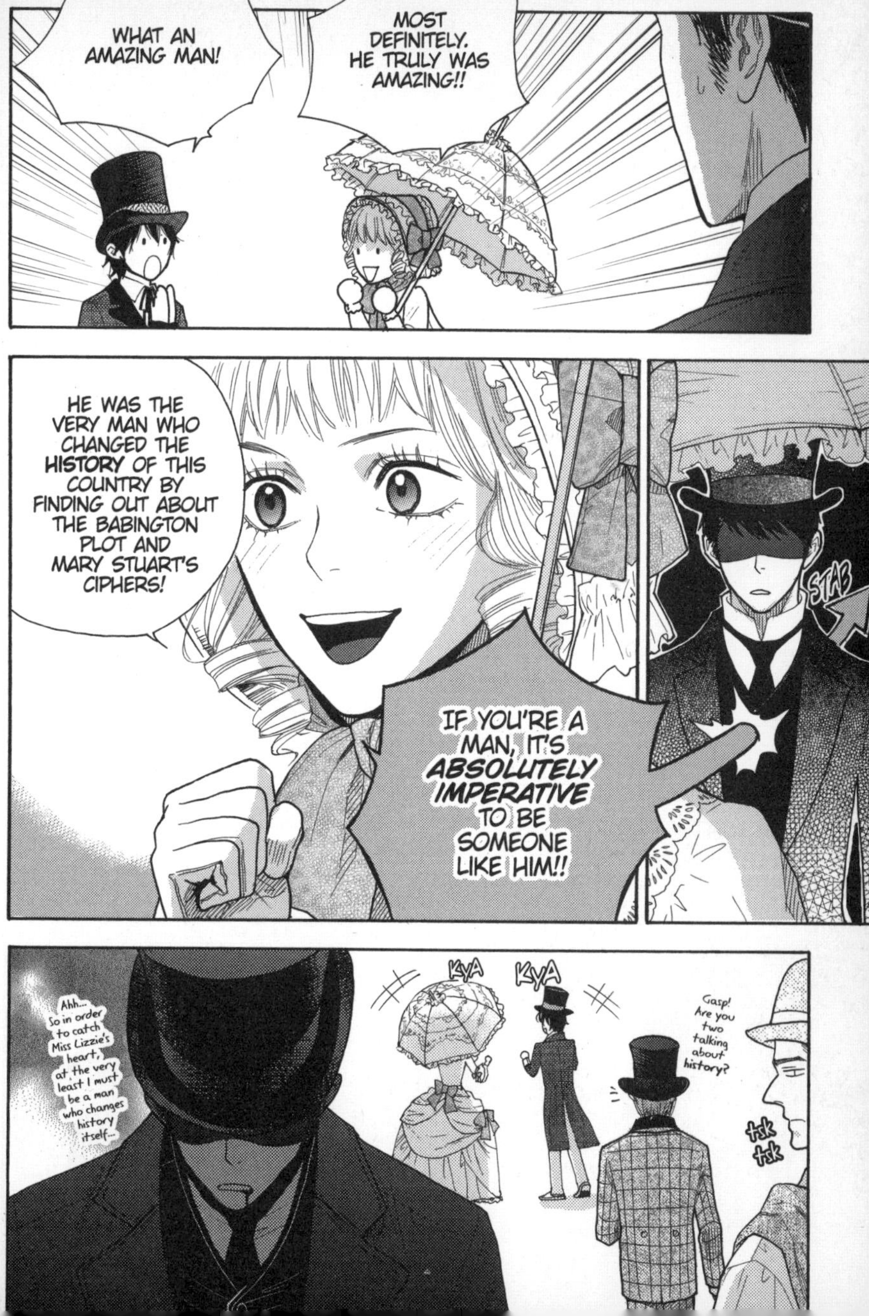
WHAT AN AMAZING MAN!
MOST DEFINITELY. HE TRULY WAS AMAZING!!
HE WAS THE VERY MAN WHO CHANGED THE **HISTORY** OF THIS COUNTRY BY FINDING OUT ABOUT THE BABINGTON PLOT AND MARY STUART'S CIPHERS!
IF YOU'RE A MAN, IT'S ***ABSOLUTELY IMPERATIVE*** TO BE SOMEONE LIKE HIM!!
STAB
Ahh... So in order to catch Miss Lizzie's heart, at the very least I must be a man who changes history itself...
KYA KYA
Gasp! Are you two talking about **history**?
tsk tsk

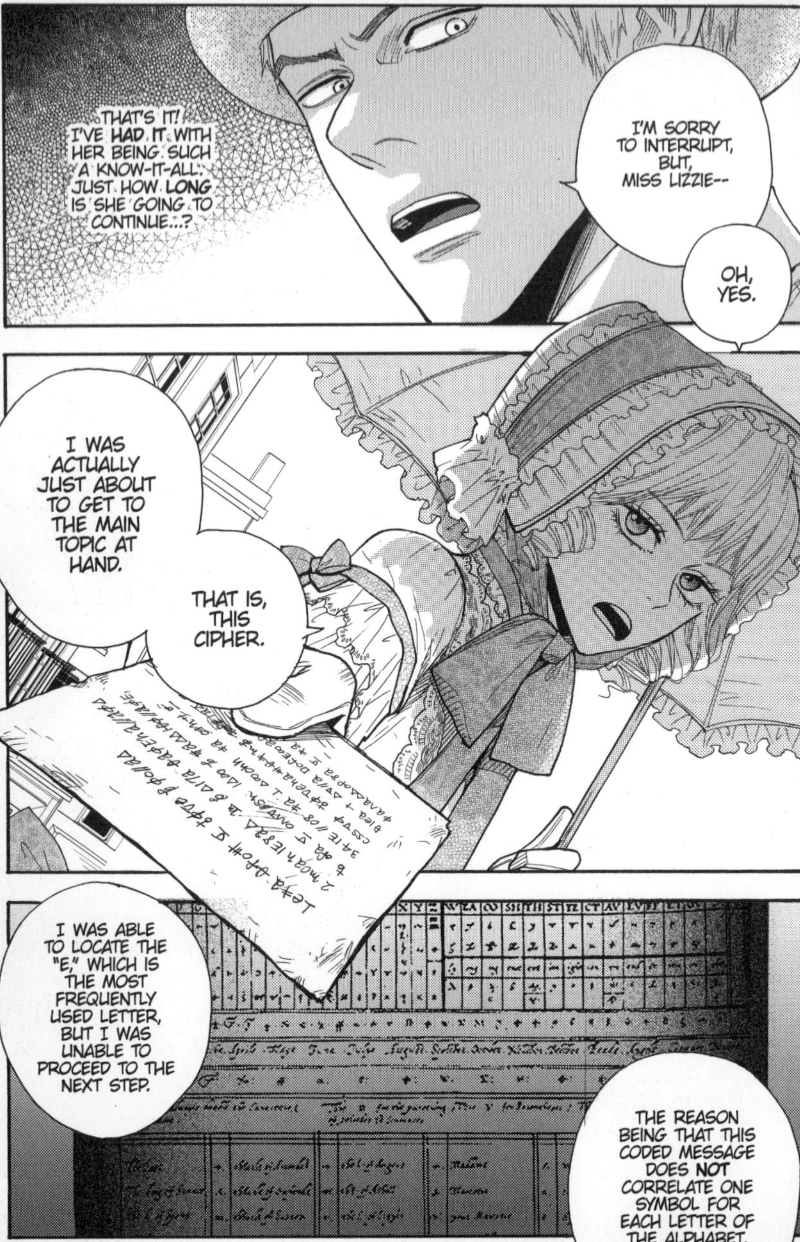
THAT'S IT! I'VE HAD IT WITH HER BEING SUCH A KNOW-IT-ALL. JUST HOW LONG IS SHE GOING TO CONTINUE...?
I'M SORRY TO INTERRUPT, BUT, MISS LIZZIE--
OH, YES.
I WAS ACTUALLY JUST ABOUT TO GET TO THE MAIN TOPIC AT HAND.
THAT IS, THIS CIPHER.
I WAS ABLE TO LOCATE THE "E," WHICH IS THE MOST FREQUENTLY USED LETTER, BUT I WAS UNABLE TO PROCEED TO THE NEXT STEP.
THE REASON BEING THAT THIS CODED MESSAGE DOES NOT CORRELATE ONE SYMBOL FOR EACH LETTER OF THE ALPHABET.

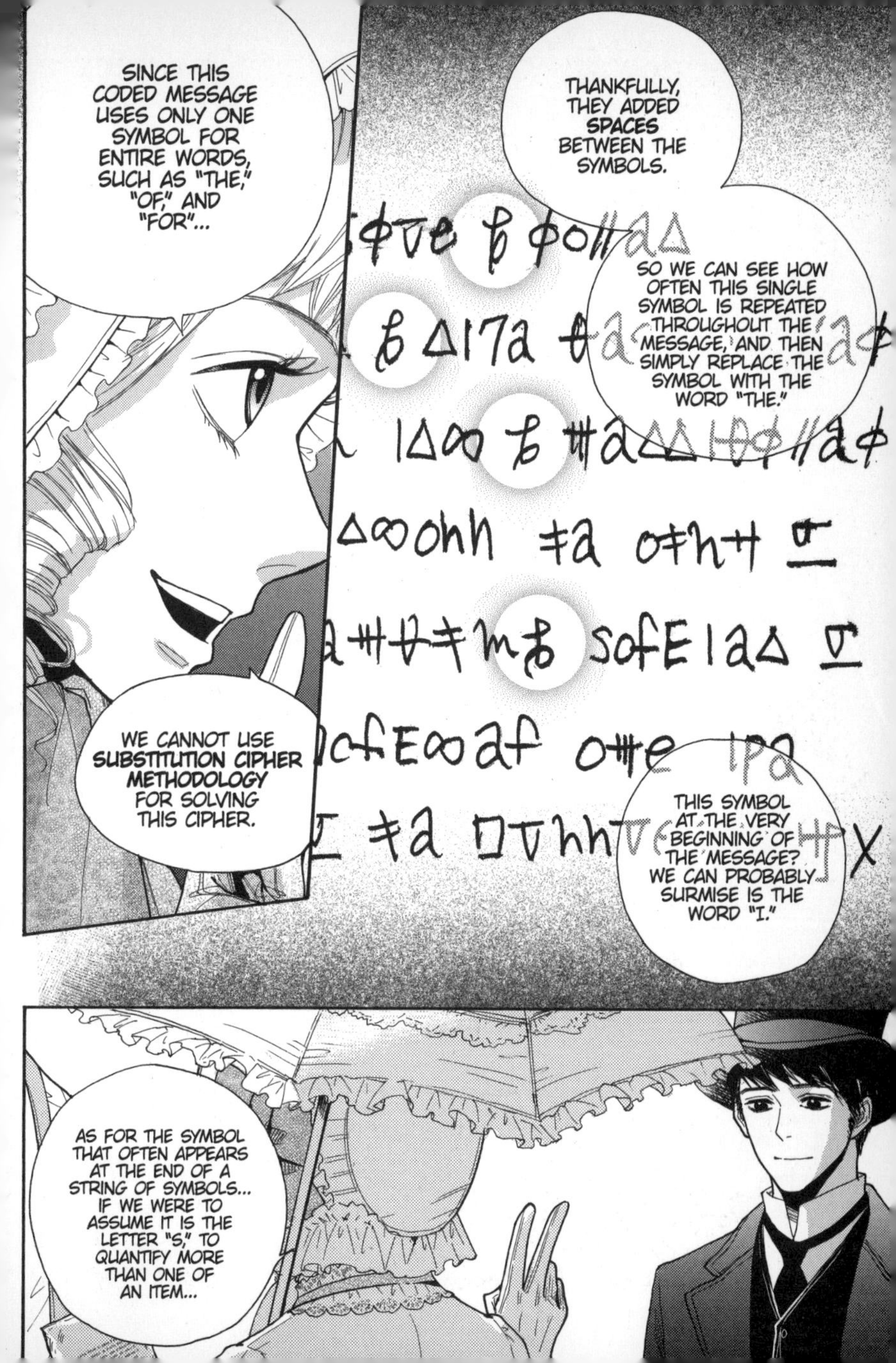

SINCE THIS CODED MESSAGE USES ONLY ONE SYMBOL FOR ENTIRE WORDS, SUCH AS "THE," "OF," AND "FOR"...
WE CANNOT USE **SUBSTITUTION CIPHER METHODOLOGY** FOR SOLVING THIS CIPHER.
THANKFULLY, THEY ADDED **SPACES** BETWEEN THE SYMBOLS.
SO WE CAN SEE HOW OFTEN THIS SINGLE SYMBOL IS REPEATED THROUGHOUT THE MESSAGE, AND THEN SIMPLY REPLACE THE SYMBOL WITH THE WORD "THE."
THIS SYMBOL AT THE VERY BEGINNING OF THE MESSAGE? WE CAN PROBABLY SURMISE IS THE WORD "I."
AS FOR THE SYMBOL THAT OFTEN APPEARS AT THE END OF A STRING OF SYMBOLS... IF WE WERE TO ASSUME IT IS THE LETTER "S," TO QUANTIFY MORE THAN ONE OF AN ITEM...

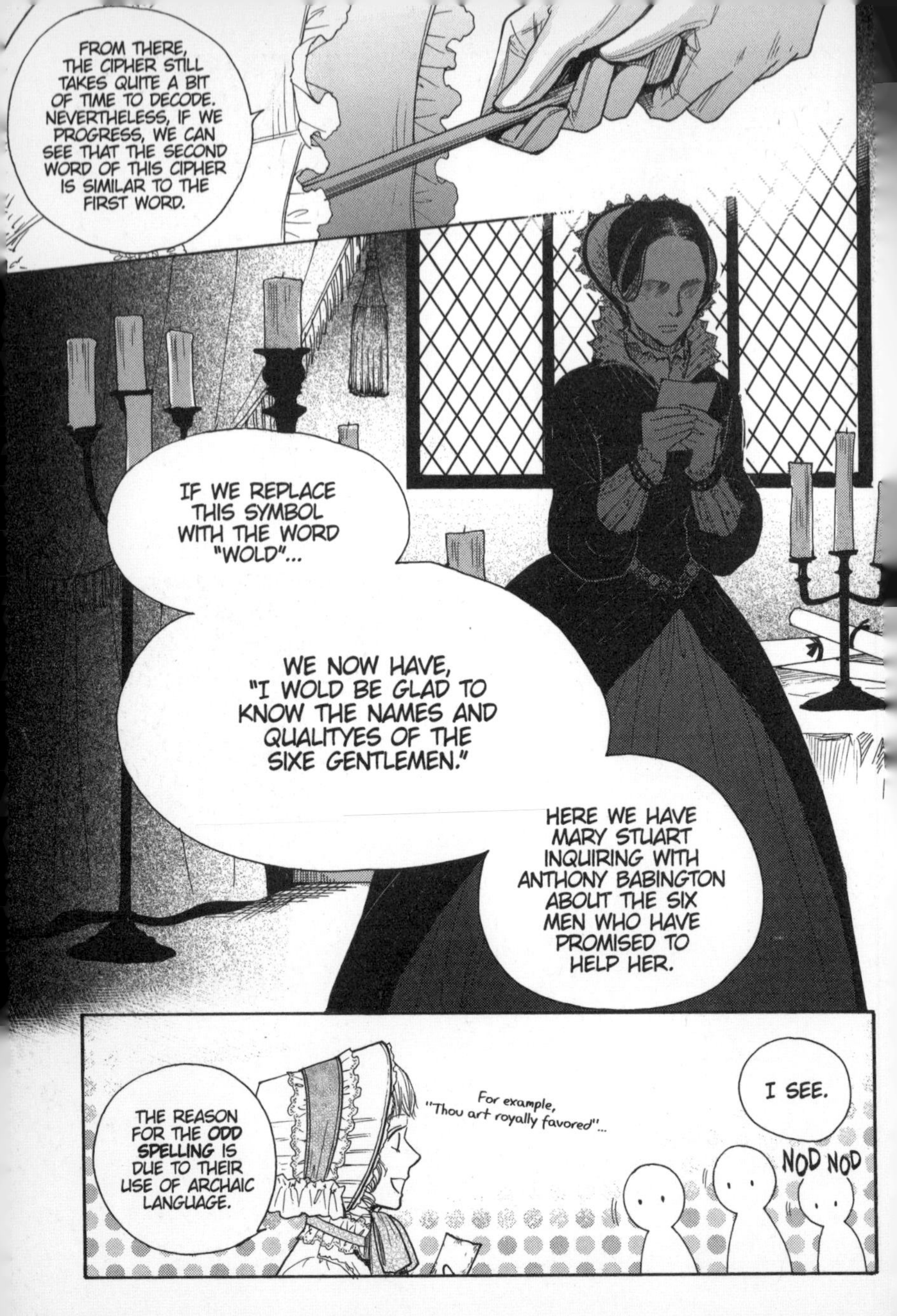
FROM THERE, THE CIPHER STILL TAKES QUITE A BIT OF TIME TO DECODE. NEVERTHELESS, IF WE PROGRESS, WE CAN SEE THAT THE SECOND WORD OF THIS CIPHER IS SIMILAR TO THE FIRST WORD.
IF WE REPLACE THIS SYMBOL WITH THE WORD "WOLD"...
WE NOW HAVE, "I WOLD BE GLAD TO KNOW THE NAMES AND QUALITYES OF THE SIXE GENTLEMEN."
HERE WE HAVE MARY STUART INQUIRING WITH ANTHONY BABINGTON ABOUT THE SIX MEN WHO HAVE PROMISED TO HELP HER.
THE REASON FOR THE ODD SPELLING IS DUE TO THEIR USE OF ARCHAIC LANGUAGE.
For example, "Thou art royally favored"...
I SEE.
NOD NOD

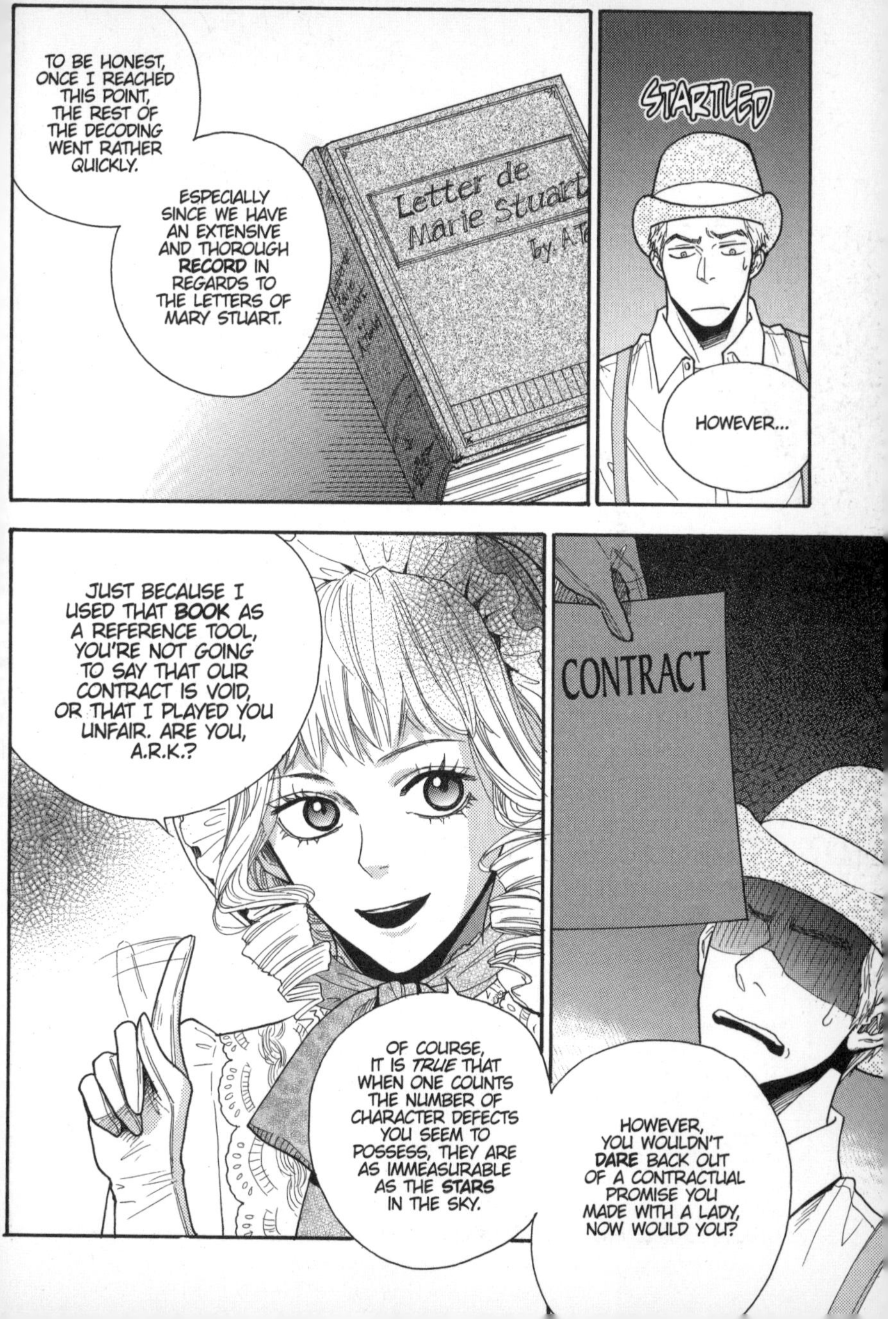
TO BE HONEST, ONCE I REACHED THIS POINT, THE REST OF THE DECODING WENT RATHER QUICKLY.
ESPECIALLY SINCE WE HAVE AN EXTENSIVE AND THOROUGH **RECORD** IN REGARDS TO THE LETTERS OF MARY STUART.
Letter de Marie Stuart
by. A.T
STARTLED
HOWEVER...
JUST BECAUSE I USED THAT **BOOK** AS A REFERENCE TOOL, YOU'RE NOT GOING TO SAY THAT OUR CONTRACT IS VOID, OR THAT I PLAYED YOU UNFAIR. ARE YOU, A.R.K.?
CONTRACT
OF COURSE, IT IS *TRUE* THAT WHEN ONE COUNTS THE NUMBER OF CHARACTER DEFECTS YOU SEEM TO POSSESS, THEY ARE AS IMMEASURABLE AS THE **STARS** IN THE SKY.
HOWEVER, YOU WOULDN'T **DARE** BACK OUT OF A CONTRACTUAL PROMISE YOU MADE WITH A LADY, NOW WOULD YOU?

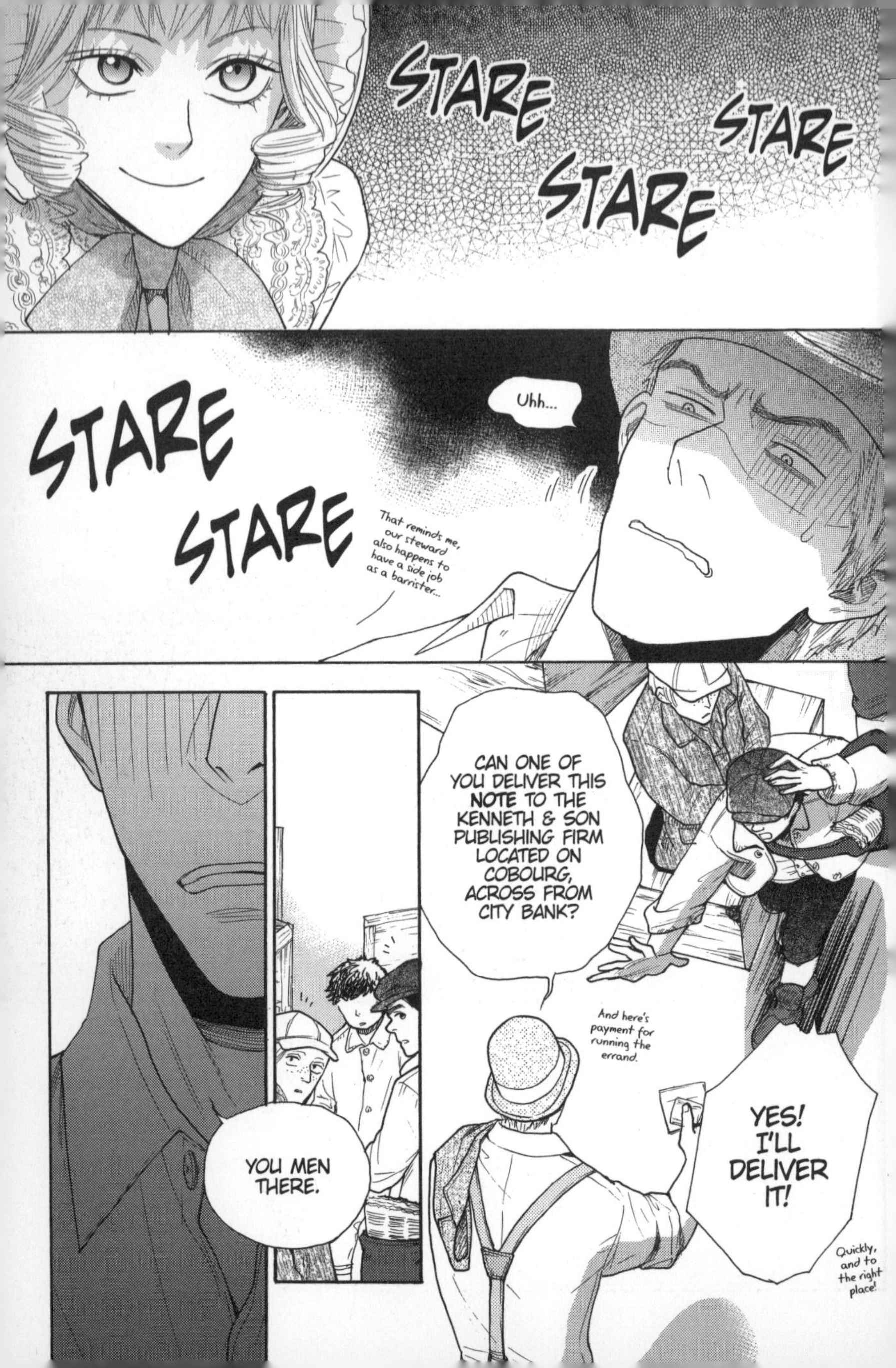
STARE
STARE
STARE
STARE
STARE
Uhh...
That reminds me, our steward also happens to have a side job as a barrister...
YOU MEN THERE.
CAN ONE OF YOU DELIVER THIS NOTE TO THE KENNETH & SON PUBLISHING FIRM LOCATED ON COBOURG, ACROSS FROM CITY BANK?
And here's payment for running the errand.
YES! I'LL DELIVER IT!
Quickly, and to the right place!

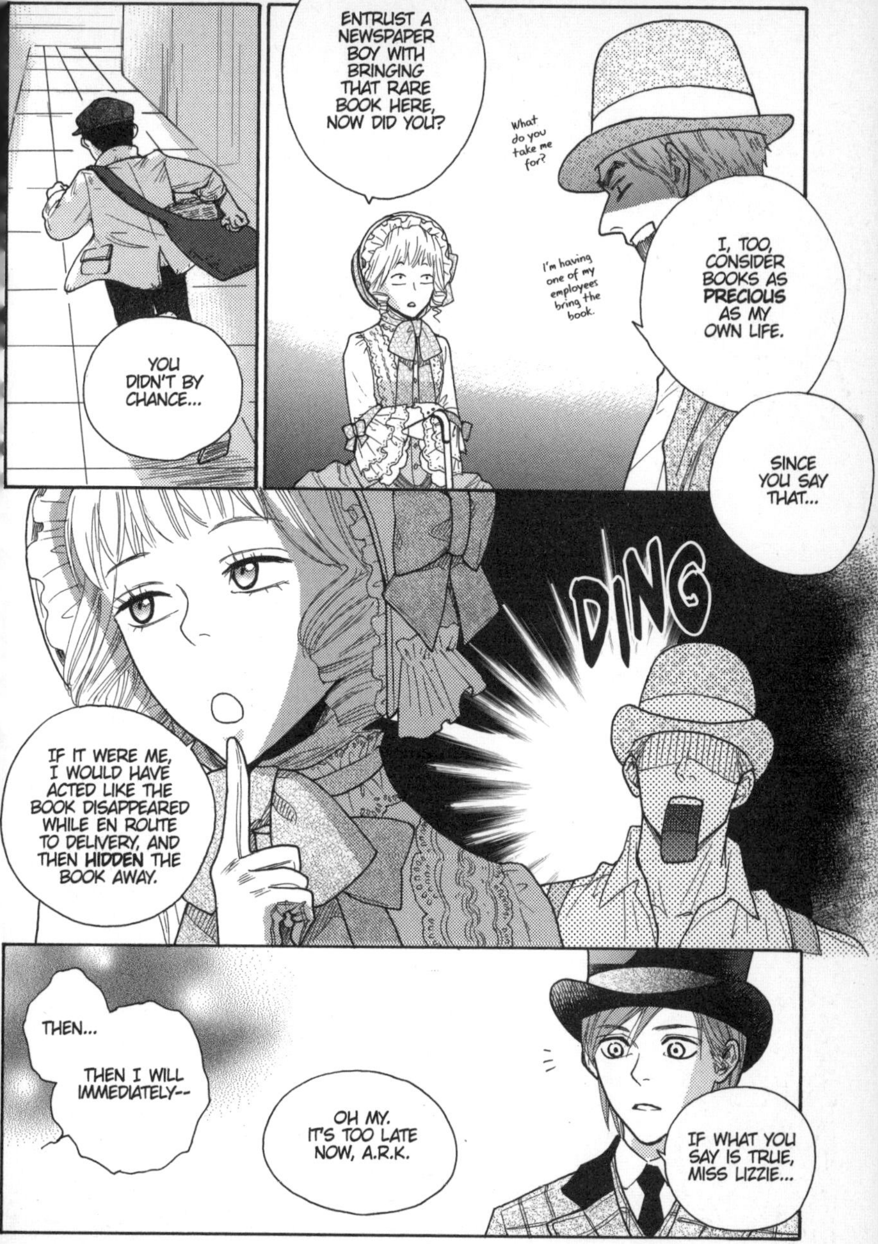
YOU DIDN'T BY CHANCE...
ENTRUST A NEWSPAPER BOY WITH BRINGING THAT RARE BOOK HERE, NOW DID YOU?
What do you take me for?
I'm having one of my employees bring the book.
I, TOO, CONSIDER BOOKS AS **PRECIOUS** AS MY OWN LIFE.
SINCE YOU SAY THAT...
IF IT WERE ME, I WOULD HAVE ACTED LIKE THE BOOK DISAPPEARED WHILE EN ROUTE TO DELIVERY, AND THEN **HIDDEN** THE BOOK AWAY.
DING
THEN...
THEN I WILL IMMEDIATELY--
OH MY. IT'S TOO LATE NOW, A.R.K.
IF WHAT YOU SAY IS TRUE, MISS LIZZIE...

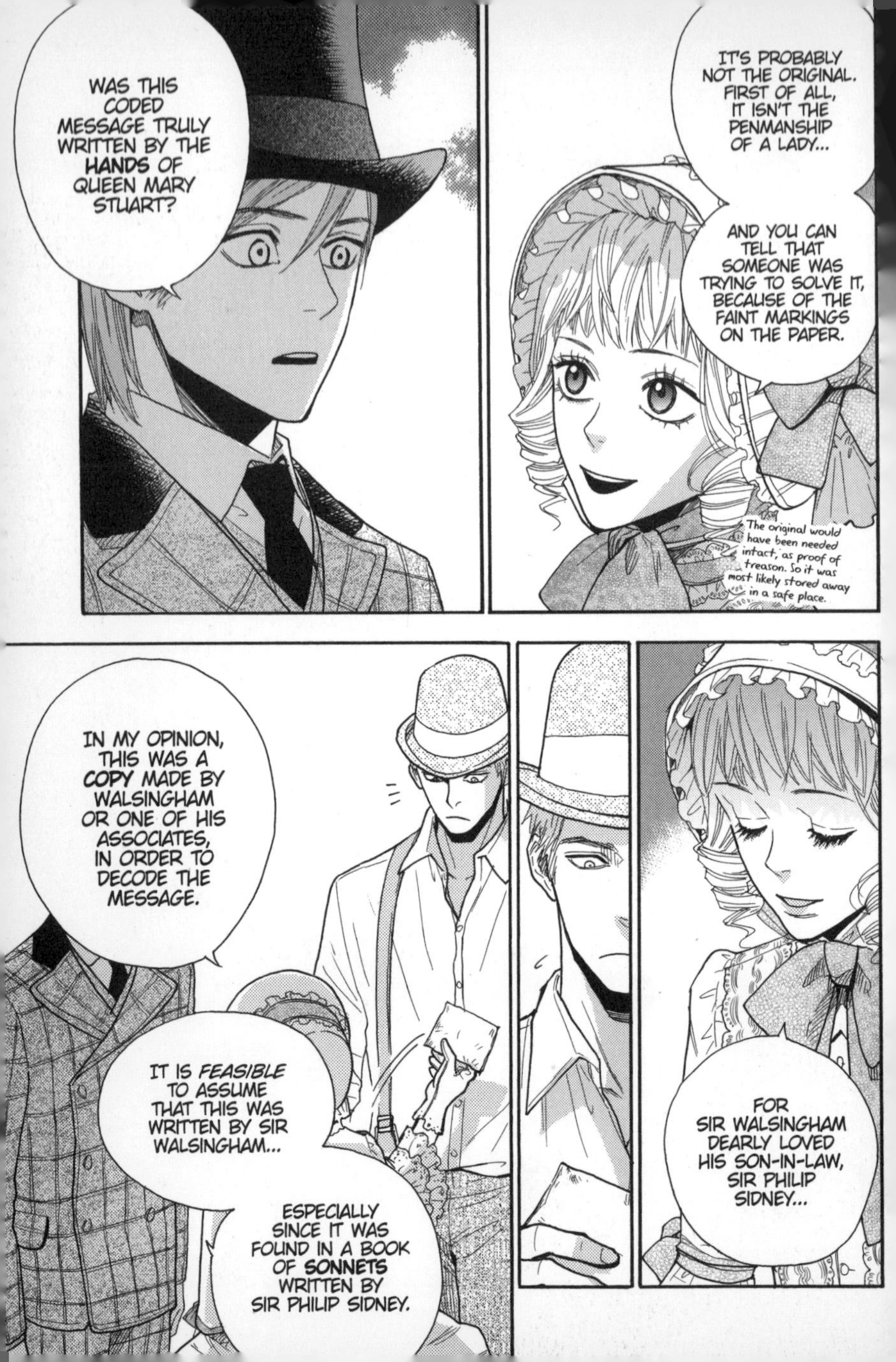
WAS THIS CODED MESSAGE TRULY WRITTEN BY THE HANDS OF QUEEN MARY STUART?
IT'S PROBABLY NOT THE ORIGINAL. FIRST OF ALL, IT ISN'T THE PENMANSHIP OF A LADY...
AND YOU CAN TELL THAT SOMEONE WAS TRYING TO SOLVE IT, BECAUSE OF THE FAINT MARKINGS ON THE PAPER.
The original would have been needed intact, as proof of treason. So it was most likely stored away in a safe place.
IN MY OPINION, THIS WAS A COPY MADE BY WALSINGHAM OR ONE OF HIS ASSOCIATES, IN ORDER TO DECODE THE MESSAGE.
IT IS FEASIBLE TO ASSUME THAT THIS WAS WRITTEN BY SIR WALSINGHAM...
ESPECIALLY SINCE IT WAS FOUND IN A BOOK OF SONNETS WRITTEN BY SIR PHILIP SIDNEY.
FOR SIR WALSINGHAM DEARLY LOVED HIS SON-IN-LAW, SIR PHILIP SIDNEY...

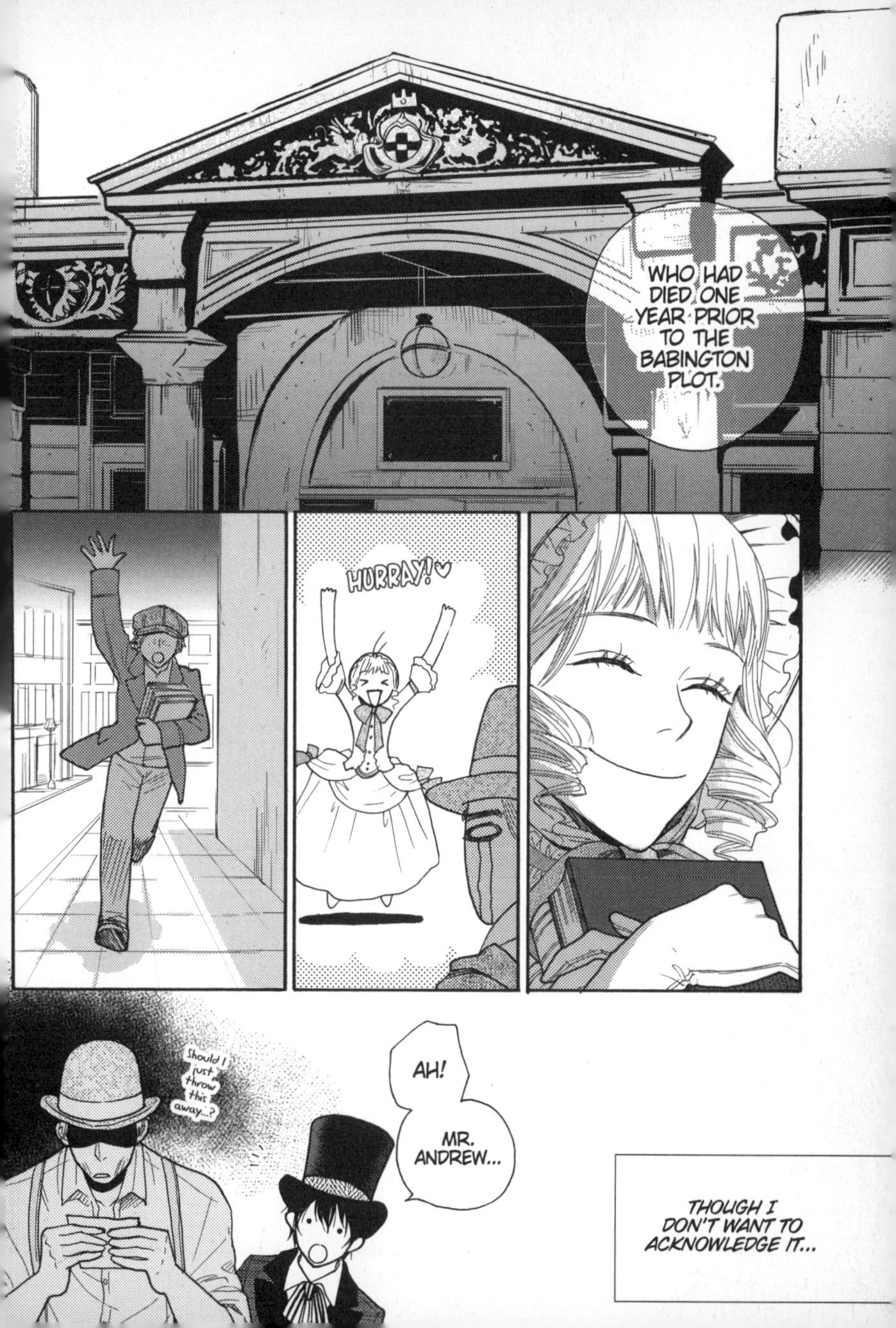
WHO HAD DIED ONE YEAR PRIOR TO THE BABINGTON PLOT.
HURRAY!♥
Should I just throw this away...?
AH!
MR. ANDREW...
THOUGH I DON'T WANT TO ACKNOWLEDGE IT...

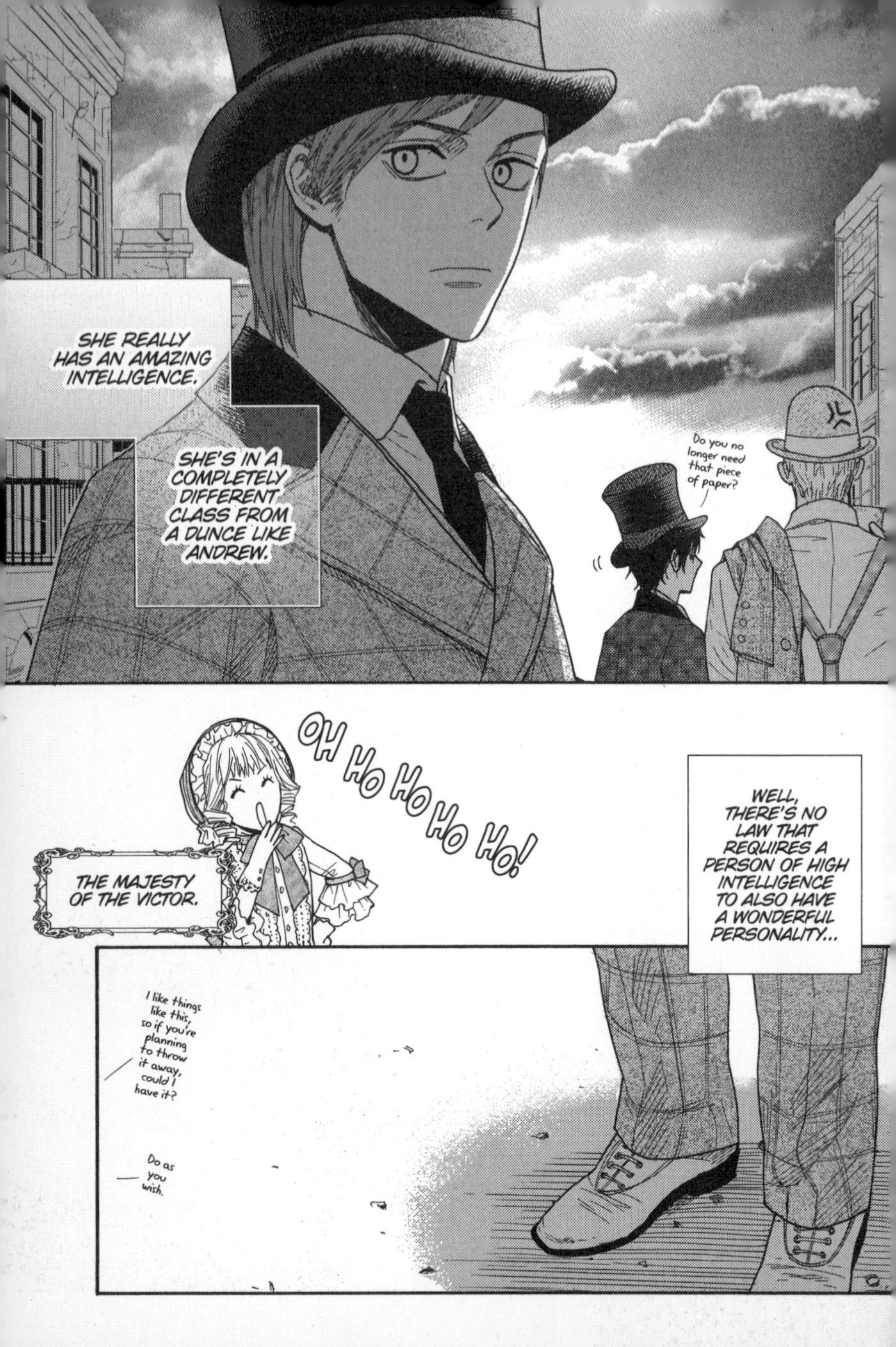
SHE REALLY HAS AN AMAZING INTELLIGENCE.
SHE'S IN A COMPLETELY DIFFERENT CLASS FROM A DUNCE LIKE ANDREW.
Do you no longer need that piece of paper?
THE MAJESTY OF THE VICTOR.
OH HO HO HO HO HO!
WELL, THERE'S NO LAW THAT REQUIRES A PERSON OF HIGH INTELLIGENCE TO ALSO HAVE A WONDERFUL PERSONALITY...
I like things like this, so if you're planning to throw it away, could I have it?
Do as you wish.

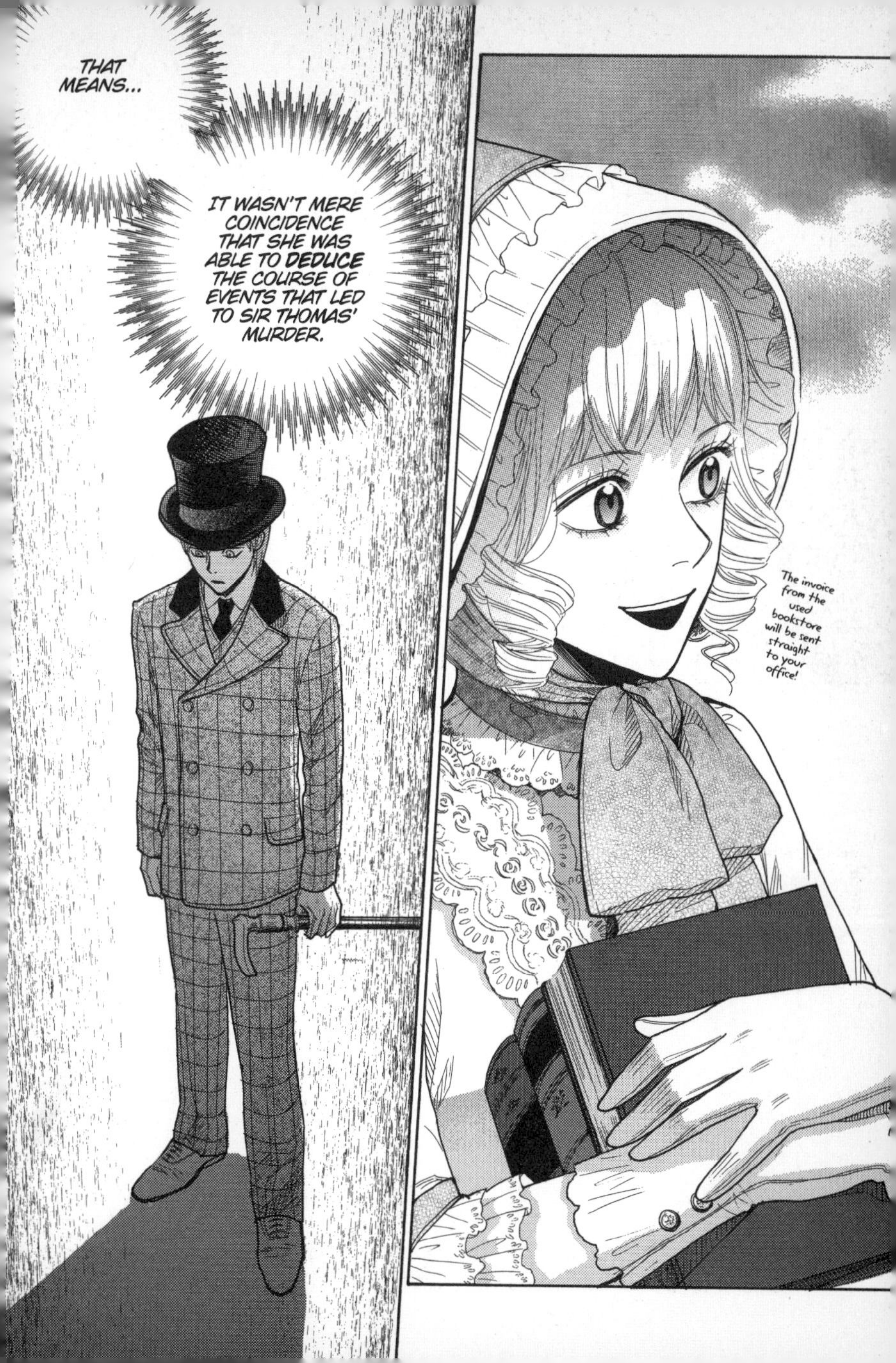
THAT MEANS...
IT WASN'T MERE COINCIDENCE THAT SHE WAS ABLE TO DEDUCE THE COURSE OF EVENTS THAT LED TO SIR THOMAS' MURDER.
The invoice from the used bookstore will be sent straight to your office!

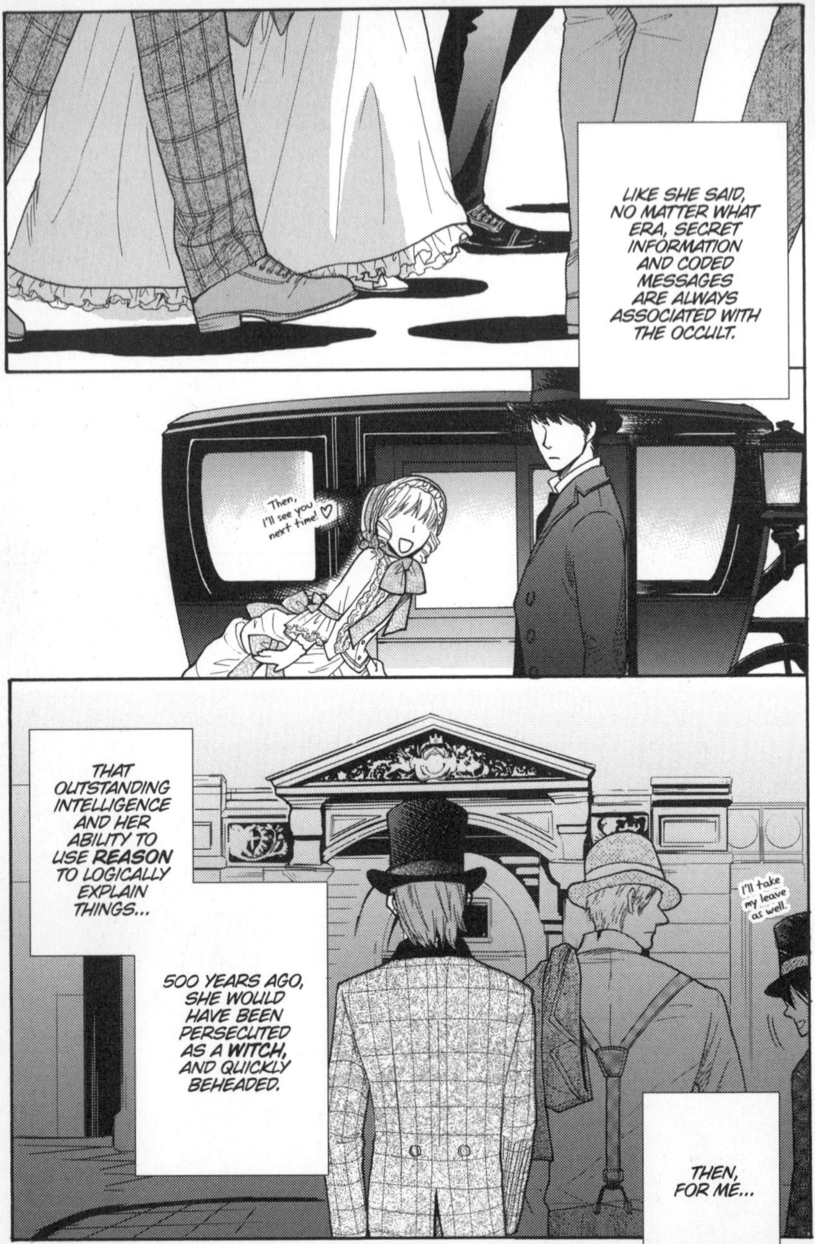
LIKE SHE SAID, NO MATTER WHAT ERA, SECRET INFORMATION AND CODED MESSAGES ARE ALWAYS ASSOCIATED WITH THE OCCULT.
Then, I'll see you next time! ♡
THAT OUTSTANDING INTELLIGENCE AND HER ABILITY TO USE REASON TO LOGICALLY EXPLAIN THINGS...
500 YEARS AGO, SHE WOULD HAVE BEEN PERSECUTED AS A WITCH, AND QUICKLY BEHEADED.
I'll take my leave as well.
THEN, FOR ME...

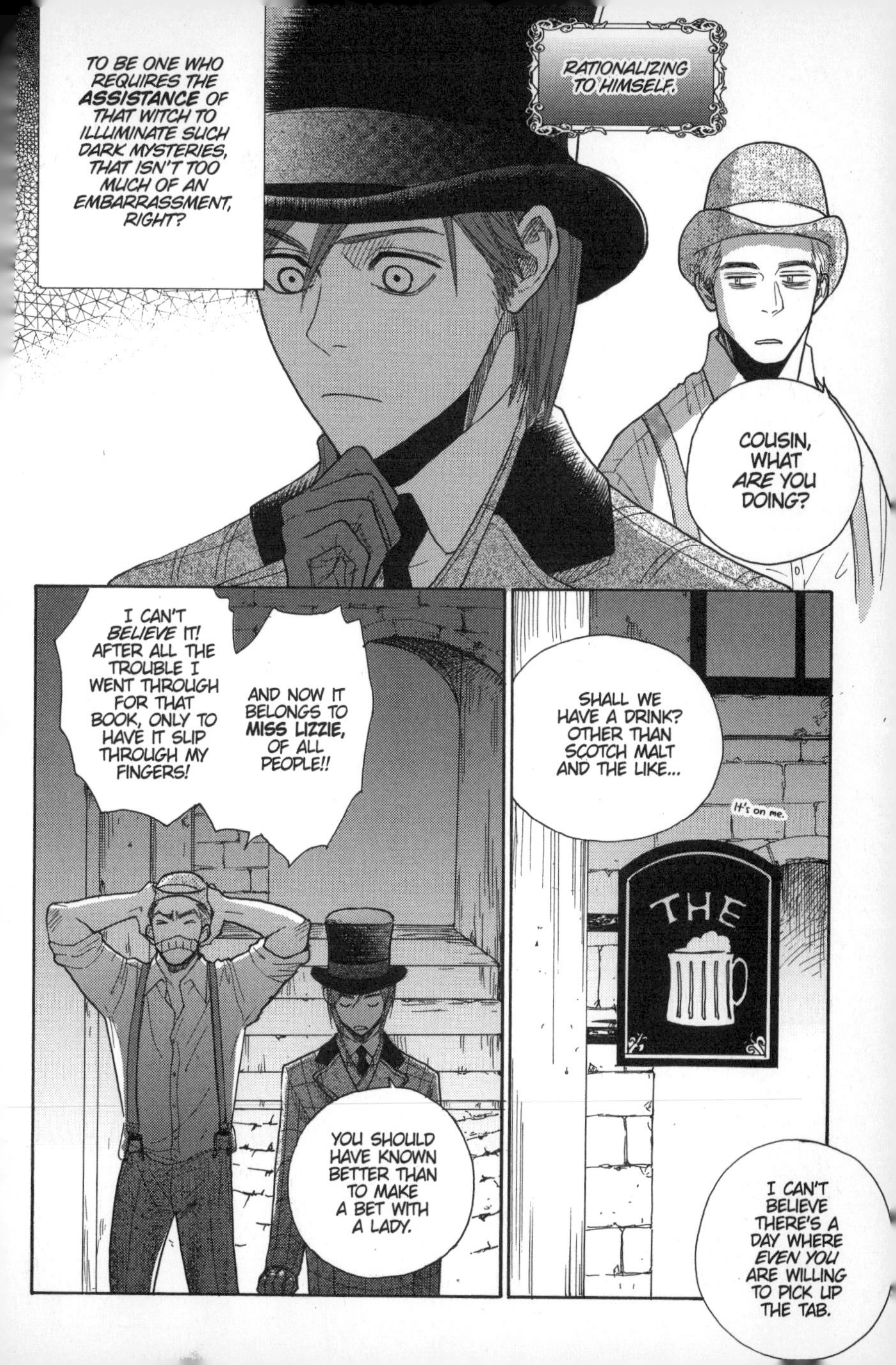

TO BE ONE WHO REQUIRES THE **ASSISTANCE** OF THAT WITCH TO ILLUMINATE SUCH DARK MYSTERIES, THAT ISN'T TOO MUCH OF AN EMBARRASSMENT, RIGHT?
RATIONALIZING TO HIMSELF.
COUSIN, WHAT *ARE* YOU DOING?
I CAN'T *BELIEVE* IT! AFTER ALL THE TROUBLE I WENT THROUGH FOR THAT BOOK, ONLY TO HAVE IT SLIP THROUGH MY FINGERS!
AND NOW IT BELONGS TO **MISS LIZZIE**, OF ALL PEOPLE!!
YOU SHOULD HAVE KNOWN BETTER THAN TO MAKE A BET WITH A LADY.
SHALL WE HAVE A DRINK? OTHER THAN SCOTCH MALT AND THE LIKE...
It's on me.
THE
I CAN'T BELIEVE THERE'S A DAY WHERE *EVEN YOU* ARE WILLING TO PICK UP THE TAB.

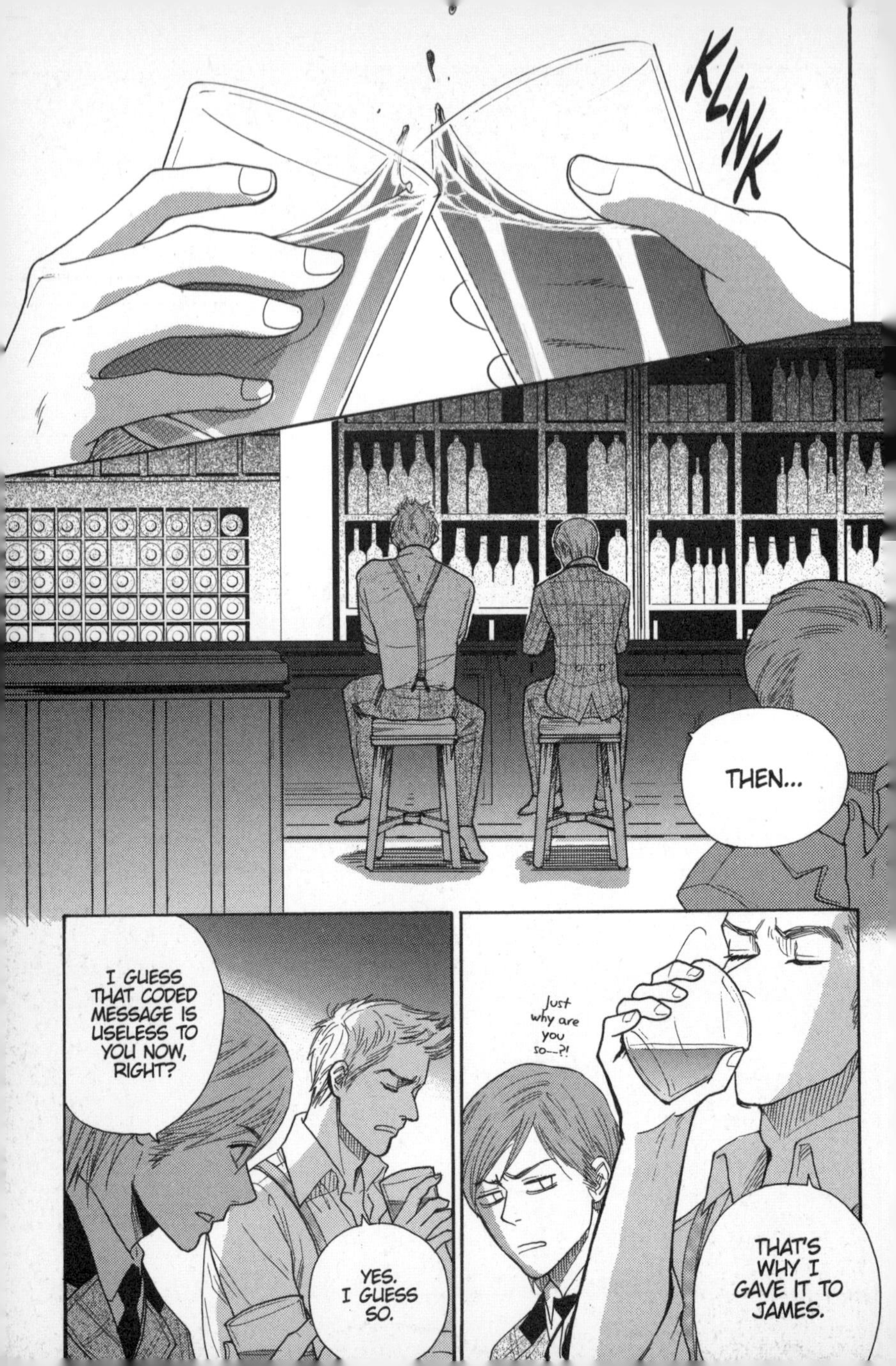
KLINK
THEN...
I GUESS THAT CODED MESSAGE IS USELESS TO YOU NOW, RIGHT?
YES. I GUESS SO.
Just why are you so--?!
THAT'S WHY I GAVE IT TO JAMES.

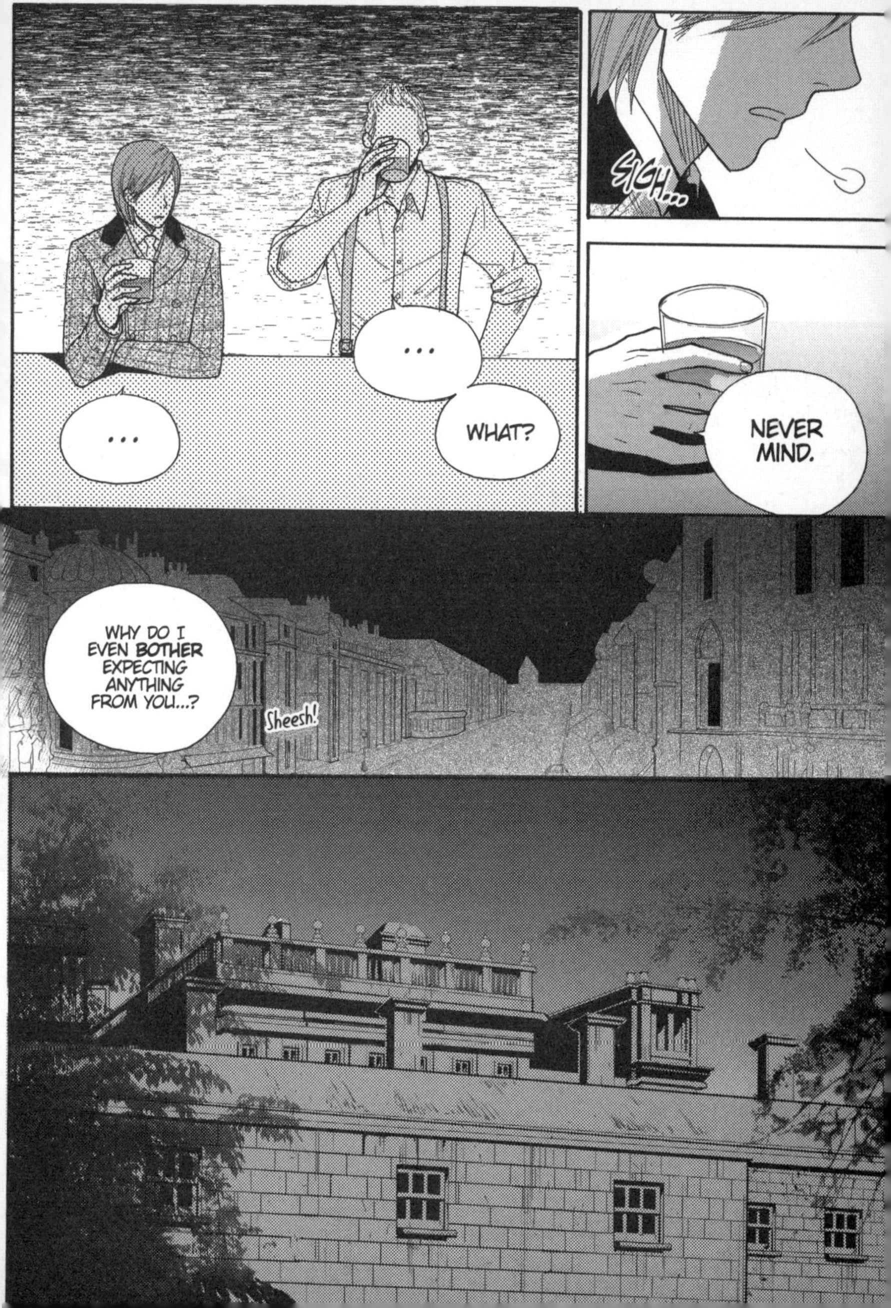
...
...
WHAT?
SIGH...
NEVER MIND.
WHY DO I EVEN BOTHER EXPECTING ANYTHING FROM YOU...?
Sheesh!

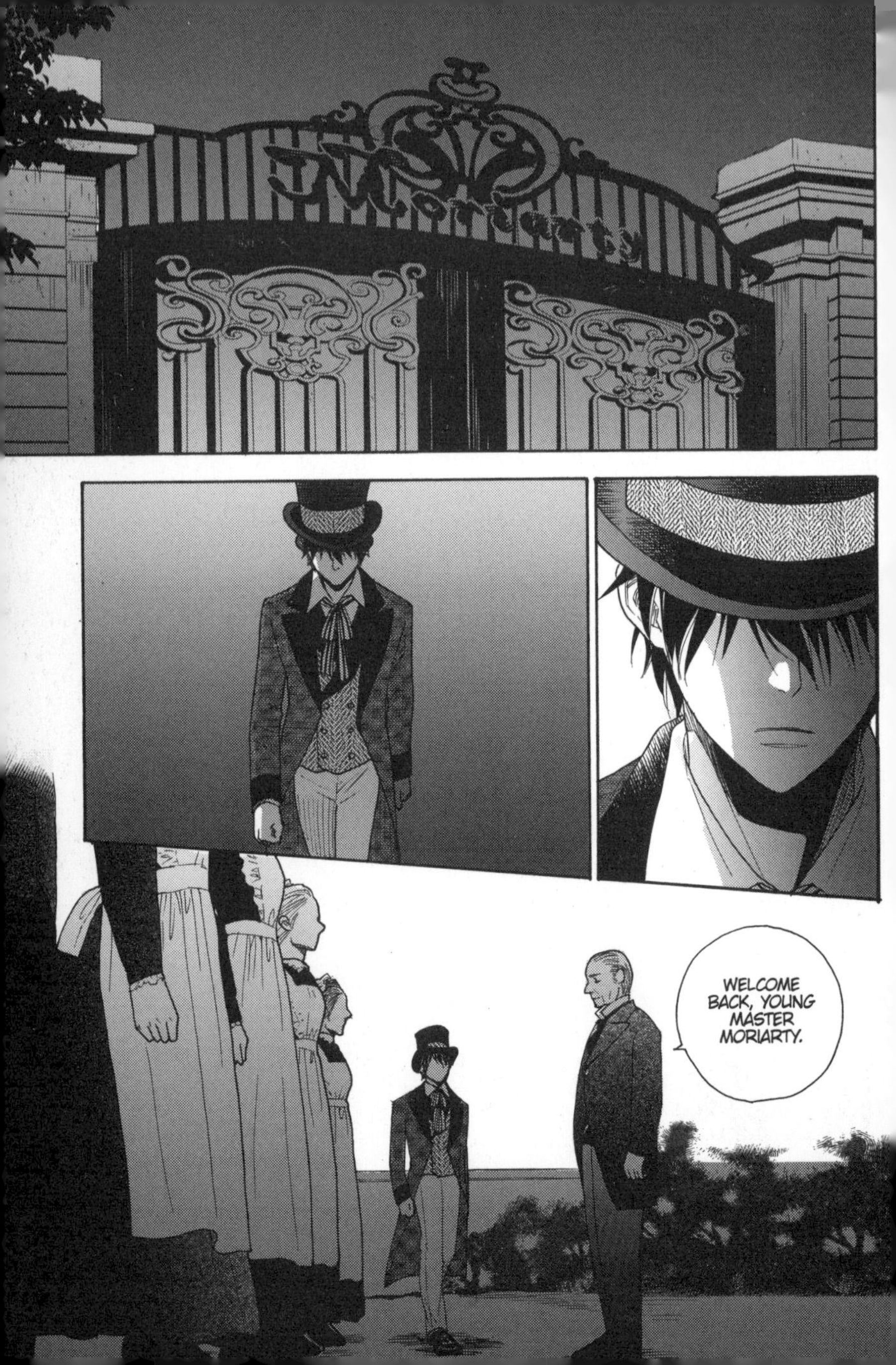
WELCOME BACK, YOUNG MASTER MORIARTY.

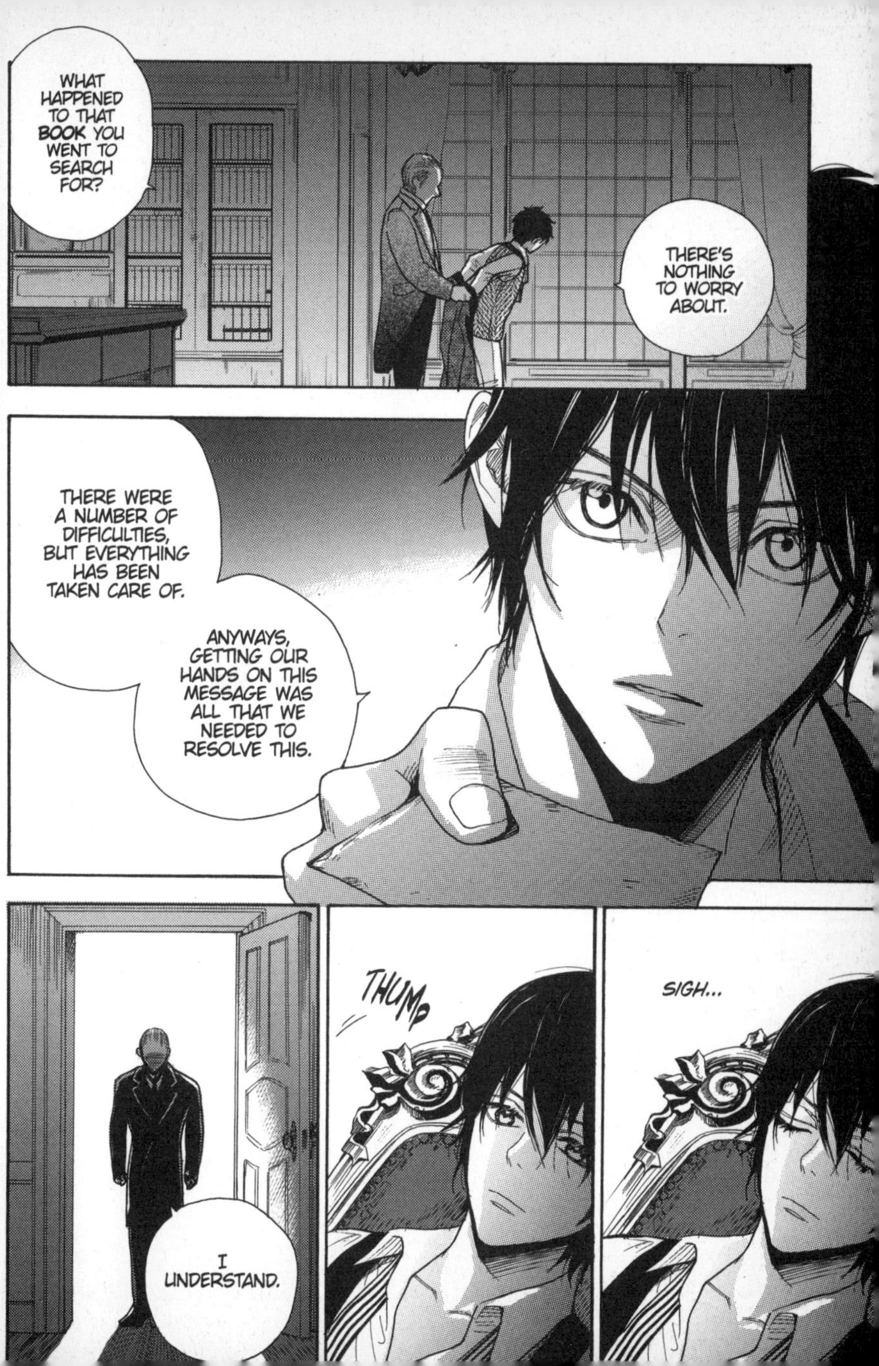
WHAT HAPPENED TO THAT BOOK YOU WENT TO SEARCH FOR?
THERE'S NOTHING TO WORRY ABOUT.
THERE WERE A NUMBER OF DIFFICULTIES, BUT EVERYTHING HAS BEEN TAKEN CARE OF.
ANYWAYS, GETTING OUR HANDS ON THIS MESSAGE WAS ALL THAT WE NEEDED TO RESOLVE THIS.
I UNDERSTAND.
THUMP
SIGH...

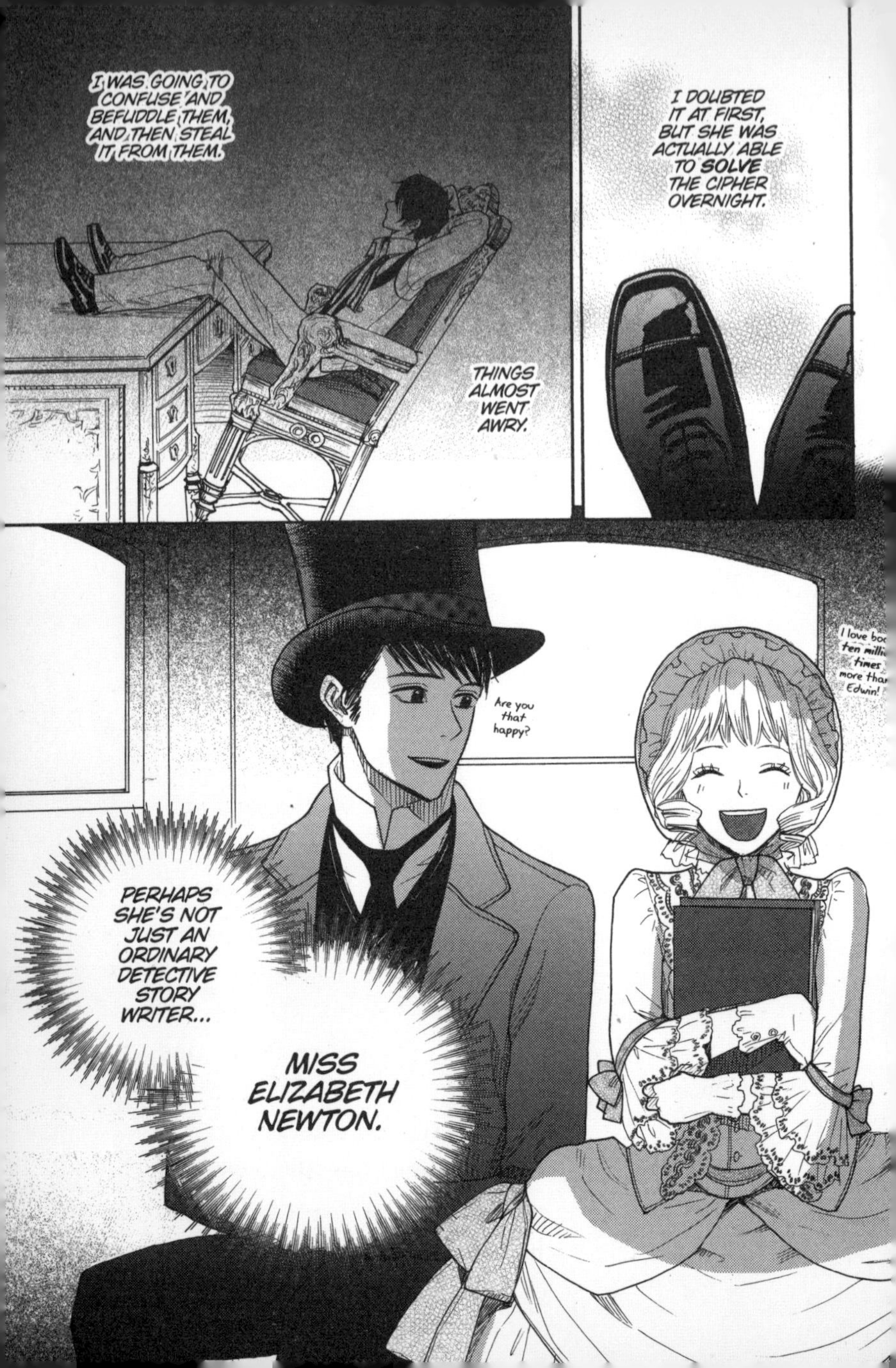
I WAS GOING TO CONFUSE AND BEFUDDLE THEM, AND THEN STEAL IT FROM THEM.
THINGS ALMOST WENT AWRY.
I DOUBTED IT AT FIRST, BUT SHE WAS ACTUALLY ABLE TO **SOLVE** THE CIPHER OVERNIGHT.
Are you that happy?
I love boo ten milli times more thar Edwin!
PERHAPS SHE'S NOT JUST AN ORDINARY DETECTIVE STORY WRITER...
MISS ELIZABETH NEWTON.

McMorning, PRIVATE TUTOR AND SLEUTH

Stepmother's Curse

By Logica Docens

While Miss Edith Fairfax was still quite young, she was already known within London society as a plaything of Dame Fortune. Even I, who remain largely indifferent to gossip within the social sets, have heard about her. She had lost her mother at birth, and was reared by one Miss Valentine, a French woman who maintained a close relationship with her father, Sir Fairfax, and later became the new Mrs. Fairfax. When Miss Edith turned three, the diamond mining company in which her father had invested the family fortune declared bankruptcy. By the time she was five years old, her father, who had been struggling with depression, worsened and soon passed away, leaving Miss Edith an orphan with no relations and very few prospects.

Dame Fortune showed pity, however: the now-widowed Mrs. Fairfax chose to raise her young ward using her own income, bequeathed to her by her French parents. And thus,

Miss Edith grew until it was finally time for her to enter society. Although her daughter had grown to maturity, Mrs. Fairfax was herself still rather young, beautiful, and far more free-spirited than our English ladies are wont to be, sometimes causing controversy with her words, and worse, with her actions. However, no one could deny that she had raised her stepdaughter well, with love and devotion. Among London's elite, it was concluded that if Miss Edith made a successful debut that Season and found an agreeable husband, it was highly probable that the widow Fairfax would follow her natural disposition and leave London to travel the world without a care.

Alas, Miss Edith's prospects for a good match appeared slim. She had hardly inherited anything from her father, and had little hope of any significant dowry from her stepmother, so she was not an ideal bride. In fact, her position was such that not even I would have considered her suitable for marriage. Perhaps if I were a bourgeoisie, made suddenly rich through commerce and industry, I might seek to legitimize my station through marriage to a daughter from a good family. But fortune smiled on Miss Edith yet again by gracing her with beauty so abundant that she was often compared with the goddess Diana. And since a woman's beauty often brushes aside obstacles such as a lack of status or wealth, she was able to make quite a splash, even meeting with the crown prince, who cultivated an interest in beautiful and talented women. The very moment she made her entrance into society, young lads, too numerous to count, eagerly lined up to rescue her from her impoverished state. But alas, as the marriage proposals increased, so too did the unfortunate rumors that she was a bearer of ill-fortune.

From whence did these tales arise? Perhaps the definitive tale regarding Miss Edith's tribulations involves an account of the young Sir Howard, the very first suitor of all the young lads desperately seeking her hand, who lost his life after falling from his horse. Sir Howard was riding with a fox hunt when his horse cast a shoe and went wild, throwing the lad and trampling him to death. Miss Edith was lucky that this happened before Sir Howard had made any formal proposal: in consequence, she wasn't compelled to waste her youth in mourning, as his bereaved fiancée. Still, she could not stop the rumors about her misfortune from spreading throughout London's social set. Even more devastating, some of these rumors attributed her bad luck to a curse, cast upon her by her very own stepmother.

"Yes, that's what they say, Iago."

I heard this account from none other than my Aunt Molly, who knew intimately every rumor that spread within London circles.

"Do you know how many people die from falling off their horses? I don't think it at all nice to ruin a young lady's prospects by spreading such poisonous rumors."

"Goodness, no, my child; but that's not all."

Whenever my aunt was conveying this or that rumor, her health appeared to improve dramatically. It was during these times that I again was reminded of my aunt's constant diatribe about the attributes of a well-bred woman. In my estimation, a true lady should not speak so joyfully about another's misfortunes, and in that same vein perhaps it was far more ladylike to be as blunt as Miss McMorning.

Returning to Miss Edith: that young lady overcame the tragedy of Sir Howard's death, and it's whispered that she has accepted the proposal of another suitor. Sir Dalton, a son of my aunt's friend, was a grand young swell who owned an extensive manor in the countryside. He had his pick of high society ladies to be his wife, but they say that he proposed to Miss Edith after being struck by her beauty, then falling for the potent combination of her misfortune and the purity of her heart. Well, this is a common enough story, one we see time and time again in those frivolous romance novels women adore.

"But then something *horrid* happened," my aunt whispered hoarsely.

"Sir Dalton had a grand engagement party with all of his relations in attendance, but of all things, Miss Edith broke out in the most ghastly freckles on that very day. My dear, everyone is saying that this is all due to that French woman."

"What could she possibly gain from giving the poor girl spots?"

"Perhaps Sir Fairfax has a hidden fortune she wanted to secure for herself."

"But everyone says that Mrs. Fairfax raised Miss Edith with her own dowry money. Wouldn't any secret fortune have been revealed when Sir Fairfax passed away? Please stop talking rubbish, and have some more tea."

"Iago, I had no notion you were such an unfeeling child. I thought perhaps your governess could be of some help regarding this matter, and that's why I've come calling today."

"You mean Miss McMorning?"

"Yes. Rumor has it that your governess is quite a remarkable young woman—I heard she was recently of great assistance to Mrs. Jones. And, as you know, Sir Dalton is the son of my dear friend Lucy, who is quite distressed over this whole affair."

Just thinking about Mrs. Jones and the jewel incident, to which my aunt was referring, gave me a headache, but I had no real recourse to escape, nor could I summarily dismiss Aunt Molly. And so, I called Miss McMorning to the study. She is an odd character, a woman of 22 who has served as our governess for about half a year.

While my aunt was relaying to Miss McMorning the recent events regarding Miss Edith, and recounting in detail the particulars of the young lady's childhood all the way to her current state, I couldn't help but wonder why such preposterous occurrences kept flying into my study and taking up residence. From the moment this governess came to my home, I have had no peace and quiet. I sat listlessly whilst Aunt Molly repeated her story to the attentive Miss McMorning, and played idly with a snuffbox from my desk. When the story finally reached the day of the engagement and the freckle incident, Miss McMorning nodded her head.

"There are a few things I would like to ask you… Was Miss Edith's engagement announcement held out of doors?"

"Well, they had it at a garden party, due to the wonderful weather. They were planning to introduce Miss Edith to all of the relatives there."

"And I presume that Miss Edith normally did not take a great deal of sun."

"No. But even so… How could someone who had a complexion as clear as snow in the morning break out so suddenly and so frightfully? The only possible explanation is that someone has cursed her."

"And Mr. Fairfax passed away after suffering from depression?"

"Yes. They say he died of an illness, but some of us think that he took his own life."

"Did Miss Edith appear to be in good spirits on the morning of the announcement?"

"I'm not sure… Miss Edith has always been a gentle, mild-mannered soul, who seldom raised her voice for any reason. And although I do believe she has feelings for Sir Dalton, on the day of the engagement, I hardly saw her speak."

"Did Mrs. Fairfax perhaps offer Miss Edith something to drink?"

"What an odd question! As it happens, my maid overheard her say to Miss Edith that it appeared her mood was going to be bad, and then saw her bring the girl some tea. I had heard that Mrs. Fairfax is the daughter of a wealthy merchant from Montereau, specializing in medicines. Now that you bring it up, I'm positive she slipped something dodgy into that tea."

"I see." Miss McMorning nodded.

As this conversation progressed, it struck me what a peculiar situation Miss McMorning had created for herself. While it is certainly inappropriate for any governess to have such familiarity with the family members of her pupil, this odd governess did have an uncanny talent in providing solutions to the many ladies who came calling on Briar Mansion with their troubles. On that note, I should not forget that it is also my duty to guide Miss McMorning so that she maintains the lady's virtue of modesty, and at the same time to carry out my judgments as the master. For the sake of her little charge Vivian, in particular, I must impress upon her that making speculations about other people's affairs is a bad habit for any lady, and far from virtuous.

As I sat deep in thought, Miss McMorning said to me, "Master, I was wondering if you wouldn't mind sending Thomas on an errand for me."

"Why are you always conscripting my butler for strange errands?"

"I'm attempting to find an answer to Madam's troubles," Miss McMorning said very matter-of-factly, her face quite expressionless. However, the saucer-eyed expression on the face of my aunt—who happened to be standing behind Miss McMorning—made turning down her request quite impossible. I had no choice but to give orders to Thomas as Miss McMorning had written them out; but all the while, I determined that one day I would make sure to show that impertinent governess who was truly the master of the house.

About an hour or so later, Thomas returned with a bag of tea, carefully wrapped in paper. Meanwhile, Miss McMorning was reading *Faust* in the corner of the room, while my aunt poured all manner of trivial stories into her inattentive ear. Although

Miss McMorning was quite obviously not listening to a word, when my aunt punctuated her stories with occasional questions, she was able to respond as though she was paying full attention the entire time. I may not care for Miss McMorning's blunt responses, or her peculiar ways, but I have often wished I could learn that skill of hers.

While this was transpiring, my aunt invited a very distressed Sir Dalton and his mother to my house. At times like this I cannot help wondering who the true master of this house is, and I find it quite vexing. It is a question to which I have no answer. Whenever those relations who now call me Sir Iago Linton, after spending years looking down upon me as a bastard love child, exercise their power in this house, it only confirms that I am nothing more than a puppet placed here to dance at their convenience. Amidst the flurry of guests constantly streaming in, I keep telling myself that I should kick that impudent governess to the curb as soon as possible—before any ridiculous and unwelcome rumors about that lady spread throughout society.

"What can you tell us, Miss McMorning?"

Mrs. Lucy Dalton's eyes were red and puffy from crying over her son's travails, and she clutched a handkerchief in her hand. Sir Dalton appeared unperturbed, but the reek of alcohol that wafted all the way to where I sat told a different story. Clearly the fellow was not so reckless a cad as to break off the engagement, but what man would be able to maintain his composure upon hearing such gruesome rumors that his bride-to-be might be cursed? Miss McMorning, quite calm and cool, disregarded the anxious question that had been put to her, and continued her examination of the tea that Thomas had delivered. At length, she put it aside, and said: "You need not worry, Mrs. Dalton. Nothing can be done about the spots that suddenly appeared on her face, but Miss Edith Fairfax has definitely not been cursed."

"Really?"

"You ought not to listen to such society gossip. These stories are poisonous lies spread by the idle rich, and have no basis in reality. After all, it would do Miss Fairfax no good for her household to say such things."

Unfortunately, there was truth to what she was saying. While Miss McMorning was utterly socially inept and blunt, just this once I was thankful that she had made this point definitively, without mincing words.

"Madame, you said that Sir Fairfax had been suffering from depression before his death. There is a high possibility that Miss Edith may have taken after her father. After all, she lost her parents at an early age, and had hardly any inheritance from her father. She has also suffered the unfortunate death of one of her suitors. So it isn't so peculiar to think that Miss Edith would be suffering from depression, don't you think?"

"It just seems so strange," Mrs. Dalton said. "She was always a gentle and quiet child; she spoke very little and never seemed to complain. Honestly, I think that was what drew my son to her."

"And it is just these quiet, introverted people that are the most likely to fall into depression. So I had Thomas ask Mrs. Fairfax's butler to share some of the tea that Mrs. Fairfax prepared for the lady. And of course, since there is nothing special about the tea, she gladly offered to share it with us."

Miss McMorning opened the bag of tea and showed it to my aunt and Mrs. Dalton.

"As you can see, it is simply St. John's Wort. A tea that is not only good for insomnia, but it also helps with depression."

Aunt Molly peered closely at the tea and then made a face. "Isn't it possible that something else could have been mixed into it?"

Miss McMorning merely shook her head. Normally, I would think it proper to reprimand her arrogance for responding in such a casual and disrespectful manner to her master's guests, but I found myself far more eager to hear Miss McMorning's explanation when she finally deigned to give it.

"I am sure that Mrs. Fairfax, as a daughter of a medicine merchant, learned one or two things about medicine from a young age. And after noticing symptoms of depression in Miss Edith, I believe it's perfectly reasonable to presume that Mrs. Fairfax would give her ward some St. John's Wort tea, particularly as it is easily obtained."

"I see…"

"It's generally agreed that Mrs. Fairfax raised Miss Edith to be a fine lady, even though she is no blood relative. Even if she were, just imagine the difficulty of raising a daughter with only a small dowry after one's husband has lost his fortune and passed away. If, by any chance, this has something to do with some hidden inheritance, all Mrs. Fairfax need do is prevent her from coming out in society. There is no reason for her to go through all this trouble and elaborate scheming."

The two women nodded their heads, and I saw a light of hope appear in Sir Dalton's despaired face. At that very moment, I witnessed with my very own eyes how vain rumors about curses and such in aristocratic society could hurt someone so deeply.

"Drinking a deeply steeped cup of St. John's Wort tea, then standing under the sun will result in skin blemishes. Although I myself have yet to experience it, I have heard that weddings and engagement ceremonies bring great joy to a woman, along with many other complicated emotions. So I surmise that Mrs. Fairfax offered Miss Edith a cup of strong tea to settle her nerves so that she might go through the engagement ceremony without difficulty. With the strong sun beating down during the garden party, it's not surprising that spots appeared on her skin. In fact, I believe that even if she hadn't drunk St. John's Wort that morning, the sun would have revealed what was hiding under her skin from having taken this tea regularly."

Miss McMorning abruptly concluded her explanation, and stood up to leave—noting, as she did, that as a mere governess, it wasn't her place to make any further speculations.

Fortunately, it all turned out exactly as Miss McMorning had concluded. Miss Edith Fairfax confirmed that she had been drinking St. John's Wort tea regularly, encouraged by her stepmother. On the day of the engagement, Miss Edith had imbibed several strong cups of tea, as it was an especially important day for her. So it was not extraordinary that Miss Edith's delicate face was dotted with blemishes, especially in light of the fact that she seldom went out in the sun (just like Diana, the moon-goddess to whom she was so often compared). However, this proved to be of no consequence to Sir Dalton; even those lamentable freckles were easily hidden by powder. This incident was a good opportunity for me to confirm, once again, how ridiculous these stories were over which aristocratic ladies wag their tongues. Through this marriage, Miss Edith became the young Mrs. Dalton, and it is my sincerest hope that she will henceforth be known as a lady of fortune rather than of misfortune.

As for us, once she had confirmed that Miss Edith, her future daughter-in-law, was not in fact cursed, Mrs. Lucy Dalton sent a short note that read: "A return courtesy to Sir Iago Linton and Miss McMorning's shrewdness" along with a nice new frock for Miss McMorning and a box of superior quality cigars for me. I was so impressed with the cigars that I found myself yet again unable to tell Miss McMorning she should abide by a lady's virtue and know her place not to meddle. But while I was mollified by the cigars, I nonetheless vowed that the day shall come where I will take this odd governess to task over propriety and her position.

– **The End** –

TEACHER HEY-JIN JEON'S POSTSCRIPT

For *Lizzie Newton Vol. 2*, I wrote a story involving a coded message, with Mary Stuart at its center. I had a blast writing this book. I hope you can tell!

If you're interested in learning more about coded messages, check out Simon Singh's *The Code Book*. It's a really fascinating read. In the postscript, I had planned on writing extensively about Simon Singh's book, but thought better of it. You will probably enjoy reading the book on your own, and it'll make a lot more sense than getting it second-hand from me.

In this volume, we have a special short story "excavated" from a 19th century *Gentleman's Own* printing of Logica Docens' detective story, "McMorning, Private Tutor and Sleuth." I believe I accurately translated the story while modernizing it, so I hope all of the readers enjoy the story of the private tutor, Miss McMorning (considered eccentric at that time) and her employer, Sir Iago Linton (whom McMorning always pesters). ^____^

For this book as well, I would especially like to thank my editor, who undoubtedly developed more dark circles because of a really disobedient otaku (me). Thank you very much~!

Teacher Ki-ha Lee's Postscript

Assistant's Revolution

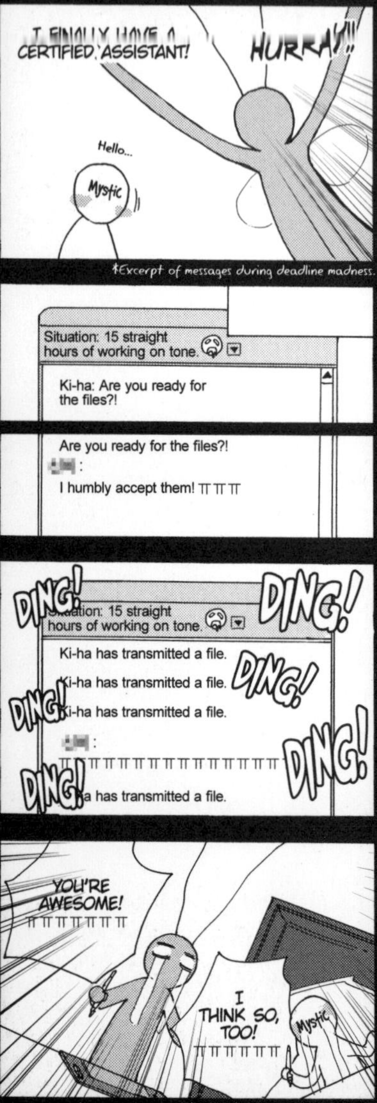
I FINALLY HAVE A CERTIFIED ASSISTANT!
HURRAY!!
Hello...
Mystic
*Excerpt of messages during deadline madness.
Situation: 15 straight hours of working on tone.
Ki-ha: Are you ready for the files?!
Are you ready for the files?!
I humbly accept them! TT TT TT
DING!
Situation: 15 straight hours of working on tone.
DING!
Ki-ha has transmitted a file.
Ki-ha has transmitted a file.
DING!
DING!
Ki-ha has transmitted a file.
TT TT TT TT TT TT TT TT TT TT TT TT TT TT TT
DING!
DING!
a has transmitted a file.
YOU'RE AWESOME! TT TT TT TT TT TT TT
I THINK SO, TOO! TT TT TT TT TT TT
Mystic

You can survive without a boyfriend,
but you can't survive without an assistant.

A Tour Through an Exhibition

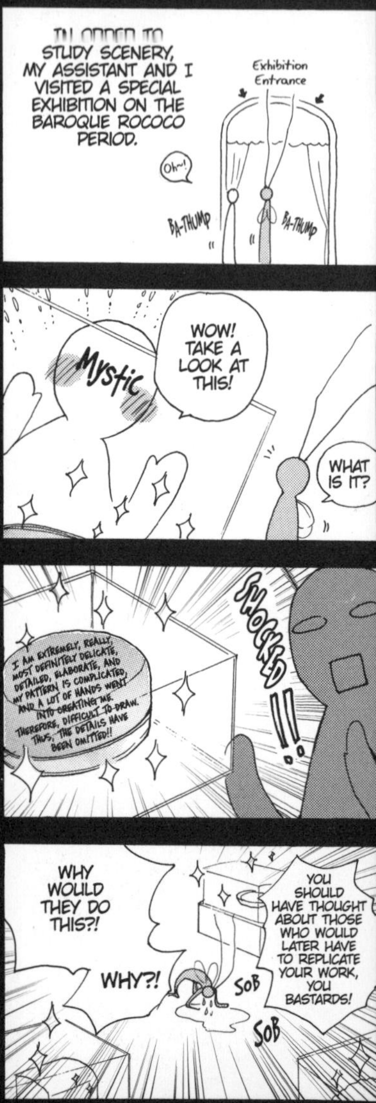
IN ORDER TO STUDY SCENERY, MY ASSISTANT AND I VISITED A SPECIAL EXHIBITION ON THE BAROQUE ROCOCO PERIOD.
Exhibition Entrance
Oh~!
BA-THUMP
BA-THUMP
Mystic
WOW! TAKE A LOOK AT THIS!
WHAT IS IT?
I AM EXTREMELY, REALLY, MOST DEFINITELY DELICATE, DETAILED, ELABORATE, AND MY PATTERN IS COMPLICATED, AND A LOT OF HANDS WENT INTO CREATING ME. THEREFORE, DIFFICULT TO DRAW. THUS, THE DETAILS HAVE BEEN OMITTED!!
SHOCKED!!
WHY WOULD THEY DO THIS?!
WHY?!
SOB
SOB
YOU SHOULD HAVE THOUGHT ABOUT THOSE WHO WOULD LATER HAVE TO REPLICATE YOUR WORK, YOU BASTARDS!

Teacher Hey-jin Jeon + Teacher Ki-ha Lee's Postscript

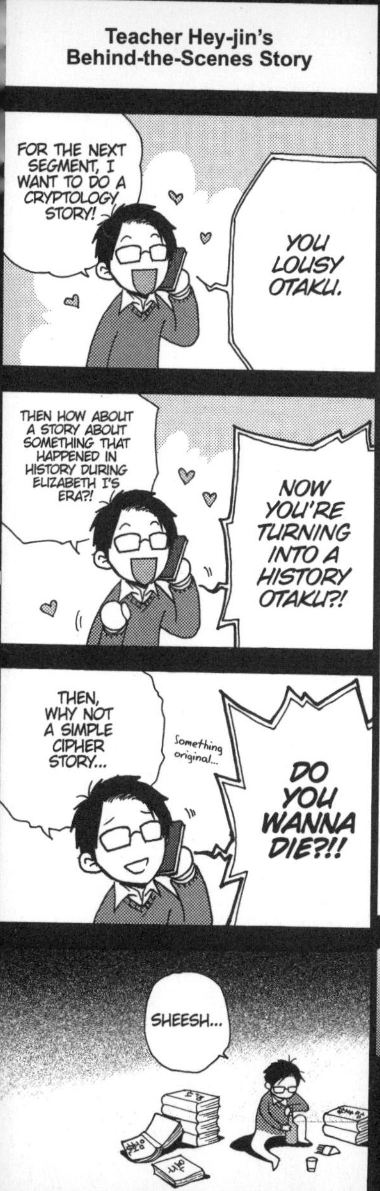

Teacher Hey-jin's Behind-the-Scenes Story
FOR THE NEXT SEGMENT, I WANT TO DO A CRYPTOLOGY STORY!
YOU LOUSY OTAKU.
THEN HOW ABOUT A STORY ABOUT SOMETHING THAT HAPPENED IN HISTORY DURING ELIZABETH I'S ERA?!
NOW YOU'RE TURNING INTO A HISTORY OTAKU?!
THEN, WHY NOT A SIMPLE CIPHER STORY...
Something original...
DO YOU WANNA DIE?!!
SHEESH...

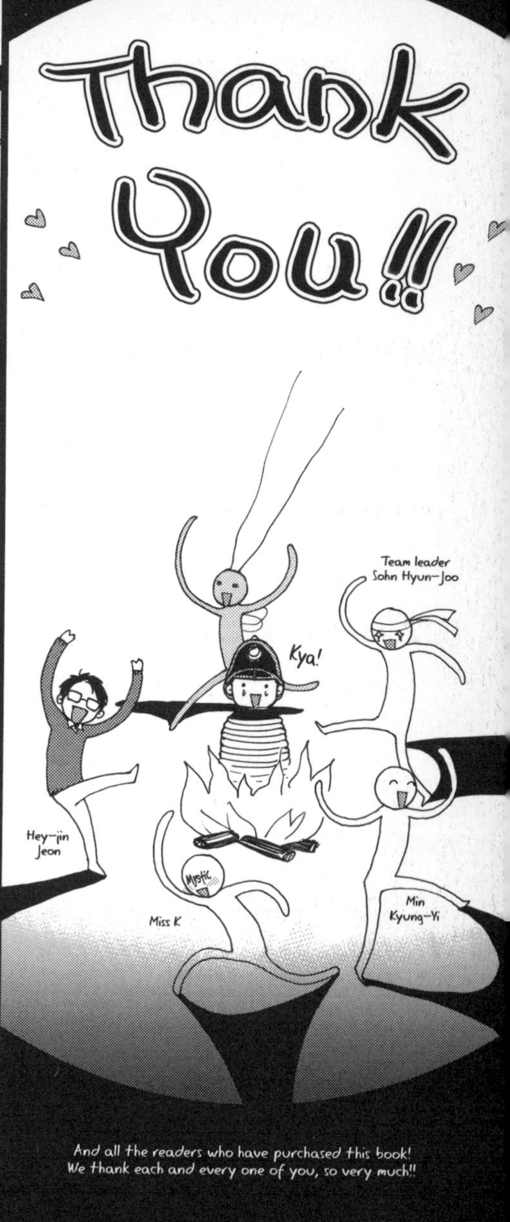

Thank You!!
Kya!
Team leader Sohn Hyun-Joo
Hey-jin Jeon
Mystic
Miss K
Min Kyung-Yi
And all the readers who have purchased this book!
We thank each and every one of you, so very much!!

A DANGEROUS EXCHANGE BETWEEN CONTRIBUTORS?!

Hey-jin:

DRAW BETTER!!! MAYBE INVEST IN SOME TIME TO GO THROUGH A PERIOD OF INTENSIVE STUDY.

Ki-ha:

UH... I JUST NEED TO DRAW TWO EYES, ONE MOUTH, AND NO NOSE!

Hey-jin:

WHY YOU--! *HA HA HA!*

SHALL I GIVE YOU A TIP ON HOW TO COME UP WITH A CHEMICAL TRICK? *HEH...* JUST OPEN UP ANY STANDARD CHEMISTRY TEXTBOOK, READ A PAGE, AND USE THE INFORMATION TO COME UP WITH A CHEMICAL TRICK FOR A STORY!

Ki-ha:

HEE HEE HEE. I SEE, SO THIS IS WHAT IT FEELS LIKE! BUT I STILL THINK MY WAY IS MORE ACCURATE! *HA HA HA!*

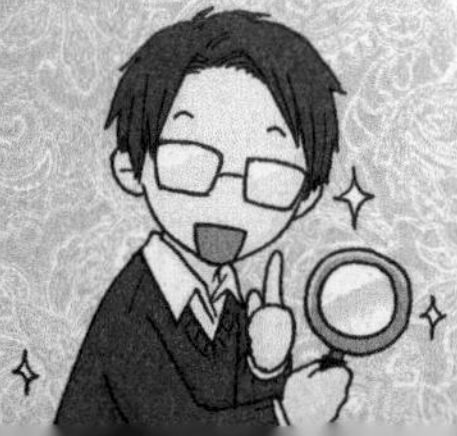

Hey-jin Jeon
http://hamadris.com

Ki-ha Lee
http://skiha.ivy.ro

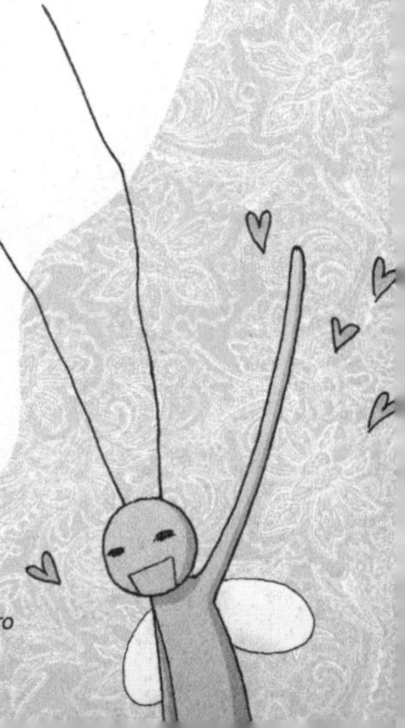

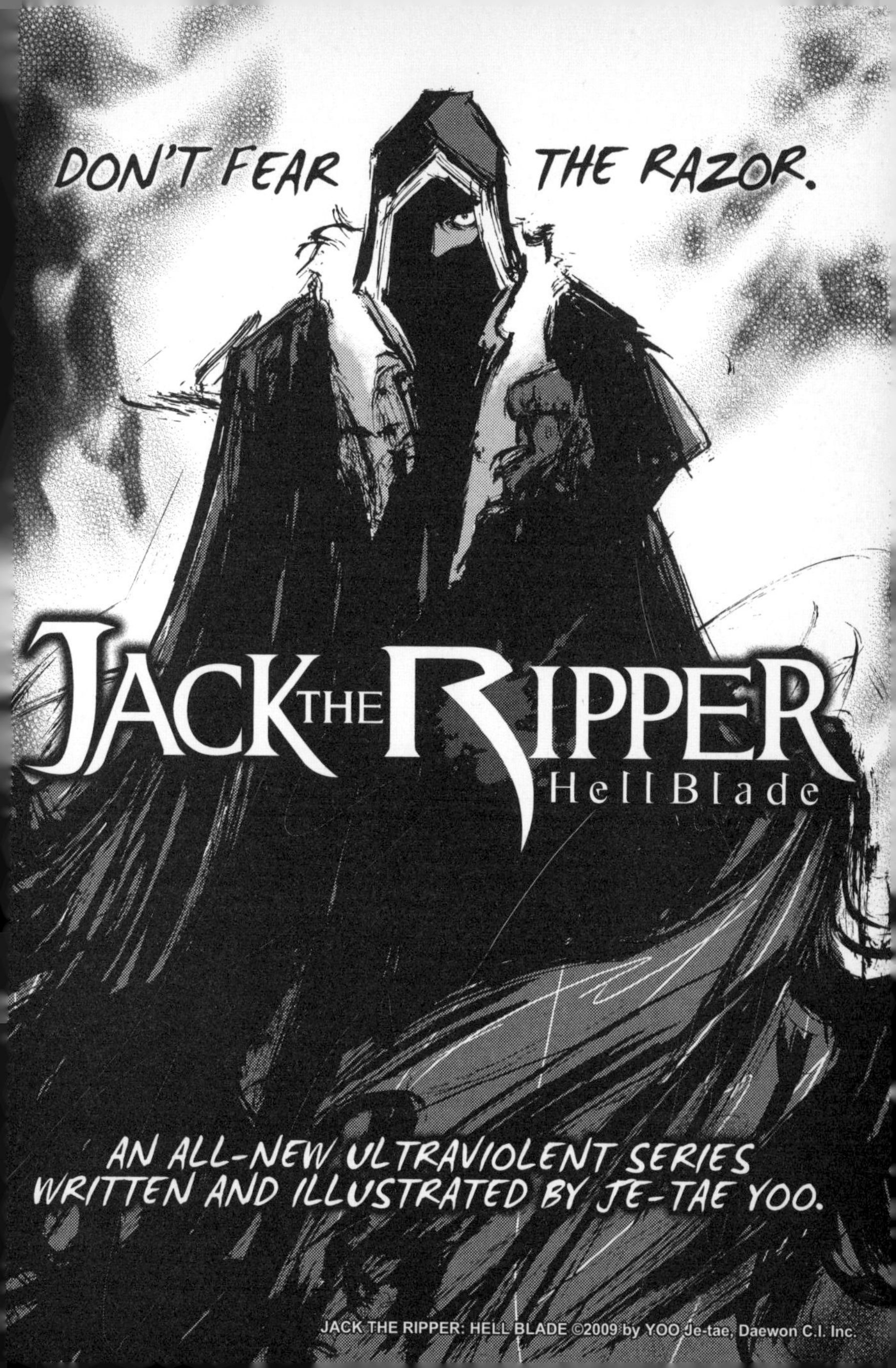
DON'T FEAR THE RAZOR.
JACK THE RIPPER
HellBlade
AN ALL-NEW ULTRAVIOLENT SERIES
WRITTEN AND ILLUSTRATED BY JE-TAE YOO.
JACK THE RIPPER: HELL BLADE ©2009 by YOO Je-tae, Daewon C.I. Inc.

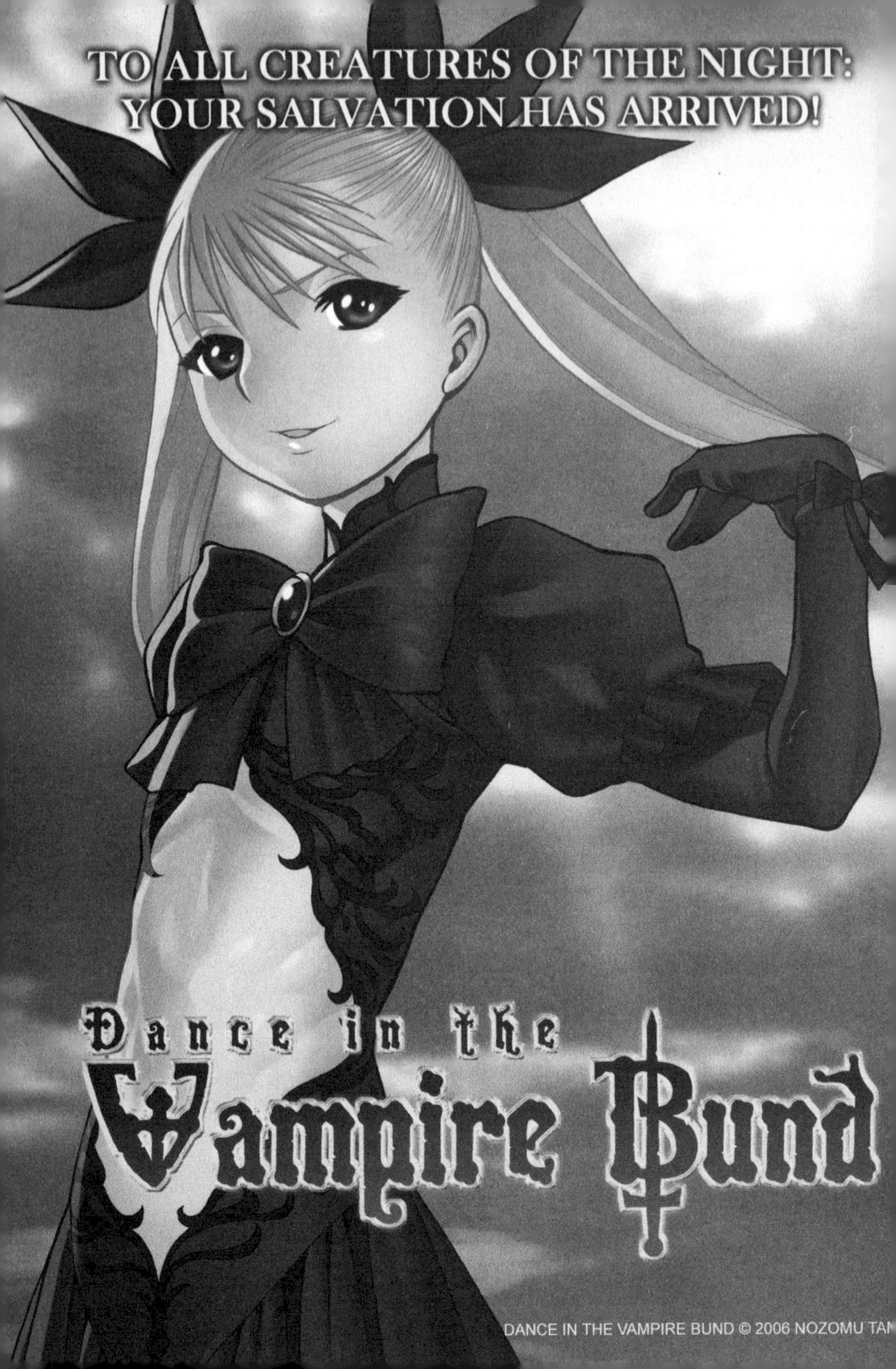
TO ALL CREATURES OF THE NIGHT:
YOUR SALVATION HAS ARRIVED!
Dance in the
Vampire Bund
DANCE IN THE VAMPIRE BUND © 2006 NOZOMU TA

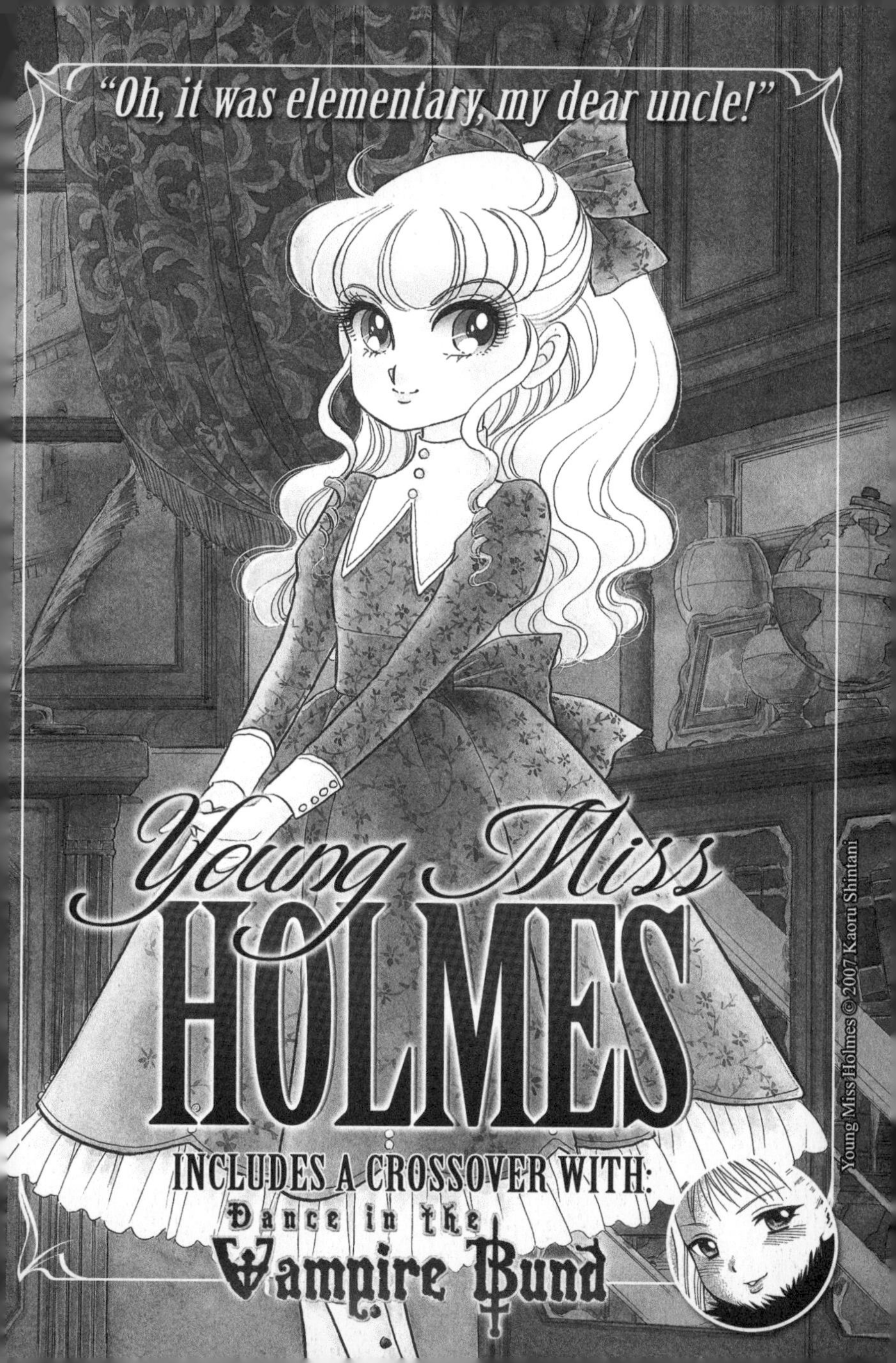
"Oh, it was elementary, my dear uncle!"
Young Miss
HOLMES
INCLUDES A CROSSOVER WITH:
Dance in the
Vampire Bund
Young Miss Holmes © 2007 Kaoru Shintani

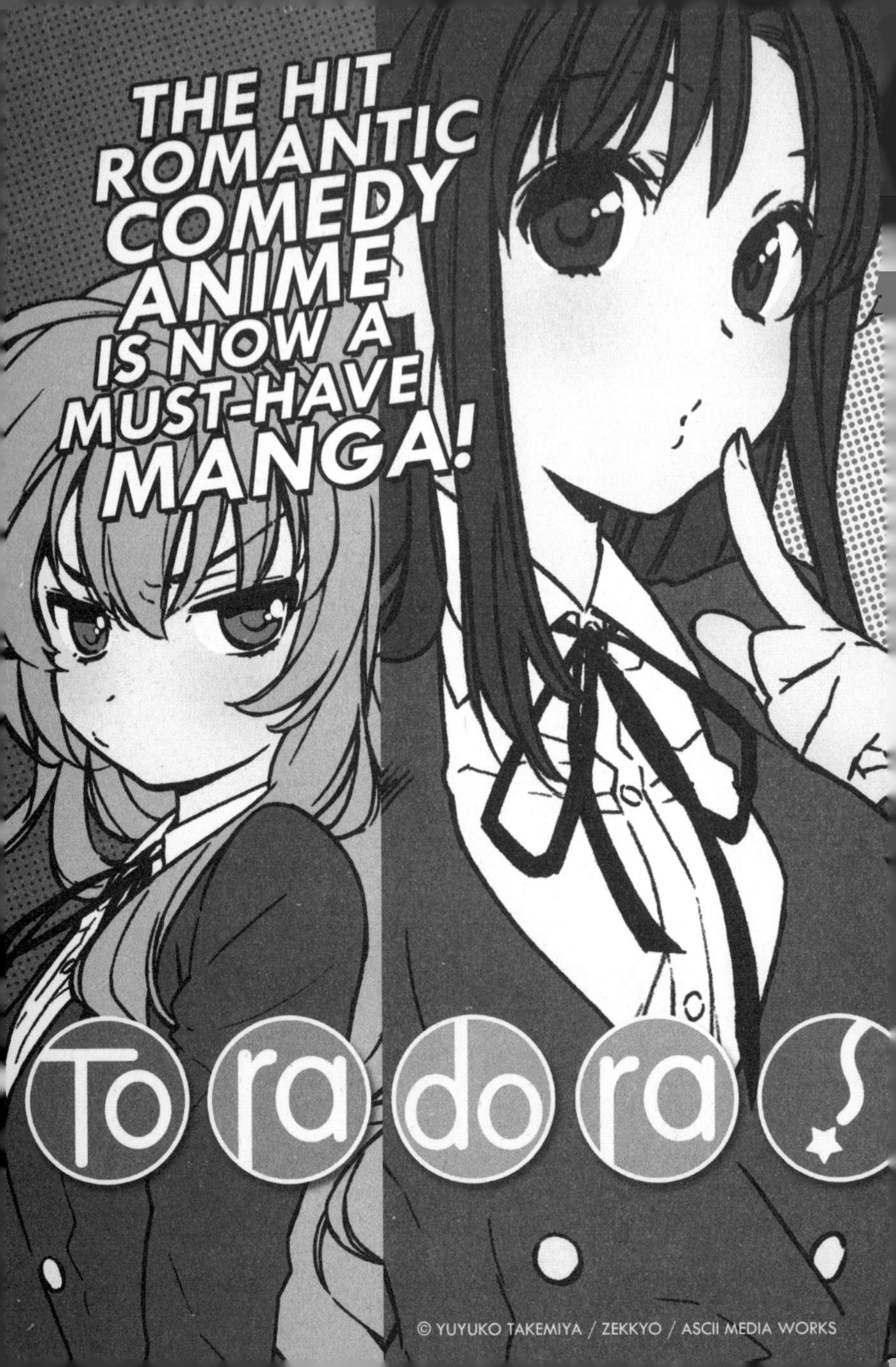
THE HIT ROMANTIC COMEDY ANIME IS NOW A MUST-HAVE MANGA!
Toradora!
© YUYUKO TAKEMIYA / ZEKKYO / ASCII MEDIA WORKS

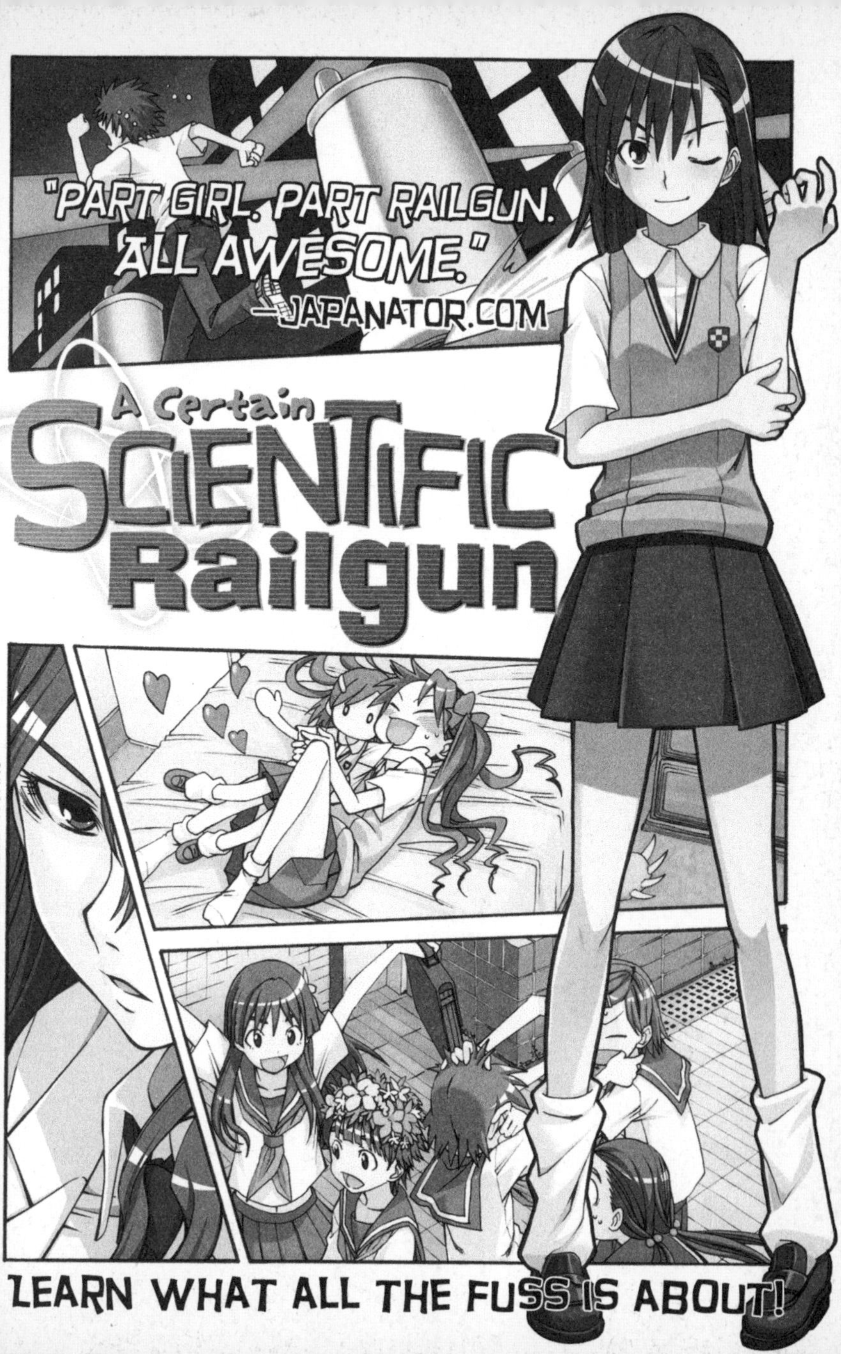
"PART GIRL. PART RAILGUN. ALL AWESOME."
—JAPANATOR.COM
A Certain SCIENTIFIC Railgun
LEARN WHAT ALL THE FUSS IS ABOUT!

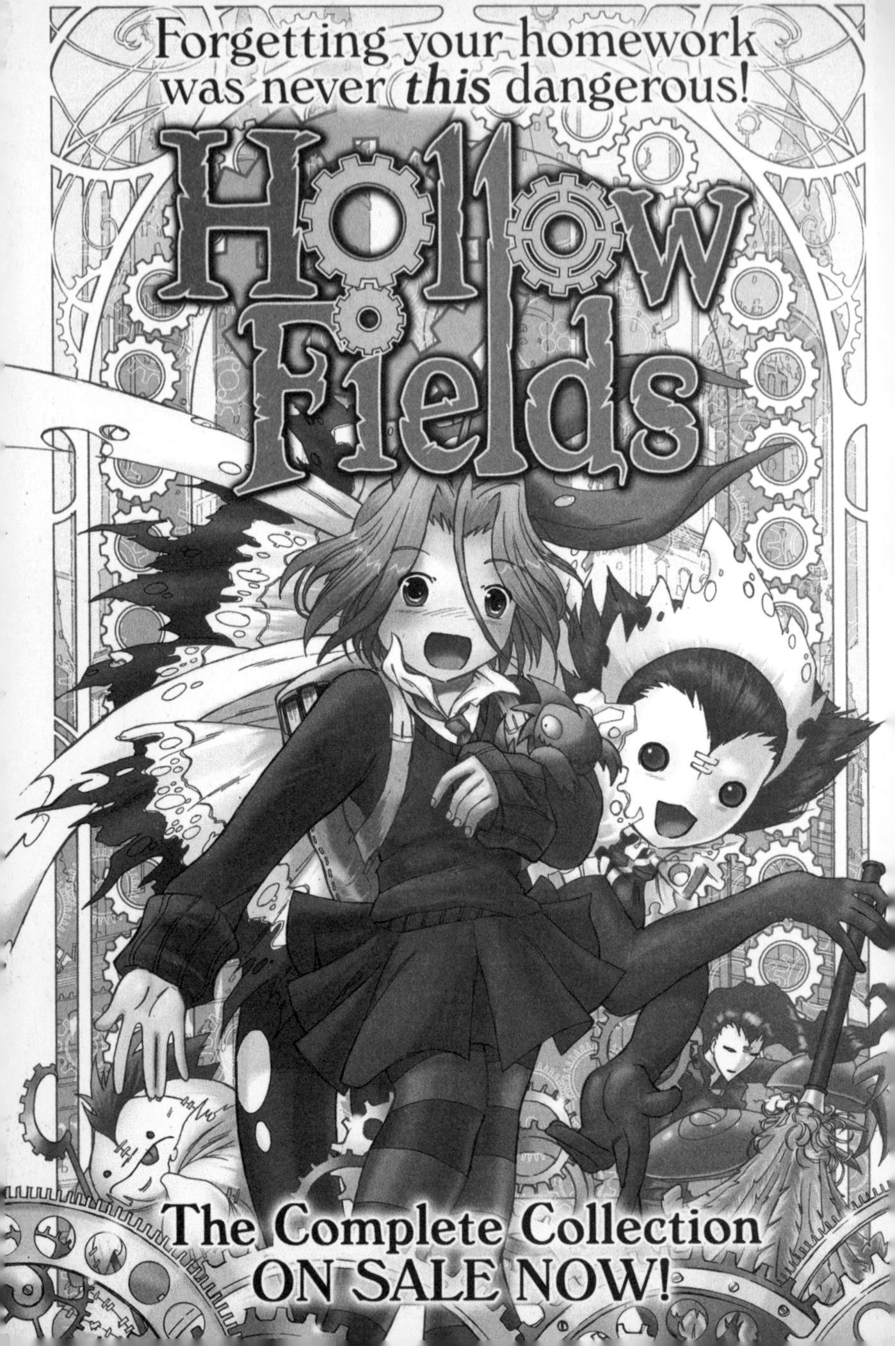
Forgetting your homework
was never *this* dangerous!
Hollow Fields
The Complete Collection
ON SALE NOW!

Amazing_Agent LUNA

Experience All 7 Exciting Volumes!

Luna: the perfect secret agent. A girl grown in a lab from the finest genetic material, she has been trained since birth to be the U.S. government's ultimate espionage weapon. But now she is given an assignment that will test her abilities to the max - high school!

story
Nunzio DeFilippis & Christina Weir • **art** Shiei

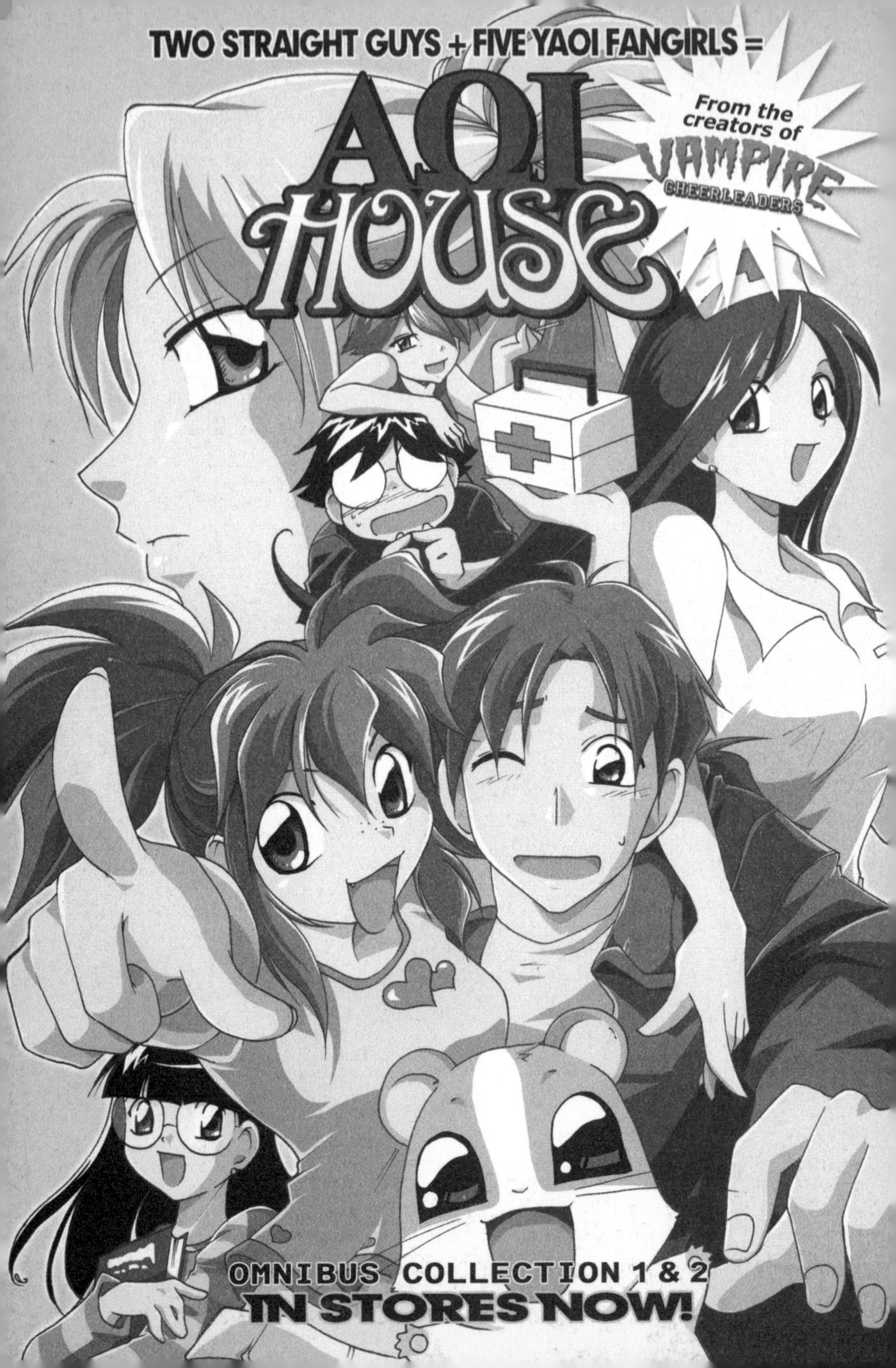

TWO STRAIGHT GUYS + FIVE YAOI FANGIRLS =
AOI HOUSE
From the creators of
VAMPIRE CHEERLEADERS
OMNIBUS COLLECTION 1 & 2
IN STORES NOW!

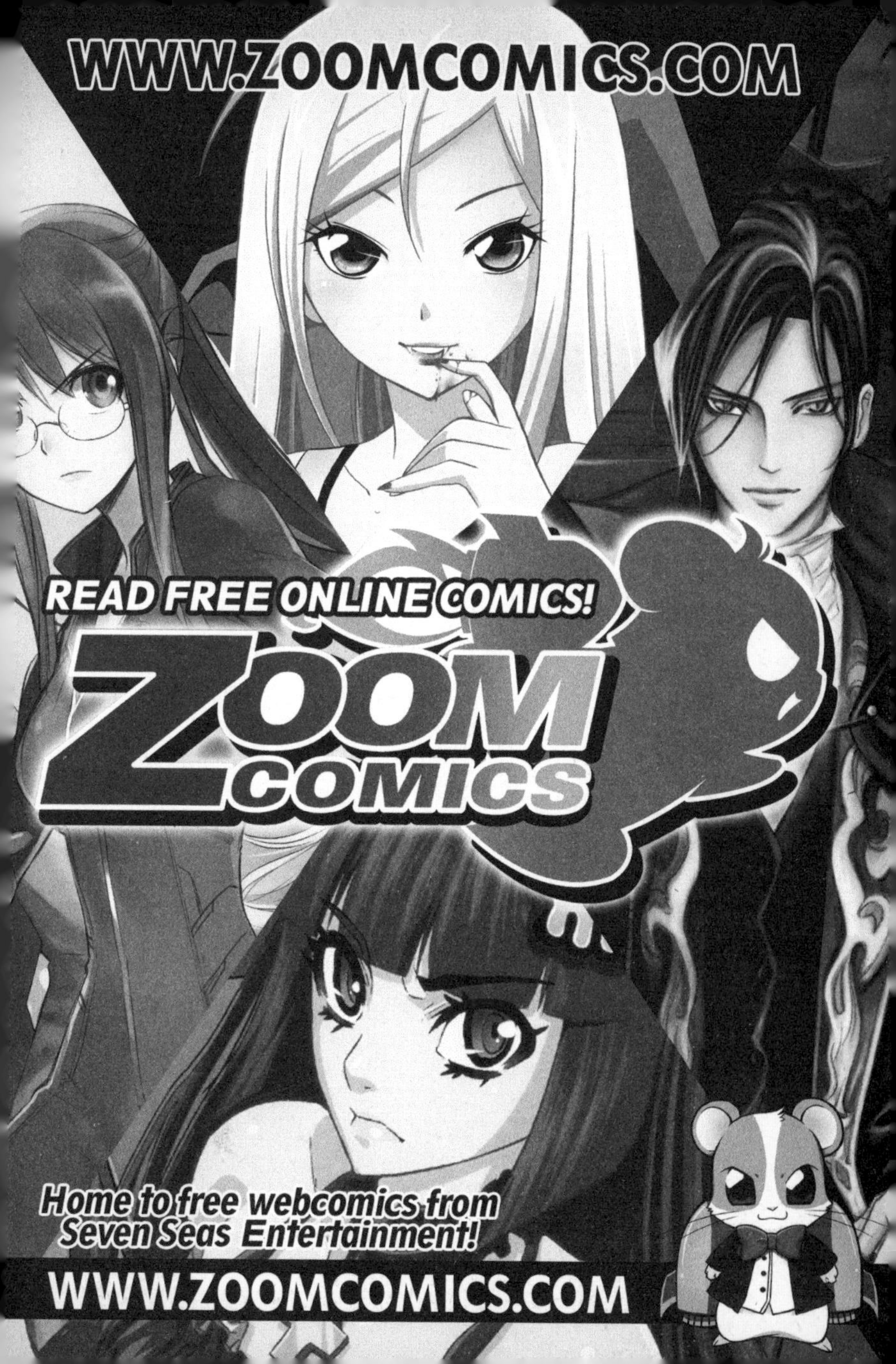
WWW.ZOOMCOMICS.COM
READ FREE ONLINE COMICS!
ZOOM COMICS
Home to free webcomics from Seven Seas Entertainment!
WWW.ZOOMCOMICS.COM